Hunt and Kill

U-505 and the U-boat War
in the Atlantic

Also by Theodore P. Savas

*Silent Hunters: German U-boat Commanders
of World War II*, editor

*Nazi Millionaires: The Allied Search
for Hidden SS Gold*, with Kenneth D. Alford

*The Red River Campaign: Union and Confederate Leadership
and the War in Louisiana*, editor, with David W. Woodbury
and Gary D. Joiner

The Campaign for Atlanta & Sherman's March to the Sea,
2 vols., editor, with David A. Woodbury

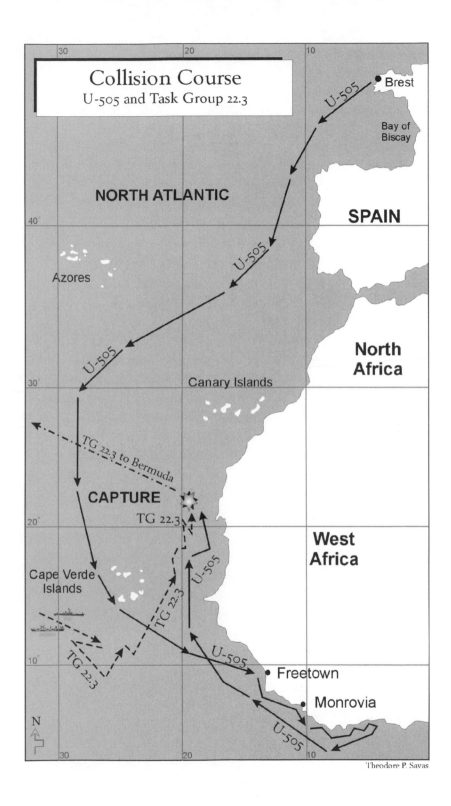

Collision Course
U-505 and Task Group 22.3

NORTH ATLANTIC

SPAIN

Bay of Biscay

Brest

U-505

Azores

North Africa

Canary Islands

TG 22.3 to Bermuda

CAPTURE

TG 22.3

West Africa

Cape Verde Islands

TG 22.3

TG 22.3

U-505

U-505

Freetown

Monrovia

U-505

N

Theodore P. Savas

For CR.

1-4-3

© 2004 by Theodore P. Savas

Cataloging-in-Publication Data is available from the Library of Congress.

First Savas Beatie edition 2004

ISBN 1-932714-01-4

SB

Published by
Savas Beatie LLC
521 Fifth Avenue, Suite 3400
New York, NY 10175
Phone: 610-853-9131

Savas Beatie titles are available at special discounts for bulk purchases in the United States by corporations, institutions, and other organizations. For more details, please contact Special Sales, P.O. Box 4527, El Dorado Hills, CA 95762, or you may e-mail us as at sales@savasbeatie.com, or visit our website at www.savasbeatie.com for additional information.

Theodore P. Savas, editor

Theodore P. Savas (signature)

Hunt and Kill

U-505 and the U-boat War
in the Atlantic

(signature)
Curator U-505

SB

Savas Beatie

Maps and Photographs

Map 1: Collision Course: *U-505*
and TG 22.3   frontis

Map 2: *U-505's* Second Patrol to the
Central Atlantic   61

Map 3: *U-505's* Third Patrol
to the Caribbean   69

*   *   *

Photograph galleries follow pages 122 and 218

U-505's remarkable history, including its astonishing transformation from frontline U-boat to Chicago landmark, is only cursorily understood by most readers—even those with a deep interest in World War II naval history. This incomplete appreciation is understandable because most published accounts highlight only narrow slices of the boat's complex three-year wartime history . . .

Theodore P. Savas

Editor's Preface

𝕴𝖓 the mid-1990s I organized and had the pleasure of serving as editor of a collection of essays written by leading U-boat scholars and published under the title *Silent Hunters: German U-boat Commanders of World War II* (Campbell, CA: Savas, 1997; Annapolis, MD: Naval Institute Press, 2003). The criteria set forth for the selection of the biographical portraits were simple: "choose a U-boat commander who has not received the scholarly treatment he deserves, one who either accomplished his record incrementally over several patrols or someone whose experiences were somehow unique and worthy of study." The result was a well-received compilation. Hopefully, others think it added something significant to the genre's literature. At that time I believed other aspects of the U-boat war needed similar treatment, but my transformation from active lawyer to the publishing world, coupled with two cross-country moves in two years, delayed the book you now hold in your hands.

U-505's remarkable history, including its astonishing transformation from frontline U-boat to Chicago landmark, is only cursorily understood by most readers—even those with a deep interest in World War II naval history. This incomplete appreciation is understandable because most published accounts highlight only narrow slices of the boat's complex three-year wartime history: Axel-Olaf Loewe's appendicitis while on patrol, Peter Zschech's gunshot-to-the-head suicide in the control room, and Harald Lange's fateful June 4, 1944, encounter with the audacious Daniel V. Gallery and his Task Group 22.3. The boat's postwar fate is similarly planed smooth, usually with little more than a sentence or two explaining that *U-505* was transported to Illinois and can be toured at Chicago's Museum of Science and Industry.

The historical record of *U-505* and its crew is much more interesting than these paltry few points and, until now, has never been fully told. After a long and thought-provoking tour of the boat in the late 1990s, I decided it was time to reassemble the team members and challenge them to tell it. The individual chapters they have prepared provide what we all hope is a broad and deep portrait of the history of *U-505*, its crew, the naval intelligence behind its discovery and seizure in 1944, and its final journey to Chicago and significance to future generations as a historical artifact and war memorial. Captain Gallery's capture of the boat off the African coast has been told and retold from his perspective, and so a conscious decision was made to weave the various threads of that event within several different chapters, which also made it easier to avoid having to present readers with what would otherwise have been an irksome overlap of coverage.

*   *   *

I remember clearly the first time I met Erich Topp. He was visiting family in Texas and was on his way to southern California before returning to Germany. Baylor University's Eric Rust provided me with his phone number. At Topp's invitation I flew down to the desert on January 27, 1996. He walked outside to greet me and flashed a broad smile. He was 82 years old but looked 55—tall, erect and handsome, with piercing ice-blue eyes, a firm handshake, and a hearty laugh. We struck it off immediately and I ended up staying many hours longer than originally planned. The honesty and forthrightness of his responses impressed me.

Admiral Topp contributed to *Silent Hunters* with a moving essay about his deep friendship with fellow ace Engelbert Endrass, written while on patrol in the North Atlantic. Topp believed a book on *U-505* was long overdue and kindly agreed to pen the Foreword for it. I have enjoyed our friendship over the years, and wish him continued good health.

Type IX U-boats played a unique role in the war. Their bulky size and slow diving capabilities rendered them less suited for convoy work than the more agile Type VII, though this was only fully realized after many good crews met their end raking North Atlantic lanes in search of clustered prey. The same girth and weight that made Type IXs clumsy convoy participants, however, furnished them with their potency as solo warriors. Their extra tanks held substantially more fuel, allowing them to operate as lone hunters for long periods of time in distant waters. First engineered in the mid-1930s, the Type IX series evolved over the years to become one of the most effective submarines in history. All of this and much more is carefully presented in our opening contribution, "No Target Too Far: The Genesis, Concept, and Operations of Type IX U-Boats in World War II," by Eric C. Rust of Baylor University. Dr. Rust meticulously explains the evolution of the German navy and naval doctrine from the First World War through the tumultuous years preceding World War II, the development and technical aspects of this U-boat series, how the Type IX was employed during the war, and its place in German naval history. He also willingly compiled the technical data related to Type IXC boats that appears as Appendix A. As he did so ably with *Silent Hunters*, Eric graciously agreed to review and help edit each of the essays that appear in this book as well as pen its insightful Introduction. Eric's keen observations, always graciously delivered, made this study stronger and more cohesive than it otherwise would have been. Over the years our friendship has grown, and for that I am both thankful and fortunate.

Timothy P. Mulligan, another veteran from the *Silent Hunters* project, switches gears from a solo biography of Karl-Friedrich Merten to something closer to a collective biography entitled "A Community Bound by Fate: The Crew of *U-505*." The title originates with Grand Admiral Karl Dönitz, "the head and soul of the German submarine service in World War II" who used the phrase to describe a U-boat crew. As an archivist working with captured German naval records and the author of a recent in-depth book about U-boat sailors, Tim is uniquely situated to write about the men who served aboard *U-505*. Although the officers are more fully developed as individuals, the common crewmen receive the lion's share of his attention. Utilizing a vast array of source material, he explores the rich diversity of these men, and in many cases is able to trace how particular individuals ended up aboard *U-505*. It is indeed a pioneering contribution. The helpful combat chronology for *U-505* that appears as Appendix B is also his work. "Success or failure for the submarine, and life or death for all on board, ultimately depended on each man performing his job, from the lowest rating to the captain," explains Mulligan. A U-boat was indeed a community bound by fate.

Surprisingly little has been published about *U-505's* history before its last voyage from Brest to its fateful rendezvous off Africa's sultry west coast. Lawrence Paterson's "From Lion's Roar to Blunted Axe: The Combat Patrols of U-505," explores this little-known and often misunderstood chapter of U-boat history. As those who read the essay will discover, its title is particularly apt. Some will be surprised to learn that *U-505* made several successful and difficult patrols in the southern Atlantic and Caribbean. As the pressures of service mounted, acts of sabotage while refitting in port repeatedly forced the boat to return to Lorient, casting a pall over those who served aboard it. It is impossible to fully appreciate and evaluate *U-505's* role in the Battle of the Atlantic without an understanding of what transpired on its first eleven war patrols. The boat's twelfth and final patrol, also related by Paterson in "Collision Course: Task Group 22.3 and the Hunt for U-505," caps his contribution to this compendium. Paterson is a native New Zealander, accomplished musician, experienced scuba diver, and the author of two outstanding U-boat Flotilla studies. Over the past two years he has provided both good advice and friendly cheer.

Most readers of U-boat history have a general grasp of the role played by Enigma in the Battle of the Atlantic, but are unaware of how Enigma and other advances in technology led to the capture of *U-505*. A thorough and thoughtful examination of this story, based almost wholly upon archival sources, is presented in "Deciphering the U-boat War: The Role of Intelligence in the Capture *U-505*." This chapter is the product of a marvelous collaboration between Mark E. Wise and Jak P. Mallmann Showell. Together, they describe more fully and forcefully than any other published account how Allied intelligence efforts melded with Daniel Gallery's perseverance and German mistakes to bring about "an event unparalleled in the history of modern naval warfare." Both know well of what they write. Wise is a graduate of the University of Minnesota and an intelligence specialist in the U.S. Naval Reserve. His Master's thesis is on the same subject as his chapter. This contribution is Mark's first foray into the ranks of the published in the U-boat field. Co-author Jak Showell is well-known to students of the U-boat war. Teacher, scientist, and computing expert, Jak is the author of some two dozen titles and like Wise, enjoys a deep interest in Enigma and intelligence-related issues. Jak also helped provide me with coordinates to map *U-505's* patrol routes.

Most accounts of the capture of *U-505* are written from the Allied perspective as related through the words and eyes of Daniel V. Gallery. Jordan Vause's "Desperate Decisions: The German Loss of *U-505*" examines the issue from the German perspective. He reconstructs (as far as such a thing is possible) what took place inside the boat from the moment the depth charges began to explode through its ascent to the surface and the terrifying minutes that followed. It is a thoughtful essay based upon eyewitness accounts, a keen appreciation of the chain of command, and the observations of other U-boat commanders and personnel. It is also the closest we shall probably ever come to understanding the German decision-making process that fateful day. Jordan, who has authored two well-received U-boat books, was present when the seeds that eventually sprouted the earlier *Silent Hunters* study were planted in the summer of 1995. Nine years have passed since that evening in his living room. Since that time he and his charming family have moved to the wrong coast. We manage to keep in relatively close contact, though I miss our face-to-face banter.

Anyone with even a cursory interest in the U-boat war learns sooner or later that a real German submarine sits outside Chicago's Museum of Science and Industry. It is by far the institution's most popular exhibit, and draws hundreds of thousands of visitors each year. How it ended up in the American heartland is set forth in meticulous fashion by the boat's curator, Keith R. Gill, in "Project 356: *U-505* and the Journey to Chicago." The boat's meandering path to the Windy City was paved with politics, money, and egos—which together conspired to nearly derail the effort and doom the submarine to a humiliating end as a target for American artillery practice. Displaying and preserving *U-505* has been both costly and difficult, but the museum has finally solved its preservation dilemma by moving the boat indoors, where it will continue to serve as a memorial and historical curiosity to generations yet unborn. The vast majority of the photos in this study would not have been available without Keith's assistance. On more than one occasion our late-night conversations wandered far a field from the Battle of the Atlantic. I have enjoyed each of them.

*   *   *

Except for its editor, every contributor to *Hunt and Kill* is a U-boat scholar. Quite honestly, my forte is a long and deep interest in the subject, coupled with reasonably good organizational skills. If this body of work adds substance and understanding to the growing literature on U-boats, it is solely because of their expertise and the strength of their work product. It has been a pleasure working with such an outstanding team. Every editor should be so fortunate.

The Chicago Museum of Science and Industry, courtesy of *U-505's* always helpful curator and contributor Keith Gill, worked overtime to help locate and prepare many of the photographs that appear in this book. The visual record makes this study much richer and easier to comprehend and appreciate. Fellow contributors Timothy Mulligan and Jak Mallmann Showell supplied map details and boat coordinates.

I would also like to thank Lee Merideth of Historical Indexes for preparing the index, and Ian Hughes of Mousemat Design in the UK for crafting such a fine cover.

Lastly, I would be remiss if I closed without thanking my wife Carol and children, Alexandra Maria and Demetrious Theodore. Somehow I always manage to stretch myself in too many directions simultaneously, and despite Carol's best efforts to tamp me back into form, she is rarely (if ever) successful. She suffers because of my frenetic existence, bearing as a result more than her fair share of the home front's daily burdens. I can only ask for my best friend's continued understanding. Alex and Demetri know what it means when papa slinks toward his library after supper: "Momma's putting us down tonight!"

Someday I will try to make it up to you both.

U-505 is best remembered, from my point of view, as a monument to all seamen from every country who never returned from patrol.

Erich Topp

Foreword

Many U-boats and their commanders and crews are celebrated or remembered for their activities and accomplishments made during their war patrols. *U-47* for entering Scapa Flow and sinking HMS *Royal Oak*, for example, or the dramatic successes of the *Paukenschlag* boats off the eastern coast of America in 1942, the desperate convoy actions and successes of the "Happy Times," and even my own accidental sinking of the American destroyer USS *Reuben James* on October 31, 1941. These events and naturally many more, stand out as accomplishments. The *U-505* story, as told in this book, is remembered for other reasons.

U-505 was found by what was called a Hunter-Killer group. If aircraft or escorts from one found you, there was almost no chance of escape. Under the influence of depth charges, *U-505* was heavily damaged and forced to surface. The commanding officer, *Oberleutnant zur See* Harald Lange, tried to defend his boat with available machine guns against overwhelming odds, bravely I might add, but was hurt severely when struck by a bullet in the knee. His brain was still working, but as I understand the case to be, he did not give orders to sink the boat by activating the prepared explosives, as has been the tradition among submariners. It was his duty no matter the circumstances, and in this he failed. The crew, of course, did what they could to survive. They left the boat probably thinking it was set to sink but somehow no one eliminated the coding and enciphering machines and enigma. The result was the Americans captured *U-505* and learned valuable information but it did not, I must say, at that late date in the war change fundamentally their war effort. From our perspective it would have been considered a shocking thing, but of course at the time we knew nothing about this activity and Allied success.

Today *U-505* has been preserved and can be seen and toured in Chicago at the Museum of Science and Industry. I have been there many years ago now, and it was very impressive. It brings back to me many memories, although I did not serve on a Type IXC boat but rather a Type II and VIIC, and at the end of the war a Type XXI.

U-505 is best remembered, from my point of view, as a monument to all seamen from every country who never returned from patrol. This collection of accounts, written by authors who know what they are writing about, will help preserve the history of this boat and the memory of these lost men, and in that regard the fate suffered by *U-505* on June 4, 1944, can be turned into something positive for mankind.

U-505's feats were more than balanced by interminable months of drudgery and flat-out failure—odysseys, if you want, without the cleverness, skill, endurance, and character of an Odysseus. The only vision the men of *U-505* are certain to have shared with Troy's legendary conqueror must have been a determination to come home for good to their Penelopes and to leave the sea to Poseidon's devious whims.

Eric C. Rust

Introduction

I still remember the day—I was then a ten-year-old Gymnasiast in the town of Kappeln on the Baltic Sea just south of Denmark—when Dr. Schnoor acquainted me with my first Latin phrase: *pars pro toto*. "Doc" Schnoor was not a particularly exciting teacher in any of the subjects he taught (German, religion and history), in large measure because, as a veteran of Operation Barbarossa, he suffered from terrible pains in the stump of his right leg which the Russians had shot away two decades before. Indeed, it would have made more sense if our school principal and director of Latin studies, Pasche Klüver, who had lost an eye in Germany's costly airborne attack on Crete in 1941, had introduced me to that majestic ancient language.

Over the years I have used both the expression and the concept of pars pro toto on more than a few occasions on my students for it suggests a method of inquiry and a path toward deeper insight as simple and as straightforward as it is effective. Translated literally it means "a part for the whole" and corresponds to the basic notion that, by studying a small segment of a much larger phenomenon in great detail and intensity, one stands to gain a solid and valid understanding of that broader entity through a process of measured and informed generalization. Applied to our case, the story of *U-505* as told in *Hunt and Kill* becomes the *pars* that holds the key to our grasp of the *totum*, that long, bloody, relentless, but also grand and epic struggle from 1939 to 1945 that transformed the Atlantic Ocean and its peripheral waters for those who were there into the most terrifying theatre of the most terrible war in modern memory.

In all likelihood *U-505* would have remained a more or less typical German submarine among hundreds of U-boats with similar war histories had it not become involved in a sequence of events that led to its capture on the high seas by American naval forces and its eventual display as the most prized exhibit of Chicago's Museum of Science and Industry. To be sure, its eleven wartime patrols before that fateful day off the West African coast in June 1944 knew moments of high suspense and fleeting glory, but those feats were more than balanced by interminable months of drudgery and flat-out failure—odysseys, if you want, without the cleverness, skill, endurance, and character of an Odysseus. The only vision the men of *U-505* are certain to have shared with Troy's legendary conqueror must have been a determination to come home for good to their Penelopes and to leave the sea to Poseidon's devious whims.

But back to the *pars* and the *totum*. This volume describes and analyzes the history of a single U-boat—its men, its activities, its adversaries, and its unusual fate—in as much detail as any reader is likely to discover in a book on naval history. Recounted by some of the foremost experts in the field today, the saga of *U-505*, by informed extension, is the story of all German submarines and submariners in World War II, and of all Allied sailors, soldiers, and airmen whose skills, wits, and courage marked the Battle of the Atlantic. When we read of the conception and deployment of Type IX boats like *U-505* in the Kriegsmarine, we feel transported to U-boat headquarters where Grand Admiral Karl Dönitz and his staff plotted their cleverly conceived but fatally doomed "tonnage war" against Allied shipping on all seven seas. The careful breakdown and scholarly scrutiny of the boat's officers and men speaks volumes about the German Navy's staffing habits and how they stacked up against the war's inexorable demands. The summary of *U-505's* prior patrols illuminates both the possibilities and limitations of Germany's raiders of the deep as their chances for meaningful success first flickered and then expired like a candle's flame out of wax and oxygen. And not least there is the masterful examination of the ever-diminishing options *Oblt.z.S.d.R.* Harald Lange and his men faced when their boat shot up from the depths to encounter certain destruction by a foe who held every trump card in the deck. No doubt, dozens of U-boat commanders must have felt exactly as Lange did when they opened their boat's conning tower hatch after surfacing and realized in an instant that the game was up.

This exercise of projecting the experience of *U-505* onto the whole of the war at sea is by no means restricted to the German side. No reader can possibly be deceived into believing the Allies were destined to win the war on account of sheer superiority in numbers, industrial capacity, and motivation. The bloodletting associated with the U-boats' assault on the United States' and Canada's Eastern Seaboard as well as the Caribbean in 1942 should cure anyone of such delusions. But numbers, economic potential, and the consistent application of human ingenuity to the necessities of combat did favor the Allied effort from the start and only grew more pronounced as the war grew old. Foremost among such endeavors must rank the extraordinary accomplishment of codebreakers at Bletchley Park in Britain who, with help from their American associates in Dayton, Ohio, broke the German Enigma cipher—known as the Ultra Secret to the Allies—which most German naval leaders in their unfathomable hubris deemed perfectly secure until the very end of the conflict. Still, reading the enemy's mail is one thing; making him pay for it in tangible ways is quite another. And here again readers will discern that history is ultimately predicated on the performance and character of individuals, in this case Commander Knowles and Captain Gallery of the U.S. Navy whose mutual trust, friendship, and singleness of purpose made a decisive difference. Sometimes historians point to independent chains of causation to account for historical events whose outcomes they have trouble understanding or explaining, typically dismissing them as products of contingency or chance beyond plausible solution. No such excuse can apply to the Allied detection and capture of *U-505*. While the boat may have made its way home to Lorient with the greatest of luck in a counter-factual scenario, the indisputable reality remains that successful codebreaking, HF/DF vigilance, relentless aerial surveillance, and the dogged determination of a hunter-killer task force commander and his men, doomed the boat days before its final encounter with destiny.

An argument can be made, as my good friend Admiral Topp reminds us in his Foreword to this work, that the capture of *U-505*, its crew and all its contents came too late to make a real difference in the Battle of the

Atlantic. Fair enough. But war is also about symbols, heroes, and yes, trophies. And here the ultimate significance of *U-505's* journey comes together for us alive today, from its encounter with Task Group 22.3 off the littoral of Africa, to its lay-over in Bermuda, its long and almost lethal sojourn at Portsmouth, New Hampshire, to its final and present-day display off the shores of Lake Michigan in the Museum of Science and Industry in Chicago, Illinois. There was nothing in the stars that destined this boat, built proudly and efficiently by the Deutsche Werft in Hamburg in 1941, to end its life as a tourist attraction and curiosity for school children and history enthusiasts in the heartland of its former enemy. By the same token, every indication suggests the Allies earned their triumph fair and square, and they continue to enjoy every right to savor a victory celebrating that eternal and inimitable recipe for victory: brains and grit.

Critical readers, especially those with a pacifist set of mind, may take issue with the title we chose for our book: *Hunt and Kill*. Upon superficial inspection it appears to convey a taste and predilection for blood and violence, for celebrating the gory side of things. We certainly do not feel that way; nor did the men engaged on either side of the U-boat campaign. They deeply respected their enemy—as we do with the benefit of hindsight—and took extraordinary care to ensure their stricken foe, once cornered beyond hope, enjoyed every chance to survive. The capture of *U-505* is a remarkable but not at all unusual case in point. At the same time both sides knew that as long as the fight was on and neither side had gained a decisive advantage, everything came down to that simple yet terrible demand: *Hunt and Kill*.

One final annotation. Not long ago I published a book review about a work on the strategic cooperation (or lack of it) between the navies of Japan and Germany in World War II. While my evaluation of the book was on balance quite positive, I felt impelled to include the following observation: "Collaborative historiography involving multiple authors often leads to an uneven product marked by gaps, duplication, imbalance in coverage, irritating changes in style and emphasis, and a less than satisfactory sense of closure, even if aimed at a knowledgeable audience." No such problems pertain to the present volume. Readers will immediately and instinctively notice that this study, thanks to the guidance of its editor and the expertise of its contributors, is carefully coordinated to focus exclusively on *U-505* and its singular but telling fate—*pars pro toto*.

One of the myths regarding German U-boats is that all submarines were created equal and looked alike. In fact, German naval architects and engineers produced a range of different submarine types, each intended for specific tactical or strategic purposes, each with its particular strengths, weaknesses, capabilities, and limitations.

Eric C. Rust

No Target Too Far

The Genesis, Concept, and Operations of Type IX U-Boats in World War II

Articles 188 and 191 of the Treaty of Versailles, which Germany's representatives signed under protest on June 28, 1919, could not have been clearer: "All German submarines . . . must [be] handed over to the Governments of the Principal Allied and Associated Powers. . . Those in course of construction shall be broken up entirely by the German Government under the supervision of the said Governments. . . The construction or acquisition of any submarine, even for commercial purposes, shall be forbidden in Germany."[1]

These stark and unforgiving clauses closed Germany's first great experiment in underwater naval warfare, an experiment which had sent twelve million tons of Allied and neutral shipping to the bottom of the oceans, had struck terror into the hearts of merchant sailors and naval crews alike, indeed had lent to the First World War a dimension nobody could in the least have foreseen when the "Guns of August" ended a spectacular century of peace, progress and prosperity in that by then distant summer of 1914. It had also cost the lives of 5,000 German U-boat officers and men, the wrecks of their sunken craft, some 200 of them, along with those of their thousands of victims, littering the waters around the British Isles, the Atlantic, the Baltic, and the Mediterranean Sea.

No profound insight is required to discern why it was primarily British (and to some extent American) pressure that reduced Germany's postwar surface fleet to miniscule proportions compared to its status as the world's second most powerful navy in 1914, or why the Anglo-Saxon powers specifically insisted on the total and permanent elimination of Germany's submarine component. On numerous occasions during the war, U.S. President Woodrow Wilson expressed his outrage over what he considered Germany's barbaric use of submarines, with the *Lusitania* case of May 1915 ranking merely as the most notorious of such incidents. Indeed, Germany's calculated resumption of unrestricted submarine warfare in February 1917 led directly to the United States's declaration of war against the Center Powers two months later and ultimately to the Second Reich's military defeat and political collapse. In a similar fashion the British Admiralty considered the submarine a decidedly ungentle-manly weapon—sneaky, stealthy, and bluntly brutal, its hit-and-run tactics and newfangled torpedo technology at odds with, and unworthy of, the western naval tradition which the Royal Navy felt called upon to preserve and to prolong. To play the game fairly, the Germans should have come out and fought in the open in time-honored Nelsonian style on the surface for all to see, as their High Seas Fleet had done briefly at Jutland in 1916 with sufficiently bloody but strategically inconclusive results. To Anglo-Saxon observers, Germany's U-boat campaign simply proved the Teutonic way of making war had indeed deteriorated ingloriously from the days of Frederick the Great and, more recently those of Otto von Bismarck, to a level akin to the terror of late antiquity's Attila and his Huns.

Upon honest inspection, even the winners of the war had to admit by 1919 that the hostilities just concluded held out a number of revolutionary lessons for future naval warfare, just as they did for their counterparts in the army who had survived the slaughter along the Western Front and elsewhere, or for those who had opened a new dimension altogether by taking the war to the air. The experience of Germany's formidable submarine campaign—by 1918 the Kaiser's shipyards had completed no fewer that 344 boats of various designs to add to the 28 U-boats in commission when the war began—would undermine the very foundations upon which western naval doctrine had rested for centuries.[2]

Among many others, the experience of the First World War raised the question of whether major naval powers such as Great Britain, the United States and Japan could or even should continue to try to exercise effective and ubiquitous control over the seas. Enemy submarines, if available in sufficient numbers and operating from convenient forward bases, stood to threaten such hegemony by endangering not only the vital lifelines of merchant shipping but the safety of the surface fleet units designed and deployed to protect them. The era in which a numerically and qualitatively dominant fleet of capital ships with its vast and superior fire power, together with a supporting cast of cruisers, destroyers, and torpedo boats, could literally chase the enemy from the seas appeared to have come to a close.

The future strategy of naval superpowers called for a considerably more sophisticated approach. Whereas domination of the seas remained a desirable and perhaps even feasible objective, it could only be attained by complex fleets consisting of as many as five different elements:

(a) mighty battleships and battle cruisers, along with the new and as yet untried aircraft carriers, would continue to symbolize and attempt to exercise maritime hegemony by destroying or neutralizing the enemy's surface fleet;

(b) a second and very differently composed set of naval units would guard one's own merchantmen against the new submarine menace with large numbers of escort craft for the defense of these commercial vessels, whether sailing in convoys or singly, and with specialized submarine chasers to hunt, locate, destroy or otherwise deter the enemy's hunters of the deep;

(c) an effective blockade of hostile ports and coasts would be required to deny use of maritime communications to the enemy;

(d) a submarine force of one's own to reinforce the blockade, threaten the enemy's remaining supply lines, and to perform reconnaissance duties for the surface fleet; and

(e) the development of a naval air arm for such diverse tasks as reconnaissance, artillery spotting, submarine hunting, ship and shore bombardment, and aerial combat, was fast becoming indispensable.

Such an approach, if realistically pursued, demanded massive outlays in terms of finance, resources, and personnel, and would be a hard sell to civilian authorities or the other branches of the military—particularly after 1918, when in most minds another war of modern dimensions was all but unimaginable.

From the perspective of middling and minor naval powers—which included Germany as the principal loser of the war—the tactical characteristics and strategic possibilities of the submarine represented a huge and quickly understood windfall. Whatever else the war that had just ended may have meant, it introduced in the submarine a weapon ideally suited for the needs of naval underdogs. With submarines, even if built and deployed in modest numbers, such lesser powers could compel their mightier neighbors to lay out vast amounts of financial, material, and human resources for their naval establishments in pursuit of a sense of national and maritime security that might prove fleeting or altogether illusory. While by their very nature submarines could never hope to gain more than partial or temporary control of the seas, they surely could *deny* any such hegemony to their adversaries. The higher their numbers—and the better supported they were by forward bases, surface raiders, aircraft, supply vessels and reliable reconnaissance of all kinds—the more lethal their threat to the enemy's oceanic lifelines would become.

In this sense Articles 188 and 191 of the Versailles Treaty not only exemplified another manifestation of Allied revenge and mean-spiritedness vis-à-vis defeated Germany in a treaty saturated with such sentiments, but mirrored the concern, uncertainty, and even fear of Allied military experts who sensed the victory of 1918 had been bought at the cost of a revolution in military technology that threatened to negate and even overturn in the long run the Allied triumph just won. Their response of denying modern weapons such as submarines, aircraft, and tanks to the vanquished powers, and engaging in arms-control and disarmament measures such as those negotiated at the Washington Conference of 1922, could be but feeble, half-hearted, and pessimistic efforts to arrest the march of modernization and innovation.[3]

Long before Adolf Hitler's seizure of power in January 1933 and his subsequent open renunciation of the Versailles Treaty, the leaders of Germany's predominantly liberal and conciliatory (but no less patriotic-minded) Weimar Republic (1918-1933) took steps to ensure that military planning and technological innovation went on even if much of it was banned on paper. As early as 1922, secret diplomatic arrangements with the Soviet Union allowed for the clandestine training of German tank crews and Luftwaffe personnel on Russian soil. Civilian aviation schools at home doubled as training facilities for future combat pilots and mechanics. At the same time, experiments and improvements in German U-boat technology continued, typically disguised as consultation or third-party construction work for shipyards in foreign countries like Holland, Finland, and Turkey. Occasional protests by the Allied powers, especially neighboring France, brought few or inconclusive results. In fact, the once reasonably solid wartime coalition fell quickly apart after 1919. Its solidarity was weakened when the United States refused to sign the Versailles Treaty and drifted into renewed isolationism. At the same time, Britain was careful not to enfeeble Germany too much so as to preserve it as a counterweight to France on the continent and as a buffer against the spread of Bolshevism from the Soviet Union. Country after country followed Italy's lead in 1922 and moved from democratic and liberal forms of government to dictatorial, typically fascist, rule. By 1939, only Britain, France, the Low Countries, Ireland, Switzerland, Poland, and most of Scandinavia remained in the democratic camp. Everywhere else authoritarianism, irrationalism, and aggressive militarism had triumphed.

Against this backdrop of treaty restrictions, ongoing technological innovations, diplomatic realignments, and the prospect of radically different domestic and international policy aims under National Socialist leadership, Germany's naval planners in the 1920s and early 1930s set out to find a formula that would redefine the size, composition, and overall concept of the Reichsmarine (Kriegsmarine after 1935) for the foreseeable future. Germany's geostrategic situation was that of a continental land power with no significant allies and difficult access to the world's oceans. Taking into consideration the fate of its High Seas Fleet in the First World War, and assuming the Anglo-Saxon powers would again emerge as Germany's most likely adversaries at sea, the most logical and plausible conclusion would have been to create a fleet whose primary function would be massive and sophisticated commerce-raiding on a global scale, together with adequate coastal defense against bombardments or invasions and perhaps the possibility of limited offensive action against weaker neighbors.

In the event, Germany's strategic planners never fully embraced, let alone implemented, this clarity of purpose. Instead they favored a *hybrid* fleet concept that married a technologically innovative but numerically insufficient and ultimately quite useless battle fleet component with a likewise underdeveloped commerce-raiding element based on surface raiders and submarines, especially the latter.[4] This early omission and failure to analyze its geostrategic strengths and weaknesses properly, and to draw clear-cut consequences from it for its naval building and training program, would cost Germany dearly and tragically. It would be an overstatement to maintain that Germany lost the Second World War in large measure because of faulty naval planning. But it is certainly a defensible claim that *U-505's* cheerless mission and inglorious end in 1944, along with the even grimmer fates of many hundreds of its fellow U-boats, can be directly linked to a disastrous breakdown in strategic reasoning and planning in the inter-war period, even and especially after the Anglo-German Naval Agreement of June 1935 restored sovereignty and flexibility to its naval building program.

How was this lapse possible? A good number of historical analysts have blamed Germany's Commander-in-Chief of the Navy after 1928, Grand Admiral Erich Raeder. He was an old-school surface fleet proponent whose apprenticeship in the Imperial Navy had equipped him neither with the mental flexibility nor with the independence of analysis to divorce his thinking from Tirpitzian illusions about German battle fleet grandeur on the high seas. In addition, the very fact the Versailles Treaty prohibited Germany from building warships of more than 10,000 tons displacement became a political challenge inasmuch as any action in defiance of this limitation translated into a reassertion of German independence, nationalism, and sovereignty. In the end Raeder remained committed to his dual-fleet concept well beyond the time when the Allies had proved it to be, just as in World War I, a costly fiasco. In early 1943, Hitler replaced Raeder belatedly, but not illogically, with Grand Admiral Karl Dönitz, the popular creator and leader of Germany's U-boat arm.

Other observers maintain Germany could not absolutely take for granted that England and the United States would be its principal adversaries at sea in the event of another war, but that Germany would have to guard against the possibility of war with countries like France, Poland, or the Soviet Union, as indeed would be the case after 1939. As it turned out, and as any planner worth his salary should have foreseen, major or even minor surface fleet actions would not be *necessary* against these powers as German land and air forces would be principally engaged in these campaigns.

In the final analysis the most compelling explanation of Germany's failure to embrace a fleet concept aimed uncompromisingly at the destruction of enemy commercial shipping—what Dönitz would call *Tonnagekrieg*, or "tonnage war," i.e. sinking more tonnage than the enemy could replace by new construction—appears to have been the result of a lethal confluence of muddled thinking by Germany's naval leaders, coupled with a massive attack of national hubris. This tragic affliction prompted an entire people to overestimate vastly its collective strength and resources while simultaneously belittling and undervaluing the accomplishments and potential of its likely military opponents. When Hitler and the Nazis seized control in 1933, this hubris would be taken to entirely new dimensions far beyond any realistic and rational assessment. As their notorious Z-Plan[5] of 1938 indicates, Hitler and the Naval High Command envisioned the construction of *both* a prestigious Tirpitzian battle fleet with super battleships, battle cruisers, and even aircraft carriers in direct competition with Britain, *and* a commerce-raiding submarine force of hundreds of boats ready to drive the enemy into humiliating defeat and submission.

For the purpose of the subject at hand it will be necessary to restrict to a few comments the discussion of the German surface fleet construction program that would produce before the end of the war, after Hitler's formal renunciation of the Versailles Treaty and the signing of the Anglo-German Naval Agreement in 1935, a small sea-going surface force. Its exact mission in a possible war with Britain or under any other circumstances was never clearly thought out. Germany built two modern battleships (*Bismarck* and *Tirpitz*), two battle cruisers (*Scharnhorst* and *Gneisenau*), three heavy cruisers (*Admiral Hipper*, *Blücher*, *Prinz Eugen*), six light cruisers, and some forty destroyers, as well as several squadrons of torpedo boats and fast patrol craft. In addition, one aircraft carrier (*Graf Zeppelin*), six battleships, three battle cruisers, six light cruisers, and scores of destroyers remained on the drawing boards or were never completed and commissioned, while ultimate plans called for the construction of an even mightier fleet.[6] There are two central points to this compilation: (a) the predictable futility of building a force clearly inferior to that of the most likely enemy and therefore essentially doomed to idleness, suicide missions, or peripheral operations such as the costly invasion of Norway in 1940; and (b) the tremendous waste and misdirection of resources (money, raw materials, personnel, research and development efforts, and shipyard capacity) that could and should have been rerouted from the beginning toward the development, design, construction, training, and deployment of a commerce-raiding force of perhaps a thousand submarines or more, representing the latest technology and ideally based on the Atlantic littoral for easy access to enemy shipping lanes.

While one can ponder the might-have-beens of this proposition, Germany was not idle in addressing the commerce-raiding aspect of its overall naval program. Among the first and in some ways most ingenious steps in this direction ranks the development and construction of three replacement "cruisers" to compensate for the retirement of obsolete pre-dreadnoughts still in the German arsenal. Under international treaty arrangements, these *Panzerschiffe* (literally "armored ships;" the British dubbed them "pocket battleships") ostensibly displaced no more than 10,000 tons, but actual figures rose considerably above that limit. Lightly armored, the *Deutschland, Admiral Scheer*, and *Admiral Graf Spee*,[7] laid down between 1928 and 1932, exemplified the concept of oceanic commerce raiders that could protect themselves against superior enemy warships on the principle of being "stronger-than-faster and faster-than-stronger" opponents. In other words, their main artillery of six 11-inch guns in two triple turrets fore and aft enabled them, in theory, to keep faster but more lightly armed (8-inch) Allied cruisers at a distance, while their top speed of up to 28 knots made it possible to run away at ease from more heavily armed but slower enemy battleships. Their operational range of some 10,000 nautical miles at an economical speed of 20 knots and the use of catapult-launched reconnaissance aircraft made them potent hunters of merchant vessels, especially in the open waters of the South Atlantic and Indian Ocean. The operations and fate of the *Graf Spee* in 1939—chased into Montevideo after sustaining combat damage from British cruisers and forced to blow itself up on the River Plate—made clear both the possibilities and the limitations of these

Panzerschiffe. German efforts to employ regular battleships and cruisers against enemy commercial shipping in North Atlantic and Arctic waters produced at best mixed results and were at first curtailed and later abandoned altogether following the loss of the *Bismarck* on such an outing.

The Kriegsmarine's second and considerably more promising initiative aimed at high seas commerce-raiding involved converted and armed merchant vessels. They were relatively fast (up to 18 knots) with virtually unlimited endurance. They were also deceptively camouflaged to resemble genuine Allied merchantmen and sported disguised weaponry that could subdue an unsuspecting enemy vessel in minutes. Nine such raiders enjoyed a charmed existence in the southern oceans in the early phases of the war. They destroyed or captured no fewer than 136 enemy freighters and tankers until, by 1943, they were either hunted down or otherwise eliminated. Their successes compared favorably with the 60 Allied merchantmen bagged by German *Panzerschiffe* and capital ships in the North Atlantic. Famous raiders such as *Atlantis*, *Orion*, *Thor*, *Pinguin*, *Komet*, and *Kormoran* refueled and reprovisioned from captured enemy ships. Occasionally they entered Japanese ports for maintenance and repairs. Not unlike the pocket battleships, these raiders amounted to a compromise and improvisation whose effectiveness depended in large measure on the Allies' inability to extend the convoy system significantly beyond the North Atlantic routes. Improved aerial surveillance, more sophisticated intelligence gathering, and the detachment of major Allied fleet units for search-and-destroy missions permanently ended their effectiveness.[8]

U-boats were the most menacing counterforce against the Allied struggle to keep the British Isles (and later the Soviet Union) properly supplied, to build up forces in Britain and North Africa for the invasion and destruction of Hitler's "Fortress Europe," and to secure shipping lanes worldwide for the safe and uninterrupted movement and transfer of people and material. Germany had mounted a formidable effort in the First World War to force Britain to its knees. Within the self-imposed limitations indicated above, it would endeavor to do so again in the Second World War.

*   *   *

There exist two common myths regarding the German U-boat campaign of World War II—myths even today cheerfully promoted by bad popular fiction and equally shallow Hollywood movies. The first one holds that all German submarines were created equal and looked alike; invariably moved and attacked in wolfpacks; could remain submerged for days without surfacing; always suffered interminable depth charge pursuits after firing their torpedoes; eluded or shot down most of the aircraft sent out to find and sink them; and their brave crews under gruff but coldly competent skippers came within a hair's breadth of deciding the war in Germany's favor. Only last minute Allied heroism, technological sophistication, plentiful resources, and worthy patriots like "Rosie the Riveter" turned matters around and won the day for freedom and democracy. The second myth suggests all Allied merchant vessels traveled in convoys; were almost immediately picked up by prowling U-boats and tracked meticulously and accurately on huge charts at U-Boat Headquarters; incurred terrible losses whenever German wolfpacks sent off their lethal "eels" at night from submerged positions with every torpedo a sure hit; abandoned all shipwrecked survivors in invariably freezing, burning, or shark-infested waters because convoys could not afford to stop for fear of inviting even greater carnage; and at the conclusion of their travails, limped into port to lick their wounds only to receive orders for another voyage through hell after a short respite for their crews.

Of all the popular misconceptions suggested above, the most serious and misleading relate to the supposedly uniform German U-boat design and ubiquitous use of convoys throughout the war. In fact, German naval architects and engineers produced a range of different submarine types, each intended for specific tactical or strategic purposes, each with its particular strengths, weaknesses, capabilities, and limitations. Convoys were in use only in the North Atlantic, Arctic, and Mediterranean, and to a lesser extent, the Gulf of Mexico, Caribbean, and along certain stretches of the South American and South African coastlines. Everywhere else, especially in the Central and South Atlantic and Indian Ocean, Allied and neutral vessels typically sailed without armed escorts and without air cover because not enough escort vessels existed in the Allied arsenals to extend the convoy system to regions where attacks by Axis forces were relatively rare.

Based on successful World War I boats, on more recent concepts developed clandestinely in the interwar period, or by the 1940s on revolutionary new ideas derived from wartime experience, between 1928 and 1945 the Construction Bureau of the German Navy created on its drawing boards no fewer than thirty-six different U-boat models.[9] Neatly numbered in Roman numerals from I to XXXVI, and usually consisting of a basic design (lettered Type IA, Type IIA, etc.) as well as more refined or specialized subversions (e.g. Types IIB, IIC, IID), six of these projects would be fully developed and mass produced. In other cases a prototype or two was built and tested, but most models never matured beyond the planning stage, or remained mere ideas sketched on paper.

The earliest and smallest class was designated Type II, which consisted of forty-eight coastal boats with limited range, endurance, and weaponry. Nicknamed *"Einbäume"* (Dug-outs) by their crews and displacing a mere 250 tons, they participated in operations around the British Isles, in the Baltic Sea and, after transfer by way of the Danube, in the Black Sea. Few were built after 1940. As the war grew old those not decommissioned, scrapped, or cannibalized for parts ended up in the various training commands.

With no fewer than 695 commissioned boats, the Type VII design in its several variations comprised the most numerous class of submarines Germany built and deployed in World War II. Its sleek lines and salient features were made famous in Wolfgang Petersen's motion picture *Das Boot*, which was based on Lothar-Günther Buchheim's novel of the same title. Sometimes called "Atlantic boats" of about 850 tons displacement when submerged, Type VII boats carried up to fourteen torpedoes, anti-aircraft artillery and a ship-ship deck gun, enjoyed a surface range of 6,500 to 9,500 nautical miles, a top surface speed of 17 knots, and a crew of some forty-four officers and men. A total of fifteen different German shipyards along the North and Baltic Seas were pressed into service to produce them. They were the U-Boat Command's true workhorses: dependable, resilient, maneuverable, quick divers, and overall well suited for either independent assignments or wolf-pack warfare west and north of the British Isles, along the great-circle convoy routes from the New World to the Old, in the Arctic Ocean, and in the Mediterranean. Refueled and reprovisioned at sea, and economically handled, they could and did operate against shipping as far away as the Eastern Seaboard of the United States and Canada, and occasionally even in the Caribbean.

Men like Günther Prien, Otto Kretschmer, Jochen Schepke, Erich Topp and many other aces grew to master this weapon to perfection. Their principal forward bases were Brest (1st and 9th Flotillas), La Pallice/La Rochelle (3rd), and St. Nazaire (6th and 7th), all in France; Bergen (11th), Trondheim (13th), and Narvik (14th), all in Norway; and Salamis (23rd) and La Spezia/Toulon (29th) in the Mediterranean.

Leaving aside for the moment submarines of the Type IX class to which *U-505* belonged, and which will be discussed in more detail below, three other designs reached the stage of full development, if not necessarily large-scale wartime deployment. The ten commissioned boats of Type XIV, all built in Kiel, were large and rather ungainly boats of almost 2,000 tons displacement when submerged and intended exclusively for the mid-ocean resupply of other German submarines for the purpose of extending their range and length of operations. Invariably dubbed "*Milchkühe*" (Dairy Cows) because of their appearance and strategic purpose, they became available for frontline assignments by 1942 and played a not insubstantial role in projecting sustained German submarine activities into waters ordinarily beyond the range of Type VII and Type IX boats. Attached to the 12th U-Boat Flotilla in Bordeaux in southwestern France, these *Milchkühe* carried no armament except anti-aircraft artillery for self-defense, were slow divers and somewhat difficult to handle even on the surface. Still, their payload of more than 600 tons of diesel and lubrication oil, large store of provisions, spare parts, four extra torpedoes, a medical staff, and even replacement personnel, made them a welcome mid-ocean sight for Germany's attack submarines low on fuel, ammunition, and foodstuffs. Type XIV boats rendezvoused with their beneficiaries in relatively remote locations away from well-traveled sea lanes because the transfer of fuel and stores (and especially torpedoes) required hours of uncomfortable exposure on the surface that rendered both supplier and recipient vulnerable to surprise attacks by enemy planes and submarines. German efforts proved ineffective when a combination of sophisticated Allied code-breaking, high-frequency direction finding techniques, and increased aerial surveillance all over the Atlantic, helped along by a considerable degree of German carelessness, dispatched every *Milchkuh* to a watery grave by the time *U-505* met its own fate in June 1944.[10]

Of a truly new and revolutionary design, but developed and deployed much too late to influence the outcome of the war, were two other classes of U-boats: Types XXI and XXIII. Both types joined Admiral Dönitz's arsenal in the fall of 1944. Type XXI was conceived as a replacement for boats of the Type IX design like *U-505*, whose basic strategic purpose and engineering concepts went directly back to World War I precedents. In many ways a technological marvel, the new boats featured all the characteristics of a true underwater craft: a hydrodynamic hull to offer the least possible resistance when moving through the water; a large and strong hull (displacement over 1,800 tons) for greater diving depths than conventional craft; high underwater speed (better than 17 knots); tremendous endurance to elude convoy escorts courtesy of a huge array of rechargeable batteries and snorkel technology; and the latest target-seeking, individually programmable torpedoes. From the beginning it was conceived that these boats would be constructed at inland locations by sections, which would be transported to a seaside shipyard for final assembly. It was not until late 1944, with Allied land forces already pushing onto German soil from East and West, that Grand Admiral Dönitz gained the almost perfect weapon (still *sans* radar and similar modern guidance systems) to challenge the enemy's ubiquitous control of the oceans. Alas, of the 828 Type XXI boats ordered, only 118 were ever commissioned—the first, *U-2501*, on June 27, 1944, three weeks after D-Day—and none saw combat before the end of hostilities. Not surprisingly, Type XXI boats captured at the end of the war inspired postwar submarine designs on both sides of the Iron Curtain. In America alone, boats from the *Guppy* class to the *Nautilus* could hardly deny their kinship to their less fortunate forerunners in Hitler's arsenal.

The much smaller Type XXIII boats were a mere 250 tons. Mimicking the basic technological features of their larger Type XXI cousins, they were essentially craft of limited range designed for coastal defense. Whereas a total of 378 such boats were at one time on order from shipbuilding facilities in places as far-flung as Hamburg, Monfalcone (Italy), Toulon (France), Linz (Austria) and Nikolaev (Ukraine), wartime realities allowed for only 62 boats to be actually delivered and commissioned. Only three managed to inflict minor losses on the enemy in early 1945 before Germany's unconditional surrender.

*   *   *

Like the smaller Type II and Type VII designs, Type IX boats were developed in the interwar period. Seven were commissioned in 1938 and 1939 by the time Hitler attacked Poland and World War II got under way. They copied many features of the *U-81* class of boats in the Kaiser's Navy, and further improved thanks to two forerunner prototypes (*U-25* and *U-26* of Type IA). This group of submarines was not designed for either coastal defense or pitched convoy battles in the North Atlantic, although occasionally individual boats were drawn into convoy actions if they were in the vicinity. Instead, the Type IX class was earmarked for long-distance missions to far-away waters where enemy aerial surveillance was comparatively weak and spotty, the convoy system absent or poorly run, and targets easily picked off. This kind of deployment was also likely to draw Allied warships and planes away from the North Atlantic and ease the job of Germany's other submarines, whose main mission was to interdict incoming ships and shipments to the British Isles.

Almost by definition Type IX boats prowled as "lone wolves" and not in packs. In most cases U-boat Command assigned to them a general geographical area of operations, but the boats' skippers enjoyed considerable leeway when it came to working out the specific details of their missions. As a German memorandum of late 1941 clearly states, these boats were to wage war "independently and without restrictions within their assigned areas of operation."[11] All this grew from Dönitz's idea of *Tonnagekrieg*, the notion that it did not really matter when, where, or how you sank enemy merchant shipping as long as Allied losses month after month and year after year outstripped the number and tonnage of new construction delivered by neutral and Allied shipyards. By this reasoning, the Allies would be starved into submission and surrender as a calculable matter of time.

Type IX boats were exclusively built and serviced by three German shipyards, all on the North Sea: the Deschimag AG Weser in Bremen; the Deschimag AG Seebeck downriver in Wesermünde, and the Deutsche Werft AG in Hamburg on the Elbe River, where *U-505* was built as a Type IXC boat. A total of 194 such boats in seven different variations were delivered and commissioned before and during the war, with most seeing deployment and combat before the end of hostilities. Those few not lost in action were either decommissioned before the surrender because of irreparable combat damage or old age, or were captured and distributed after May 1945 as booty among the winners of the war. Most of the latter boats, in turn, were quickly scrapped or otherwise used up by the Allies, or simply scuttled as part of "Operation Deadlight."[12] Some saw a few more years of service under new flags before meeting a similar fate. Besides *U-505* in Chicago, only one other Type IX boat exists. In 1993, *U-534* was raised from a watery grave off Denmark and restored as a museum boat in Birkenhead, England.

Depending on individual features in their seven distinguishable design variations labeled IXA through IXD42, the double-hulled Type IX boats measured some 252 feet in length, 22 feet in width, drew a little over 14 feet of water, and displaced between 1,200 and 1,800 tons when submerged. They carried between 22 and 25 torpedoes (some in special containers outside the hull on the upper deck) that could be launched from six separate tubes, four forward and two aft. A 10.5-cm gun in front of the conning tower on the main deck could take on surface targets, while a 3.7-cm gun and a 2-cm battery were arrayed on platforms on and behind the bridge for moderate protection against enemy aircraft. After 1943, when suitable targets for surface artillery had practically vanished, the 10.5-cm guns were removed and additional 2-cm anti-aircraft weaponry installed on the platform behind the bridge. Every version carried periscopes for scanning the surface, for submerged attacks, and to search the sky for enemy aircraft.

Two 4,400 HP diesels produced a respectable top speed of 18 to 19 knots on the surface, while battery-powered electric motors moved the boat more or less quietly along at speeds of up to 8 knots submerged. The maximum safe diving depth is variously reported between 150 and 200 meters, but some boats survived accidental dives well beyond that mark while others, obviously, did not. An extended range of at least 10,500 nautical miles—up to 31,500 miles for the special Type IXD U-cruisers operating in the Indian Ocean and the Far East—at an economical speed of 10 to 12 knots, permitted Type IX boats to roam the oceans for months at a time. This range could be extended by mid-ocean refueling and reprovisioning from German surface vessels early in the war, or special Type XIV U-tankers later in the conflict. Occasionally, combat boats returning from operational areas transferred surplus fuel, provisions, and unused torpedoes to outbound boats to top off their stores and weapons. Four officers (including the engineer), 15 senior and junior petty officers, and 29 ratings made up the standard Type IX crew strength of 48. Often, however, extended missions included additional personnel, such as a medical officer, cadets-in-training, war correspondents, extra gunners to man the ever-growing array of anti-aircraft artillery, and so-called "confirmands," or officers slated to command a boat of their own but in need of acquiring practical hands-on experience.

Versions IXA, IXB, IXC and IXC/40 resembled each other in all central features except effective range, which was gradually extended from about 10,500 nautical miles in the early boats to almost 14,000 miles in later variations. This was achieved by adding more fuel capacity in the space between the two hulls. In addition to swapping the largely superfluous deck gun for more anti-aircraft artillery after 1943, most boats also received snorkels at that time, a tube-like device originally invented by the Dutch to pull in fresh air from the surface while expelling noxious diesel fumes. In theory, with relatively good weather snorkels allowed the boats to run their diesels while running at periscope depth. This advantage not only increased speed but made it possible for the boats to recharge their electric batteries without having to fully surface and face the increased possibility of detection. Unfortunately for the crews, snorkel technology was never perfected. The snorkel's head often cut under the surface (especially in ugly weather), abruptly stopping the flow of fresh air into the boat. The sudden immersion triggered dangerous pressure variations in the boat that often popped eardrums and filled the hull with toxic gases.

Type IXD boats in their variations D1, D2 and D42, and with their amazing range of more than 30,000 nautical miles, were specifically created for operations in the Indian and Pacific oceans. Some doubled as transporters of precious raw materials between Japanese-controlled ports in the Far East and German bases in western France. When the war ended in Europe, *U-181*, *U-195*, and *U-862*, Type IXs all, refused to surrender and were instead taken over by the Japanese and renamed I-501, I-506, and I-502, respectively. Their change of ownership did not prevent them from sharing the fate of their fellow boats that had ended the war under the swastika rather than the Rising Sun.

The numbering system of Type IX boats, and indeed that of all German submarines in World War II, at first glance defies logic and continues to confound anyone except the most knowledgeable of experts or those with a superbly developed memory. Instead of numbering boats in the chronological order in which they were commissioned and joined active service, the German Navy designated its submarines more or less according to the sequence in which construction orders were allocated to individual shipyards. This arrangement led to some confusion, because some boats carrying high numbers had been commissioned (and sometimes sunk) before a boat with a lower number ever hoisted its battle ensign. Thus, a Type IXC boat with a relatively high number like *U-505*, for example, was commissioned on August 26, 1941, while *U-176*, of the same class and design, entered service on December 15, 1941, eight days after Pearl Harbor. This hiccup in the numbering sequence occurred because U-505 belonged to the first batch of Type IXC boats allocated to the Deutsche Werft in Hamburg, whereas *U-176* belonged to a long series of boats built in Bremen by Deschimag. Other events only served to complicate this situation. As the war wore on, the Navy cancelled a number of construction contracts issued earlier for Type VII and Type IX boats in favor of the more promising Type XXI and XXIII designs. It did so, however, without canceling and reusing the numbers allocated under the original orders. As a result, the few boats of the Type XXI and XXIII classes commissioned in 1944 and 1945 carried designations beginning with *U-2501* and *U-2321*, respectively.

By any measure Type IX boats are one of the most successful submarine designs in history. Called *Seekühe* (Sea Cows) because of massive saddle tanks in their mid section reminiscent of bulging bovine stomachs, they enjoyed solid sea-going characteristics, more elbow-room and creature comforts for their crews than smaller Type II and VII models, and a longer life expectancy (generally speaking) than German submarines thrown against North Atlantic convoys. Their crews tended to serve together for longer periods of time under commanding officers with considerable experience. It was customary for junior officers trained as watch officers in Type IX boats to eventually move up to captain boats of this class. *Oblt.z.S* Oskar Kusch, for example, an outstanding watch officer with several remarkably rewarding tours of duty as second and first watch officer in *U-103* (Type IXB), took over command of *U-154* (Type IXC) in early 1943 at the unusually young age of twenty-four. Sometimes, however, successful skippers of Type VII craft were rewarded with command of the larger model boat. Thus, after impressive service in the Mediterranean as skippers of *U-83* and *U-81* (Type VIIB and VIIC boats), *Kapitänleutnants* Hans-Werner Kraus and Fritz Guggenberger received command in 1943 of the Type IXD2 and

IXC boats *U-199* and *U-513*, respectively, for operations in South American waters. In some cases officers of the rank of commander and even full captain were placed in charge of boats and given special or unusual assignments, including operations in the Indian Ocean or supply missions to and from Japanese bases in East Asia. Both Hans Ibbeken (*U-178*) and Kurt Freiwald (*U-181*), as seasoned *Kapitäne zur See*, fell into this category when they took their Type IXD2 boats into Asian waters late in the conflict.

Despite its many solid features, Type IX boats suffered from a number of drawbacks. One was their comparatively slow diving speed, a by-product of their mammoth size. It took a Type IX at least 35 seconds to dive (calculated as the time between the order to crash-dive and the time the boat reached periscope depth or better). Boats were utterly defenseless during those precious few moments. Until fully submerged or at a relatively safe depth they were completely vulnerable to enemy aircraft dropping bombs and depth charges. By 1943 some Allied planes were equipped with an acoustic homing torpedo that could be released into the wake of a diving (and unsuspecting) U-boat. The Mk 24, known as "Fido" by the Allies, followed the boat into the depths where it often rendered the plunge a permanent one rather than merely a temporary evasive maneuver.

Another factor limiting the effectiveness of German submarines of every classification was their nearly complete reliance upon visual means to locate suitable targets. Because they usually operated far from the somewhat predictable convoy routes and movements, encounters between Type IX boats and Allied merchantmen were almost always a matter of chance and luck—or misfortune, if you happened to be the victim. At no time during the war did the German Luftwaffe supply Dönitz's U-boat Command with sustained reliable information about the location of enemy vessels, nor did the Kriegsmarine's radio intelligence service fill this void with radio intercepts or high-frequency direction finding feats that could in any sense rival what the Allies managed to accomplish in this field. In short, the U-boats were essentially limited in their hunts to information derived from the lookouts scanning the horizons from the low conning towers of their boats, unstable and pitching platforms as they usually were in the ocean swell, the range of their binoculars even under ideal meteorological conditions restricted to perhaps ten miles in every direction and the airspace above. Underwater listening devices, such as hydrophones, turned out to be highly unreliable and only worked over a limited range, as did underwater telephony as a means of communicating with other submarines in the vicinity.

Submarines were also highly susceptible to depth charge damage. While their pressure hulls rarely cracked under the impact of these explosive canisters, the interior of the boats suffered heavily from the shockwaves. By 1944, the U-Boat Construction Bureau seriously considered installing additional shock-absorbing devices such as rubber and steel springs in the hope these alterations would limit combat damage inside the hull.[13]

Because of these frustrating conditions the Germans turned to a number of improvised techniques and devices to improve their chances of harming the enemy while reducing their own vulnerability. While German submarines had no active radar of their own, many carried a passive receiver called METOX. If properly tuned, it could in some cases detect whether enemy warships in the vicinity but beyond visual range were emitting radar beams. In theory a useful contraption, METOX became more or less useless when the Allies switched to higher radar frequencies. The receiver not only could not detect these shorter wavelengths, but produced dangerous emissions itself. Each time the boat surfaced the unwieldy reception antenna had to be carried up to boat's bridge, where cables connected it to the receiver in the radio room below. This time-consuming setup posed a hazard when the boat had to crash-dive, and the antenna was sometimes simply tossed overboard in the interest of saving the boat. At least one Type IX boat, *U-126*, appears to have been lost in an emergency dive when the conning tower hatch could not be completely closed because someone forgot to cut the METOX antenna cable in time.[14]

Yet another improvisation available by 1943 was a one-man mini-helicopter or gyro kite. The Fa 330 (also called *Bachstelze* after a popular, long-legged bird) could be assembled in less than three minutes and launched from the stern of a Type IX. Because it did not have an engine of its own, the reconnaissance craft was towed on a long steel cable. Depending on the boat's speed and wind velocity, it could reach an altitude of 700 feet. At this height maximum visibility increased to more than 30 miles—almost three times the distance enjoyed from conning tower level. Most Fa 330 launches, however, achieved altitudes closer to 500 feet with visibility in clear weather stretching up to 25 miles. As was often the case, however, practical performance lagged woefully behind theoretical expectations. The *Bachstelze* showed up prominently on enemy radar, which severely restricted its effective use. Because no submarine skipper was eager or likely to risk a surprise attack by surface units or aircraft while trailing the unwieldy device, deployments were limited to waters far distant from concentrations of Allied shipping, such as the South Atlantic and the Indian Ocean. Actual use in frontline situations appears to have been minimal. According to surviving war diaries only two boats, *U-177* and *U-861*, actually launched the Fa 330. Both were in the waters near Madagascar. Only one Allied ship came to grief as a result of these flights.[15]

Type IX boats participated in World War II from their first deployment into the Atlantic in August 1939 in anticipation of Hitler's attack on Poland, until the last of them, by then flying the Japanese flag, surrendered to the Allies in the Far East after VJ Day. Type IXs accounted for less than one-third of the Type VII boats that saw action, but are credited with 37 percent of the enemy tonnage sunk by German submarines. Nine of the ten most successful patrols undertaken between 1939 and 1945 were carried out by Type IX boats, and eight of the ten most successful boats overall were *Seekühe*. In the final analysis, these accomplishments had less to do with the experience or bravery of the boats' commanders and crews than with the fact they found and disposed of their victims under less dangerous circumstances than those experienced by Type VII boats, which were often forced to carve their prey out of heavily guarded convoys.

As originally conceived, Type IX boats usually operated as independent contractors, each with its own specific mission and broadly allocated area of operations. Three times during the war, however, U-Boat Command pulled together greater numbers of these larger boats for more concerted action. The first occasion was in the spring of 1940, when Type IX boats participated in Operation Weserübung, the hastily arranged German invasion of Denmark and Norway designed to gain a major geostrategic edge and to forestall an identical Allied countermove. German submarines gained little glory in these operations, largely because Norway's high geographical latitude and peculiar geomagnetic characteristics played havoc with the detonation mechanisms of their torpedoes. They did, however, help consolidate the German foothold ashore by transporting vital war materiel north, including several hundreds of tons of aviation fuel—a cargo crews were eager to pass on to Luftwaffe personnel ashore.

The second period of closely coordinated activities by Type IX boats is much better known than the frustrating Scandinavian interlude, and justifiably so. While this is not the proper place to recount in detail Operation Paukenschlag (or Drumbeat, as Michael Gannon translated the term in his outstanding book by the same title[16]), it should be noted the terrific carnage inflicted upon American shipping along the Eastern Seaboard in the first half of 1942 was almost exclusively the work of Type IX boats. Crossing the Atlantic from their bases at Lorient and Bordeaux, the boats picked off hundreds of juicy targets almost at will against token and poorly coordinated resistance. Their success demonstrated the wisdom of keeping a sizeable number of long-distance submarines in the German arsenal. It also highlighted the inexcusable folly and hubris on the part of American authorities, who had apparently learned nothing in terms of anti-submarine preparedness after witnessing daily for more than two years what Dönitz's U-boats could accomplish if given the opportunity to strike. To America's credit, the implementation of a regular convoy system and increasingly effective shore-based aerial reconnaissance tamed the menace by mid-1942. This, in turn, forced U-Boat Command to disperse its Type IX boats to waters less traveled—and generally less rewarding when it came to winning the tonnage war.[17]

The withdrawal of Type IX boats from the East Coast of the United States and Canada led directly to the third instance of concerted activity by these long-range commerce raiders, operations lasting intermittently from the fall of 1942 until the conclusion of the war. The boats were dispatched to the waters around the Cape of Good Hope and into the Indian Ocean, culminating by 1944 and 1945 in Operation Monsoon, when a handful of German U-cruisers began operating out of Penang in Japanese-occupied Malaya against Allied shipping in the region. Strategically, Dönitz found himself in a push-pull situation. The North and Central Atlantic had become increasingly dangerous for submarines of all types, whereas raiding Allied sea lanes around the tip of Africa, in the Indian Ocean, and in the approaches to the Red Sea and Persian Gulf represented virgin territory and the possibility of inflicting considerable damage to the enemy's seaborne traffic. Type IX boats, and especially

U-cruisers of the Type IXD variety, were ideally suited for such an undertaking.[18]

In retrospect it is not easy to judge the efficacy of Dönitz's decision to employ these boats in this manner, except perhaps to observe that he had very few alternatives. With the help of U-tankers and against weak Allied defenses, his boats did very well in the waters stretching from Capetown to Madagascar, particularly during the initial phase of these operations. Enemy defenses and convoy protection stiffened quickly, however, and by 1943 every Type XIV supply submarine had been sunk. Their loss limited the effective range of regular Type IX boats. Thereafter, long distance patrols had to cruise all the way into Japanese-controlled territory to refuel and reprovision, or resources had to be shared among incoming and outgoing boats. Many U-boats fell victim to air attacks; others suffered mechanical mishaps and fatigue in the unaccustomed tropical climate. Several commanding officers also succumbed when the challenging months-long assignments overtaxed their physical and mental endurance. While individual boats (like *Kapitän zur See* Wolfgang Lüth's *U-181*) could boast of solid and even spectacular successes, the majority of Type IX boats dispatched into the Indian Ocean never reached their destination or once there, hunted with but meager results. By the last year of the conflict several boats in Penang had run out of torpedoes and were reluctantly converted into improvised transport submarines to carry precious raw materials back to Europe from East Asia.

By this late date *Grossadmiral* Dönitz's overall strategy had long since shifted from his initial concept of waging a global tonnage war to a rearguard action. While sinking ships was still desirable, finding and sending them to the bottom of the sea had become very difficult and dangerous. During the war's final year U-boats were dispatched under increasingly lengthening odds against success (and even survival) to both hunt the enemy and attract and tie down as many Allied ships, planes, and resources as possible. The once proud raiders of the deep had become mere decoys in a desperate effort to postpone what loomed evermore as inevitable, namely the invasion of the heartland of Europe and the end of Hitler's Germany. The tonnage war was effectively lost by late 1942. After that time Allied shipyards consistently produced through new construction more ships than U-boats could sink at sea. The loss of no fewer than forty-one U-boats to a variety of Allied countermeasures in the month of May 1943 signaled the effective and dramatic end of the Battle of the Atlantic as it had been fought since 1939.[19]

These massive losses were directly related to what was perhaps the greatest handicap then facing German submarine operations: the deadly transit through the Bay of Biscay to and from bases in western France. The growing numerical and technological superiority of the Allied arsenal of weapons only made the journey that much more difficult. The Atlantic bases constituted a significant and obvious geostrategic improvement over having to fight the U-boat campaign from bases in Germany or Scandinavia. That advantage, however, was offset by the absolute predictability of submarine operations. German boats had to pass through the Biscay waters in order to reach their operational areas, and these waters could be easily patrolled by Allied aircraft and surface vessels. The approach to the French bases, therefore, posed a supreme navigational hazard and outright nightmare for the U-boats and their crews. By 1943, the Bay of Biscay—which earlier in the war offered one of the most lucrative hunting grounds for German submarines—rapidly took on the features of a permanent and ever-lurking death trap.

Unfortunately no alternatives, save a complete strategic retreat, presented themselves. After the defeat of France in June 1940, Germany developed a network of submarine bases along the Atlantic coast, with each installation servicing boats either of the Type VII or Type IX designs. Virtually all Type IXA, IXB and IXC boats belonged to the 2nd and 10th U-Boat Flotillas stationed at picturesque Lorient in southwestern Brittany, while the Type IXD boats with their globe-spanning range made Bordeaux their new home (in company with several large Italian submarines temporarily detached from the Mediterranean for service in the Central Atlantic). The ports themselves were well protected against enemy activity. In addition to heavy antiaircraft batteries, massive concrete pens with almost thirty individual berths in Lorient alone protected the boats against aerial bombardment, which allowed for unimpeded repair and maintenance work. Getting into port or out into the open sea through the vulnerable approaches to the bases, however, posed the Achilles heel of German submarine operations in the last three years of the war. Not only could the coastal channels be mined from the air, but the around-the-clock patrolling by Allied planes and warships of a north-south cordon of ocean netted almost daily U-boat sightings and large numbers of sinkings. This simple stratagem was effective because every departing or inbound submarine had to come up for air at regular intervals to vent out the interior of the boat. Just as important was a U-boat's need to recharge its batteries with the help of generators by running their diesels on the surface. During the six to eight hours it took to fully reenergize their electric plants, the boats were subject to detection even at night, when Allied hunters used shipboard and airborne radar, together with the famous Leigh Light—a powerful searchlight mounted beneath airplane wings—to spot their prey and deliver sudden and often lethal attacks at close range. With almost mathematical precision the Allied patrol pattern yielded scary or frequently deadly results for Dönitz's submariners, a fact surveys of U-boat war diaries make painfully clear. The entries reflecting this phase of the war are full of reports of daily aircraft sightings, crash dives, near misses by bombs, and lengthy depth charge pursuits.

Foremost on the U-boat men's minds were not the glorious successes scored during the "Happy Times" so long ago but mere survival, the simple but uncertain hope of returning to their bases and hometowns, which Allied bombers were turning systematically to ash and rubble. The Normandy Invasion of June 1944 forced most surviving submarines, after a brief and abortive effort to hurt the Allied armada in the English Channel, to abandon their bases in western France and retreat to Norway or German waters. Except for more deaths, bloodshed, and foolish but brave sacrifice, ostensibly in the name of binding enemy resources, the U-boat campaign was over.

*   *   *

The story of the Type IX boats is one of solid, even brilliant, performance until the turning point of the war in 1942/43, with a clearly defined mission under the guiding *leitmotif* of a worldwide tonnage war against Allied merchant shipping. After that time, with their strategic concept defeated or rendered immaterial given Allied superiority everywhere at sea and in the air, the boats' plight turned inevitably to tragedy. The life and fate of *U-505* and its men mirrors this transformation from hope to despair, from winning to losing, with haunting accuracy.

The NCOs and enlisted men constituted the great majority of the men who served aboard *U-505*. Collectively identified as a single entity, individually they varied greatly in background, experience, age, rank, shipboard function, and even in number. Reflecting the general turnover in U-boat crews, many men departed for additional training and reassignment, their places taken by new men. Still, a core of veterans remained intact aboard throughout the submarine's history.

Timothy P. Mulligan

A Community Bound by Fate

The Crew of U-505

Grand Admiral Karl Dönitz, the head and soul of the German submarine service in World War II, once described a U-boat crew as a *Schicksalsgemeinschaft*, "a community bound by fate." Success or failure for the submarine, and life or death for all on board, ultimately depended on each man performing his job, from the lowest rating to the captain.[1] Applicable to any submarine in any navy, this observation holds even more true for those who manned *U-505* in the service of the *Kriegsmarine*, the German Navy of Hitler's Reich.

From commissioning in August 1941 through capture by the U.S. Navy in June 1944, *U-505*'s crew represented both the continuity and evolution of German submariners during the war. From the original all-volunteer, hand-picked elite that still lingers as a propaganda image, German U-boat crews grew less voluntary and more generally

representative of the Navy and of their society as a whole. The men of
U-505 reflected this process, at the same time enduring a series of unique
events that marked their history: sustaining extraordinary damage in an
air attack, enduring the suicide of their commanding officer during a
depth-charge attack, and finally suffering the capture of their U-boat.
These events earned *U-505* the reputation as a "Pech-Boot," an unlucky
boat, extending even to her appellation in a recent history as "the sorriest
U-boat in the Atlantic force."[2] Over the course of three years, 11 officers
and approximately 100 noncommissioned officers (NCOs) and enlisted
men experienced the extraordinary history of this unique vessel. This
essay examines who these men were, and the community they
represented.

Officers

Over *U-505's* operational history, 11 officers served regular
assignments aboard her: three commanding officers (*Kommandanten*),
who held ranks ranging from *Oberleutnant zur See* (equivalent to a
Lieutenant (j.g.) in the U.S. Navy) to *Korvettenkapitän* (Lt.
Commander); two chief engineers (*Leitende Ingenieure*, abbreviated
L.I), holding ranks of *Oberleutnant (Ingenieur)* and *Kapitänleutnant
(Ingenieur)*, equivalent in the U.S. Navy to Lieutenant (j.g.) and
Lieutenant, Engineering); five watch officers (*Wachoffiziere*), usually
with the rank of *Leutnant zur See* (Ensign); and one naval surgeon.
Except for the last, these men occupied key leadership roles during the
vessel's history, and as officers their lives and careers are more
extensively documented than other crewmen. Their careers represent a
microcosm of the naval officer corps caught in the vise of a world war.

The rapid evolution of the U-boat war can be seen in the collective
backgrounds of *U-505's* three commanding officers. When war began
with Germany's invasion of Poland on September 1, 1939, all three were
on active duty, but none were in the submarine service, nor had any
received submarine training. By November 1941, however, as *U-505*
began her fourth month of training, all three had become *U-boot-Fahrer*
(submariners). This was typical throughout the Navy, as seen in the
example of the class of German naval officers who entered service in
1934: as of autumn 1937, only 36 of 318 officers had entered the U-boat

force (compared with 51 for the naval air arm), but by 1941, most of the class had become submariners.[3]

U-505's original commander, *Kapitänleutnant* (Lieutenant) Axel-Olaf Loewe, represented a direct link to the traditions of the Imperial Navy of World War I. Born January 3, 1909, in Kiel, Loewe belonged to an extended naval family. His father served as a gunnery officer aboard the battlecruiser S.M.S. *Seydlitz* at the Battle of Jutland in 1916, ending the war as first gunnery officer on battlecruiser S.M.S. *Von der Tann.* Two of his uncles commanded U-boats in that conflict: one died with his crew in the English Channel, while the other survived to attend his nephew's commissioning of *U-505* into service at the Deutsche Werft shipyard at Hamburg on August 26, 1941. Also attending the ceremonies was a former gunner of the *Seydlitz,* the chapter president of the ship's veteran's association in 1941. By that time Loewe's younger brother, also a U-boat officer, was already a British prisoner following the sinking in May 1941 of his boat, *U-110,* commanded by Loewe's cousin *Kaptlt.* Fritz-Julius Lemp.[4]

But Loewe had no need to rely solely on his pedigree during his naval career. He survived a stringent battery of mental and physical examinations to qualify for the highly select naval officer class of 1928 ("Crew 28"). Ranked second among 39 executive officers in his class, he received his officer's commission in October 1932 and served tours aboard cruisers *Emden* and *Königsberg* and *Panzerschiff* (most commonly translated as "pocket battleship") *Deutschland,* seeing his first action during the Spanish Civil War. At war's outbreak Loewe held a post at the naval academy, but his intellectual abilities soon led to his transfer as a staff officer to Armed Forces High Command (*Oberkommando der Wehrmacht,* or OKW), the command headquarters most directly associated with Adolf Hitler. During his year's stay at headquarters Loewe likely demonstrated considerable staff skills that would later be employed by Dönitz, but the needs of the ever-expanding submarine fleet resulted in his reassignment in October 1940 to the *U-Boot-Waffe.* After six months' training and a one-month stint aboard *U-74* as a "commander-in-training," he reported to Hamburg to familiarize himself with his first operational command, *U-505.*[5]

An initially unimpressed crewman described his commander as "medium height, with a head of thick, unruly hair. . . . He seemed very casual, in both dress and demeanor." It soon became apparent, however, that Loewe's appearance belied a "first-rate professionalism" and the ability of "a natural leader with a keen understanding of how to deal with men. . . . He led us by his personal example . . . like a father to us."[6] These traits were essential in any submarine commander, but particularly for those in command of Type IXC U-boats that operated for lengthy periods in distant operational areas. After leading his crew through a five-month period of training and shakedown cruises, Loewe led *U-505* on a transit passage from the Baltic to Lorient, France, then conducted two combat patrols into the waters off Western Africa and the Caribbean lasting 86 and 79 days, respectively. Through the long patrols Loewe maintained high morale through his command style, keeping the crew informed of his intentions, exercising a light touch in place of harshness to remedy crew lapses, and respecting maritime traditions and superstitions, including the traditional elaborate ceremony when the boat first crossed the Equator. Only in his preference for tea over coffee did Loewe part company with his crew.[7]

Loewe's operational success also boosted crew morale. Though inexperienced as a submarine commander, Loewe proved a quick learner. During the West African patrol he attacked six targets, sinking four with eight torpedo hits out of 14 fired. In the Caribbean *U-505* attacked and sank three vessels, achieving four hits in five torpedo shots and finishing two victims with gunfire; more would likely have followed had not Loewe's appendicitis curtailed the patrol. The crew proudly recorded their victories in white paint on the bulkhead aft of the electric motor room, and fashioned the traditional pennants hung from the periscope on returning to port. The success inspired one crewman to devise the conning tower insignia of an axe-wielding lion, combining the commander's name ("Loewe" = lion) with the axe, the symbol of his naval officer class. The seven vessels sunk (totaling 37,800 tons) fell short of Loewe's expectations, who considered his totals "nothing better than average at the time . . . I myself was definitely not satisfied with my success in the Freetown (Sierra Leone) area."[8] Yet, he had laid a foundation for the future.

For the performance of his vessel Loewe relied on his experienced Chief Engineer, *Kaptlt. (I)* Fritz Förster. A native of Krefeld who was only a year old when his father was killed in World War I, Förster had entered the Navy in 1933 as a simple stoker, but his abilities soon won him promotion into the engineering officer cadets of "Crew 33." He passed his examinations in April 1935 and thereafter logged engineering assignments aboard the cruiser *Leipzig* and pocket battleships *Deutschland* and *Admiral Graf Spee*. In the planned expansion of the surface fleet Förster doubtless would have held an important position, but by 1941 he, too, found himself reassigned to U-boat duty. Like Loewe, he reported to *U-505* while the vessel was still under construction, and the two developed a good relationship. As chief engineer Förster was almost equal to Loewe, responsible for maintaining the submarine's capabilities and seaworthiness. Loewe considered him "a real pro who mastered the complicated instruments and technical installations on board."[9]

Serving with Loewe were two very able watch officers. The *I.W.O.* or First Watch Officer, *Oblt.z.S.* Herbert Nollau, held the same rank and was older as Loewe's subordinate than would be *U-505's* later commanding officer. A graduate of the 1936 class of naval officers, Nollau survived the sinking of the heavy cruiser *Blücher* during the Norwegian campaign, then put in nine months with a harbor defense flotilla at Oslo before transferring to submarines. Popular with the crew, Nollau once led *U-505* in a fruitless two-hour pursuit of a herd of sea tortoises to try to catch a fresh dinner. Although Nollau's relations with his captain were not particularly close, they worked effectively together through Loewe's departure. When the latter fell ill with appendicitis on the third cruise, Nollau effectively assumed command of *U-505* for the final month of the patrol. Three months later Nollau received command of the Type IXC/40 boat *U-534*, which he would captain for the rest of the war.[10]

Second Watch Officer Gottfried Stolzenburg came to *U-505* from the merchant marine as a 29-year-old reservist on his first combat assignment, but whose experience in seamanship and navigation proved invaluable to Loewe. He moreover represented the first of the submarine's officers to have been a member of the Nazi Party (officially the "National Socialist German Workers' Party," *Nationalsozialistische Deutsche Arbeiterpartei*, or NSDAP), which he joined in May 1933 as member no. 1,540,181.[11] German naval officers have often been characterized as "Nazis" on the basis of impressions of their wartime captors and interrogators—hardly impartial sources—or because of their expressed loyalty to Hitler, a criterion not only variable by degree and time, but too vague in meaning.[12] With the availability of microfilmed Nazi Party membership records formerly held by the Berlin Document

Center, concrete documentation of a specific choice offers a firmer basis for evaluation. Yet even here we lack knowledge of the context in which an individual chose to join the Party.

Stolzenberg's decision possibly reflected the growth of the Nazi-affiliated SA (*Sturmabteilung*, storm troopers) within the rank-and-file German merchant marine, which pressured many officers to also join either the SA or the Party to maintain their positions— particularly in a profession rendered increasingly insecure by the collapse of world trade during the Great Depression. (Germany's premier ace in the early days of the war, Günther Prien, also came to the navy as a former merchant marine officer and had also joined the Nazi Party in 1932.) In accordance with Wehrmacht regulations then in effect, Stolzenburg surrendered active membership in the Party upon activation from the reserves in 1938, although his Party membership doubtless played a key role in his nomination as a reserve officer. He remained aboard *U-505* until wounded in November 1942, and eventually exercised command of training boats *U-11* and *U-554*, ending the war as captain of the Type XXI submarine *U-2543*.[13]

Also of note were two young midshipmen (*Fähnriche zur See*), Horst Doedens and Werner Jacobi, who shipped aboard *U-505* in Danzig on September 26, 1941, as part of their training. Although they were officer candidates, their onboard status equaled that of NCOs subordinated to the watch officers. They remained aboard until May 1942, enduring their baptism of fire in *U-505's* patrol off West Africa. Doedens eventually became Second Watch Officer aboard *U-845* and survived its sinking on March 10, 1944, to spend the rest of the war in captivity. Jacobi was apparently responsible for failing to provision *U-505* with the proper soap supply before an early patrol, thereby earning the wrath of *I.W.O.* Nollau. When Jacobi later discovered he had been assigned as watch officer to *U-534* under Nollau, he immediately requested a reassignment, which unhappily led to his death aboard *U-973* in March 1944.[14]

Förster's and Stolzenburg's service aboard *U-505* outlasted their commander, whose appendicitis cut short his second combat patrol and forced a quick return to base. Following his recovery, Loewe—now promoted *Korvettenkapitän*—returned to staff duties at Dönitz's headquarters, where he continued to play a role in the Battle of the Atlantic in evaluating weaponry and tactics reports and directly interviewing captains of returning U-boats for their experiences. In this capacity Loewe could at least follow the fate of his old command.[15]

U-505's second commanding officer represented the wartime generation of U-boat officers needed for the rapidly expanding U-boat fleet, men who enjoyed successful apprenticeships as watch officers but would encounter far greater difficulties as captains. At the time of *U-505's* commissioning in August 1941, Dönitz's front-line strength amounted to 64 U-boats, with 120 engaged in training or trials. By September 1942, when *Oblt.z.S.* Peter Zschech assumed command, front-line strength had nearly tripled to 172 submarines, with 194 in training.[16] Providing this fleet with officers and men necessitated the promotion of younger, less-experienced men. Yet, the choice for *U-505's* new captain did not seem to represent a compromise.

Nine years Loewe's junior and two years younger than Nollau, Zschech was born October 1, 1918, in Constantinople (now Istanbul), where his father, Dr. Bernhard Zschech, served throughout World War I as a naval surgeon to German naval forces assisting their Turkish allies. His son entered as the youngest of the naval officer class of 1936, whose 560 members dwarfed the select "Crews" of Loewe's period. Curtailed training also characterized the younger officer's early service: where Loewe and his colleagues spent 54 months as cadets, the members of Crew 36 received their commissions in only 30 months. Nevertheless, Zschech's ranking of 82nd among more than 350 executive officers (the class included 200 engineering, medical, weapons, and administrative officer cadets) testified to an above-average ability that led him to the Navy's destroyers, where he saw combat aboard the *Hermann Schoemann* (July 1939-April 1940) and the *Friedrich Ihn* (April-October 1940).[17]

Zschech's transfer to the U-boat arm in October 1940 brought Dönitz a young but seemingly self-confident and accomplished officer. After completing his submarine training, he distinguished himself as an instructor at the torpedo school in Mürwik. Zschech, a colleague later recalled, "was one of the most intelligent officers of his Crew. I heard from a *Crewkamerad* that, if there was anything to write, often they looked for what Peter did, and followed his lead . . . after some months he effectively led the training flotilla during exercises, the actual commander gave Peter free rein to do what he wanted."[18]

In late August 1941, Zschech joined *U-124* as the *II. W.O.* (Second Watch Officer) under its new commander, *Kaptlt.* Johann Mohr, who would continue the success bequeathed him by the boat's original captain, Wilhelm Schulz. Zschech served aboard *U-124* for four patrols (the last three as First Officer), in the course of which the U-boat sank the British light cruiser *HMS Dunedin*, a Free French corvette, and 20 merchant vessels totaling nearly 90,000 tons, as well as torpedoing three additional merchantmen and participating in the rescue of survivors of the German raider *Atlantis* and supply ship *Python*. As *I.W.O.* Zschech assumed much responsibility and personally conducted the torpedo attacks made on the surface, and thus could claim a fair share of this success. When he transferred at the end of June 1942, Zschech could take pride in his role in making *U-124* the third most successful U-boat of World War II.[19]

Doubtless *Oblt.z.S.* Zschech expected to expand this legacy when he assumed command of *U-505* on September 6, 1942. A crewman described him as "young, handsome, and cultured . . .intelligent but a little aloof...very eager to get at the enemy," leading *U-505's* veterans to suspect their new commander of suffering from *Halsschmerzen*, the "sore throat" that afflicted young U-boat captains and could only be remedied by the award of the Knight's Cross.[20] Zschech never suspected the first vessel he sank would also be his last.

U-505's fourth operational cruise brought her back to the Caribbean, where Zschech dispatched a 7,200-ton British merchantman on November 7, 1942. Three days later a British Hudson aircraft surprised the boat on the surface southeast of Trinidad, dropping a depth-charge that detonated on the U-boat's aft deck. The explosion was so strong it destroyed the attacking aircraft and caused severe damage to the submarine's hull, engines, and many of her operating systems. The attack also injured *II.W.O.* Stolzenburg, who suffered head wounds, broken ribs, and a punctured lung, and another crewman who also sustained serious injuries. *U-505* just managed to limp home on one diesel engine, reportedly the most severely-damaged U-boat ever to return to base during the war. The extent of the damage was, if anything, underestimated through the remarkable feat of the crew in nursing their crippled craft more than 4,700 nautical miles home; they even managed to restore a limited diving capacity. The aggressive Zschech even attempted an extreme-range torpedo attack on a freighter during the return voyage.[21]

Still, little satisfaction accrued from this achievement. Although Zschech retained the axe-symbol on the conning tower to maintain continuity with Loewe (adding the Olympic rings on the front of the conning tower to represent his own "Crew 36," the year of the Olympics), he sharply broke with many of his predecessor's practices relating to the crew. A far more formal relationship between officers and other ranks now characterized the crew of *U-505*, doubtless reinforced by the submarine's protracted stay in port to undergo repairs and refitting. From December 1942 through the end of June 1943, *U-505* received 36 square meters of new pressure hull plating, a rebuilt port diesel engine, extensive interior repairs, and a new conning tower with an extended platform for a battery of new antiaircraft guns. But the extent of repairs necessary, combined with dockyard sabotage by French workers, severely curtailed *U-505's* effectiveness: the next six attempts at departure from July through September 1943 resulted in returns to port with continuing mechanical problems or easily-sustained battle damage. During these three months *U-505* managed only 32 days at sea.[22]

These delays and aborted sorties preyed on the crew's morale, and above all on the captain. Far more significant, the boat and its crew began to earn a reputation as malingerers among submariners at Lorient: verses were composed about "the U-boat that sailed out every morning and was back every evening," *U-505* became known as a "drydock goat" (*Werftbock*), and Zschech himself came to be considered as a "true master of authentic sabotage" to avoid the risks of combat.[23] Such remarks reflected a bitterness born of increasingly heavy losses. Of the 27 Type IXC U-boats that comprised the 2nd U-boat Flotilla with *U-505* at Lorient in early March 1943, 13 had been sunk by early August. One of these was Zschech's former *U-124*, which was lost with all hands in April. At the same time the scale of casualties became evident to Zschech through the loss of so many of his classmates and friends. From late April through August at least 24 officers from "Crew 36" were killed or captured while in command of U-boats.[24]

Professional disappointment, damaged prestige, and grief over the loss of comrades affected *U-505's* commander despite his promotion on April 1, 1943, to *Kapitänleutnant*. Unfortunately he could not look to support from his crew, whom he had largely alienated by his conduct.

According to crewman Hans Goebeler, Zschech treated his men in an arrogant manner, constantly running extra drills and exercises, insisting on formalities in the officers' mess, and often displaying anger at subordinates. Where Loewe had respected "good luck" traditions and superstitions for crew morale, Zschech ignored them. His style did not encourage a sense of community with the crew. For example, on one occasion a soiled and sweating torpedoman moving through the wardroom was informed, "Get your filthy carcass out of the officer's quarters!" Machinist's Mate Karl Springer recalled, "Zschech was not an officer you could talk to, instead he just gave orders. . . . I suspect he had it in for us petty officers, because of some bad experiences he'd had as a midshipman."[25]

Zschech lost his strongest support onboard with the transfer of his First Watch Officer, *Oblt.z.S.* Thilo Bode, in August 1943. Bode, slightly older than Zschech and a member of the same 1936 class of officers, had joined *U-505* with his commander and immediately renewed their close prewar friendship. If relations with the lower ranks were strained, the captain at least enjoyed a sympathetic ear with his first officer. Moreover, at the time of his transfer Bode had begun to develop a better rapport with the crew, which might have helped bridge the emotional gulf between Zschech and his men. When he departed *U-505*, Bode paid tribute to "the splendid crew whose spirit I wish to see duplicated on my ship," and praised the "enthusiasm, high courage, and good humor" they displayed. Unfortunately Bode could no longer assist an isolated Zschech as the captain approached his ultimate challenge.[26]

U-505 sailed again on October 9, 1943, and this time successfully traversed the Bay of Biscay. Within two weeks, however, the pressures building up inside Zschech boiled over. At 7:54 p.m. (Berlin time) on October 24, 1943, *Kaptlt.* Peter Zschech shot himself in the control room. He lingered more than 90 minutes before death overtook him at 9:29 p.m. The next morning his body, wrapped and sewn inside a hammock, was put over the side. The only U-boat commander to commit suicide in an action not involving the loss of his boat at last had found peace.[27]

As with many other aspects of *U-505's* history, some mystery attends the circumstances of Zschech's death. The U-boat's war diary and all subsequent accounts of German eyewitnesses assert that the suicide occurred during an intensive pursuit and depth-charging by Allied vessels.[28] Yet a review of all available Allied antisubmarine warfare operations on that date fails to reveal any actions, by either warship or aircraft, in the area of *U-505's* location (approximately 600 miles west of Lisbon, Portugal).[29] Such a discrepancy is not easily resolved, and the date of the event does not seem in question. If Zschech's suicide did not result from an unnerving underwater attack, its attribution to such circumstances hardly makes the captain's decision more justifiable or comprehensible, certainly not to his crew. Today the mystery may only be noted, and will likely never be solved.

In any case, Loewe offers perhaps the best verdict on the fate of his successor:

> As an officer up to that time, he might have been considered a good average. Without doubt he was a capable seaman. . . But command of a sub demands a strong constitution, both physically and psychologically, and Zschech had reached a point where he no longer possessed either. Add to that his bad luck and lack of success . . . so it came about that at the end of his moral and physical strength, in a situation that was in no way critical, he lost his nerve and killed himself. The main responsibility for this lies not with Zschech, but with the leadership who failed to take him out of combat and did not recognize his condition. Here was a man asked to give more than he had.[30]

The officer who assumed command of *U-505* at Zschech's death was 26-year-old *Oblt.z.S.* Paul Meyer, the new First Watch Officer after Bode's departure. Meyer represented an entirely different type of U-boat officer, one risen through the ranks. Enlisting in the Navy in 1936, the native of the Baltic town of Zoppot (now Sopot, Poland) first saw action aboard a German commerce raider, where his performance as a member of a prize crew that brought a captured Allied vessel to Germany earned him promotion as an officer. After eight months of duty aboard destroyer *Z30*, he received his U-boat training and joined *U-505* in December 1942 as Second Watch Officer. He got along well with Zschech, whom he found "very comradely." At the same time Meyer proved very popular with the crew, his origins as an enlisted man permitting an ease and familiarity with the ranks not accorded to naval academy graduates. With more time as *I.W.O.* he, too, might have bridged the gap between Zschech and the crew. Instead, he found himself the acting commander of *U-505* on the evening of October 24, 1943. To settle a shaken crew, Meyer promised to bring them safely back to port, if in return they did their utmost in fulfilling their duties. All promises were kept as Meyer carefully guided the boat back through the hazardous Bay of Biscay, arriving at Lorient on November 7.[31]

During Zschech's tenure a complete turnover had occurred among *U-505's* officers. The changes at First Watch Officer with Bode and Meyer have already been noted. Gottfried Stolzenburg, the original Second Watch Officer so badly wounded in the air attack on November 10, 1942, had been transferred to a "milk cow" U-boat for medical attention; Meyer had first replaced him after *U-505* returned from that patrol. Following Meyer's promotion, *Lt.z.S.d.R.* reservist Kurt Brey joined the crew as *II.W.O.* and, at age 36, was the oldest man (temporarily) on board. Also assigned to *U-505* from October 1943 was Dr. Friedrich-Wilhelm Rosenmeyer, one of 243 naval surgeons who served on German U-boats during the war (the majority on the long-range patrols of Type IXC boats), 117 of whom would perish with their boats.[32]

Most significantly, the original Chief Engineer, *Kaptlt. (I)* Förster, served only 18 days on Zschech's first patrol before transferring to *U-514* and returning to Lorient for a shore assignment. His foreshortened final war cruise was merely to supervise the new chief engineer, *Oberleutnant (Ingenieur)* Josef Hauser, who assumed his duties on October 22, 1942, and would remain chief engineer through the day of *U-505's* capture. Nicknamed *der Waschbär* ("the Raccoon") for his preoccupation with his beard, Hauser was only 22 when he came aboard, several years junior to two NCO machinists under his command; Thilo Bode would later recall he displayed a very forward manner, although he looked more like a Boy Scout than an officer.[33] Also on board for the first Zschech patrol was engineering midshipman Erich Altesellmeier, who received his promotion to *Leutnant (I)* only 11 days after the air attack that so badly damaged *U-505* in November 1942. Altesellmeier later became chief engineer on *U-377* and was lost with that vessel in January 1944.[34]

For the *Kriegsmarine*, the immediate problem after Zschech's death became what to do with the crew. After a summary investigation and the swearing to secrecy of *U-505's* officers and men about their captain's suicide, flotilla headquarters—perhaps U-Boat Command itself—determined to keep the boat and crew together (this is discussed further in the "Crewmen" section below). The selection of a new captain became paramount. Meyer's impressive performance notwithstanding, he had accumulated only 62 days' sailing experience as a submariner during a year aboard *U-505*.[35] On November 18, 1943, *Oblt.z.S.d.R.* Harald Lange assumed command.

At age 40, the Hamburg native became not only the oldest member of the crew, but the oldest captain of a front-line U-boat at the time. More important, he emerged from a different milieu than his predecessors. Lange also chose the sea as a profession, but as a civilian with the merchant marine. An officer with the Hamburg-America Line between the wars, Lange often visited the United States, where his first cousin and boyhood friend Johannes Messmer lived in Indiana as a contractor. Lange's frequent visits to New York introduced him to his future wife, Karla, who had come to America as a professional nurse and might have remained had she not fallen in love with Lange and returned to Germany with him. In 1935 he joined the naval reserves, but remained a merchant sailor until activated in 1939.[36]

When war came Lange commanded first a barrage- and mine-sweeper, then took over a patrol boat in the western Baltic from May 1940 through September 1941. In November 1940 he depth-charged and apparently damaged a British submarine operating in the Kattegat, and one year later transferred to the U-boat arm. His first combat assignment as a submariner came as First Watch Officer aboard the Type IXD1 submarine *U-180*, which featured a unique propulsion system of six Mercedes-Benz water-cooled diesel engines—a design that provided more surface speed, but proved unusable due to the excessive smoke and heat generated. Lange participated in the historic patrol of February-July 1943, when *U-180* rendezvoused with a Japanese submarine in the Indian Ocean to transfer Indian nationalist leader Subhas Chandra Bose and his adjutant to their Axis ally in an effort to promote Indian discontent against British rule. After returning from this 144-day voyage Lange temporarily assumed command of *U-180*, then attended U-boat commanders' school before replacing Zschech on *U-505*.[37]

Lange's six-foot height and deep baritone voice immediately impressed his crew, but it was his character that completely won them over. "He was a father figure who quickly gained our trust," recalled one crewman; "You could talk with him, he was very approachable," remembered another. Crewman Hans Goebeler wrote, "Like our first commander Axel Loewe, his main concern was the good of the boat, everything else was small fish . . . he exuded an air of calm confidence," to which the crew eagerly responded.[38] Lange's was truly a remarkable achievement in salvaging the morale of a crew wracked by a year's worth of chronic technical problems, aborted missions, and their commander's suicide. Goebeler's comparison to Loewe is particularly revealing in view of the differences in background. Of the three executive officers (commander and watch officers) who commissioned *U-505* in 1941, two were naval academy graduates and the third a reservist; two years later, none of the three were academy graduates, two were reservists and one was promoted from the ranks.

Thus *U-505's* final set of officers constituted a third generation of U-boat officers encompassed by the boat's history. Loewe represented the select professionals of the inter-war period, with direct links to the Imperial Navy; Zschech exemplified the younger breed promoted by the harsh demands for success. Now Lange and his subordinates succeeded to command, not as career officers but as reservists advanced through the decimated ranks of Dönitz's corps. Their mission concerned much less the sinking of Allied tonnage than mere survival as a fighting force, to continue to tie down Allied resources while German scientists and technicians raced to develop a new generation of submarines to renew the battle in the future.[39] That such variations existed over less than three years indicates the turmoil and turnover within an officer corps increasingly transformed into submariners and fed into the maw of superior Allied forces.

But another shared characteristic of *U-505's* final set of officers commands even more attention: like Stolzenburg, three of the five had joined the Nazi Party prior to entering the Navy. Harald Lange entered the Party as member no. 3,450,040 on May 1, 1934. Like fellow merchant marine officer Gottfried Stolzenburg before him, pressures within his profession doubtless contributed to Lange's decision. When Josef Hauser joined the NSDAP as member no. 6,956,390 in September 1938, he was an 18-year-old engineering student in Zweibrücken who had been only 12 when Hitler came to power. By contrast, Kurt Brey, a commercial salesman before the war, applied for Party membership at age 33 in November 1939, and was accepted in January 1940 as Party member no. 7,381,657.[40]

How these facts figured into the collective history of *U-505* can never be fully determined. The reasons behind these personal choices accompanied their authors to the grave. For Lange, Brey and Stolzenburg the link between Party membership and reserve officer status was not coincidental, but increasingly standard throughout the Wehrmacht—a nexus of political-military relations that has not yet received the study it deserves.[41] Thus, if professional concerns lay behind their political choices, the latter also advanced their military careers as reserve officers. Whether through professional pressure, opportunism, conviction, or youthful zeal, it is also true that all joined the NSDAP only after Hitler had assumed power. Neither does the available evidence suggest any proselytizing for National Socialism or overt propaganda among the crew (that Lange had even been a Party member surprised a friend and former *U-180* comrade). Yet, the oft-asserted independence of the German Navy from Nazi influence appears ever less convincing, and if the four officers' decisions to join the Party did not play a part in bringing Hitler to power, their actions nevertheless contributed to consolidating that power and National Socialism's grip on German society. Moreover, they collectively illustrate the process of increasing politicization of the Navy and Wehrmacht as a whole as the war entered its final stages.[42] As an interesting contrast, Thilo Bode's marriage one month after he left *U-505* led him into contact with German resistance circles and to undertake some discrete efforts on behalf of Admiral Wilhelm Canaris, the head of German intelligence eventually executed for treason against the regime.[43]

Perhaps it was thus fitting these officers led *U-505*, now sporting a seashell as her conning tower insignia, on her final missions. On December 25 the boat departed on patrol but was diverted three days later to search for survivors of German surface forces sunk by British cruisers in the Bay of Biscay. Lange rescued 34 survivors of torpedo-boat *T25* and brought them to Brest January 2, 1944. (This rescue, ironically, returned *T25*'s favor nearly five months earlier in recovering survivors of another 2nd U-boat Flotilla boat, *U-106*, at virtually the same spot.[44]) Following several weeks of repair to replace the diving plane shaft, *U-505* sortied on March 16, 1944, en route to familiar hunting grounds in West African waters off the ports of Monrovia and Freetown. *U-505* found few opportunities there while constantly dodging Allied aircraft and warships, yet her mere presence accomplished Dönitz's proclaimed strategic mission of tying down superior Allied forces while new U-boat models were developed.[45] *U-505* exemplified this strategy at the moment of her capture on June 4 by the disparity of forces involved: opposed to

Lange and his 59 men was Capt. Daniel Gallery's Task Group 22.3, comprising one escort aircraft carrier and five destroyer escorts with about 3,000 crewmen.

In *U-505's* brief final action, American gunfire badly wounded Lange in his face and both legs; he survived but eventually lost his right leg at mid-thigh. By incapacitating Lange, these wounds prevented him from overseeing the sub's scuttling and thus probably secured the U-boat's capture. Meyer also received a wound (to his scalp), but the other officers passed into captivity unhurt. To conceal the boat's capture from German authorities, no mail was sent or received by *U-505's* crew at Camp Ruston, Louisiana, where they were held as prisoners of war, and thus their families in Germany knew only that all were missing in action. Karla Lange maintained contact with the families, encouraging them that her husband would do everything he could to look after their sons and husbands and save them. Events did not prove her wrong.[46]

In a combat branch distinguished by the death in combat of more than half of all who served, association with *U-505* proved most fortunate for its officers. Of the 11 officers regularly assigned to duty aboard the U-boat over the course of the war, only one—Zschech—died, and that by his own hand. The five officers captured in June 1944 gradually returned home after war's end. None of the officers who departed *U-505* for other assignments suffered death or capture during the conflict. Herbert Nollau survived the sinking of his own command, *U-534*, on May 5, 1945, and eventually took a position with the German Postal Service in Frankfurt; ironically, his *U-534* was salvaged in August 1993 and is currently being restored at Birkenhead outside Liverpool. Thilo Bode took command of the Type IXC/40 *U-858* on September 30, 1943, which he led through the end of the war, surrendering at sea to US destroyer escorts *Carter* and *Muir* on May 9, 1945. After returning from captivity he became a journalist, a profession that eventually took him to India, Singapore, and London. *Kaptlt. (I)* Fritz Förster, *U-505's* original chief engineer, returned to Krefeld after the war as an engineer for an industrial firm.[47]

Harald Lange returned to his native Hamburg in May 1946, eventually becoming the docks and warehouse manager for a fruit import company. In 1964 he returned to the United States for ceremonies commemorating the twentieth anniversary of the boat's capture. The first commander, Axel-Olaf Loewe, became naval liaison officer to Albert Speer's Ministry of Armaments in August 1944 and remained there until the war's last month, when he briefly commanded a naval ground unit in Schleswig-Holstein. With his own home in Berlin destroyed and his family's estate in Mecklenburg lost to Soviet occupation, Loewe gradually worked his way back from a farmhand to the manager of a sawmill near Flensburg, then moved to the Ruhr and eventually became an executive with a housing construction firm in Duisburg.[48]

Crewmen

The NCOs and enlisted men constituted the great majority of the men who served aboard *U-505*. Collectively identified as a single entity, individually they varied greatly in background, experience, age, rank, shipboard function, and even in number. Reflecting the general turnover in U-boat crews, many men departed for additional training and reassignment, their places taken by new men. Still, a core of veterans remained intact aboard throughout the submarine's history. Together they not only represent the "below decks" story of *U-505*, but offer a study of the men of the U-boat service in microcosm. Our purpose here is to identify where these two stories come together, and differentiate where the two stories divide.

In terms of numbers, the crew size constantly grew over the boat's history. As of early 1942, *U-505* carried a crew of four officers, four senior NCOs (*Feldwebel* or *Oberfeldwebel*, depending on the rank, collectively also designated *Unteroffiziere mit Portepee*, "noncommissioned officers with sword-knot"), two midshipmen whose official status equaled that of the senior NCOs, 12 petty officers (*Unteroffiziere*), and 28 enlisted men (*Mannschaften*), for a total crew of 50. By early 1943, that total had only increased by two, but altered in structure with the departure of the midshipmen and one *Feldwebel*, the increase in petty officers to 13, and the addition of four enlisted men. Beginning in the late summer and autumn of 1943, each Type IXC crew grew by about 10 men, to provide more radiomen to monitor the fragile, idiosyncratic radar detectors that became standard equipment aboard German submarines, and to provide needed gunners for the expanded anti-aircraft platforms added to each bridge.[49] In addition, a naval surgeon often joined the crew because of the extended length of Type IXC patrols and the increased risk of casualties among flak gunners. Thus, on its final patrol *U-505* carried a total of five officers (including a naval surgeon), four senior NCOs, 13 petty officers, and 37 enlisted men for a total of 59. Throughout *U-505's* career, however, individual crewmen were constantly reassigned or transferred while new crewmen came aboard. Altogether a review of the available data indicate approximately 101 NCOs and enlisted men served on *U-505* from the time she completed training to the boat's capture in June 1944. Forty-seven of these 101 crewmen eventually transferred to other subs or commands, but 11 were aboard from beginning to end.[50]

Such turnover derived in part from the organization of NCOs and enlisted men in the submarine service. Every U-boat crew was roughly equally divided between seamen (*Seemänner*), the most common classification in the German (or any other) navy, and technical specialists, who included engineering personnel (officially designated *Techniker*), radiomen, and torpedo mechanics. Even within the cramped confines of a submarine, a crewman most commonly interacted with others of their career-track who shared onboard responsibilities. The seamen usually stood four-hour watches, standing as lookouts on the bridge while surfaced, performing maintenance work on torpedoes, manning the steering controls when submerged, and preparing meals. Engineering personnel stood six-hour watches operating and maintaining the two 2200-hp MAN diesel engines, the two electrical motors, and performing a variety of associated functions. Radiomen (*Funker*) worked variable watches ranging from four to eight hours in the radio and sound rooms, sending and receiving signals, listening to the hydrophones when submerged, and monitoring the all-important radar search receivers and primitive radar that provided warning of approaching Allied aircraft. Torpedo mechanics, who bunked and worked with the regular seamen, supervised the maintenance and operation of the U-boat's torpedoes. Near the end of *U-505's* career artillery mechanics also joined the crew to man the anti-aircraft guns on the platform extension of the bridge.

Within these classifications, however, the same structure of ranks prevailed. At the top stood the *Feldwebel* and *Oberfeldwebel*, senior NCOs whose experience and expertise were essential to the functioning of men and machinery. (In the U.S. Navy of World War II, these ranks were equivalent to warrant officers and some chief petty officers.) The senior NCOs exercised their authority through the petty officers, always designated in rank by the suffix *Maat* (Mate) . The enlisted men mostly held the ranks of Seamen or Firemen 1st or 2nd Class, expressed in

German as *Matrosen-* / *Maschinen-obergefreiter* or *-gefreiter*. The accompanying Table 1 (below) provides an overview by classification and rank, with approximate U.S. Navy equivalents, of the 54 crewmen aboard *U-505's* last voyage as a German warship.

TABLE 1.
Classification of Crew by Function / Rank

SEEMÄNNER	*TECHNIKER/SPECIALISTS*
Obersteuermann (Chief Helmsman's Mate)	*Diesel Obermaschinist* (Diesel Machinist)
Bootsmann (Boatswain's Mate, 1st Class)	*Elektro Obermaschinist* (Elec. Machinist)

(*Oberfeldwebel / Feldwebel*, Senior NCOs) = 4

Oberbootsmannsmaat (Chief Bosun's Mate)	*Obermaschinenmaat* (Chief Machinist's Mate)
Two *Bootsmaate* (Bosun's Mates)	Six *Maschinenmaate* (Machinist's Mates)
	Two *Oberfunkmaate* (Radiomen)
	Obermechanikersmaat (Torpedoman's Mate)

(*Unteroffiziere*, Petty Officers) = 1 3

Eleven *Matrosenobergefreite* (Seamen 1st Class)	Thirteen *Maschinenobergefreite* (Firemen 2nd Class)
	Three *Mechanikerobergefreite* (Seamen 1st Class)
	Funkobergefreiter (Radioman 3rd Class)
Matrosengefreiter (Seaman 3rd Class)	Three *Maschinengefreite* (Firemen 3rd Class)
	Mechanikergefreiter (Seaman 3rd Class)
	Two *Funkgefreite* (Radiomen 3rd Class)
	Sanitätsgast (Apprentice Seaman)
Matrose (Apprentice Seaman)	

(*Mannschaften*, Enlisted Men) = 3 7

With this overview of onboard rank and function, we may organize the total number of 101 crewmen who served on *U-505* as follows:

Senior NCOs = 4 (two Seamen, two Engineering)
Petty officers = 24 (nine Seamen, ten Engineering, three Radio, two Torpedo)

Enlisted Men = 73 (28 Seamen, 32 Engineering, 6 Radio, 6 Torpedo/Artillery, 1 Medical)

From this data, it is evident the greatest amount of turnover occurred among the largest category—enlisted men. Only four men from the ranks remained aboard from the first patrol to the last, indicating the nearly complete change in enlisted personnel over two and one-half years. Several crewmen who joined after the first patrol had already transferred off before the final mission. Most went to other U-boats, and some doubtless rose to petty officer rank. Those so promoted did not return to *U-505*, almost certainly a standard *Kriegsmarine* practice to provide new boats with proven crewmen. From early 1942 to March 1943, 20 of the original 28 enlisted men departed *U-505*.

A somewhat different picture emerges for the petty officers. Over the same year that saw nearly 75% of the enlisted men transfer, only one-third of the 12 original petty officers moved on to new assignments. Even by the time of *U-505's* final patrol, five of the original 12 *Unteroffiziere* remained on board (one of whom had been promoted to a senior NCO). Of greater significance in transfers was the particular career-track: the torpedoman's mate, one of the radiomen, and both of the original *Seemänner* petty officers served on *U-505* from beginning to end, but six of the seven engineering petty officers who began the submarine's career had departed before the end. Again, the overriding demand for qualified specialists in the most technical of warships ensured the constant movement of personnel within the U-boat arm.

These conditions prevailed almost from the beginning of the war. Although the prewar submarine force represented an all-volunteer, hand-picked elite of 3,000 officers and men, Dönitz quickly drew up plans for a massive expansion of the U-boat fleet that necessitated a more general recruitment of submariners from within the Navy. Drafted in October 1939, the expansion plans called for 881 U-boats to be commissioned by autumn 1943, with precise timetables for training specific numbers of needed officers, NCOs and petty officers, and enlisted men among the seamen, engineering, radio, and torpedoman classifications. To meet these goals required such measures as shortening U-boat training, culling surface units for new submariners, accelerating the promotion of petty officers, and a regular turnover of 15% of each U-boat crew after every second patrol.[51]

The last practice is evident in the turnover we have noted. All the other measures, however, can be seen in *U-505's* earliest period, while training in the Baltic. Loewe's original crew included only three U-boat veterans from other submarines. Two of the boat's new *Maschinenmaate* came directly from the battleship *Scharnhorst*, their transfer preceding the arrival of their decoration with the Fleet War Badge each had earned. Another engineering petty officer proved a constant disciplinary problem from the start, yet Loewe's efforts to arrange his transfer were rebuffed by higher authority—a reflection of the shortage of qualified personnel. When Loewe did depart on his passage patrol from the Baltic to Lorient, the lack of adequate training time and the recent arrival of six new crewmen compelled him to proceed with extreme caution (e.g., remaining submerged by day while close to the British isles) and continue onboard drills and exercises to try to whip his crew into shape.[52]

Another but much smaller cause of turnover lay in the German Navy practice of allowing new captains the prerogative to take or bring with them one or two selected crewmen from their former commands. Thus when Zschech became commander, he brought with him two boatswain's mates from his former boat, *U-124*. One of them, *Bootsmaat* Hannes Bockelmann, later transferred back to *U-124* only to die with that submarine. After Nollau departed *U-505* for his new command, he took with him to *U-534* two enlisted engineering men from the original crew, Aloysius Hasselburg and Heinrich Klappich. In February 1944, Willi Jung, another original crewman just promoted to engineering petty officer, accompanied *Kaptlt.* Thilo Bode to his new command, *U-858*. And when Lange assumed command of *U-505*, he brought along Otto Dietz, another veteran from *U-180* whose indiscretions had led to his transfer and severe wounding in an Army punishment battalion on the Eastern Front before being restored, at reduced rank, to the Navy.[53]

However, after the middle of 1943 the rapid turnover in *U-505's* crew dramatically decreased. Whereas only 18 of the original 50 officers and men remained aboard after the first year of operations, 36 of the

52-man complement from early 1943 were still serving with *U-505* more than a year later when she was captured. Even more instructive is the crew list for August 9, 1943, which reveals that three officers and 39 men of a total crew of 54 would still be on board ten months later. Why?

Part of the answer may lay in the relative contraction of the U-boat fleet after the middle of 1943. Into June of that year Dönitz still planned accelerated production of existing submarine models and ever more crewmen to man them, until even Navy authorities acknowledged the proposed numbers of submariners simply could not be produced. The heavy U-boat losses that summer convinced Dönitz by August to focus instead on the advanced Types XXI and XXIII, with much reduced personnel demands as the new models entered production. *U-505's* prolonged repairs and inactivity during this period may have spared it a greater turnover in personnel. It must be noted, however, that *U-172*, another veteran Type IXC boat stationed at Lorient, endured major changes in her crew in October-November 1943 before departing on what proved to be her last mission.[54]

Another answer is suggested by reviewing those who represent the longest link of continuous service aboard *U-505*, the senior NCOs. *Obersteuermann* Alfred Reinig (age 28 in June 1944), *Stabsobermaschinist* Willi Schmidt (age 31), and *Obermaschinist* Otto Fricke (age 29) served on board the submarine from beginning to end. The fourth *Feldwebel* at the time of capture, *Bootsmann* Heinz Möller (age 29), had also spent his entire U-boat career on *U-505*, most of it as a petty officer. Only one senior NCO ever transferred off the boat. Granted that their seniority and expertise precluded frequent transfers, the retention of all four NCOs on one submarine for its entire operational career remains unusual. This suggests a specific decision, probably by the 2nd U-boat Flotilla but very likely approved—if not initiated—by higher authority, to keep these men together on *U-505*.

Former commander Axel-Olaf Loewe later concurred with Daniel Gallery's opinion that after Zschech's suicide, the crew of *U-505* should have been broken up and redistributed among a dozen other U-boats. He speculated that "organizational reasons" lay behind the determination to keep them together.[55] It is quite possible the decision to keep the original engineering senior NCOs on *U-505* resulted from the severe damage sustained in November 1942, that their experience and long familiarity with the engines combined with the extensive nature of needed repairs and replacement parts compelled their retention. With Zschech's suicide, however, this probably broadened to include the *Seemänner* senior NCOs and perhaps First Officer Meyer as well. Unable to determine (or confront) ultimate responsibility for a U-boat captain's taking his own life at sea, *Kriegsmarine* officials decided to keep the boat's officers and senior NCOs together with most of the crew, almost certainly to restrict knowledge of the incident to the smallest possible circle. Moreover, if doubts remained about the other officers and senior NCOs in their support of Zschech, keeping them together offered the best means of allowing them to prove themselves in the future. If this hypothesis of naval rationale is accurate, the German Navy itself first determined *U-505's* crew was indeed a community bound together by fate.

Beyond the questions of turnover and continuity, several other general characteristics provide insights into the character of *U-505's* crew. One is the question of age. Several writers have characterized the 1943-45 U-boat campaign as a "children's crusade," in which Dönitz increasingly sacrificed ever-younger crews to superior Allied forces.[56] In the case of *U-505*, this interpretation can be examined by a comparison of the available crew list for March 1943 (which includes birthdays) and the prisoner-of-war (POW) data for crewmen recovered by the U.S. Navy in June 1944 (Table 2, below).

TABLE 2.
Average Ages, U-505 Crew

	Crew List March 1943	POW Data June 1944
Officers	24	31
Senior NCOs	28	29
Petty Officers	24	24
Enlisted Men	20	21

This information demonstrates *U-505's* crew actually grew older rather than younger in every category from 1943 to 1944. Lest it be thought this represents a special case, the author's own research among 611 U-boat officers and crewmen killed, captured, or surrendered in May 1945 confirms the average age at war's end was *older* than that for the 1942-44 period.[57] Sacrificed they might have been, but German submariners in the last year of the war proved more likely to be uncles rather than teenagers.

Some of *U-505's* crew had indeed begun families. By March 1943, eight of the crewmen were married, four with children. Of the latter, two were among the relatively few transferred off over the next year, perhaps one of the criteria used in such determinations. Sadly, one of the remaining married men, *Oberfunkmaat* Gottfried Fischer, proved to be *U-505's* only fatality on the day of her capture.

Granted this more mature age profile, it is appropriate to consider the lives of the crewmen before they entered the German Navy. During the war British intelligence officials noted an interesting class distinction between their Luftwaffe and U-boat POWs: German Air Force pilots and crewmen were solidly middle-class in background and more likely to have completed a secondary education, while the submariners demonstrated a working-class character in which a primary education was followed by apprenticeship in a craft or trade.[58] Subsequent research expanded these findings to reveal a heavy reliance on metalworkers— particularly targeted for Navy recruitment for the skills they brought to the service—and consequently a geographic bias toward the industrial regions of central Germany, the great coal and steel cities of the Ruhr and Westphalia, and the diverse light metals plants of Saxony and Thuringia.[59]

The previous occupations listed by 29 of *U-505's* enlisted crewmen (the only ones for whom interrogations are available) conform to this pattern. Only two of the 29 listed occupations that might be considered unskilled or semi-skilled labor (a farm worker and a coal miner); only four held jobs that qualified them as members of the *Mittelstand*, the lower- and middle-middle class (a draftsman, a railway employee, a warehouseman, and a merchant seaman). All the rest belonged to the elite of the working class: 16 metalworkers and skilled industrial workers (mechanics, machinists, toolmakers, lathe operators, electricians), and seven skilled craftsmen (three in woodworking, one each among painters, tailors, bakers, and butchers).[60]

For the crew's geographic diversity within Germany, POW data for the entire crew are available. Here we have the advantage of the author's previous study of this proportionate representation by birthplace from a sample of 937 U-boat noncommissioned officers and enlisted men who responded to background questionnaires during the period 1991-94. The comparative results of this data with that for the listed residences (places of birth were not recorded) of *U-505's* 48 crewmen in the March 1943 crew list are provided in Table 3 (below). The evidence in the general sample indicates northern and central Germany were over-represented, and south Germany definitely under-represented; the evidence for *U-505* not only strengthens these trends, but exaggerates them even more.

But if German submariners more likely originated from the old Kingdom of Prussia, the fact remains every crew included individuals from every corner of the Reich, thus guaranteeing the U-boat service reflected a truly national character. At a time when the German Army still relied on regional identification for its units, this quality contributed to the sense of a military elite.

TABLE 3.

Geographic Distribution of General Sample
of U-boat Crewmen and *U-505's* Crew

(German boundaries as of May 1939)[61]

AREA	POPULATION (millions)	NO. IN GENERAL SAMPLE	NO. IN U-505 CREW
Northern Germany	20.64	265	16
(port cities, Schleswig-Holstein, Hanover, Oldenburg, Mecklenburg, Pomerania, East Prussia, Brandenburg, Berlin)			
Pct. of Total	26%	28%	33%

AREA	POPULATION (millions)	NO. IN GENERAL SAMPLE	NO. IN U-505 CREW
Central Germany (Rhineland, Westphalia, Saxony, Thuringia, Anhalt-Dessau, Hesse, Silesia, Sudetenland)	36.75	489	26
Pct. of total	47%	52%	54%
Southern Germany (Saar, Pfalz, Baden, Württemberg, Bavaria, Austria)	21.43	148	148
Pct. of Total	27%	16%	16%

Born outside of Germany = 18 in general sample, 1 from U-505

Therefore, the available collective data reveal much of the background and character of *U-505's* crew, particularly in comparison with German submariners as a whole. But what led them to the U-boat arm to begin with? How did they become submariners? "By no means were submarine crews made up of volunteers," Loewe observed after the war. "In general U-boat duty was by command."[62] For answers to questions about motivation and morale, we must examine individual cases.

Many early members of *U-505's* crew could trace an active personal interest in the Navy, though sometimes for different reasons. Hans Goebeler's boyhood fascination with German U-boats in the Great War ultimately led him to volunteer in August 1941. His performance at boot camp drew the attention of the submarine recruiters who approached him and the best of his recruit class to volunteer for submarines. Similarly, Aloysius Hasselberg developed an interest in the Navy as a youth in a small East Prussian village, ultimately leading to his enlistment in 1940 and volunteering for the U-boat arm. By contrast, Werner Reh was advised as an adolescent by a family friend to develop his technical skills and join the Navy as a way to see the world. He followed this advice and rose to the rank of *Maschinenmaat* while serving in various posts before being assigned to U-boat duty.[63] Willy Englebarth had gone to sea as a cabin boy in the merchant navy at age 14, and simply changed uniforms three years later when he enlisted.[64] Karl Springer, a veteran of *U-565* before joining *U-505* in late 1942, planned to serve his 12 years in the *Kriegsmarine* and then finish his career as a policeman or customs official; he only opted for U-boat duty as an alternative to serving on battleship *Gneisenau*. Heinrich Klappich, another of *U-505's* original crew, chose the Navy simply because he did not "want to be in the infantry—I saw them drilling in Darmstadt and it shook me. My father," he continued, "who had been in the Navy in World War I, told me 'go with the Navy, it's better than the Army.' In training I volunteered for the U-boats, I would rather have been aboard a battleship but I went to the submarine service."[65]

For those who joined *U-505* later in her history, however, the U-boat arm was more likely to find them than the reverse. Torpedoman Wolfgang Schiller, who came aboard with Zschech, had already learned that his career-track involved involuntary assignment to submarines. Yet as a petty officer and a specialist, he understood and accepted the situation.[66] More interesting are the claims of at least six enlisted crewmen—all of whom entered the Navy in 1941-42, and came to *U-505* after January 1942—that they were not volunteers, but drafted into U-boat service.[67] One of these, Ewald Felix, left his American captors with the impression he was a Polish conscript (although Polish surnames were common in the Wehrmacht, Allied interrogators assumed they were Polish nationals drafted as cannon fodder), but apparently offered his assistance in salvage efforts as well. The degree and significance of the aid he provided the Americans in keeping *U-505* afloat during the first days after her capture remains a matter of some uncertainty, yet there is no doubt Admiral Gallery separated Felix from his erstwhile comrades with an invented story of his "death" from a stomach ailment, and that Gallery later praised Felix for his assistance.[68] Whatever the truth, Felix's case raises the question of motivation for members of an involuntary military elite.

This question becomes even more significant in connection with German Navy discipline. Men of the *U-Boot-Waffe* usually enjoyed considerable latitude in this regard in "letting off steam," as the occasion in June 1942 when the off-duty crews of *U-505* and *U-154* became so intoxicated they could not be aroused to take shelter during an air raid, for which they were punished with only two days' denial of shore leave and canteen privileges.[69] When individuals transgressed against basic regulations, however, they received no sympathy. One submariner who stole some coffee spent four months in prison before being reassigned to *U-505* at reduced rank. Another who had been AWOL for three days served three months in prison and six months of combat duty in a punishment unit on the Eastern Front, after which he was returned to submarine duty and joined *U-505*. With the already-cited example of Lange's protegé Otto Dietz, at least three of *U-505's* final crew had thus experienced considerable time in military prison.[70]

These examples of draftees and discipline cases further alter the notion of submariners as a select elite, but perhaps reinforce a perspective of qualified but otherwise ordinary seamen placed in the role of warrior elite. The harsh punishments reflect less on the character of the offenders or the offenses: theft of military supplies ranked first among wartime infractions committed by U-boat personnel (even more so than the *Kriegsmarine* as a whole), and overstayed leave was not uncommon among submariners (though more typical for the rest of the Navy).[71] Rather, harsh discipline became an increasingly striking feature of the regime they served as the war entered its final years. On November 13, 1943, the Headquarters of the 2nd U-boat Flotilla announced the execution of seaman Johann Mainz, from the headquarters staff of another U-boat flotilla, for stealing personal property of a deceased submariner and using it as a gift for a French girlfriend.[72] Two months later the *I.W.O.* of *U-154*, another boat in *U-505's* flotilla, denounced his commander for "undermining military morale" through remarks opposed to Germany's political and military leadership. As a result, *Oblt.z.S.* Oskar-Heinz Kusch was arrested in Lorient on January 21, 1944, court-martialed, convicted, and shot by a firing squad less than a month before *U-505's* capture.[73] Kusch joined as many as 30,000 members of the German armed forces who were executed by their own military tribunals and courts in World War II.[74]

As the worst of this slaughter fell on German Army personnel during the last year of the war, motivation and morale for *U-505's* crew, and German submariners in general, rested on a foundation other than that built by fear alone. If *U-505's* crew followed selected patterns of age, skills, and geographic origin, they nevertheless represented more of a general cross-section of German society in motivation and political attitudes. Among the boat's five senior NCOs and petty officers who were 18 or older when Hitler came to power, only one had joined the Nazi Party.[75] The average age of the enlisted men, on the other hand, was 10 at the time Hitler came to power, and nearly all of them passed through the "Hitler Youth" program that became compulsory in December 1936. One, Wolfgang Schiller, belonged to a unit pledged to join the Party on "graduation," but his father—an old member of the Catholic Center Party—arranged to have his son transferred to another unit to avoid this.[76] A review of the 97 book titles in *U-505's* 1944 library reveals not a single political tract among a mix of fiction, adventure, and humor that included such authors as Theodor Fontane, Herman Hesse, Hans Grimm, and Antoine de Saint-Exupéry. Similarly, the boat's collection of 88 phonograph records (each with two musical pieces) consisted overwhelmingly of popular songs, tangos, waltzes, and foxtrots; only six discs presented traditional military marches, one of which was eventually replaced by a Spanish melody.[77]

Perhaps Hans Goebeler spoke for most of his comrades when he observed:

> Whether one was a Party member or not didn't matter a bit. Everyone I knew, without exception, was willing and eager to fight . . . a depth charge exploding over your head did not care about your politics . . . we considered ourselves patriots, pure and simple. Ideology at that point was irrelevant.[78]

The truth of these observations must also be balanced by an awareness of the motivation through fear that characterized National Socialist rule. Some tasted punishment directly, but all understood its reality and potential. Allied material and technological supremacy assured their defeat; Nazi intransigence compelled them to continue. The only question that remained concerned the circumstances of how they would meet their end.

And here we return to the unique fate of *U-505*. Not only the boat itself, but all save one of her crew survived the action of June 4, 1944. As with the officers, this good fortune extended as well to former crew members: of 47 senior NCOs, petty officers, and enlisted men who transferred from *U-505* to other boats or commands, only nine are known to have been lost during the war.[79] Combined with the officers and midshipmen, the final record reveals that of 115 officers and men identified as having been assigned to *U-505*, only 13 (11 %) died in the conflict. As not less than 57 percent of all who served in the Dönitz's *U-Boot-Waffe* were killed in action, *U-505* belied her reputation and proved indeed to be, at least in this regard, a very lucky boat for those who served aboard her.[80]

Conclusion

To conceal the submarine's capture, American authorities did not inform the International Red Cross of the survival of her crew and denied them any mail or other communication with their families in Germany. Thus, when *U-505's* crew gradually returned home in 1946-47, they truly seemed to have returned from the dead. But unlike so many of their comrades, they had come back to rebuild their lives and their society. Three of them eventually resettled in the United States: Hans-Joachim Decker, who worked as a guide at the Museum of Science and Industry where his former home became the star attraction, eventually moving to New Mexico; Werner Lüdecke, who settled in Oneida, New York; and Hans Goebeler, who also resided in Chicago before moving to Florida. By 1980, the boat's veterans had begun organizing annual reunions. Two years later 11 of them, accompanied by Frau Lange and 12 family members, visited Chicago to see once more the submarine that had defined their wartime community. As her former commander Axel-Olaf Loewe later remarked, "It is an odd feeling to consider that every month thousands of people enter the boat and stroll through the places where we so often stood while sweating out depth charges and bombs falling upon us."[81]

Like their vessel, the men of *U-505* were spared for a future unimaginable in the period that had brought them together. Their own lives and work contributed to forging the present, just as *U-505* stands as silent testimony to their mutual past. Though time thins their ranks, the U-boat at Chicago preserves their memory, even as it symbolizes the victory of their earlier opponents. More than sixty years after her commissioning, *U-505* and her crew—in their shared experiences and mysteries—remain a community bound together by fate.

Meyer immediately assumed command of U-505 in an effort to save the boat. *Bold* capsules were fired from the *Pillenwerfer* as the boat began a series of evasive maneuvers. The sonar decoy's chemical bubble cloud hampered the enemy's ability to track the boat. With their small window of opportunity fractionally opened, Meyer pushed through and U-505 somehow stole away to safety. At 2129, when the din of the British depth charges was nothing more than a distant murmur, a brief two-word entry into the boat's War Diary was made—a tragic epitaph for a troubled man: "*Kommandant tot.*" (Commander dead).

Lawrence Paterson

From the Lion's Roar to Blunted Axe

The War Patrols of U-505

On Saturday, May 24, 1941, the large Type IXC U-boat *U-505* slid laterally down prepared ramps into the turbid waters of the Elbe. Hamburg's *Deutsche Werft* had just launched the fifth of a small series of Type IX boats ordered earlier that year. Constructed as work order 295, *U-505* had not yet received her finishing work and still faced three months of shipyard incarceration before she would be released into the *Kriegsmarine*. Workmen swarmed over the stripped hull to begin their myriad tasks to prepare the boat for frontline duty.

The country it would soon serve was about to receive news of a stunning naval victory. During their attempt to enter the Atlantic Ocean by breaking through the Denmark Strait, the battleship *Bismarck*, the symbol of pride for Germany's new surface navy, together with the heavy cruiser *Prinz Eugen,* were pursued by Royal Navy warships. The engagement in the frigid waters ended abruptly when the British battle cruiser HMS *Hood* exploded, ripped apart by German artillery fire. It went under so quickly only three of its 1,419 crewmen escaped the fatal plunge. *Hood's* stunned consort, HMS *Prince of Wales*, retired with damage.

Germany's military star was in the ascendant. Much of Europe was already under the control of the Third Reich's *Wehrmacht.* While German troops stood guard over conquered land stretching from Norway's Arctic Circle to the balmy climate of the Franco-Iberian border, elsewhere the seemingly unstoppable German military machine marched unchecked. In North Africa, General Erwin Rommel led his Afrika Korps eastward across the Egyptian border, his goal of the Nile delta tantalizingly close. In the Aegean, Greece teetered on the verge of surrender, with German paratroopers and other forces poised to begin an ambitious airborne invasion of Crete. The fight at sea was also going well as Admiral Karl Dönitz continued his tonnage war of attrition against Allied shipping. His U-boats raked across convoy lanes leading to Britain and elsewhere, sending hundreds of thousands of tons to the bottom of the sea. *Bismarck's* initial success augured well for surface raider operations against those same vulnerable convoys. Victory was the watchword of the hour.

*   *   *

On August 26, 1941, a young and energetic crew stood quietly on deck and listened while *Kapitänleutnant* Axel-Olaf Loewe addressed them from the conning tower of *U-505* during the commissioning ceremony. A *Kriegsmarine* ensign was hoisted for the first time on her standard. "Comrades," began Loewe's concise speech, "as commandant of *U-505*, I have come here to Hamburg in order, with your help, to take our boat to the front after our short shake-down and combat training exercises. It will be a hard life—have no illusions about that. But with a well-disciplined crew, we'll have our successes."[1]

Though none of those listening to his words could have known it, the face of the war had already changed irrevocably against Germany in just a few short months. Soon after its victory over *Hood, Bismarck's* career ended following a dramatic and protracted chase across the expanse of the Northern Atlantic. The air war was also faltering. Royal Air Force operations targeted military installations within occupied Europe, defying German proclamations that such a thing would never occur. The land war had also reached what in hindsight would be recognized as a critical phase of its operations when Hitler launched Operation Barbarossa—the invasion of Russia. The summer advance opened on June 22 and rolled victoriously across the seemingly endless landscape of that immense country. Many German officers feared the Wehrmacht had finally taken on an adversary capable of stopping even tried and tested German tactics and skill. German casualties from the Russian campaign approached half a million men—more killed, wounded, captured, and missing than had fallen from the opening of hostilities in September 1939 to the beginning of the Russian operation.

U-505 was Loewe's first U-boat command, but the Kiel native of German and Dutch parentage was no stranger to the sea. Loewe was a veteran naval officer and appeared well prepared to take on this new challenge. A member of The Crew of 1928, he graduated at age nineteen as *Leutnant zur See* when the navy was still known as the *Reichsmarine*.[2] He had recently completed a central Atlantic war patrol aboard *Kapitän-leutnant* Eitel-Friedrich Kentrat's *U-74* as a *Kommandantenschüler* (commander-in-training). Loewe's chosen *Wappen* (or emblem) reflected both his own lineage and the "vintage" of his officer's crew: a shield bearing a raging Lion (*Loewe* in German) clutching an axe, which was also the symbol of Crew 28. From his Dutch mother Loewe inherited a love of tea rather than coffee—a distinctly un-German trait. His unyielding desire for properly brewed tea would soon become the bane of "Toni" Walbrol, *U-505's smutje* (cook), whose ongoing struggle with the alien dried leaves more often than not produced a thick bitter sludge even the most hardened U-boat man could barely stomach.

Once the commissioning ceremony was complete *U-505* slipped away from Hamburg toward the Kaiser Wilhelm Canal, which linked the North Sea with the Baltic. It was time for Loewe and his crew to endure months of training exercises as part of Stettin's 4th U-training Flotilla. Together with a dozen other boats and new crews, the men aboard U-505 engaged in gunnery, torpedo, and tactical exercises. "Our surface playmates even gave us our first taste of the realities of war," remembered machinist Hans-Joachim Decker, "They dropped depth charges—Wabos, we called them—one day while we were on a submerged run. So now we knew what they sounded like." Once this training ended, *U-505* returned to the builder's yard at Hamburg for alterations and minor repairs that consumed much of December 1941. By the end of the year the boat transferred once more to Stettin to take on fuel and torpedoes in preparation for its first journey into dangerous waters. At noon on January 19, 1942, Loewe's boat sailed from Kiel through the canal and into the North Sea in transit from the Fatherland to its new flotilla base in Lorient, Brittany. The new submarine was attached to the 2nd Flotilla, a unit equipped entirely with long-distance Type IX boats, including those spearheading the attack against the eastern seaboard of America."[3]

The voyage to France proved relatively uneventful. For Loewe it offered a final opportunity to meld boat and crew. Those unused to the harsh swells of the North Atlantic soon found their sea legs, though on some occasions only after days of torturous seasickness. Skirting the north of England and running between the Shetland and Faeroe Islands, *U-505* was pounded by the worst of winter weather. These atrocious conditions, however, eliminated the threat of an air attack and rendered ineffective the few Royal Navy forces encountered. On January 25, for example, *U-505* spent several minutes running in full view of a British destroyer. Both protagonists were so focused on their own struggle against the elements they were unable to undertake combat operations.[4] Each day Loewe submerged his boat for two hours to allow his crew to rest and make minor repairs to components shaken loose by the atrocious conditions.

After being buffeted about for more than two weeks Loewe brought his tired but elated men into Lorient on a cold and snowy February 3, 1942, trailing in the wake of a single *Sperrbrecher* and a pair of minesweepers. The port offered the crew but a brief respite of eight days to savor the delights of conquered France before new orders sent them into the Atlantic. *U-505* would take part in a timely renewal of operations against shipping off the coast of West Africa in general, and the sea lanes leading to and from Sierra Leone's main port of Freetown in particular. The most important British colonial outpost between South Africa and Great Britain, Freetown lay on the southern bank of the Rokell River estuary. Ramshackle and shabby, Freetown was hemmed on three landward sides by heavily forested and mosquito-ridden swamps. Its value was a large harbor capable of sheltering a sizable deepwater fleet.

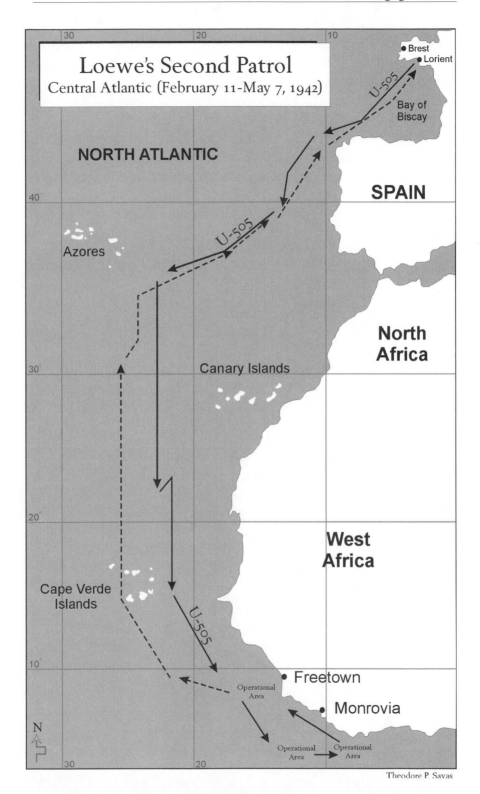

Loewe's Second Patrol
Central Atlantic (February 11–May 7, 1942)

NORTH ATLANTIC

Brest
Lorient
Bay of Biscay

U-505

SPAIN

Azores

North Africa

Canary Islands

West Africa

Cape Verde Islands

U-505

Freetown

Monrovia

Operational Area

Operational Area

Operational Area

N

Theodore P. Savas

Facilities in the port enabled ships to undergo minor repairs and be watered and coaled. As a result, the harbor quickly became an important assembly and stopover point for shipping bound for points both north and south.

Freetown's merchant traffic had been under fire since November 1940, when future ace Hans-Gerrit von Stockhausen in *U-65* made the first of several outstanding patrols off the humid African coast.[5] His successes made the area a popular destination for U-boats—particularly those of the 2nd U-Flotilla. Between May and June 1941, seven boats made some of the most successful sorties of the war into this region, sinking seventy-two ships for 387,671 tons. Ace Jürgen Oesten in *U-106* came within a whisker of capping this performance with the sinking of a capital ship when he pumped a torpedo into the "old British battlewagon" HMS *Malaya*. The explosion did not sink the powerful warship but it did take her out of commission for the better part of one year. Further success there, however, eluded the U-boats. Results dwindled until there was little to be hunted in the sweltering equatorial heat. The Allies learned their lesson well (though slowly); ships were increasingly herded into well-defended convoys where once they had sailed solo and vulnerable.

The declaration of war against the United States in December 1941, however, had made escort vessels and submarine hunters an increasingly scarce resource, which prompted Dönitz to make the U-boat presence felt once more off Freetown. America's entry marked virtually all merchant traffic steaming between Freetown, Bathurst, Monrovia, Lagos, and Takoradi as fair game. Dönitz also correctly surmised that by reopening the West African combat theater, he could pin escort vessels to that region rather than allow them to cross the Atlantic and enter the American arena of combat.[6]

And so *U-505* sailed for Africa, escorted by a minesweeper escort from Lorient alongside *Korvettenkapitän* Karl-Friedrich Merten's *U-68*. Land was still in sight when Loewe turned to his executive officer and said, "Nollau, throw the flowers over the side." Nollau complied, agreeing "that be be best." According to "sea lore, at least in German sea-faring tradition, it was bad luck to carry flowers," explained Decker. "No hexes for us, so over the side they went." The boats made good time through the Bay of Biscay, although forced several times to submerge in the face of enemy aircraft. Attacks from the air were becoming increasingly effective n the Bay of Biscay, which would soon be called the "Valley of Death" by U-boat crews.[7] Loewe spotted a "fast" convoy but was chased off by the escorts before he could set up for a shot. Both boats reached their operational area in early March after nearly a month in transit, some of the time on one diesel engine to conserve fuel. The nearly continuous harassment by aircraft, coupled with the draining tropical heat, frayed tempers aboard the boat. The stifling temperature of the southern Atlantic was radically different than the cold Baltic waters to which the crew had become accumstomed. The hourly drudgery, too, wore steadily at the nerves of the new sailors. "It was quiet, peaceful, and desolate," remembered Decker. "The war seemed far off." Loewe's quiet but firm authority held his men together as they began the difficult transition from new boat to veteran warriors.[8]

After days spent dodging heavy air cover their threadbare patience was finally rewarded when lookouts spotted the British steamer SS *Benmohr* on the evening of March 5. Belonging to the Ben Line, *Benmohr* was approaching Freetown from Durban on the second leg of a journey scheduled to end in Oban, Scotland. The ship's large cargo included silver bullion, pig iron, and rubber. Loewe set up his prey but missed with an initial two-torpedo spread. His roaring diesels ran the 5,920-ton *Benmohr* down and he hit the vessel with a third shot under a brightly shining moon. The British Master, David Boag Anderson, knew his vessel was done for when it slowly began to list. All hands were ordered to abandon ship after a swiftly morsed distress signal. Loewe conned *U-505* closer while the merchant crew made good their escape from the crippled steamer. Although holed, the ship stubbornly refused to go completely under. Once the sailors were clear Loewe decided to finish the ship off instead of risking the chance salvage tugs might save the crippled freighter. His fourth torpedo hit and snapped *Benmohr*'s spine, sending the doomed cargo vessel on a "long death glide" to the seabed below. Now only debris and a forlorn shipwrecked crew floated on the gentle Atlantic swell. Loewe ensured the lifeboats were provisioned and watertight before backing his boat away and making good his escape. He did not want to linger in the area lest the moonlight reveal the U-boat to Allied forces responding to *Benmohr*'s SOS. The success restored spirits aboard *U-505*. "We took it as a good omen and hoped for more like it," Decker recalled. [9] With their first sinking behind them the crew—who just days before had argued over the slightest provocation—were once again the closest of comrades. Infractions against one another, real or imagined, were forgotten and morale soared as *U-505* slipped away to seek new targets.

Loewe sank another ship the next day when the 7,600-ton Norwegian tanker SS *Sydhav*, engaged on a voyage from Trinidad to Freetown, crossed his path. Torpedoes smashed into the ship, the first into the engine room and the second a bit forward. Unbenownst to the Germans, *Sydhav* carried 11,400 tons of oil. She exploded in a massive fireball of bright flame and thick black smoke. The blast engulfed *U-505* (Decker remembered it as a "gentle" shock wave) which luckily received nothing more than minor damage to its clutch. *Sydhav*, meanwhile, sank so quickly her crew was forced to jump overboard. Many were pulled under by the suction of the sinking ship. Captain Nils O. Helgesen and eleven of his thirty-five men never resurfaced. The two dozen survivors were subjected to the terrifying prospect of being eaten alive when sharks arrived. The predators made their presence known by dragging a man clinging to a mattress to his death. The others, meanwhile, managed to right a lifeboat and bail out the seawater. They rowed back and forth until darkness fell, calling out the names of their missing comrades. Loewe surfaced nearby and gave the survivors fresh water, food, and bandages to treat their burns. When a Sunderland was spotted Loewe ordered *U-505* to dive for cover. The lifeboat rowed north and the men were picked up by a British escort ship on March 7.[10]

Both *U-505* and Merten's *U-68* became the victims of their own success. British authorities feared Vichy-controlled Morocco was about to be handed over to the Germans and had begun to thicken the defence of Freetown traffic against potential threats from that quarter.[11] After *U-505's* two sinkings, newly established RAF planes began air patrols to hunt down the German submarines. A decision was also made to put a stop to ships sailing alone from Freetown in order to form convoys that could be more effectively protected. These moves cleared the eastern Atlantic of potential targets and forced Loewe into frequent crash dives to escape the eyes of circling bombers. The danger from the skies kept the majority of the crew confined to the boat's damp, mildewed interior. The only respite from the RAF "bumble bees" (as they were called by the crew) was the brief torrential tropical rainstorms, which added a different misery for the men. Days passed without even a glimpse of a surface ship. A foul mood spread through the boat. Loewe's request to cross the Atlantic and hunt in Brazilian waters was denied by BdU because of the fragile political situation in that country. The pro-American government of Brazil had broken off diplomatic relations with Germany on January 27, and Dönitz was concerned sinkings off the coast would aggravate an already volatile situation.[12]

Merten's successes scored along the way to the Nigerian coast, however, prompted Dönitz to order Loewe to trail *U-68* to this fresh hunting ground. Loewe complied but fortune did not smile on *U-505*. Instead of finding tankers and freighters, the boat sailed into stiff opposition from escort ships and aircraft. Several attempted attacks near Cape Palmas were foiled. Frustration mounted when *U-505* briefly tangled with a suspected Q-ship operating in tandem with two aircraft. After hurriedly diving away from the trap *U-505* was rocked by the explosion of nearby depth charges, which rattled the crew's nerves but caused no lasting damage or panic. If nothing else, they had finally passed their baptism of fire as a target instead of a hunter. Loewe expressed his satisfaction at their performance as the boat quietly crept away to safety. The near miss did little to ease frustration aboard the boat. Loewe pulled away from the coast, stretching his operational instructions slightly by crossing the equator (with all due ritual humiliation for those "lowly pollywogs" who had never crossed the line) and heading southeast. The spell of bad luck was soon to be broken.

Late on the afternoon of April 3 lookouts sighted a single steamer. The arrival a few minutes later of a small escort ship, the armed trawler HMS *Copinsay*, convinced Loewe to hold back until the blanketing camouflage of nightfall would allow him to make a surface attack. Amidst intermittent heavy tropical squalls *U-505* raced ahead of the ship's projected path. Loewe decided to submerge and wait for the unsuspecting ship. The steamer was the 5,775-ton SS *West Irmo*, an American vessel carrying 4,000 tons of general cargo to West Africa. In a daring attack Loewe closed to within about 400 meters from the steamer's starboard side and released a pair of torpedoes. Even though the range was very close the first "eel" either ran wide of the mark or too deep. The second, however, impacted with a terrifying roar slightly forward of the bridge. Within seconds the *West Irmo* began sinking by the head, and within a few minutes it was gone. Ten African stevedores, unable to make it to the deck with enough haste or killed in the explosion, rode it to the bottom. The balance of the crew—36 merchant seamen, an 8-man armed guard, and 55 longshoremen—was rescued by the escort

HMS *Copinsay* while Loewe wisely turned tail and skimmed away at high speed.

Playing a hunch he would intercept more traffic in the area, Loewe lingered in the general vicinity. He was rewarded the next afternoon when he chanced upon SS *Alphacca*, a 5,760-ton Dutch cargo ship en route from South Africa to Freetown with a cargo of wool. Trailing the steamer Loewe once more waited until nightfall before hitting the Dutch merchant with a single torpedo shot. The fourteen-year-old Rotterdam-built ship shuddered as the impact tore into its stern. It, too, went down quickly. Fourteen of the ship's 72 crew and passengers did not make it into the bobbing lifeboats that were all too quickly the only evidence *Alphacca* had ever existed. Loewe nosed *U-505* gently among them to question the survivors and render whatever aid he could. After providing the shipwrecked unfortunates with a course for the nearby Ivory Coast he sped away from the site.[13]

Despite long stretches of empty water and occasional failures, the patrol thus far had been a successful one. The sinking of the Dutch ship, however, ended *U-505's* triumphs even though Loewe had been given complete freedom of action by Dönitz. Two days later the U-boat was nearly destroyed when a British Sunderland flying boat hurtled out of the sun before a startled watch could bellow for the boat to crash dive. During the hurried blowing of the tanks several valves jammed, which resulted in only partially flooded diving cells. As *Kaptlt. (I)* Fritz Förster, the boat's chief engineer, struggled to free the obstructed hand wheels, the imbalance of weight within the submarine's diving tanks caused the bow to dip under while the stern rose into the air, leaving the boat fully exposed to destruction while its propellers spun without effect. Loewe ordered his crew to stampede aft in an attempt to drop the screws back into the water. The crew, meanwhile, waited in terror for the explosions they knew must follow. Miraculously, there were none. The stern slowly slid beneath the surface, the screws bit into the dense seawater, and *U-505* pushed deeper with painful sluggishness—and escaped. "All sorts of gallows humour enlivened our work as we repaired the relief valve," recalled crewman Hans Goebeler. "The best joke was that the English pilot failed to attack because he thought *U-505* was an ostrich, with its head buried in the water and its tail in the air."[14]

It was not the last time *U-505* would brush with enemy aircraft as it continued to scour the now empty seas for merchant traffic. During the return voyage to France two planes attacked out of the sun on May 5, forcing the boat under on both occasions. This time, however, depth charges rocked the boat with several near misses. *U-505* finally arrived home on May 7, guided into Lorient by minesweepers after a round trip of 12,937 miles—less than three percent of which had been spent submerged. The mission was deemed a complete success because of the ships sunk and the considerable disarray that once more reigned off West Africa. Statistically, *U-505* had expended fourteen torpedoes for eight hits, sunk four ships, dived on twenty-four occasions to avoid aircraft, and was only bombed twice. The mission, noted Dönitz inside the boat's War Diary, had been "well and thoughtfully carried out. . . . Despite a long time in the area of operations, [a] lack of traffic did not permit greater success."[15]

Extensive overhaul work on the boat's diesel engines was required before *U-505* was once again ready for war. This time her destination was the distant hunting grounds of the Caribbean, which had been under assault by German U-boats since February 1942. The first torpedoes launched in that heavily travelled Allied tanker arena took the enemy completely by surprise. Hundreds of thousands of tons were dispatched to the seabed in what remains the single most successful surprise attack operation undertaken by Dönitz's U-boats.[16] The Allies were working to toughen their defenses there and the easy pickings were becoming harder to find. Still, effective anti-submarine countermeasures were slow to come on line. Not a single U-boat was lost until June 13, when Wolf Henne's *U-157* was caught and depth-charged to destruction by USS *Thetis* off the Cuban coast. An oil slick, a few pairs of pants, large deck splinters, and an empty tube stamped "Made in Düsseldorf" were all that remained.[17]

U-505's crew knew few of these facts when they sailed on June 7 from Lorient amid the customary fanfare accorded Germany's undersea warriors. Loewe conned his boat out of the harbor for the "Golden West" alongside *Kapitänleutnant* Heinrich Schuch's veteran *U-105*, which was also heading for the Caribbean. By 2000 hours they had cleared the French coast and were skirting the southern fringes of the Bay of Biscay, hoping to evade the Allied aircraft that were making transits across that body of water more difficult by the day. The air threat was more than amply illustrated four days later when a sudden burst of radio messages from *U-105* (which was west of Loewe's position) reported that boat under heavy aircraft attack and unable to dive. Loewe immediately changed course to render whatever assistance he could. With flak weapons manned he charged towards his crippled flotilla-mate. All too quickly the appeals abruptly halted, followed shortly thereafter by instructions from BdU to close on *U-105's* last reported position and hunt for survivors. Less than an hour later the order was cancelled. An unspoken understanding of depressing significance coursed through *U-505's* crew. As they thankfully discovered, they were mistaken. Radio problems had interfered with Schuch's transmissions. An Australian Sunderland had badly damaged the U-boat, but the plane was low on fuel and out of ammunition and forced to leave the scene. Schuch's crippled submarine limped into the neutral port of El Ferrol, Spain, where emergency repairs were performed so it could return to France. The boat would be out of commission for five months.[18]

U-505, meanwhile, made good time crossing the Atlantic by travelling surfaced virtually the entire way. A smattering of neutral merchant ships crossed the boat's path before Loewe was at last able on June 28 to order action stations north of the Leeward Islands. An armed American freighter had been sighted running fast and straight southeast. Loewe gave chase. After seven hours at high speed he submerged during the early evening, closed to within 800 meters, and delivered a two-torpedo attack. Both ran straight and true, exploding on either side of the 5,447-ton SS *Sea Thrush*'s bridge. The freighter went down slowly by the bow, which was jammed with heavy aircraft parts. Because the merchant's brave and tenacious gun crew continued to man their weapon Loewe remained submerged to watch the drama unfold. At the last moment the gunners abandoned their piece and took to the lifeboats. Once the boats had pulled clear Loewe decided to hasten the inevitable. A third torpedo was fired and the wreck slipped quickly beneath the water. Loewe, of course, could have fired the torpedo much earlier. By not doing so, he allowed the entire crew to climb aboard the lifeboats for a chance of survival. This act of humanity eventually saved everyone aboard.[19]

Loewe sailed on. The crew's confidence and spirits soared when a second American steamer, this one the 7,191-ton Liberty ship SS *Thomas McKean*, was spotted the next day. The ship had left New York for Trinidad, a port it would never reach. *U-505's* captain once again demonstrated substantial skill by running the freighter down,

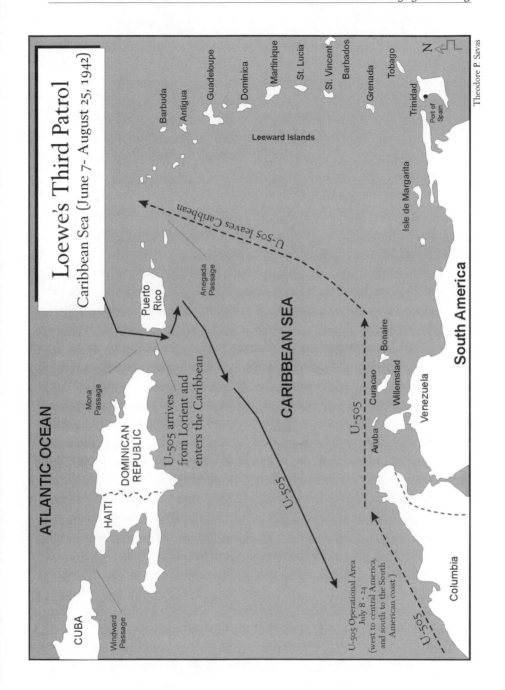

Loewe's Third Patrol
Caribbean Sea (June 7- August 25, 1942)

ATLANTIC OCEAN

CUBA

Windward Passage

HAITI

DOMINICAN REPUBLIC

Mona Passage

Puerto Rico

Anegada Passage

Barbuda

Antigua

Guadeloupe

Dominica

Martinique

St. Lucia

St. Vincent

Barbados

Grenada

Tobago

Leeward Islands

U-505 arrives from Lorient and enters the Caribbean

U-505 leaves Caribbean

CARIBBEAN SEA

Isle de Margarita

Trinidad

Port of Spain

N

U-505

U-505

Aruba

Curacao

Bonaire

Willemstad

Venezuela

South America

Columbia

U-505 Operational Area July 8 - 24 (west to central America, and south to the South American coast)

U-505

Theodore P. Savas

submerging his boat, and attacking with another two-torpedo spread. The explosions triggered a fire and five men perished in the flames of the dying steamer, four of them members of the Naval armed guard that had manned the ineffectual stern artillery piece. When it appeared safe to do so Loewe surfaced among the drifting lifeboats near the slowly settling merchant ship to provide medical aid and inquire about his latest triumph. "A lot of people think German U-boat men sank ships without mercy, but if we had a chance, we always tried to help their crews," Hans Goebeler wrote after the war. "After all, they are humans, too. It was only later in the war, when the airplanes were attacking, that we couldn't wait around after firing torpedoes. . . . We never hated the Americans; we were just doing our duty, just like the boys on the ships hunting us."

This time the *coup-de-grace* was delivered by artillery when Loewe ordered *U-505's* 10.5 cm. deck gun to pound the hulk into oblivion. It took 80 high-explosive shells before the stationary and burning steamer finally turned turtle and sank. Floating wreckage included bomber fuselages and other airplane parts from the ship's deck cargo (ultimately bound for Russia). These, too, were destroyed—this time by Loewe himself on the 2 cm. flak weapon.

In a repeat of the previous patrol, the boat's success appeared to empty the sea of targets. *U-505* cruised north of Puerto Rico for a full week before traversing the Canal de la Mona (Mona Passage) into the Caribbean. There, the humidity and high sea temperature transformed the boat's interior into a dripping fetid hell, even while submerged. Matters only worsened when the sea, too, began rising, leaving *U-505* to buck and plough its way westward when Loewe opted to head toward the Panama Canal in search of targets. Two muggy, unfruitful weeks of patrolling followed as *U-505* cruised toward Colombia in the face of thunderous tropical storms. Newly deployed Liberator bombers carrying centimetric radar hounded the boat day and night, and served as a reminder the Allies were rapidly improving their once porous defenses. The constant aircraft alerts depressed the boat's fractious crew.[20]

Finally, on July 21, a large three-masted schooner was spotted near Isla de San Andrés. The sailing ship was zigzagging in a manner more akin to anti-submarine maneuvers than tacking into the wind. Loewe ordered his men to battle stations and the main deck gun manned. "Fire a shot over her bow, so we can find out who she is," said Loewe to *Lt.z.S.* Gottfried Stolzenburg, the boat's *II.W.O.* (Second Watch Officer).

Unfortunately, the shell took down the schooner's main mast. In a panic, the ship attempted to flee while a Colombian flag was run up the yard: a neutral ship! Loewe guided his boat around the wildly zigzagging schooner, perplexed by its reluctance to halt and present papers to prove its nationality and status. Frustrated and thinking he had little alternative other than to finish the work the single shell had begun, Loewe ordered Stolzenburg to open fire: "Sink that thing—but quick!" Two shots later the 110-ton *Roamar* from Cartagena was nothing but splintered debris. Goebeler put it more succinctly: "We couldn't leave the evidence floating around, so we sank her with the deck gun." *U-505* departed the area hastily. The boat's fortunes were about to dip even lower.

It was about this time the experienced and respected Loewe was seized by a sudden depression and nervousness, the cause of which seemed to the crew related to the sinking of *Roamar*. Some of the more superstitious aboard related his condition to the sailor's persuasion that destroying a sailing ship would bring bad luck. *Oblt.z.S.* Herbert Nollau, the boat's *I.W.O.* (First Watch Officer) assumed more of the mantle of command. Whatever the cause of Loewe's condition, *U-505* dieseled back and forth along the South American coast while the weather continued deteriorating. No other targets were spotted. The commander's irritability and melancholy infectiously spread through the entire crew. It soon became clear to everyone that Loewe was indeed physically ill. On August 1 he requested and was granted permission to return to Lorient.

En route to France *U-505* gladly accepted 12 tons of fuel from the *Milchkuh U-463*, a large Type XIV boat, and transferred surplus supplies to the outbound *U-214* (including its excess supply of tea, a love of which Loewe had been unable to instill in his crew). *U-505* made the return trip without mishap and made landfall in France on August 25 to an enthusiastic reception from Lorient's sailors, soldiers, nurses, and prostitutes. Once safely ashore Loewe was hospitalized and diagnosed with appendicitis; the infected organ was safely removed. Loewe, however, could not shake the despondency he felt over the way he handled the schooner. He deeply regretted sinking *Roamar*, which he later learned had been the property of a Colombian diplomat. The attack triggered outrage in the small South American country and may have hastened Columbia's decision to declare war on Germany. The declaration opened additional airfields to the Allies and helped ring the Caribbean with enemy planes. Dönitz, who noted in the War Diary the sinking "had better been left undone," respected Loewe and recognized his excellent leadership abilities and keen intellect. Loewe was relieved of his command and assigned to the staff of *Korvettenkapitän* Hans-Rudolf Rösing (FdU West) as Referent W (attached as Rösing's representative to BdU Ops to deal with armament logistics for the western U-boats).[21]

U-505's deployment to the Caribbean was the third consecutive poor return for the expensive and time-consuming commitment of a Type IX boat to the far western Atlantic. Although there had been periods of tremendous frustration during his brief tenure, Loewe had proven himself a capable captain. His crewmen were distraught at the loss of their commander, with whom they had developed a close and trusting bond. Their mood lifted somewhat when news reached them that their new captain, *Oblt.z.S.* Peter Zschech, had served as *I.W.O.* aboard Johann "Jochen" Mohr's fabled *U-124*. Better known as the "Edelweiss boat," *U-124* had carved out a formidable reputation within the U-boat service and in newspapers across Germany. At age 26, Mohr was as renowned for his ability in combat as his irrepressible sense of humor. Zschech had served at Mohr's side for nearly a year, during which time Mohr had earned a coveted Knight's Cross.[22]

Peter Zschech, a native of Constantinople, was nine years younger than Loewe and the youngest member of the Class of 1936. After service with destroyers (he saw combat aboard the *Hermann Schoemann* and *Friedrich Ihn* during the war's early months) Zschech transferred to the U-boat service in the fall of 1940. Superiors and comrades alike found him intelligent, thoughtful, friendly, and a natural leader. His four patrols aboard *U-124*—during which the boat sent nearly 100,000 tons of shipping (including a light cruiser and corvette) to the bottom—served to confirm these estimations of his abilities. Zschech was more than ready for his own boat, and everyone aboard *U-505* hoped his impressive credentials would bring them renewed success. "We all felt we were in good hands," wrote Hans Decker after the war.[23]

But the crew developed serious misgivings about their new captain even before leaving on their next patrol. Zschech's style of command was radically different from Loewe's. Gone was the unruffled and often informal atmosphere of authority the latter had utilized. Unlike Loewe, Zschech remained aloof from his crew and aristocratic in his mannerisms and attitude toward them. As the men quickly discovered, his detachment masked a mercurial temper that flared with the slightest provocation. His first order to them did nothing to endear him to his men: they would undertake training in infantry combat while U-505 was being refitted (a lengthy procedure that also included the installation of a new Metox radar detection system).[24]

While his men grumbled about the pointlessness of their repetitive drilling, marching, and shooting, the officer structure aboard U-505 also changed. Herbert Nollau, the boat's I.W.O., left to begin his own commander training. He was replaced by Oblt.z.S. Thilo Bode, a member of Zschech's 1936 officer's crew.[25] Bode did not endear himself to U-505's men, either. A former Flak artillery battery commander and division chief aboard the destroyer Theodor Riedel, Bode was a harsh disciplinarian who rode those beneath him without pause while maintaining a strong and rather secretive friendship with his crewmate Zschech. Goebeler, in his compelling autobiography of his time as a Maschinenobergefreiter aboard U-505, makes clear his own strong dislike of both Zschech and Bode, and believed their friendly relationship and inability to relate well to the men made it difficult on the crew and hurt morale.[26] In time, Bode matured as an officer and later commanded his own boat (U-858) during the war's final year. It is entirely possible his early attitude aboard U-505 would have been markedly different if he had served under the direction of a more effective captain.

Oberleutnant (Ing) Josef Hauser also transferred aboard as an engineering officer in order to develop his hands-on experience under Förster, the boat's chief engineer, before potentially replacing him in that capacity. Hauser, too, was unpopular with the majority of the crew. The addition of a freshly trained engine room Maat who also enjoyed exercising his own authority over the most mundane of matters further served to divide the boat's company, leaving the lower ranks largely critical of their superiors. Förster and II.W.O. Stolzenburg were the only commissioned men the crew still viewed with respect. The transformation of U-505 into a vehicle for its new officers was continued when the conning tower emblem was changed. Zschech felt it necessary to make a clear statement he was now in charge. Gone was the rampant lion emblem of Loewe's era, which was replaced by the Olympic Rings of the Officer's Crew of 1936, alongside the large battle axe—the only part of Loewe's Wappen Zschech allowed his new crew to keep.

On October 4, 1942, *U-505* received the traditional send-off from well-wishers ashore and headed under minesweeper escort for the Bay of Biscay, its conning tower and deck festooned with flowers. The boat's destination was again the western Atlantic. As France ebbed from view several sailors began throwing the garlands overboard, maritime superstition maintaining that flowers be removed from the boat before losing sight of land lest they bring bad luck. An outraged Zschech screamed at them to stop. A bewildered Stolzenburg, who had ordered their removal, tried to explain but was silenced by an irate Zschech, who had swiftly turned his rage on him. The flowers remained as *U-505* sailed west. The relationship between commander and crew dipped still lower.

Zschech and Bode kept the crew busy during their Atlantic crossing with whatever mundane chores they could provide. The last obstacle to Zschech's complete domination of the boat was removed on October 22. Once *U-505* reached the western fringes of the Atlantic, BdU radioed that Förster was to transfer to Hans-Jürgen Auffermann's *U-514*, a new boat with the 10th U-Flotilla. Auffermann's boat had suffered severe depth charge damage following successful torpedo attacks, and Förster's experience and mechanical expertise were needed to repair the nearly crippled boat and keep it at sea. Hauser took charge of *U-505's* engineering crew. His inexperience and grating personality continued to irritate his comrades.[27]

Zschech's combat inauguration as commander finally arrived on November 7 while patrolling east of Trinidad. His alert watch sighted a solo steamer a little after midnight. The diesels pounded into high gear as he took up the chase. After about one hour Zschech launched a pair of torpedoes but both missed, probably because the target's speed had been incorrectly estimated into the firing solution. *U-505* bucked through choppy seas as Zschech tried to close the range for a second attack. Alerted to the danger, the quarry ran hard and the new commander attempted a long distance shot. At 2,000 meters two more torpedoes sped on their way, a distance that ensured a nail-biting wait for the German crewmen. At two minutes and thirty-seven seconds the distinctive sound of the steel torpedo striking its target was heard, followed a moment later by a deafening explosion. The 7,173-ton British Liberty-type ship SS *Ocean Justice* had been fatally holed. Traveling from Karachi to New York via Trinidad, the large steamer carried 600 tons of Manganese ore as ballast. The second torpedo sealed the ship's fate when it exploded slightly forward of where the first torpedo had impacted. Its master, Captain Thomas Edward Daniel, ordered his crew and naval gunners to abandon ship. As *Ocean Justice* slipped below the waves red-hot boilers exploded when the cooler seawater washed up over them. Two men were carried into the depths.[28]

U-505 left the area and continued the hunt. The boat was routinely hounded by aircraft for the next several days. A single attack was attempted during this period with four torpedoes against a distant freighter on November 9, but the effort was foiled by air escorts and the target's prudent zigzagging. The next day Zschech made a prolonged submerged run away from the aerial plague and surfaced during daylight east of Trinidad beneath a low overcast canopy. Stolzenburg was first on watch and eyed the overhanging grey cover with justifiable apprehension. Sailing exposed only 150 miles from Trinidad's RAF airfields provided good reason for his fear, and he requested the bridge watch be doubled and *U-505* trimmed down to enable a swift dive if needed. The low cloud cover also favored their aerial adversaries. This prudent request inflamed Zschech's temper; *U-505* motored on without any extra security measures in place.

At 1514 local time, a Hudson bomber from Trinidad's RAF 53 Squadron dropped from the clouds without warning and straddled *U-505* with depth charges. The attack took the boat completely by surprise. The bomber's pilot, Flight Sergeant Sillcock, had perfected a technique that turned the Germans' reliance on Metox against them. When searching the area of a suspected U-boat sighting, Sillcock would acquire the target at range by radar and then switch off his set and approach at high altitude until he could see his quarry. At that point he would cut his engines and silently glide out of the sun until he reached bombing height just above sea level, when he would restart his engines and swoop over the startled U-boat like a giant bird of prey. The depth charges dropped perfectly and exploded with a thunderous roar around *U-505*. Unfortunately for Sillcock and his crew, his attack was too precise. A single deadly canister landed on the stern deck and prematurely exploded there, but most of the force of the blast was directed upward against Sillcock's aircraft, which broke apart and plunged into the sea, killing its entire crew. The pilot's body was later spotted by the Germans lying spread-eagled on one of the bobbing wings.[29]

Pandemonium gripped the interior of the boat. The explosions shook the submarine as if grasped in a giant's fist, throwing its crew about and temporarily stunning and deafening them. The bombs, remembered Decker, felt like "a series of rapid shocks and explosions [that] literally lifted us off our feet. The lights went out and the engine room watch stared unbelievingly as a jet of water sprayed against the port diesel. We were hurt." Zschech raced white-faced to the conning tower and bellowed for the crew to prepare to abandon ship—an order belayed by the grim-faced and seething *Obermaschinist* Otto Fricke, who stormed into the control room and angrily declared that everybody else could jump overboard if they wanted to, but he and his technical crew were staying aboard to keep *U-505* afloat. His retort spoke volumes about the lack of respect the men had for their new commander.

Fricke's instincts proved correct: *U-505* was not sinking. A large hole had been ripped in the pressure hull, but the *Obermaschinist* and his engineers managed to plug it, as they did the numerous small leaks around the port diesel engine. Bilge pumps brought flooding under control and thick acrid smoke was sucked away by switching the starboard diesel air supply to the choking interior. "Other boats with the same damage might have sunk," recalled a member of the engineering team, "but our crew knew what to do, and we did keep her afloat." Order was restored while a bewildered Zschech stood in his control room. Although the conning tower was covered in blood, miraculously none of the bridge watch had been killed by the blast, although several had been seriously injured. In a twist of irony, the most severely wounded was Stolzenburg, who had suffered severe injuries to his head and body. After he was carried below it was discovered several of his ribs were broken and a lung had probably been punctured. The young officer spit up blood and a moderate fever soon overtook him. Difficulty breathing added to the considerable pain that wracked his body. Stolzenburg desperately needed medical attention.

The crew, meanwhile, began to take in the enormity of their narrow escape. "The wooden planks of the upper deck aft of the conning tower looked as if a bulldozer had ploughed across them," remembered Goebeler:

> In the centre of the damage, an enormous hole gaped half way across the entire topside hull of the boat, exposing a jumble of

smashed and broken equipment below. . . . Fully half of the steel
side plates of the conning tower were either gone or hanging limply,
clanging against each other in time with the gentle rocking of the
waves. One depth charge had exploded on the pressurized tubes
where the spare torpedoes were stored, completely destroying one
of the torpedoes except for the warhead section. If that torpedo
warhead had gone off, none of us would have survived.[30]

Radio appeals for medical assistance were made to BdU while the
crew spent hours laboring over their injured boat. Unable to dive, the boat
was completely at the mercy of any passing enemy bomber or
approaching escort. The port diesel, knocked out of action by the blast,
refused resurrection, although the pressure hull was successfully patched
with steel salvaged from the upper decking and conning tower. Work had
barely begun when someone on the bridge watch shouted "Aircraft to
starboard!"—a second plane! "There we were, helpless, and not a gun in
operation," remembered Decker. Zschech immediaely ordered a change
of course to put the boat's "stern to the enemy to present the smallest
silhouette. It worked, and we breathed deeply as the plane disappeared."
The next days, recalled one crewman, "were a nightmare."

After four days of lying dangerously exposed Zschech eased *U-505*
beneath the surface. "It was deathly still in the boat when we shut down
the diesels. No one moved," Decker recalled years later. Zschech ordered
the boat's chief to flood the tanks. The 20 meter mark was reached. "All
clear! 30 meters—all clear; 40, 45." The boat was sinking too rapidly.
Decker was in the engine room when " a loud clank sounded . . .The
battered pressure hull had buckled inward a few centimeters." Zschech
ordered the boat up, announcing, "We can only dive to thirty meters with
any safety!" A collective sigh was exhaled throughout the boat. "We
could dive!" Decker explained. "We had a chance!"

While the hull proved generally water tight, it would obviously be
unable to withstand the pressure generated by a deeper dive. Although it
trailed a thick oil slick, *U-505* was otherwise sound. BdU responded
quickly to Zschech's request for medical assistance: "Nearest Doctor
with [Kurt-Eduard] Engelmann [*U-163*] in ED90. Also Doctor with
[Bruno] Vowe [*U-462*] in EH60. Rendezvous with latter no sooner than
13th. Report nature of injury at once. Also whether very prolonged
rendezvous seems necessary."[31]

Whatever relief the crew may have felt at their narrow escape vanished when Zschech made his desire known to take the crippled boat into Trinidad's Port of Spain harbor in search of prey. The move was not without precedent. In February 1942, *Kapitänleutnant* Albrecht Achilles had slipped *U-161* into the harbor and attacked shipping at anchor there. He repeated his unique offensive style against Saint Lucia and Costa Rica. But Zschech was no Achilles, and *U-505* was not in any condition to launch an offensive operation, let alone one against a heavily defended harbor. Undeterred, Zschech headed toward Trinidad. On the way he attempted an unsuccessful attack against a distant freighter that brought swift and accurate retribution from RAF bombers. The boat was lucky to escape once more. Stormy weather followed. The crew cursed the horrible conditions while continuing to carry out repair work. Their only respite was the lashing rain and high winds, which at least kept enemy aircraft at bay. Stored torpedoes from the damaged topside canisters were jettisoned. Eventually Zschech had a change of heart and abandoned his bizarre scheme, reinforced by radio messages from Lorient directing *U-505* to rendezvous with Schuch's *U-154* in grid square EE60. The two boats met on November 13, but the only help Schuch could offer was twenty ampules of morphine for the injured Stolzenburg, who languished below in pain.

That same day BdU again ordered the crippled boat to rendezvous with Vowe's *Milchkuh U-462*. Two days after Vowe brusquely radioed BdU to question when *U-505* would arrive. Zschech's damaged submarine made its appearance on November 22. The tanker U-boat was in the act of refueling Merten's *U-68* when *U-505* arrived. *Kptlt.* Johannes Liebe's *U-332* was also present. Vowe's doctor transferred aboard to check Stolzenburg and the other less severely wounded men while Merten passed over a small quantity of spare torpedoes. As diesel fuel pumped through the heavy hoses trailing from the tanker and crewmen transferred food and mechanical equipment, *Lt.z.S.* R. Knocke, a replacement *II.W.O.*, shipped across on a dingy to replace the unfortunate Stolzenburg, who was removed to *U-462* for immediate and probably lifesaving surgery.[32]

After the rendezvous *U-505* continued her homeward trek. The aggressive Zschech attempted to attack distant shipping but was foiled, his single functioning diesel being unequal to the task. The journey was hard on the battered boat and crew. The men experienced one of the most frightful days of their war in early December and only a few days short of Lorient and safety. A distant ship was spotted and Zschech did his best to set up for a long torpedo shot. The torpedo, however, malfunctioned and the bridge crew watched in horror as it circled back toward *U-505*, striking the boat at an angle too oblique to trigger the contact detonator. "That's enough for this trip!" Zschech exclaimed. It was a narrow escape, but the impact cracked some of the repair welding and the boat began to leak again. One cannot help but wonder how many of the men speculated whether any more luck was left in their battered Type IX.

The crew's torment ended on December 12 when Lorient was reached. A large crowd of awed spectators was on hand to welcome the boat back to port. "The whole 2nd Flotilla staff came aboard," to inspect the damage, said Decker, who remembers the flotilla's chief engineer's remark, "This is the most damaged boat ever to come back under its own power." The crew was just relieved to be once again on friendly *terra firma*. Drunken celebrations stretched into the night, followed by an awards ceremony and the lifting of the crippled *U-505* on the Kéroman slipway for extensive and time-consuming repairs. It would be months before *U-505* would be fit enough to sail again.

Admiral Dönitz had been battling deadly Allied aircraft since the beginning of the war, but the danger from the air was only getting worse. At a Paris conference on June 16, 1942, BdU and various OKM department heads discussed several important matters, one of which was U-boat anti-aircraft strategy. The development and testing of radar detectors was given top priority, but plans to increase and improve the flak weaponry carried aboard U-boats was also an important agenda issue. A decision was reached to attach an additional conning tower kiosk aft of the existing flak station on every U-boat. Construction was scheduled to begin as soon as materials became available.

U-505's silhouette changed completely during its extended stay at Kéroman. The entire conning tower had been replaced with new shielding, and an extended lower platform *Wintergarten* was added to carry the firepower of a four-barrelled *Vierling* anti-aircraft weapon. Completing the powerful array of flak weaponry were two twin-barrelled 2cm. cannons mounted on the platform above. The deck gun, once so important for sinking ships, was now essentially superfluous because remaining on the surface was no longer viable and its top-heavy load posed a danger of overweighting the increasingly top heavy superstructure. It was removed.

Not until June 1943 was *U-505* released from the dockyards to re-enter active service. During the six months of repair the face of war had irrevocably changed. By the middle of 1943 Germany had suffered what are now recognized as irreversible defeats on nearly every front. In the Soviet Union, Stalingrad was lost together with more than 100,000 Sixth Army survivors, few of whom would ever see their homes again. Further north, Russian advances lifted the cruel siege of Leningrad. The massive Allied invasion of North Africa late in 1942, tagged "Operation Torch," had trapped the Axis forces operating in that theater in a constricting vise, leaving Rommel and his vaunted Afrika Korps with a powerful enemy on two fronts. The Germans and Italians finally surrendered in Tunisia in May 1943. Even more devastating for Zschech, his crew on *U-505*, and their flotilla mates, was what had transpired at sea during their half-year hiatus. That May, the *Kriegsmarine* lost forty-one boats in a bloodletting that clearly signalled the U-boat tonnage war was a forlorn hope. Dönitz had little choice but to admit defeat and withdraw his boats from the Atlantic. Decker wrote what many of his comrades were thinking at that time when he observed, "This was getting to be a suicidal trade we were following."[33]

Despite these horrific defeats the spirit of "Uncle Karl's" men remained largely unbroken. Realizing convoy battles were no longer possible until new weapons and boats were developed, Dönitz focused his energies instead on distant lone-wolf operations in which the bulky Type IX boats excelled. The nature of the U-boat war, however, had changed even more dramatically than Dönitz realized. Not only had the threat of aerial attack significantly increased, but enemy advances in radar and improved anti-submarine tactics and weapons—coupled with the ability to decipher German wireless transmissions by the breaking of the Enigma code—had utterly tipped the scales in favor of the Allies. Even the ports themselves had become a killing ground, with overworked minesweepers constantly clearing ground mines sown by RAF bombers during their many raids over naval bases.[34]

Promoted to *Kapitänleutnant* that April, Zschech finally put to sea on July 1. With little fanfare the boat eased from port on electric motors. Every crewman except those essential below decks were assembled on the forward casing, kneeling and wearing life jackets—a new directive thought to provide the greatest chance of survival should the boat activate a magnetic mine. Tribulations began almost immediately. As dusk fell both diesels sputtered and died. Mechanics eventually coaxed the engines back to life and *U-505* ploughed forward once again. As was customary, the submarine made ready for a trial dive once past the 200-meter depth curve, beyond the threat posed by magnetic ground mines. The boat eased down to forty meters, its electric motors purring quietly. To Hauser's dismay a stream of water was discovered jetting into the pressure hull through the starboard propeller shaft. Zschech and his officers discussed the problem and opted to continue, hoping the flow would ease or stop once the shaft expanded slightly from the heat generated by the friction of normal use. Unfortunately it was not to be and *U-505* made an ignominious return to base.

After undergoing repairs *U-505* left Lorient on July 3 in company with *U-168*, *U-183*, *U-514* and *U-533*. This time events took an even darker turn. The boat's Metox unit failed shortly after the standard trial dive. As far as the men were concerned, the failure left them incapable of detecting approaching radar-equipped aircraft. One calamity followed another. The GHG hydrophone array failed, leaving the boat deaf as well as blind. Still Zschech pressed forward. On July 8 the boat was cruising submerged during daylight when Allied aircraft spotted the submarine's outline and dropped down to attack. Six rapid explosions rocked *U-505*. The near-misses ripped a small split in an external fuel bunker. Thick oil seeped from the damaged tank and left a spreading oil slick in the boat's wake. Zschech finally admitted defeat and aborted the patrol, turning *U-505* for home.

The oil leak almost proved fatal when *U-505* became the object of an extended hunt by Royal Navy destroyers homing in on its shimmering trail. The warships pounded the sea with depth charges in search of the elusive submarine emitting the telltale fuel slick. Zschech demonstrated considerable skill and slipped free of his hunters by combining high speed surfaced runs at night near the Spanish and French coastlines while running submerged by day. The battered *U-505* entered Lorient on July 13 for repair. Once inside the vast Kéroman pens it was discovered that most of the seals on the emergency valves, batteries, air relief valves, and fuel bunkers were corroded to the point of failure. The suspicion arose that battery acid had been poured over them. The realization was a chilling one: sabotage had nearly doomed the boat. The new threat only added to the burden of their failure. It would not be the last time suspected sabotage within the French dockyard would cause *U-505* to cut short her patrols.

After more than two weeks of repairs *U-505* put to sea once again on August 1, only to be forced into a premature homecoming by yet more deliberate damage discovered aboard. Loud noises crackled through the pressure hull in the course of the customary test dive. This time Zschech immediately aborted and headed back to Lorient, a decision that left 2nd U-Flotilla staff unfairly skeptical of his judgment. Zschech was exonerated when closer examination revealed several welded seams had been weakened by pushing in strips of oakum and covering them with light soldering to disguise the caulking rope. A deep dive may well have flooded *U-505* beyond recovery, for the ruined seams would not have been capable of withstanding much pressure—particularly if depth-charged.

Twelve more days of repairs ensued before *U-505* slipped yet again from port, this time with orders to head for the western Atlantic. Unfortunately for Peter Zschech and his men, the patrol was again short-lived and eerily reminiscent of their last effort to leave the French coast behind them. The boat was only hours out of the harbor and undertaking its test dive when strange banging noises shuddered through the hull. By this time everyone knew the drill. *U-505* turned around yet again and returned to France, this time with an external air supply duct crushed and flattened. Another attempt at departure on August 21 alongside Werner Henke's *U-515* also ended in failure when the same noises echoed through the boat during an attempt to submerge. Trailing a thick oil slick *U-505* returned once more to Lorient. A small hole had been drilled into one of the exterior fuel bunkers. The constant threat of fatal sabotage gnawed away at the crew and indeed every German stationed at Lorient. Guards were doubled aboard every boat and several French workers were arrested as saboteurs.[35]

For the sixth time in three months *U-505* put to sea on what would be yet another short-lived patrol. Zschech sailed on September 18 in company with 2nd flotilla-mate Gustav-Adolf Janssen and his *U-103*, Erwin Christophersen's *U-228* of the 6th Flotilla, and Adolf Piening's *U-155* from the 10th Flotilla. Once again during the test dive water gushed from the starboard diesel exhaust. Thereafter the boat's radio direction finder soon failed, followed by the starboard electric motor, which shorted out. Hoping his technical crew could repair the electric motor, Zschech ran surfaced through high seas as *U-505* shipped tons of water through the open conning tower hatch until, on September 23, a permanent failure of the main bilge pump occurred; it was unable to stand up to the strain of handling so much water. Zschech wired the discouraging news to BdU: "Motor of main bilge pump cracked by closed armature circuit and short circuit in newly installed Siemens switch board. Armature burnt out. . . . Reversed course."[36]

The brief radio list of woes indicated *U-505* was again unserviceable. The boat trekked across the treacherous Bay of Biscay yet again, arriving in Lorient on the last day of September. This time few were present to greet the boat as it entered port on its electric motors and was ignominiously placed into dry-dock. The new flotilla chief, *Fregattenkapitän* Ernst Kals, was on hand to receive the distraught and demoralized commander while his crew boarded buses for Lager Lemp, a newly established home for submarine crews. Lorient now rarely hosted the glorious receptions for returning boats that had been typical in years past. Indeed, even departures were looked upon as somber and grim farewells. The chance of returning was slim and growing slimmer each month, and everyone knew it. Lorient was a devastated ruin, bombed into oblivion by RAF and USAAF attempts to interfere with U-boat operations at their source.

Despite the constant menace of bombing and sabotage within port, and the regular loss of comrades at sea, morale among the U-boat crews proved remarkably resilient. *U-505's* repeated aborted patrols, however, coupled with an already fragile state of mind, wrought havoc on Peter Zschech. Rumors of his heavy-handed method of command and doubts about his personal bravery circulated in Lorient. The latter was utterly unfounded, but malicious whispers relentlessly plagued the young commander. Zschech's friend Thilo Bode was no longer with *U-505*. He was transferred to commander training school and would eventually take command of *U-858*. His replacement was *Oblt.z.S.* Paul Meyer, who had initially come aboard as *II.W.O.* in Lorient after Stolzenburg had been injured, and was now promoted to Bode's empty post. *Lt.z.S.* Kurt Brey, in turn, transferred to *U-505* to serve as the boat's new *II.W.O.* While in port the crew rarely saw their reclusive and morose commander. As they were soon to discover, even at sea Zschech had become but a shadow of the man he had once been.

U-505 departed from the wasteland of Lorient on October 9, 1943, creeping submerged through the Bay of Biscay ("the suicide stretch," was what Decker and his comrades now called it) with the constant rumble of distant depth charges a reminder of omnipresent death. Zschech refused to surface any more than absolutely essential—even when the Bay of Biscay was behind them and *U-505* began crossing the Atlantic. The boat's dank interior dripped with chilled moisture and reeked of rotting food, unwashed bodies, and the stinking contents of toilet buckets stashed away in the diesel compartment. As *U-505* crept west at a depth of 100 meters, ambient water pressure made it impossible to use the two water closets. Slop buckets were placed in the engine room for forty-nine men to use.

On October 24 the faint thunder of depth charges was picked up by the boat's hydrophones. The muffled explosions moved closer and at 1948 the hydrophone operator reported the ominous sounds of a destroyer in his headphones. Zschech had thus far been virtually absent from the control room through much of the voyage. Brooding behind the green curtain that sealed off his commander's bunk, he finally emerged and walked silently to the conning tower ladder and ascended to the small compartment above. The men in the control room exchanged puzzled looks. They were too deep to use either periscope, and no orders had been issued to ascend to periscope depth. Paul Meyer hovered below at the foot of the ladder pleading through the open hatch for instructions from his captain as the escort's propellers swished close enough to be clearly audible to every ear in the boat. The probing fingers of ASDIC began to play over the iron hull and with chilling certainty the crew realized they had been located. It came as a surprise to no one when the hydrophone operator reported the sound of large canisters hitting the water. The depth charges drifted silently downward until their pressure-sensitive triggers activated. Hundreds of pounds of Torpex detonated near the boat, the violent concussion throwing men to their knees when the incompressible layers of water pummeled the U-boat's hull. Lights blew out, glass splinters flew through the air, and everything loose joined the growing mess on the rattling steel floor plates. "We thought this was the end . . . we were in total darkness this time," admitted Decker. "Still, no reports of a ruptured hull came."

After this initial barrage ended the men picked themselves up and braced for a further onslaught. An expressionless Zschech climbed slowly down the ladder into the control room. His glassy eyes reflected the ghostly illumination of fluorescent paint daubed on essential equipment within the boat. He stood without making a sound, as if he did not see the chaos around him. As the crew looked on Zschech disappeared inside his small commander's nook. Another round of charges battered the barely moving target as warships circled above intent on finishing off the trapped U-boat. Amidst this cacophony of explosions and flying debris Zschech reemerged to crouch in the control room hatchway. "All the lights were out, and we had been knocked off our feet by the explosions," remembered Goebeler years later. "I looked over and noticed the *Kapitän* and saw him slowly begin to lean over. . . . When the lights came on, I saw the blood and found out he had shot himself in the head with his pistol during the depth-charge attack. The depth charges were so loud I never noticed the sound of the pistol."

Funkobergefreiter Erich Wilhelm Kalbitz, the boat's chief radio operator, lifted his commander onto his cot. Small pieces of Zschech's brain were discovered in the blood flowing from the wound. A second shock gripped the men when they discovered their captain was still alive. Even death did not come easily to Peter Zschech, whose botched suicide attempt had left him contorted and issuing grotesque noises from deep within his throat. They were the sounds of a slowly dying man. While more depth charges fell about them, the men gathered around their unpopular commander in a macabre final act of a drama no one could have foreseen. To hasten the inevitable and end his suffering, four strong hands reached out and pushed a thin pillow over his face, holding it firmly in place until the groaning and writhing ceased. Peter Zschech, a man tormented by his own inner demons, was dead.

Meyer immediately assumed command of *U-505*. An announcement crackled over the intercom: "First Officer speaking. The captain is dead. We are going to 150 meters. Silent running." Decker and his comrades were stunned. "Zschech dead? We hardly had time to think about it, because as we started down a new attack commenced and continued without let up for the next two hours." *Bold* capsules were fired from the *Pillenwerfer* as the boat began a series of evasive maneuvers. The sonar decoy's chemical bubble cloud hampered the enemy's ability to track the boat. With their small window of opportunity fractionally opened, Meyer pushed through and *U-505* somehow stole away to safety. At 2129, when the din of the British depth charges was nothing more than a distant murmur, a brief two-word entry into the boat's War Diary was made—a tragic epitaph for a troubled man: *"Kommandant tot."* (Commander dead).

Meyer eventually surfaced briefly at 0400 to bury Zschech at sea without ceremony or remorse. As far as the majority of the crew was concerned, Zschech had abandoned them when they needed his firm command the most. No one mourned aboard *U-505.* "It was not much of a service for the man who had held such great hopes for us and our boat—and we for him," wrote Decker. Meyer radioed their situation to Lorient on October 30 and headed home once more.[37]

Although the consequences of Zschech's suicide could have been disastrous to the morale of the crew, their confidence did not break in the face of their former commander's bizarre action. Once they arrived in Lorient they received a brief visit and morale-boosting speech from Admiral Hans-Georg von Friedeburg, who was accompanied by FdU West *Fregattenkapitän* Hans-Rudolf Rösing. A majority of the crew received home leave to Germany while the remainder enjoyed the relative peace of the Breton countryside and village of Caudan near Lager Lemp. For those who had returned to the Fatherland, Germany's battering at the hands of the Allied air forces left a deep impression. For many it stiffened their resolve to take the war to the enemy once more.

In Lorient, meanwhile, *U-505's* complement awaited the arrival of a new commander. He was not long in coming and officially assumed charge of the boat that November. *Oblt.z.S. der Reserve* Harald Lange was an experienced sailor, graduating in 1925 at age twenty-one from the Mürwik Naval Academy. After his military service in the *Reichsmarine* Lange became a member of the naval reserve and joined the peacetime *Handelsmarine* (merchant navy), plying the Far Eastern trade routes aboard various freighters. At the outbreak of war Lange found himself once more in naval uniform serving aboard *Sperrbrecher* (mine-detonators) and *Vorpostenboote* (patrol boats) until his transfer to the U-boat service in 1941. His pre-war experience in the Far East soon put him in good stead when he was assigned as *I.W.O.* and later commander of *U-180,* a Type IXD1 he took into the Indian Ocean in early 1943. The arrival of a new commander changed *U-505's* exterior once more: Zschech's Olympic Rings and Loewe's axe were removed and replaced with a freshly painted shield bearing a large scallop shell on either flank of the conning tower. Whether Lange would have any better luck with *U-505* remained to be seen.

The first effort to leave Lorient did not bode well for the new commander. *U-505* departed on December 20, 1943, only to be forced back into port when water poured through a leaking flange around the hydrophone cables because of deliberately faulty welding. Five frustrating days of repair followed before the boat sailed once more, this time slipping from the harbor on Christmas Day—two days after Lange celebrated his 41st birthday. Tall, calm, and able to relate easily with all ranks, Lange insisted on shooting the stars with a sextant himself. He was every inch a professional seaman and swiftly earned the unconditional respect of his new crew. He was the direct opposite of Peter Zschech in many respects, and his refreshed subordinates appreciated his courtesies.

The Lorient *U-505* left behind was quiet and desolate. A single seaman played the boat on its way with his accordion, the 2nd U-Flotilla staff completing the small but enthusiastic dockside farewell party. Around them was nothing but ruin. Lorient in 1943 was the most heavily bombed French Atlantic U-boat base. The installation was the recipient of 6,102 tons of Allied ordnance that flattened everything around the U-boat pens and dockyards, which had somehow remained largely intact. Evacuated by most of its French population, Lorient on Christmas 1943 was a city of ghosts.

After three days at sea *U-505* was still ploughing through the Bay of Biscay's cold wind-whipped water, with thick, low-hanging cumulus layers threatening rain. Through the boat's steel walls and above the roar of the twin "jumbos," Lange's crew could hear the distant resonance of gunfire. Tension within the boat rose. At 1900 on December 28 an urgent message from BdU directed *U-505* and three other outbound boats to form group "Hela" and head at all speed for grid square BE6938. Shortly afterward *Fregattenkapitän* Kals radioed again from Lorient: the German destroyer *Z27* was dead in the water while other German surface ships were attempting to fight their way to the French coast and coastal artillery support. The details provided by Kals were not encouraging:

1. Enemy cruisers, destroyers and aircraft took part in engagement at 1500 hrs, otherwise no information as to enemy dispositions;
2. Own destroyers and torpedo boats are attempting to return in groups and singly;

3. According to weather and direction of wind start from *Z27*'s battle area in BE6938 and search for survivors.

A chilling four-word postscript arrived a few minutes later: "Beware of enemy aircraft."

By the time *U-505* reached the coordinates provided by BdU in the early morning darkness of December 29, the sea was rising, icy winds were throwing spray over the bridge crew, and visibility extended a scant handful of meters beyond the bow of the boat. Blankets were accumulated within the central control room and coffee boiled on the stove within the cramped galley while binoculars scanned the tumbling sea. Of *Z27* there was no sign. More ominously, the first shipwrecked Germans the boat discovered were from the torpedo boat *T25*. Lange was still on the bridge, lashed by spray and stubbornly attempting to chain-smoke one damp cigarette after another, when the first of several red distress flares sputtered into view. The submarine turned in their direction and soon came across a scattering of rafts holding a miserable collection of freezing sailors. Lange eased his boat alongside to provide some shelter from the high wind and seas while the survivors, who were barely able to hold the ropes thrown to them, were lifted aboard. The last man saved was *Korvettenkapitän* Wirich von Gartzen, *T25's* commander. Von Gartzen was devastated about the loss of so many of his men. He refused treatment for his own injuries until the search was reluctantly abandoned when the weather further deteriorated and all reasonable hope of finding additional survivors passed. Several distant red distress lights faded into oblivion as their owners slipped below the icy water to their graves.

When he had done all he could Lange submerged. He had pulled thirty-four men from the sea. None of the half-frozen sailors were used to the violent yaw of a U-boat, and most spent their first several hours aboard vomiting into the bilges the diesel oil and seawater they had swallowed. The initial downward tilt of the boat caused several delirious casualties to become hysterical with panic. Some had to be tied to bunks to prevent their interference with the boat's crew. Order was gradually restored within the overcrowded U-boat as *U-505* began its return journey to France, diverted to the 5th T-Flotilla's homeport of Brest instead of Lorient.

Lange ran submerged as much as possible. An emergency crash dive would be virtually impossible with the overladen boat because men were crouching, standing, and lying everywhere, blocking the wheels and levers vital for a fast dive. However, without ventilation the odor generated by so many extra men rose to hideous proportions. The swallowing of seawater and diesel oil from their sunken ship caused many of the rescued men to suffer from stomach cramps and diarrhea. There was no way of ridding the boat of human waste while travelling at depth, so the fecal matter and urine accumulated in the odiously familiar overflowing waste buckets.

Lange peered through the periscope as *U-505* approached Brest and discovered they were some miles off course; the boat's direction finder was malfunctioning. He radioed the headquarters of Brest's 1st U-boat Flotilla for instructions and the glaring beam of the lighthouse at Pointe de Penmarc'h was illuminated for his benefit. Escort ships shepherded the U-boat past Pointe St Mathieu and into Brest harbor on the morning of January 2, 1944. En route through the entrance channels a barge loaded with war correspondents pulled alongside *U-505* and, much to the crew's chagrin, climbed aboard with heavy camera equipment to film the confined interior. As they did water leaked into the electric motors' accumulator panel and a massive flash and huge blue bolt of electricity arced across the starboard motor, sending thick white smoke billowing through the U-boat and starting a small fire. The terrified newsmen rushed headlong for the control room and the exit hatch, their panic infecting the *T25* survivors as well. For *U-505's* crew it was business as usual, for the problem had happened once before. With CO_2 fire extinguishers in hand the small conflagration was quickly smothered. The U-boat men shook their heads in weary resignation. "It just wouldn't have been the *U-505* if something like this hadn't happened," explained Hans Goebeler.[39]

When the chaos subsided *U-505* eased its way toward Brest's huge U-boat bunker, similar to those they had left not so long ago in Lorient. The headquarters staffs of the 1st U-Flotilla and 5th T-Flotilla were present, as were many other blue uniforms and even a brass band, harking to the bygone age of earlier days. One final indignity awaited *U-505* as it entered wet-pen C1. A group of torpedo boat sailors, overjoyed to be nearing their home base, rushed to disembark from the boat. In their haste to climb outside one of them slipped from the vertical ladder and landed squarely on the helmsman, causing *U-505* to swerve to starboard and brush the concrete mooring bay. The crash bent the forward dive plane's shaft, a serious injury that would require dry-docking and two weeks of repairs before it could put to sea again. Later, as Lange pondered the bizarre twist of his boat's latest misfortune, insult was added to injury when he was informed the nearest replacement shaft was in Bordeaux. It would be considerably longer than a fortnight before *U-505* sailed again.

In fact, it was not until March 16 that *U-505* was able to leave port on its twelfth war patrol. The boat sailed at 1835 from Brest alongside *U-373* and *U-471*, a pair of Type VIICs skippered by Detlef von Lehsten and Friedrich Kloevekorn. Lange entered the Bay of Biscay before separating from his escorts at 1025 the following morning, the departure of the *Vorpostenboote* marking the official beginning of what was to be *U-505's* last war patrol. His fellow U-boats submerged to begin crossing the Bay of Biscay, the "Valley of Death" where so many boats and men had been lost to enemy aircraft and naval forces. Unlike his companions, however, Lange elected to remain surfaced as much as possible, risking extended diesel sprints rather than creeping continually submerged beneath the heavily patrolled waters. His gamble paid off and *U-505* cleared the "Valley" in good time. He emerged from the outer Bay of Biscay on March 25. According to Hans Decker, the boat came upon the incoming *U-154* and "passed the new radio code on to her." In the exchange of information "we heard, too, for the first time of the new Allied Hunter-killer groups, composed of small aircraft carriers and destroyers, that were raising havoc with our U-boats."[40]

And so *U-505* headed for the hunting grounds off Freetown, the west coast of Africa—and a fateful rendezvous with a Task Group 22.3.

The staff of the Supreme Naval Command repeatedly told Karl
Dönitz—and he believed it—that the use of high frequency radio would
make direction finding impossible. *Kriegsmarine* scientists were even more
reluctant to consider the possibility that the Allies were installing HF/DF
gear aboard ships. Not until June 15, 1944, when *U-505* was already en route
to Bermuda under tow, did BdU send a message to the fleet warning of the
threat from shipborne HF/DF. By that late date, of course, much of the
damage had already been done.

Mark E. Wise and Jak P. Mallmann Showell

Deciphering the U-boat War

The Role of Intelligence in the Capture of U-505

from its earliest days of construction through its final hours of
life as a frontline *Unterseeboot*, *U-505* had been the
subject of Allied intelligence reports. It was regarded as just another
enemy submarine, however, until Captain Daniel V. Gallery reported her
capture on June 4, 1944.

Photographic intelligence alerted the Allies to *U-505's* early
existence when aerial reconnaissance revealed in early 1941 another
Type IXC U-boat under construction at the Deutsche Werft shipyard
along the Elbe River in Hamburg. At that time, of course, the photo
interpreters of the RAF Reconnaissance Unit had no way of knowing its
hull number.[1] The last time *U-505* became the subject of Allied interest
was during its final war cruise, when signals intelligence in the form of
high-frequency direction finding (HF/DF) and decrypted Enigma

messages revealed to the U.S. Navy *U-505* was on patrol. This intelligence indicated its general operating area with enough precision to allow U.S. Navy analysts to predict the boat's position more accurately than Karl Dönitz's BdU staff. Earlier intelligence gleaned from prisoner interrogations had allowed the Office of Naval Intelligence to draw up deck plans, copies of which had been given to Gallery's boarding parties to study should the opportunity to board a U-boat arise.

Intelligence continued to figure into the *U-505* story after its capture. The submarine and its contents, together with interviews with members of its crew, provided a colossal windfall for the Allies. In particular, the Enigma keys discovered aboard freed up U.S. naval cryptanalytical assets, which were thereafter devoted to decrypting *Luftwaffe* and *Wehrmacht* message traffic as the Allied invasion of Europe progressed.[2]

It is impossible to understand how all this came about, however, without a full appreciation of the key organizations, people, and history leading up to *U-505's* final war patrol.

United States Naval Intelligence Organizations Relevant to the Capture of U-505

The organization and reorganization of U.S. naval intelligence during World War II arose directly from Admiral (later Fleet Admiral) Ernest J. King's dissatisfaction with the existing structure when America entered the war. King was appointed to the post of Commander in Chief, United States Fleet (COMINCH) on December 20, 1941. Within a month he established a Fleet Intelligence Officer billet in the Plans Division of his headquarters, effectively ignoring the Office of Naval Intelligence (ONI).[3] Over the next eighteen months King, who had been pulling double-duty as Chief of Naval Operations (CNO) since March 12, 1942, reorganized his intelligence staff and established some unity of command between his COMINCH intelligence staff and ONI.[4] On May 20, 1943, he established the Tenth Fleet under his direct control as an administrative organization to direct the U.S. antisubmarine effort. These disparate entities—COMINCH, ONI, and Tenth Fleet—cooperated with each other and with parallel British units to support the operating forces in their successful campaign against the U-boats.

COMINCH

Because King believed ONI was too large and too slow to respond to the demand for operational intelligence, he put together a lean fleet intelligence staff of approximately 30 people to handle the task.[5] The original staff, dubbed F-11, stood a continuous U-boat plotting watch. The officer in charge presented a daily briefing to King, his chief of staff, and all COMINCH officers working in antisubmarine warfare (ASW).[6] King also brought an operational intelligence section of ONI, known as OP-38W, under his control in mid-January 1942. King named it F-35, the Operational Information Section of the Operations Division of COMINCH Headquarters. A tracking system based on available intelligence was set up in F-35 to detour convoys around known or suspected U-boat positions. Since access to F-35 was less rigidly controlled than access to F-11, highly classified operational details were plotted in the latter staff organization.[7]

On July 1, 1943, a major reorganization of naval intelligence occurred. F-11 was converted into F-2, the Combat Intelligence Division, under Rear Admiral Roscoe E. Schuirmann. The tracking system formerly known as F-35 was dismantled and divided into three sections: F-21 (Atlantic), F-22 (Pacific), and F-23 (Operational Summaries). These three sections reported to F-20, Captain Henri H. Smith-Hutton, the Assistant for Combat Intelligence.[8] Admiral King intended F-2 to be a small organization optimized for the rapid handling of operational intelligence, in contrast to ONI, which King saw as an organization better suited to handle noncombat-related information.[9]

F-21: The Atlantic Section, COMINCH Intelligence

Commander Kenneth A. Knowles, a 1927 Naval Academy graduate whom King personally recalled from medical retirement, served as the head of F-21.[10] Early in his career, Knowles had served as gunnery officer aboard the destroyer *Paul Jones* (DD-230) under the command of Francis S. "Frog" Low, who was greatly impressed by the young officer. When the need for an antisubmarine intelligence entity became apparent, Low, by now a captain on King's staff, convinced King to recall Knowles to the Atlantic unit of F-11, which (as noted above) evolved into F-21.

Knowles sailed to England as soon as possible after his return to active duty. There, he worked closely with Lieutenant Commander Rodger Winn, the commander of the Admiralty's Submarine Tracking Room, learning the half-science and half-art of submarine tracking.[11] Returning to the United States, Knowles assembled F-21 on the British model. To reduce security risks and bureaucratic inertia he deliberately kept his unit small, with four male officers, eight Wave (Women Accepted for Volunteer Emergency Service) officers, two or three yeomen, and a "handful" of enlisted Waves.[12]

Knowles's most important initial duty was to track U-boats in the Atlantic, issue daily position estimates, and advise the staff responsible for routing convoys.[13] Knowles and his staff would later combine Ultra intelligence from F-211 (when it became available; see below) and information from the high frequency direction finder network (HF/DF, or Huff-Duff), prisoner interrogations, action reports from Allied merchant ships and warships, air reconnaissance, and any other available source.[14] Knowles also maintained a liaison with operational intelligence centers in Britain and Canada, communicating daily by teleprinter with Commander Winn in London and Canadian naval reserve officer Lieutenant Commander John B. McDiarmid, who performed a similar function in Ottawa.[15] When the Tenth Fleet began operations, F-21 served as its operations plot. Its U-boat position estimates would prove vital to the Allied effort against Dönitz's submarines.[16]

F-211: The "Secret Room"

Commander Knowles's F-21 began operating during the Enigma blackout of 1942, after the *Kriegsmarine* added a fourth rotor to its Enigma machine. Until the Allies could break into the more complex coding system, there were no decryptable messages to exploit for their intelligence value, and thus no requirement for F-21 to handle this traffic during the section's early months of existence. By December 1942, however, the codebreakers at the deceptively-named Government Code and Cipher School (GCCS) at Bletchley Park were furnishing four-rotor Enigma solutions to their American counterparts, and COMINCH had to make arrangements for the security of Ultra intelligence. Although Knowles set up tight security measures for F-21 and kept his staff intentionally small, task group commanders and other non-COMINCH personnel frequented the room.[17] Obviously, more stringent precautions would be necessary for the protection of Ultra.

The solution was the "Secret Room," later known as F-211. The Secret Room was established on December 27, 1942, "to provide for the processing, from the operational standpoint, of special U/B intelligence obtained from radio intercepts."[18] Lieutenant John E. Parsons, USNR, served as officer in charge, assisted by Lieutenant (j.g.) John V. Boland, USNR, and Yeoman First Class Samuel P. Livecchi.[19] In addition to Parsons and his assistants, only Knowles, who used the room constantly, and Ensign R. B. Chevalier, who acted as relief yeoman, had routine access to F-211. King, Vice Admiral Richard S. Edwards (King's chief of staff), Low, Schuirmann, and Smith-Hutton visited occasionally, and rare visitors were admitted "with the approval of the Chief of Staff."[20]

F-211 worked closely with the Enigma section of ONI known as OP-20-GI-2, keeping abreast of the availability and interpretation of intercepted Enigma traffic. A secure telephone connected the two sections, and its users spoke in a voice code to enhance communications security. F-211 also maintained a liaison with OP-16-Z, the Special Activities Branch, to obtain the most current possible intelligence derived from the interrogation of prisoners.[21] Officer messengers delivered Enigma traffic in sealed double envelopes. The staff abstracted the special intelligence for a daily location list that was used to maintain a plot in F-211 as well as the main board in F-21.[22]

In addition to the daily plot, F-211 maintained a monthly plot of U-boats sunk and a 10-day plot of DF fixes.[23] Sinkings were noted with the date, time, position, type of attack, and attacking forces involved. If prisoners were taken, a summary of the final action was added as F-211 received interrogation reports from OP-16-Z.[24]

F-211 routinely shared intelligence with the British. The Admiralty's Operational Intelligence Centre sent an "Ultra serial" to F-211 "almost daily."[25] Winn would add comments and queries before sending the message, and F-211 would draft replies and comments, which were sent in turn by F-21 serials. This two-way message traffic allowed Winn and Knowles to share information and keep each other fully informed of what the other was thinking. This practice began in 1942, when Bletchley Park was breaking Enigma traffic faster than OP-20-G, and continued even after the U.S. Navy outstripped Bletchley Park's capabilities.[26]

Office of Naval Intelligence

Several important departments and sub-departments were developed to meet the requirements necessary to battle the Axis forces. An understanding of these organizations is necessary in order to appreciate fully the intelligence offensive waged against the U-boat war, though the names and descriptions of these departments can become difficult to keep straight.

OP-16-Z: The Special Activities Branch

The Special Activities Branch, or OP-16-Z, came into existence on August 5, 1942, the successor to the Special Intelligence Section (OP-16-F-9). OP-16-Z was responsible for interrogating prisoners of war and for foreign materiel exploitation.[27] In addition to disseminating intelligence to Knowles's F-21 and operating forces, OP-16-Z compiled and published reports for its own internal use. Interrogating officers used these reports, which detailed active U-boats, officers, and bases, as starting points from which to obtain additional information from new prisoners.[28]

OP-20-GI-2 (A): The Enigma Section

The responsibility for decrypting and translating Enigma message traffic belonged to the Enigma Section of the Office of Naval Intelligence, or OP-20-GI-2 (A).[29] In addition to its decryption work, the Enigma Section maintained a card file on matters pertaining to U-boats. This file primarily served the translators and watch officers answering questions from F-21 and F-211, but was also used to find suggestions for "cribs," or clues that could be used to speed the decryption of intercepted Enigma traffic.[30] OP-20-GI-2 (A) also disseminated a daily U-boat summary, produced by Lieutenant Willard Van Orman Quine, USNR.[31]

OP-20-3-GI-A: *The Atlantic Section*

Yet another department that played an integral role in subduing the U-boat menace was the Atlantic Section, also known as OP-20-3-GI-A. This organization, a unit within OP-20-G, dealt more broadly with the operational intelligence situation in the Atlantic. Enigma provided but one of its many sources. OP-20-3-GI-A began operations in January 1943, with responsibility for translating U-boat message traffic, performing traffic analysis, and correlating D/F reports.[32] The section's primary mission was to furnish Knowles's F-21 with an accurate interpretation of each message—a task complicated by the *Kriegsmarine*'s system of double-encoding U-boat positions. The Atlantic Section met this difficult challenge, but the code would require substantial extra analytical effort until a key to the *Kriegsmarine* grid-square system, the so-called *Addressbuch,* was captured with *U-505.*[33]

To support Knowles, the Atlantic Section supplied its intelligence output to F-211 ("The Secret Room") as quickly as possible. Operational use of Ultra intelligence was entirely Knowles's responsibility, and he had his own system for analyzing Ultra and fusing it with information from other sources. In addition, the Atlantic Section supported Knowles's work by preparing any special studies or reports he requested.[34]

While Knowles shared intelligence with the Admiralty's Operational Intelligence Centre, the Atlantic Section shared intelligence with the codebreakers working at Bletchley Park. With its coverage of local *Kriegsmarine* circuits as well as its greater experience with U-boats, Bletchley Park provided information and expertise that the Atlantic Section was unable to obtain elsewhere. In turn, as American bombes (machines built to read encrypted German transmissions) began breaking the four-rotor Enigma, the Atlantic Section shared the resulting Ultra intelligence with their British counterparts.[35]

The Tenth Fleet

Against the background of the tradition-rich United States Navy, the Tenth Fleet was notable for its oddities. It was the only fleet in the

American Navy without ships. Its numerical designation was much higher than any other numbered fleet, and not a single other approached that integer. The commander of Tenth Fleet was none other than Admiral King, a position adding yet a third responsibility to his roles as Commander in Chief, United States Fleet, and Chief of Naval Operations.[36] The Tenth Fleet had a remarkably small staff and most of its enlisted personnel were Waves.[37] Tenth Fleet was indeed a unique organization.

King believed that unified control over antisubmarine operations in the part of the Atlantic for which the United States was responsible was essential to victory. To meet that need, he established Tenth Fleet under COMINCH control on May 20, 1943.[38] King took command of the fleet believing supreme naval authority was required for the ASW mission. Still, he usually left day-to-day command authority to "Frog" Low, Tenth Fleet chief of staff, whom he promoted to rear admiral. Orders from Tenth Fleet to the operating forces, however, were issued in King's name, a procedure that left no room for argument from subordinates.[39]

King and Low set out to create a unit composed of highly intelligent people, both regular navy and reservists, officers and enlisted, in a small, flexible, responsive organization.[40] Its elements included a Convoy and Routing Division, made up of a staff Tenth Fleet inherited from the former F-35; an ASW Organization (ASWORG), consisting of approximately 100 civilian experts, and a core staff of approximately 50 officers and enlisted.[41]

There was a reason Tenth Fleet did not possess a single ship: it did not have a need for them. By King's explicit order, Tenth Fleet had the power to commandeer any U.S. naval forces as needed for antisubmarine operations.[42] These Allied hijacking directives were normally dispatched as "suggestions" to Commander in Chief, Atlantic Fleet (or CINC-LANT), though King fully expected CINCLANT to comply immediately.[43] The end result was that CINCLANT's commander, Admiral Royal E. Ingersoll, virtually relinquished command of his escort carrier task groups, allowing Frog Low to coordinate their operations.[44]

For his part Low fully appreciated that Tenth Fleet required intelligence support to perform its tasks. While the organization had unrestricted access to the British Admiralty's ASW resources, most of Tenth Fleet's intelligence was obtained from U.S. naval sources.[45] Both Low and King agreed Tenth Fleet did not need its own intelligence division. Therefore, Knowles's F-21 was tasked with fulfilling the fleet's intelligence requirements since it was already devoted almost exclusively to issues relating to U-boats.[46] The division of labor worked well. F-21 maintained the operations plot for Tenth Fleet, which in turn passed its "suggestions" to CINCLANT, which complied.[47] F-21's output was also forwarded to Tenth Fleet's Convoy and Routing Division (or F-0), which used the intelligence to direct shipping away from U-boat infested waters.[48]

In addition to its daily contact with the operating forces through CINCLANT, Tenth Fleet issued a regular publication. Commonly known as the "Yellow Peril" after the color of its cover, *U.S. Fleet Antisubmarine Warfare Bulletin* was issued every month from June 1943 to June 1945, serving as Tenth Fleet's primary method of communication with commanding officers at sea. It provided a wealth of reliable and useful information about new enemy weapons, U-boat tactics and capabilities, and ASW developments and doctrine.[49]

Small yet multifaceted, Tenth Fleet labored largely in obscurity, as did the various elements of COMINCH and ONI that supported the antisubmarine effort. Any glory in the Battle of the Atlantic went to the operating forces. Still, those chasing down U-boats in the wide expanse of the Atlantic or escorting convoys safely across the sea fully understood the value of the intelligence they received and unstintingly praised the naval intelligence organizations that made their exploits possible.[50]

Allied anti-submarine warfare in the Atlantic benefited from a strong spirit of cooperation among the United States, Great Britain, and Canada. This relationship, however, took some time to develop because codebreakers at Bletchley Park were reluctant to share Enigma intelligence with their American counterparts.[51] It took an exchange of visits between Bletchley officials and the Office of Naval Intelligence and a written agreement to establish a solid foundation for the sharing of intelligence gleaned from Enigma. The British influence in anti-submarine warfare was also put to use when the U.S. Navy built its ASW organization on the Royal Navy's model, a result that largely came about with Knowles traveling to England to meet with Winn to learn the science and art of submarine tracking and how the Royal Navy set up its ASW organization.[52]

Intelligence Sources and Methods:
The Role of All-Source Intelligence in the Capture of U-505

The publication of F. W. Winterbotham's *The Ultra Secret* in 1974, detailing for the first time the story of how the Allies had broken the Enigma machine cipher, captured the popular imagination of people around the globe. The Allies' success in keeping the secret for nearly three decades after the end of World War II only added to the mystique of the accomplishment. Less romantic intelligence disciplines, although vital to the Allied antisubmarine effort, passed largely ignored.

In the case of *U-505*, as it was with the greater anti-submarine war effort, the reality was more complex. Radio direction finding technology matured quickly and was used for tactical intelligence both ashore and aboard ship. Less sophisticated codes and ciphers were exploited both for the information they held and as aids to decrypting Enigma traffic. Human intelligence stripped from the interrogation of prisoners of war yielded information that was used in defeating the U-boats. Material captured from enemy surface ships and submarines was exploited profitably in signals intelligence (SIGINT) operations and in the development of countermeasures.

High Frequency Direction Finding:
Unglamorous, but Effective

The British initiated efforts to obtain high frequency direction finding (HF/DF, or Huff-Duff) bearings on U-boats as early as January 1941. By that time seven radio intercept stations were operational in the Atlantic area.[53] Within four months the U.S. Navy and the British Admiralty began exchanging DF information, and the Americans quickly demonstrated skills comparable to those of the British.[54] As the war continued improvements in equipment, training, and doctrine made direction finding at least as important to the defeat of the U-boats as any other single intelligence asset, with the possible exception of Ultra.[55]

At its peak the Atlantic HF/DF network consisted of 51 shore stations along the coasts staffed by American, British, and Canadian operators. Their first task was to copy the text of any radio traffic to or from U-boats at sea. Their second task was to obtain a bearing on the source of the transmission. With six or seven bearings (known as "cuts"), a U-boat's location could sometimes be plotted to within 25 miles of its actual location.[56] Because of the peculiarities of radio-wave propagation, most fixes were less precise. Still, knowledge of the approximate location of a U-boat often allowed the Allies to guide antisubmarine forces to an area where the submarine could be attacked, or route target ships away from the stalking submarines.

Unlike other technical intelligence assets, HF/DF had the advantage of rapid exploitation. Because of the time required for decryption, Ultra remained too slow for tactical use. In contrast, improvements in communications eventually made it possible to transmit a fix to COMINCH within 30 minutes of a U-boat's transmission.[57] When shipborne equipment became widely available, HF/DF became a true tactical asset. Fixes were often forwarded immediately to every ship and aircraft in a task group, improving the chances of a successful antisubmarine operation.[58]

U-boats Highly Vulnerable to HF/DF

Admiral Karl Dönitz, the commander of German U-boat operations, insisted on a centralized system of control for his U-boat fleet and frequent reports from his captains. This system allowed for the organizing of "wolf pack" task groups directly from his headquarters. Unfortunately for the German war effort, Dönitz's system generated a tremendous amount of radio traffic between submarines at sea and BdU, Dönitz's headquarters. Even during the Enigma blackout, HF/DF profitably exploited the radio waves themselves.[59]

Dönitz was a sailor, not a technical man. Born outside Berlin in 1891, he entered the Navy in 1910 and cut his military teeth aboard the cruiser SMS *Breslau* during the war's early years before transferring to U-boats in 1916. The younger Dönitz made five successful patrols in the Mediterranean aboard *U-39* as *I.W.O.* (First Watch Officer) before getting his own boat, *UC-25*, a minelayer and attack craft of 417 tons. He made two patrols between late February and September 1918 with *UC-25*, sinking several ships and earning the highly coveted Cross of

Hohenzollern with Swords. His calm demeanor, "competence and energy" brought him respect and the command of a larger boat, *UC-68*. These early boats, Dönitz would later note, had a tendency to dive sharply; they also tended to be manned by largely inexperienced crews. These two factors probably came together on October 4, 1918, during a convoy encounter. While submerged the boat experienced a stabilization problem and plunged deeply by the bow. When the tanks were blown the boat went out of control and broke the surface near enemy destroyers. Out of compressed air and thus unable to dive, he ordered the boat abandoned while under fire and spent the next nine months as a prisoner of the British. Dönitz, however, had time to think about and analyze the entire U-boat experience. The result was the formulation of the early doctrine of what would evolve into his 1939-1945 U-boat tonnage war.

During the height of the Second World War the staff of the Supreme Naval Command repeatedly told Dönitz—and he believed it—that the use of high frequency radio would make direction finding impossible. *Kriegsmarine* scientists were even more reluctant to consider the possibility that the Allies were installing HF/DF gear aboard ships.[60] Not until June 15, 1944, when *U-505* was already en route to Bermuda under tow, did BdU send a message to the fleet warning of the threat from shipborne HF/DF. By that late date, of course, much of the damage had already been done.[61]

The large volume of radio traffic, much of it inconsequential, facilitated Allied direction finding and helped bring about the destruction of 22 U-boats between May 1943 and April 1945.[62]

HF/DF Technology

Throughout the war, American HF/DF benefited from technological advancements. For example, the electronics firm International Telephone and Telegraph (IT&T, now known as ITT) developed a shore-based system far superior to previous units, and the Naval Research Laboratory (NRL) created a practical shipboard system; both yielded faster and more accurate bearings than had been possible at the beginning of the war.

How, exactly, were bearings obtained? In 1941, obtaining a bearing meant rotating a directional antenna until the received signal was at its weakest (known as a "null") and plotting a bearing at right angles to the null. Bearings were taken from several stations located at some distance from each other, which were then plotted on a chart to determine the location of the transmitting station. The margin of error averaged 25 miles under good conditions, but a transmitting boat 500 miles offshore could be as much as 60 miles from where the DF indicated it was operating.[63] A wide number of variables affected these bearings, including cold fronts at sea, electrical storms, improper electrical grounding of DF stations, weather conditions between the transmitting U-boat and the DF station, radio propagation conditions (influenced by the height of the ionosphere and the aurora borealis, among other phenomena), and the skill of the operator. As the Allies soon discovered, a better system was available.[64]

In 1936, IT&T engineer and French émigré Henri Busignies had developed Model DAJ, an instantaneous-reading HF/DF.[65] His DAJ used a fixed Adcock antenna array for distant stations and a quadrature loop antenna for signals transmitted within 200 miles. In either case it was unnecessary to rotate an antenna because the Adcock and quadrature arrays sensed the difference in phase as the signal traveled between antennas, and converted the phase shift into a line of position.[66] A cathode-ray tube displayed the bearing as a glowing line on the screen. It was a stunning advancement in HF/DF technology.[67] The Army and Navy did not become aware of the DAJ system until a conference with IT&T in January 1941. The only catch was that it was necessary to modify the system to use standard American vacuum tubes and 110-volt, 60-Hz alternating current, which was not the European standard. As a result, the system did not become operational until 1943.[68]

The new technology did not eliminate errors, however. When compared to the locations logged in *U-505's* war diary, for example, the positions shown in the U.S. DF log were off by distances ranging from 81 to 299 nautical miles. Much like anti-submarine warfare in general, in many ways direction finding was an art as much as a science, and intelligence analysts had to bring their abilities to bear to produce more accurate position estimates than those available through DF alone.

HF/DF at Sea

Because of the delay involved in relaying a fix to COMINCH and then disseminating that fix to forces in position to make use of the intelligence, land-based direction finding was too slow to be a true tactical asset.[69] Therefore, the development of shipborne HF/DF gave escorts and hunter-killer groups an important advantage because the information was immediately available to the officer in tactical command, and the effective range of ship-borne HF/DF was approximately 30 nautical miles—far exceeding either radar or sonar.[70]

The first shipboard HF/DF to employ a cathode-ray tube to display bearing information was called FH4, an experimental system installed on HMS *Culver* (Y-87), the former U.S. Coast Guard cutter *Mendota*, in October 1941. Unfortunately, the ship was torpedoed and sunk in January 1942.[71] The British also began installing less sophisticated HF/DF aboard escort vessels. These detection units were initially used primarily for evasion, but were occasionally employed to set up attacks on U-boats. The first HF/DF-directed sinking of a U-boat occurred on March 27, 1942, when escorts from the convoy WS-17 sank Kptlt. Ulrich Borcherdt's *U-587* in the North Atlantic.[72]

Despite the loss of *Culver*, the Navy decided to proceed with further development of shipboard HF/DF.[73] On June 26, 1942, Admiral King ordered half of all new U.S. destroyers (DD) and destroyer escorts (DE) to be fitted with the IT&T DAQ (shipborne) system or any improved models developed thereafter.[74] Larger ships were also fitted with HF/DF, including the escort carrier USS *Bogue* (CVE-9), which carried an operational DAQ by May 1943.[75] IT&T went on to produce about 4,000 HF/DF sets before the end of the war.[76] High frequency direction finding aided in the sinking of 22 German submarines between May 22, 1943, and April 8, 1945. This credible figure is in addition to the capture of *U-505* and damage inflicted to many other U-boats that were not sent to the bottom.[77] By comparison, Ultra information was used in 54 sinkings.[78] Clearly, HF/DF was no panacea, but it did play an important role in the Battle of the Atlantic and the capture of *U-505*.

Top Secret ULTRA: Enigma and the Bombe

"An extraordinarily important component"

Earlier in the war, before the Allies broke the Enigma cipher, Royal Navy hunter-killer groups scoured vast expanses of the Atlantic in search of U-boats. Shore-based direction finding was a useful tool, but a U-boat whose presence was first revealed by a HF/DF fix in the middle of the North Atlantic was likely to be well out of range of the nearest available ASW assets. The British recognized the importance of the Enigma cipher and devoted enormous resources to its solution. Through statistical analysis, foreign material exploitation, and their extension of Polish work in decryption by machine, the codebreakers at Bletchley Park eventually kept pace with the three-rotor Enigma machine. When the four-rotor Enigma was introduced to the U-boat fleet in February 1942, outstripping Bletchley's capabilities, the U.S. Navy cooperated with American industry to develop a high-speed machine capable of solving the new problem.

The eventual availability of Ultra intelligence tipped the scales for the Allies, largely because of BdU's (U-boat headquarters) meticulous accountability and control. BdU routinely sent operational orders by radio after U-boats had sailed, which in turn made the orders available to the Allies as soon as they were decrypted. BdU also required periodic reports from U-boats at sea, which often included position information.[79] The U.S. and Royal navies used this information to send carrier groups into promising areas, from which airborne patrols and shipboard HF/DF were used to pinpoint a U-boat's location, after which it was often hunted to destruction.[80] When combined with intelligence from other disciplines, Ultra truly became "an extraordinarily important component that orchestrated a vast symphony of technological achievements that would defeat the U-boat."[81]

German Overconfidence and Mistakes

In theory, the Enigma had 3 x 10 to the 114th power (or 3×10^{114}) ciphering possibilities.[82] German experts estimated a team of 1,000 cryptanalysts working continuously would require 900 million years to test every possible key—even if each analyst was working with a captured or copied Enigma machine.[83] The overconfidence implied by these numbers induced the Germans to make serious mistakes in operating procedure and communications security. In addition to facilitating HF/DF, BdU's system of centralized control and frequent reporting provided Allied codebreakers with enormous amounts of raw material for analysis.[84] Even when the four-rotor Enigma was introduced in 1942, the keys were identical to those of the three-rotor machine; only the fourth rotor setting was different, which simplified the task of Allied cryptanalysts.[85]

Worse yet for the *Kriegsmarine*, senior officers refused to consider the possibility Enigma had been compromised. After the introduction of the four-rotor Enigma, neither Dönitz nor any other high commander ever ordered technical or procedural changes that might have blunted the Allied cryptanalytic attack.[86] German experts studied radio and heat radiation from U-boats, transmitter radiation while tuning, the intermediate frequency oscillators of radio receivers, direction finding of U-boat transmissions, and the possibility of an undetectable Allied radar, but apparently never gave serious thought to the possibility of decryption intelligence. It was a serious oversight that had far-reaching conse-quences for the German war effort.[87]

Early Success against Enigma

The internal workings of the Enigma machine were "cracked" by Marian Rejewski, a young Polish mathematician employed by his country's *Biuro Szyfrow* (BS), or Cipher Bureau. He began his work in September 1932 using higher mathematics than had ever been employed in cryptanalysis, as well as information purchased from German spy Hans-Thilo Schmidt. By the end of the year he had broken the code for the first rotor.[88] Rejewski worked out a mathematical method for determining Enigma keys when the indicators in three messages met certain conditions. AVA Radio Manufacturing Company built the first *bomby* machines designed to exploit Rejewski's work and delivered them to BS in November 1938.[89]

When Germany invaded Poland in 1939, Rejewski and several colleagues escaped the country. News of their work eventually reached the Allies. Britain and the United States advanced Rejewski's efforts and built more advanced "bombes," as they were called in English, using them for the duration of the war.[90] By the spring of 1941, the British Tabulating Machine Company had delivered eight bombes to GCCS at Bletchley Park; that number rose to 12 by the end of the year.[91]

Foreign Material Exploitation and Enigma

The Royal Navy assisted Bletchley Park both inadvertently and intentionally. The sinking of Kptlt. Hans-Wilhelm von Dresky's *U-33* by the minesweeper HMS *Gleaner* on February 12, 1940, yielded three Enigma rotors from the pockets of a German seaman who had forgotten to throw them overboard. Two of the rotors, known as VI and VII, were previously unknown to GCCS.[92] Three weeks later the converted whaler *Krebs* fired on a Royal Navy task force, which proceeded to run the German ship aground. A boarding party from HMS *Somali* collected two rotors and the Enigma keys for February. Analysis yielded February, April, and some May Enigma traffic, and also demonstrated naval Enigma could be broken—even in the months before British bombes began operating.[93]

On April 26, 1940, a boarding party from the destroyer HMS *Griffin* captured a 394-ton German "fishing trawler" armed with torpedoes. Before the party could board, however, a German crewman threw two canvas bags overboard, one of which was recovered by a British gunner. The bag held naval Enigma keys for April 23-26, providing the codebreakers at Bletchley Park another break into naval Enigma.[94]

Harry Hinsley, a traffic analysis expert assigned to Bletchley Park's Hut 8, realized Germany needed weather information for air operations and planning, and that the *Kriegsmarine* stationed ships in the North Atlantic to observe and report the weather.[95] Hinsley suggested the Royal Navy send a task group to capture a weather ship, hoping it could be taken before its crew could send a distress call. The subsequent capture of *München* on May 7, 1941, yielded the Short Weather Cipher and the inner and outer Enigma settings for the Home Waters keys for June.[96] A repeat mission succeeded with the capture of the trawler *Lauenburg* on

June 28, 1941, which yielded the July home waters key, *Stecker* (plugboard) settings, and a sheet of internal settings.[97]

The chance capture of Kptlt. Fritz-Julius Lemp's *U-110* off Iceland just two days after the capture of *München* (during which Lemp was killed under circumstances yet to be fully understood or univerally accepted) yielded a bonanza of codebooks, instructions, key lists, an Enigma machine, and all eight rotors then in use by the *Kriegsmarine*.[98] This capture reduced the Enigma solution time for June from eleven days to an average of just six hours.[99] This new ability to read Enigma traffic lasted until the introduction of four-rotor Enigma on February 1, 1942, the beginning of an Enigma "blackout" that would last until December 1942.[100]

The final capture of note in the Enigma story took place on October 23, 1942, when several escorts and an aircraft depth charged and crippled Kptlt. Hans Heidtmann's *U-559* in the Mediterranean. A three-man boarding party from HMS *Petard* climbed onto the heavily damaged submarine and removed the current edition of the short signal book for weather reports, as well as the short signal book for reporting enemy ships, battle results, and other tactical information. The U-boat sank with two of the men still aboard.[101] The weather codebook gave Bletchley Park cribs that would be useful in the solution of four-rotor Enigma. By the time this edition of the codebook expired, Hut 8 had developed a method of taking cribs from the tactical short signal book. This method was used until the end of the war.[102]

Four-rotor Enigma

The Enigma blackout began with the introduction of four-rotor Enigma on February 1, 1942. The fourth wheel theoretically introduced a multiple of 26 into the solution time for Enigma, requiring either 26 times as many bombes or a bombe which would run 26 times as fast as the existing British bombe.[103]

However, many three-rotor Enigma machines remained in use, and Bletchley Park's analysis of four-rotor Enigma messages eventually showed that four-rotor Enigma keys were identical to three-rotor keys, with only the fourth rotor setting being different. Therefore, once a three-rotor solution was found, only 26 tests were required to determine the position of the fourth rotor. Successful solutions based on this principle reduced the number of ships sunk in convoy in January and February 1943 by fully one-half when compared to November and December of 1942.[104]

Development of the American Bombe

The Enigma problem assumed critical importance to the U.S. Navy when the United States entered the war in December 1941. Although Bletchley Park had promised their American counterparts a bombe, they were unable to produce a workable high-speed machine. Therefore, Commander Joseph Wenger, deputy chief of OP-20-G, "felt obliged to recommend to higher authority that we take the matter in our own hands and proceed as we felt proper."[105]

The urgency of the U-boat situation in the Atlantic, coupled with the failure to receive any equipment or reassurance from the British, led to a development contract between the U.S. Navy and the National Cash Register Machine Company (NCR). The contract, signed on September 4, 1942, committed the parties to research and development of "an extremely high-speed cipher machine of the Enigma type."[106] Two months later on November 11, 1942, letters from the Vice Chief of Naval Operations to the Chief of Naval Personnel (via the Chief of the Bureau of Ships) and the Commandant of the Ninth Naval District established the U.S. Naval Computing Machine Laboratory (or NCML) to assist NCR in the production of bombes and the training of personnel.[107] The Navy located NCML at NCR's plant in Dayton, Ohio, under the direct control of OP-20-G with funding from the Bureau of Ships.[108]

Everyone associated with the bombe project understood it to be a gamble, both because of its technical difficulty and because of the possibility that German changes to equipment or procedures might render their hard work useless. They were also aware that while the high-speed bombes would theoretically work, practical engineering had not yet caught up with theory. Also, Bletchley Park had expressed doubts about the success of the project, as the American plan was "at variance with British experience and recommendations."[109]

Shortages of critical materials also affected the bombe project. The Radio Division of the Bureau of Ships indicated that "serious difficulties were being experienced in getting certain critical materials necessary in radio manufacture," many of which were required in bombe construction.[110] Because of the material shortages, project officers had to decide whether to delay production until a high-speed commutator (a critical component in the bombe's operation) became available. Against the advice of the engineers, the officers decided to start construction before receiving any commutators. The gamble worked when commutators arrived in time to be installed in the first bombes.[111]

Discussions with the British led to the decision early in 1943 to build 96 bombes, a number that eventually grew to 120.[112] To assist in the construction of bombes, the Navy sent 600 newly inducted Waves and 200 men to Dayton, where they worked in Building 26 of the NCR plant. As the first bombes were completed, the sailors and Waves began training to operate and maintain the new machines.[113] Navy bombes were large and heavy machines—seven feet tall, two feet wide, 10 feet long, and 5,000 pounds. Both the front and the back sides contained eight columns of four commutators, also known as "rotors" or "wheels." The top wheel of each column corresponded to the fourth rotor of the Enigma machine, while the bottom rotor represented the rightmost rotor of the Enigma. The bottom wheel spun at 1,725 revolutions per minute, allowing the bombe to complete a "run" in 20 minutes.[114]

U.S. Bombes in Operation

On May 28, 1943, the first two prototype bombes, known as "Adam" and "Eve," were put into operation at U.S. Naval Computing Machine Laboratory.[115] The first production bombes followed that August.[116] Secure communications were set up between Dayton and Washington, and the bombes were operated in Ohio for the first few months to remain within easy reach of the maintenance and design engineers.[117] When the new "Laboratory Building" at the Naval Communications Annex was completed in September 1943, four bombes per week were shipped to Washington.[118]

Bombe menus were made up by cryptanalysts on site and sent to the Laboratory Building by pneumatic tube. The bombe operator, always a Wave, used a menu to set up the machine, with help from a supervisor.[119] The operator started the machine and monitored its operation for the twenty minutes required for a run. As the bombe sped through every possible rotor setting, it would stop just long enough to print the rotor settings that met the conditions required by the menu (also called "hits"). When the run was complete the operator gave the printout to her supervisor. The supervisor checked the results on an M-9 machine, known appropriately as a "checker," which verified the results of the bombe run and permitted the supervisor to determine any unknown *Stecker* settings. The supervisor took this complete and verified solution to the watch officer.[120] The solution, known as a "story," was logged and sent to the cryptanalysts via the pneumatic tube.[121]

By the end of 1943, 77 bombes were operating continuously at the Annex. OP-20-G and NCML kept pace with German changes to their communication procedures, and by the time *U-505* was captured in early June 1944, a collection of 96 bombes routinely broke U-boat message traffic with an average delay of 12 hours from the time the message was intercepted.[122]

Producing and Using Ultra Intelligence

The Waves used M-9 machines to decrypt short messages. Longer messages were transferred to paper tape and run through an M-8, a converted Navy cipher machine containing rotors wired to match those of the Enigma machine. Linguists in another section of OP-20-G translated the German text into English.[123] Watch officers from F-211, the "Secret Room," read the intercepts as they arrived at COMINCH and made sure the information was posted on U-boat and convoy maps.[124]

The U.S. Navy began using Ultra intelligence offensively at approximately the same time "Adam" and "Eve" began operations (May 1943), although much of the Ultra at that time came from Bletchley Park. Early in June 1943, aircraft from the carrier USS *Bogue* sank two U-boats with the aid of Ultra. Between January 1943 and the end of the war, U.S. naval forces sank 54 U-boats with direct assistance from Ultra intelligence; approximately 30 more were sent to the bottom with the indirect aid of Ultra.[125]

Human Intelligence

The majority of human intelligence (HUMINT) relevant to the capture of *U-505* came through the interrogation of prisoners of war. Naval POWs were interrogated by OP-16-Z, the Special Intelligence Section of the Office of Naval Intelligence, which was also responsible for "foreign material exploitation" (FME). OP-16-Z interrogated prisoners from no fewer than 43 U-boats *before* the capture of *U-505*.[126] Internal drawings of various types of U-boats derived from some of these interrogations were distributed to the boarding parties of Dan Gallery's Task Group 22.3 before the cruise ending in the capture of *U-505*.[127]

OP-16-Z also blended HUMINT with FME after USS *Roper*'s (DD-147) sinking of Eberhard Greger's *U-85* north of Cape Hatteras on April 14, 1942. No one survived the sinking (those who managed to exit the boat were killed in the water by additional depth charges), but an engine room petty officer's notebook was recovered. This notebook provided OP-16-Z with details on the submarine's construction, the layout of its engineering spaces, and its operations, all of which was used during subsequent interrogations to obtain more details from captured U-boat crewmen.[128]

On June 12, 1943, aircraft from USS *Bogue* sank *U-118*, a 1,600-ton Type XB minelayer under the command of Werner Czygan, west of the Canary Islands. Sixteen survivors were plucked from the water and interrogated. By the middle of July OP-16-Z interrogators had obtained scale drawings of the submarine, as well as technical information on the mines and how they were used. Interrogation techniques had improved, and some prisoners were more willing to divulge information than their counterparts had been earlier in the war. This made it possible for OP-16-Z to obtain information on new enemy technologies that were often still in experimental stages. Interrogators acquired information and drawings on new types of German torpedoes, data on radar detection equipment and methods, modification of armament, and operating tactics.[129]

Allied operational and technical personnel considered much of the information derived from POW interrogations to be of immediate importance for modifying ASW equipment and tactics to improve their performance against the U-boats.[130]

Tracking U-505's Position

F-21, the group Commander Knowles established to track U-boats in the Atlantic Ocean, appears to have taken no notice of *U-505's* final departure from Brest until the boat's commander, Harald Lange, sent his first position report on March 25. Lange reported his position to BdU at 3:34 a.m. on March 25, as "CG 17."[131] This message told his superiors *U-505* was leaving the Bay of Biscay. It may or may not have been useful to BdU, but F-21 and the Allied HF/DF network made use of the information. The direction finders obtained a fix on Lange's signal, placing *U-505* at 44-39N 14-30W, or 290 miles from its actual location when Lange sent the message.[132] The codebreakers read CG 17 as 40-39N 14-30W, 45 miles from the center of grid square CG 17.[133]

Just before midnight on March 28 Lange received orders from BdU.[134] These orders were countermanded the next day, but Lange's radio operators never received the second message canceling the new orders.[135] Lange waited until April 1 before sending a position report using the Short Signal codebook.[136] The message was garbled, but HF/DF placed the transmitter at 34-00N 18-00W—a difference of 110 miles from the KTB position of 33-57N 20-12W. OP-20-G assessed the contents of the message and determined if the radio operator had intended to send the code group "OKQD" instead of "OKXD," (the Morse Code for *Q* is *dah-dah-di-dah* while *X* is the closely related *dah-di-di-dah*), a position of 34-03N 19-42W would be obtained. This point was only 26 miles from *U-505's* logged position.[137]

U-505 ran southeast on the surface in darkness, submerging in daylight. On April 4 Lange received orders to rendezvous with *U-123* the next day to deliver new Enigma keys (code books).[138] Early the next morning, he sent a message reporting he was on schedule, only to be informed an hour later the rendezvous had been cancelled.[139] Shortly after noon Lange received new instructions and the two U-boats effected their rendezvous on April 7. *Oberleutnant zur See* Paul Meyer, the boat's First Watch Officer, carried the new keys to *U-123* in a rubber boat.[140]

Lange continued south and on April 10 again reported his position, this time in square DS 63.[141] He requested orders in the same message, which he received a few hours later. No DF fix was obtained, but the position report was decrypted as 23-33N, 28-27W. The position shown in the KTB, DS 6353, was only 23 nautical miles from the decrypted estimate.[142] Lange received his final operating orders—to patrol west of *U-190*, between 3-42W and 14-30W.[143]

Knowles and his staff paid little attention to *U-505* as it traveled to its operating area. Any mention of *U-505* on the daily location lists for March 26 through April 14, 1944, is limited to brief summaries of the decrypted message traffic and the HF/DF fixes discussed above.[144] No effort appears to have been made to predict *U-505's* actions, although it should be noted Lange was receiving orders and sending position reports frequently enough that no predictive analysis was necessary.

Lange's superiors in BdU kept a daily position estimate for all U-boats at sea. Each position estimate was listed in the same grid square system that U-boat captains used to log and report positions, although the BdU estimate was given to a lesser degree of precision than the reports in the KTB. For example, BdU's position estimate for March 19 was "BF 41" when Lange logged his position as "BF 7333." Even so, at that time *U-505* was no closer than 138 miles to any point in square BF 41.[145] Other position estimates vary similarly, with BdU typically over-estimating *U-505's* progress, sometimes by more than 400 miles, until receiving the next position report from Lange.

Lange sent a situation report during the night of May 19. The report described the lack of traffic or patrols off Freetown, told of his attempt to catch a British steamer, and announced his intention to head for home on May 21.[146] BdU was unable to copy *U-505* clearly because of interference, but Allied HF/DF intercepted the message—the first such traffic from *U-505* in weeks. The HF/DF network fixed *U-505's* position at 3-00N 6-00W, 118 nautical miles from the KTB position of 4-51N 5-21W.[147] BdU's position estimate for *U-505* placed it in square EU 80, which at its closest point lay 164 miles from the submarine.[148]

Renewed Interest in U-505

F-211's U-Boat Intelligence Summary for April 28, 1944, warned of *U-505*, *U-190*, and *U-155* patrolling "close to the coast in the Gulf of Guinea," citing BdU's message 1253/13/340 as its source.[149] At this time Knowles was not yet making a daily estimate of *U-505's* position on the F-21 submarine plot, and the submarine does not appear in the next summary dated May 13.[150] F-21 began paying closer attention to *U-505* after intercepting Lange's May 14 situation report. Knowles included a summary of Lange's message on the May 15, 1944, location list and included the HF/DF fix for the boat.[151] In addition to position estimates for other U-boats in the Atlantic and Mediterranean, F-21's daily message to the operating forces contained this notice: "DFs over past several days suggest that three U-boats estimated patrolling off African Coast are now homebound from Cape Palmas area."[152] The May 16 location list repeated the DF position, adding, "Will return 21 May."[153] The lists for May 17 through 20 all contained the legend, "Cape Palmas returning 21 May."[154] F-21 began estimating *U-505's* noon position on May 21, assessing the submarine's location as 2-00N 10-00W. Knowles was off by 267 miles from *U-505's* actual position, 5-57N 12-03W. However, this figure compared favorably with BdU's own estimate of square ET 12 (closest point 9-36N 18-36N), an error of 452 miles.[155]

Pursuit

The accurate position estimates from Tenth Fleet had astonished Captain Gallery during USS *Guadalcanal's* first two war cruises. Since he was not, of course, cleared for Ultra intelligence, Gallery had no idea how Knowles made his uncanny predictions. Gallery chose to regard Knowles as a "soothsayer" and based his operations on the estimates coming from Knowles and his staff.[156] Gallery traveled to Washington before departing on the third cruise. Stopping by the offices of COMINCH, he visited Smith-Hutton, a onetime shipmate and fellow turret officer on the battleship USS *Idaho* (BB-42), who now occupied the post of Assistant for Combat Intelligence (F-20). Gallery told Smith-Hutton of his intention to capture a German submarine on his next cruise. In addition to promising Gallery reports on submarine activity (on which Gallery had come to rely), Smith-Hutton took him to the head of ONI's Technical Section, who gave him interior plans of two types of U-boats known to be operating in the Atlantic.[157]

Gallery's Task Group 22.3, consisting of *Guadalcanal* (CVE-60) and Escort Division Four, the destroyer escorts *Chatelain* (DE-149), *Flaherty* (DE-135), *Jenks* (DE-665), *Pillsbury* (DE-133), and *Pope* (DE-134), departed Hampton Roads on May 13, 1944. The task group sailed to York Spit Channel, where *Guadalcanal* calibrated its DAQ

HF/DF gear.[158] A burst boiler tube forced the carrier to return to port the next day, but the damage was promptly repaired and the task group set out again on May 15 for what would become one of the U.S. Navy's most celebrated operations.[159]

Daily Operations

Task Group 22.3 proceeded to its operating area south of the Cape Verde Islands, flying daytime antisubmarine searches and qualifying pilots in night operations along the way.[160] Air searches turned up nothing promising, and the only sonar contacts the destroyers reported were evaluated as fish or seaweed.[161] A torpedo plane reported a radar contact 10 miles from the task group shortly before midnight on May 27, and a HF/DF bearing was obtained by *Pope*'s DAQ an hour later, but the contact was lost.[162]

Closing in on U-505

As Gallery's Task Force steamed through Atlantic waters, Knowles and his staff continued tracking *U-505*, as well as a dozen or so other submarines. F-21 continued predicting *U-505*'s position more accurately than BdU, placing it 230 miles southeast of its actual position on May 22, while the square in which BdU placed the submarine was no closer than 377 miles east-southeast of its true location. Knowles continued to include three homebound submarines near Cape Palmas in his daily broadcasts.[163] The May 23 dispatch specifically included *U-505*'s estimated position, 4-30N 12-30W, for the first time. The message included no hull numbers (the daily broadcast was classified Secret, but estimates with hull numbers were Top Secret Ultra), but the position corresponds to that listed for *U-505* on that day.[164] *U-505*'s logged position at 10:00 a.m. was 7-33N 14-51W, 231 nautical miles to the northwest.[165]

Neither Knowles nor anyone on his staff showed any particular excitement over *U-505*, as demonstrated by the F-211 summary of May 24, 1944: "Cape Verde Islands . . . Three U/Boats, now homebound after fruitless patrols in the Gulf of Guinea, are expected to pass between the

Cape Verde Islands and Dakar shortly."[166] *U-505* was just another enemy submarine to be located and, if possible, exterminated.

Broadcasts mentioned *U-505* in general terms until May 28, when Knowles reported, "One homebound and one moving SE within 200 miles of 10-00[N] 18-00[W]."[167] Knowles actually estimated *U-505's* position to be 10-45N 19-00W, 74 miles from the center of the circle, while the KTB records the submarine's position as 15-03N 19-39W, or 318 miles from the center.[168]

Messages from May 29 through June 1 include word of a submarine heading north along 19-30W, starting at 12-30N 19-30W on May 29, figures corresponding to Knowles' estimates of *U-505's* position.[169] The messages until June 5 show a submarine continuing north along 19-30W, advancing two degrees (120 nautical miles) per day. F-21's Ultra estimate for June 1, the last day for which a location list has been found, placed Lange's *U-505* 175 miles south-southwest of the position in the KTB, while BdU's estimate was 503 miles northwest of the actual position.[170] Both sides were now overestimating *U-505's* progress home.

Since TG 22.3 was running low on fuel, Gallery set a course for Casablanca on May 31. It was a simple matter to head north within aircraft range of 19-30W.[171] Gallery's airplanes flew day and night searches over an area 100 miles to either side of *U-505's* estimated track. On June 2, Lange despaired over the "continuous night patrols" saturating the airspace, as evidenced by radar emissions detected by his *Naxos* warning system.[172] Although shipborne enemy radar occasionally surprised crews operating *Naxos* (which was carried aboard most U-boats at this time of the war), the radar detection gear was very sensitive to aircraft radar. As a result, it often provided warnings of airplanes operating far too distant to pose a threat. This was probably true in Lange's case, for on June 2 the task group's closest planes were more than 200 miles away. During the next night, a torpedo plane reported disappearing radar contacts east of the carrier at 18-45N 19-10W. The pilot dropped two sonobuoys into the water and reported hearing motor noises. After listening for two hours, the pilot dropped depth charges without observing any results. *U-505's* logged position at that moment was 20-03N 18-33W, or 85 miles to the northeast.[173]

During the morning of June 3, Commander Earl Trosino, *Guadalcanal*'s chief engineer, warned Gallery that their fuel level was below safe limits. Gallery decided to risk one more day of operations, confident the task group was closing in on a U-boat. Another frustrating night of operations followed. *Guadalcanal* and *Pope* picked up HF/DF bearings at 5:20, an hour before sunrise on Sunday, June 4. *Guadalcanal*'s DAQ operator picked up a U-boat signal bearing either 024 or 200 degrees at 6:29 a.m., but nothing came of the contacts.[174] At about the same time, Trosino advised Gallery, who was Catholic, "You better pray hard at Mass this morning, Cap'n. You used more oil than I figured on last night."[175] Gallery resumed course, seething over his failure to find a submarine and hoping he had enough fuel to reach Casablanca. Less than six hours later *Chatelain* picked up *U-505* on sonar.[176]

Intelligence Exploitation of U-505

Document Exploitation

The capture of *U-505* provided the Allies with a treasure trove of intelligence riches. Gallery obviously appreciated the significance of the items removed from the boat. On June 6, with the Allies landing in Normandy, he apparently believed the captured material assumed even greater importance. That night he sent a Top Secret Operational Priority Message to CINCLANT advising he possessed "material which should be examined by communication experts immediately." He suggested communications experts and personnel from the Bureau of Ships (BUSHIPS, now the Naval Sea Systems Command, or NAVSEA) fly out to *Guadalcanal* by seaplane to collect the half-ton of documents and equipment his men had taken from the captured German U-boat, which was now being towed to a safe haven by the Allies.[177]

Gallery's plan was not adopted, and *Jenks* carried the captured material to Bermuda at top speed. As soon as *Jenks* arrived, the captured documents were loaded on an airplane and flown to Washington. The Atlantic and Indian Ocean Enigma keys for June arrived at OP-20-G on June 12.[178] For the rest of the month OP-20-G was able to read this traffic just as quickly as the Germans. Additionally, possession of these keys freed up 13,000 hours of Navy bombe time in June, allowing OP-20-G to work on *Wehrmacht* and *Luftwaffe* keys, an important consideration as the invasion of Europe progressed.[179]

Other documents were also of immediate use. OP-20-G copied *U-505's* "cipher charts" (*Addressbuch*) and sent them to F-21 on June 22.[180] These charts allowed F-21 to strip the second layer of encipherment from U-boat position reports directly, with no analysis necessary. Possession of the *Addressbuch* also gave Knowles and his assistants a greater degree of confidence in their position estimates.

OP-20-G also obtained the Short Signal Cipher that was due to go into effect on July 15. This cipher was used for tactical signals, and experience showed OP-20-G would have required about four months to reach a point where short signals could be read with no delay.[181] The reserve Bigram Tables taken from *U-505* were scheduled to take effect on August 1, 1944, which would have introduced a delay of 24 hours to 10 days in decrypting all Enigma traffic until the tables were reconstructed.[182] Of less importance, but still valuable, was the Short Weather cipher, which allowed OP-20-G to determine the position of any U-boats sending weather reports.[183]

The Office of Naval Intelligence lacked the resources to translate any but the most critical documents with any haste. As late as October 21, 1944, Commander B. F. Roeder of OP-20-GI-A sent a memo to Frog Low explaining his section had only one translator available, that no more translators would arrive until December, and the only assistance he had been able to enlist was that of OP-16-Z, which had agreed to translate three items from Low's own priority list.[184]

OP-20-G became the custodian of *U-505* documents. The collection contained approximately 1,200 items, 800 of which were technical documents and navigational charts. The remaining 400 items, *U-505's* document library, were categorized as follows:

Torpedoes: 15%
Radio Communications (operational and technical): 12%
Codes and ciphers: 13%
Manuals for the C.O., orders, etc: 4%
Ship and A/C recognition: 3%
Ships logs, receipts, and papers: 10%
U/B technical documents (including periscopes,
    diesel and electric machinery): 27%
Navigation: 13%
Miscellaneous (personal, etc.): 3%.[185]

Material Exploitation

Inspection

Low arranged a flight from Washington National Airport to Bermuda on June 20. The R5D (a naval version of the Douglas DC-4) carried officers from COMINCH (including Knowles), ONI, the Submarine Design and Sonar Design sections of BUSHIPS, and the Bureau of Ordnance's (BUORD) Torpedo Design section and Mine Disposal Group. The ONI contingent included three officers from OP-16-Z and one from OP-20-G. These experts made their own examination of *U-505*, interrogated prisoners, and removed the torpedoes from the submarine. Most members of the party completed their work within a day and returned to Washington on June 21.[186]

The Submarine

Inspection of *U-505* revealed a hole in the number 7 ballast tank caused by a 20mm shell. The port bow plane had been torn off in a collision with *Pillsbury* during the capture, but a copy could be made in Bermuda.[187] By August 31, the submarine was ready for surface operations, with an American crew of one ensign, two warrant officers, and 30 enlisted men.[188]

A memorandum dated December 11, 1944, describes *U-505's* electronic equipment from bow to stern, concentrating on the radio gear and hydrophones.[189] The anonymous writer thought well of nearly all of the German electronic equipment, with the exception of the design of the low-frequency direction finder antenna. "This is considered extremely poor practice in the U.S. Navy," he concluded.[190]

The U.S. Navy used "Nemo" (as *U-505* was code-named), as a training submarine for the rest of the war, which provided naval operating forces an opportunity to learn the characteristics of the U-boats and antisubmarine experts an opportunity to develop and improve ASW tactics.[191]

The Torpedoes

While any information that could be obtained from *U-505's* torpedoes would be valuable, the Bureau of Ordnance was particularly anxious to examine the T-5 acoustic homing torpedo, a significantly more dangerous weapon than earlier models. The T-5 followed a ship's propeller noise to the target, which defeated the traditional counter-measure of steering a zigzag course when a ship's lookouts spotted a torpedo in the water. Via COMINCH, the Bureau of Ordnance requested the team in Bermuda to send a T-5 by ship to the Naval Mine Warfare Test Station (NMWTS) at Solomons, Maryland.[192] In fact, the Bureau of Ordnance was so anxious to obtain a T-5 that if two were available, the bureau would send an airplane to collect the first one. [193]

Although the torpedo board in *U-505* indicated the inspectors would find T-5 acoustic torpedoes in tubes 2, 5, and 6, only two T-5s were located.[194] A quick review of prisoner interrogation records revealed the crew of *U-505* fired the torpedo in tube 5 shortly before abandoning ship.[195]

Although no messages directly confirming air shipment of a T-5 have been located, a message from Low directed CINCLANT to "Send *remaining* torpedoes from Nemo . . . via water transportation."[196] Other messages indicate USS *Chaffee* (DE-230) departed for Solomons on June 29 with a T-5 on board.[197] Over the next three weeks *Rudderow* (DE-224), *Sperry* (DD-697), and *Fessenden (DE-142)* departed Bermuda with 12 torpedoes, 11 detonator pistols, *U-505's* scuttling charges, and ammunition for the deck guns.[198]

The testing of the torpedoes began immediately. By early September, extensive tests of the two acoustic torpedoes recovered from *U-505* indicated that the FXR ("Foxer") Mark IV countermeasure device used by U.S. warships might be ineffective against the T-5.[199]

Water-Soluble Ink

On May 3, 1944, British aircraft located and heavily damaged Heinz-Wilhelm Eck's *U-852* in the Arabian Sea off the east coast of Somalia. Hard aground, the Germans abandoned the boat without effectively destroying its valuable contents. Inside, Allied boarders recovered eight secret communications publications wrapped in a tablecloth. Five were printed in water-soluble ink on special paper. Unable to recover any information from the documents, Bletchley Park forwarded them to American Army chemists in Washington for evaluation. Several of the documents taken from *U-505* were printed with the same water-soluble ink. OP-20-G forwarded samples of the ink and paper to the Army, which eventually recovered usable intelligence from the *U-852* material.[200]

Interrogation and Disposition of the Crew from U-505

Low's June 18 memorandum does not specify which of the representatives from OP-16-Z—Lieutenant Commander H. T. Gherardi, Lieutenant T. H. Erek, or Lieutenant H. H. Hart—interrogated the crew of *U-505*. The handwritten notes taken during the initial ("rough") interrogations appear to be in the handwriting of at least two individuals.[201] Perhaps all three officers interrogated the prisoners in an effort to complete their work before flying back to Washington on June 21.

Some of *U-505's* crewmen limited their answers to name, rank, and serial number, as required by the Geneva Convention. Others, however, more willingly provided additional information. Many told of *U-505's* history as well as their own. One man told his interrogator where to find the T-5 acoustic homing torpedoes on board the captured boat.[202] Two men provided ONI with the first details of former commander Peter Zschech's suicide during a patrol in the fall of 1943—news that must have startled the examiners.[203] Others offered the welcome news that the crew had abandoned *U-505* too quickly to send a distress signal.[204] The men from OP-16-Z recorded their impressions of the men for use during subsequent interrogations. These notes are usually variations on a few basic themes:

> "Will answer anything."
> "Completely OK."
> "A nice lad."
> "Completely OK but dumb."
> "Refuses all answers and is to be treated as a bastard."[205]

National Archives

"It will be a hard life—have no illusions about that. But with a well-disciplined crew, we'll have our successes." *Kplt.* Axel-Olaf Loewe's honest observation was spoken during *U-505's* commissioning ceremony on August 26, 1941. He knew of what he spoke—it was a hard life indeed.

U-boot- Archiv, Cuxhaven

Kplt. Axel-Olaf Loewe as he appeared while commanding *U-505*, wearing the standard denim battledress blouse and distinctive white cap associated with U-boat captains. He was later promoted to *Korvettenkapitän* and served as a staff officer in Admiral Karl Dönitz's headquarters. Loewe ended the war in command of a naval antitank unit. The Kiel native of Crew 28 died in December 1984. He was the boat's most successful captain.

Museum of Science and Industry, Chicago

Salvage parties struggle to keep the pumps operating. The signalman dressed in white awaits instructions to pass along to the task group. Captain Harald Lange's shell insignia is clearly visible on the port side of the conning tower.

Museum of Science and Industry, Chicago

Washington dispatched USS *Abnaki* and two other vessels to take *U-505* in tow and refuel the task group. They arrived on the morning of June 7. *U-505* was in tow by 1015. Salvage parties removed loose gear and worked *Abnaki's* electric pumps to keep *U-505* dry. Eventually the boat's stern rose almost level. Once underway, the submarine's propellers spun on their own, which turned the boat's generators and produced enough electricity to run compressors and blow the ballast tanks.

Museum of Science and Industry, Chicago

Several days after the capture Commander Earl Trosino, *Guadalcanal's* chief engineer, decided that all loose gear had to be removed from the boat in an effort to lighten it and make more room for the ongoing salvage efforts. In the torpedo room salvagers discovered the Germans had been using this large bucket as a toilet while *U-505* was being hunted. Nobody wanted to remove the disgusting bucket and dump it overboard, so Trosino demonstrated leadership by doing it himself.

Captain Daniel V. Gallery poses proudly on the conning tower of his war trophy. *U-505's* antenna cable and wind deflector on top of the tower were damaged in the depth charge attack. Chipping paint reveals the tower's aluminum outer skin. Several veterans recall that Gallery had the large American flag made in the sailmaker's shop for the tow into Bermuda. This flag is today housed at Memorial Hall in Annapolis. The German flag, one of perhaps five found on board, was installed beneath the U.S. flag as a traditional sign of victor over vanquished. Barely visible between *U-505's* shell emblem's are the words "CAN DO JUNIOR," which were painted by the salvage crew in recognition of *Guadalcanal's* motto "CAN-DO," which meant the ship could handle any tough job assigned to it. "The tougher the job, the better we'll like it," was how Gallery motivated the men under his command. The capture of *U-505* was indeed a tough job well done.

When the crewmen arrived in the United States they were transported to a prisoner of war camp in Ruston, Louisiana. In violation of the Geneva Convention, they were held incommunicado for the rest of the war. Their families had no knowledge of their fate until they returned home.[206]

Intelligence Sharing

Not surprisingly, the codebreakers at Bletchley Park were eager to examine the cryptographic materials from *U-505*. They sent off a bold request to OP-20-G the morning after the capture:

> Be most grateful if you could arrange for Navy Department to instruct CTG 22.3 . . . to report . . . details of any code and cipher . . . documents captured, and to forward *originals* to U.K. by fast air after photostating.[207]

Evidently the British saw an additional advantage to be gained by examining original documents rather than copies.

Commander Wenger, head of OP-20-G, forwarded the message to Captain Smith-Hutton, F-20, with a note: "Attached dispatch will require your action. We want copies of all material."[208] Smith-Hutton passed the message along to Knowles, who wrote, "We will do nothing in this regard until situation clarifies."[209] Eventually, Bletchley Park received originals or photographic copies of cryptographic and communications material, grid charts, and current technical documents not already in the Admiralty's possession.[210]

Conclusion

The intelligence support provided to Gallery began even before Task Group 22.3 departed on the fateful cruise. When Gallery traveled to Washington and told his old friend Smith-Hutton of his intent to capture a German submarine, he returned to Norfolk with interior plans for two different types of U-boat (the result of human intelligence gleaned from prisoner interrogations) and assurances of accurate position estimates.

After his Task Group put to sea, the daily operational intelligence estimates Gallery received from Tenth Fleet provided him with solid intelligence, a product of HF/DF, Ultra, and the analytical skill of Knowles and his staff. This estimate specifically included *U-505* every day from May 23 until the submarine was captured, and was routinely more accurate than the *Kriegsmarine's* morning estimates. While Knowles, like BdU, overestimated *U-505's* progress home, his estimates convinced Gallery to sail north roughly along 19-30W. If Gallery had instead steered a direct course to Casablanca to refuel, it is unlikely he would have passed close enough to *U-505* to capture it. If his airplanes had found the submarine outside of the destroyers' gun range, a capture would have been impossible and the aviators would have had to attempt to sink it instead.

As is always true in human events, chance played a role in shaping Gallery's operation. Task Group 22.3 might have stumbled across *U-505* while enroute to Casablanca, or perhaps while on the way home to Norfolk after refueling. In the event, Gallery made an operational decision based upon intelligence received from F-21. And his operational savvy, combined with years of outstanding intelligence work on both sides of the Atlantic, led to an event unparalleled in the history of modern naval warfare.

It was about this time Lange began to suspect he was the focus of a Hunter-Killer group, at the hub of which was an aircraft carrier supplying the irksome airplanes that were tormenting his boat. Events revealed his hunch was indeed correct, but by a quirk of fate he chose a most unfortunate course of action. . . .

Lawrence Paterson

Collision Course

Task Group 22.3 and the Hunt for *U-505*

far away from the north Atlantic convoy routes a chess game of detection and interception was being played by Allied naval strategists. The U.S. Navy's U-Boat Intelligence Summary for April 28 deduced from intercepted BdU radio traffic that at least three submarines—*U-190*, *U-155*, and *U-505*—were patrolling "close to the coast in the Gulf of Guinea." Enigma decryptions had betrayed the general area in which *U-505* was unsuccessfully operating. Further radio transmissions from *Oblt.z.S. der Reserve* Harald Lange provided additional intelligence, as had HF/DF fixes, all of which served to narrow the span of ocean within which *U-505* was patrolling. An American Task Force was despatched from Norfolk, Virginia, to take up the hunt.

At the core of this group steamed a *Casablanca*-class escort carrier and its invaluable aircraft contingent. Together, these carriers and planes provided the vital air cover that had helped turn the tide of the long and bitterly-fought U-boat war. The first escort carriers had entered action during 1943. Through precision intelligence provided by the Allied breaking of the Enigma code, the carriers were combined with destroyer escort groups to take the offensive against U-boats. Their effectiveness is difficult to dispute: between them the carriers USS *Bogue* and USS *Card* destroyed more than twenty U-boats before the end of the year. The deployment of these carriers in speedy and lethal "hunter-killer" groups eliminated the last small safe-haven pockets for U-boats operating in the Atlantic. Within three weeks one less U-boat would be threatening Allied shipping.[1]

*   *   *

Captain Daniel V. Gallery's Task Force 22.3 comprised the escort-carrier USS *Guadalcanal* and its aerial contingent, Composite Squadron Eight, plus five destroyers of Escort Division Four: USS *Pillsbury* (carrying the Escort Division's commanding officer), *Chatelain*, *Flaherty*, *Pope*, and *Jenks*. The entire Task Group put to sea on May 13, 1944, with the express intention of finding *U-505*. A burst boiler soon forced the return of USS *Guadalcanal* and delayed the mission for two days.

Captain Gallery was no stranger to hunting German submarines. His previous combat mission had killed two veteran boats—*U-68* and *U-515*. The former went down with all hands. The success against the latter captured most of the crew, including its captain, Knight's Cross holder Werner Henke. It also prompted Gallery to consider a bolder approach. "We had thrown everything but the galley ranges at *U-515* before she up-ended and sank," Gallery remembered. "For a while I thought we were going to have to ram her to put her on the bottom." Another option, however, presented itself. "Suppose we hadn't been quite so bloody minded about sinking her?" he pondered. "Suppose we had sent a party of stout hearted characters over there, to go aboard and make a survey of the situation after the Germans had shoved off?" The manner in which *U-515* had been sunk convinced Gallery that U-boats that chose to surface during an attack rather than perish deep beneath the sea likely had little or no intention of fighting. The skipper's primary objective, as he put it, was "to save his hide."[2]

Therefore, explained Gallery,

> We ... determined, in case opportunity arose in this cruise, to assist and expedite the evacuation of the U-boat by concentrating anti-personnel weapons on it, to hold back with weapons that could sink the sub, and to attempt to board it as soon as possible. This was discussed at the departure conference of all Commanding Officers before sailing, and all ships were ordered to draw up plans for capture and to organize boarding parties."[3]

With *Guadalcanal* repaired Task Group 22.3 put to sea again on May 15. Although he had lost two days, Gallery had lost none of his desire to bring home an enemy boat.

While in Norfolk, Gallery had ordered each ship in his task force to provide a boarding party for use in the event *U-505* could be brought to the surface. Rigorous daily practice drills were held. The signal to launch each drill began with the cry "Away Boarders!" Small floods of volunteers then rushed to their ship's designated whaler from whatever station they occupied. Once assembled, the men were lowered into the sea, rowed around their ship, and were hauled back aboard. Outwardly the practice session seemed like so much busy work, but the training would pay off sooner than anyone thought possible.

The man who was about to leave empty-handed and return to his superiors towing a U-boat that would one day end up displayed in his hometown was born and raised in Chicago, Illinois. After graduating from the United States Naval Academy at Annapolis, Gallery began flight training at the naval flight school in Pensacola, Florida. With this background he was attached as an observer to the American Embassy in London and slated to take command of a U.S. Navy airbase then under construction. The Japanese attack against the United States on December 7, 1941, spun Gallery's career in a different direction.

"I was ordered to Iceland to take command of Fleet Air Base, Reykjavik," Galley recalled. If he was hoping for a short posting there he was disappointed. "I was there from December, 1941, until May, 1943 ... There were very primitive living conditions there when I first arrived, but within six months we had a very comfortable base built with excellent facilities for operating airplanes, for living, and for recreation." As the war in the Atlantic grew more intense, Gallery worked closely with the

British "under the operational control of the air officer commanding the Royal Air Force Iceland." The arrangement worked fairly well until June 1943, when Gallery was ordered back to the United States to commission USS *Guadalcanal* [CVE-60] at Astoria, Oregon. "We left on our first ASW cruise in January 1944, and . . . got our first two U-boat kills when we surprised a refuelling operation and depth charged and sank a big refueller and a small U-boat alongside of it," wrote Gallery with some exaggeration. In fact, only *U-544* was sunk on January 16, but even that success was worth writing home about. "On our second cruise, which began late in March," he continued, "we got two more kills. We sank the *U-515* and picked up 40-some prisoners, including the captain, and sank the *U-68* the next day, getting one survivor and one dead man and a great deal of wreckage."[4]

Gallery's determination to capture a U-boat intact remained doggedly unwavering as Task Group 22.3 headed into action. While still in Norfolk he had shared his plans with Captain Henri Smith-Hutton, Assistant for Combat Intelligence (F-20) at COMINCH (office of the Commander in Chief, U.S. Navy, Admiral Ernest J. King). Smith-Hutton had been one of Gallery's shipmates aboard the battleship USS *Idaho* during their years as junior officers, and the two men had remained firm friends over the intervening years. Smith-Hutton, in turn, promised Gallery he would receive up-to-date intelligence reports of U-boat activity, as he had during his previous two cruises. Interior plans of two types of U-boats known to be operating within the region were also provided by Smith-Hutton so Gallery could familiarize himself and his prospective boarding parties with their interiors—should they be fortunate enough to ever see one.[5]

ULTRA, the source of the splendidly accurate intelligence that enabled such precise targeting of U-boats at sea, remained unknown to Gallery. Indeed, the cracking of the German code was the Allies' most jealously guarded secret. Commander Kenneth A. Knowles, USN, was responsible for monitoring the ongoing ULTRA decryptions as head of the U.S. Navy F-21 "Atlantic Section Tracking Room," which was attached to the Tenth USN Fleet. Knowles had established a close working relationship with Commander Rodger Winn, his better-known counterpart in charge of the Royal Navy's submarine tracking room. Since Operation Drumbeat, the devastating attack on the United States' eastern seaboard in early 1942, Knowles and Winn had cooperated so they could maintain a comprehensive database of Axis operations in the Atlantic, as well as other theaters where U-boats were known to be active.

It was Knowles who would have authorized the passing to Gallery of whatever intelligence material was deemed to be useful to him. These included drawings highlighting specific and vital systems found aboard U-boats depicting not only the boat's operation but how to prevent its scuttling. Gallery was also familiar with German patterns of operation based upon past knowledge gleaned from direct access to BdU's most secret communications. Germany's unsuspected Achilles Heel would soon reap disaster for *U-505*.

*   *   *

U-505 had left port for its last operational patrol on March 16, 1944, and crossed the Bay of Biscay on the surface. Lange's sealed orders directed him to hunt the waters off Freetown, West Africa. On April 7, *Oblt.z.S* Horst von Schroeter's *U-123* hove into view. The two boats ran alongside one another for more than half an hour so a copy of the so-called *Adressbuch* from his homebound flotilla-mate could be transferred by rubber dinghy to Lange. This small book provided updated cipher keys for disguising grid references, part of BdU's instructions on tightened security of the U-boat codes. Dönitz had suspected (but doubted) the Allies had breached the supposedly impenetrable Enigma code, but his suspicions could never be proven. In the face of vehement disagreement from his superiors and those within BdU responsible for cipher integrity, measures such the *Adressbuch* were adopted—the best Dönitz could implement to increase complexity of the Enigma system.

The weather worsened as *U-505* approached the equator. Heavy seas took their toll on the boat's crew, forcing Lange to submerge regularly to provide his men some relief. Towering waves were finally replaced by a long slow swell that, although less dramatic, slowed their progress considerably. New crewmen remained in the iron grip of sea sickness. Thus far the journey had been a difficult one. The tropical heat raised the temperature of both the boat's interior and individual temperaments. Regular crash dives, usually the result of air alarms triggered by the boat's radar detector, kept the men on edge and their stress level high. The daily monotony of long-distance cruising, meanwhile, was aggravated by a famine of merchant shipping. Lange did his best to locate targets by patrolling as aggressively as he dared, scouring the seas and even lingering near the harbor mouths at Freetown, Monrovia. Other than small fishing boats and a single well-lit neutral Portuguese steamer, however, nothing of value was found. Lange's KTB (War Diary) entry for April 28 evidenced his desire to slip farther south in search of prey: "Intention: The conditions encountered off Freetown and the entire absence of escort vessels at the roadstead of Monrovia permit the conclusion that there is at present no traffic moving. This is indicated also by the extremely weak air patrol."[6]

Lange continued hugging the coast of Liberia scanning for opportunities near several more vacant harbors. Nothing was seen. The enemy was conspicuous only by its absence. Frustrated, Lange decided to draw away from the coast and head south to search for merchant ships off the Cape Town or Ascension areas. The move would also allow him to more safely undertake external repairs on bow torpedo tube two, which had stubbornly refused to completely close and made it difficult for the boat to dive properly. The work was successfully completed on May 5 and *U-505* cruised slowly back toward Liberia for another five languid days before lookouts finally spotted a potential target: "Smoke plume in sight . . . battle stations!"[7]

The ship was estimated as a "fat morsel [of] 8 to 9,000 tons," and Lange gave chase on the surface. The vessel managed to maintain the eleven-mile gap between hunter and hunted, matching the U-boat's speed. Eventually it slipped from sight. Lange, however, was determined to do everything he could to catch the ship. *Obersteuermann* Alfred Renig was ordered to plot a projected interception course. The move paid off when the ship's smoke plume was once again spotted on the distant horizon later that day. Lange was thrashing his diesels in an attempt to close the range when the sudden appearance of an enemy escort vessel homing in on *U-505*'s plume of diesel exhaust forced him to abort the hunt. The wily escort waited for a while outside the range of *U-505*'s T5 *Zaunkönig* escort-killer torpedoes before mysteriously turning away and disappearing to rejoin the now vanished steamer. Although no one onboard could have known it, *U-505*'s last chance to sink an enemy ship had slipped away.

Frustrated in what had been a noteworthy effort to catch his prey, Lange continued to creep along the coastline and investigate empty harbors. *U-505* last brief situation report, transmitted on May 15, was received largely garbled in Lorient by the 2nd U-Flotilla. Eight days later a disgusted Lange threw in the towel. "We were down on oil and having some real battery trouble," recalled Hans Joachim Decker, one of *U-505's* machinists. "What a dismal trip—not a sinking to our credit." The "battery trouble" mentioned by Decker was the result of the frequent air alarms that had plagued the boat in recent weeks. "The batteries were in bad shape because of the abbreviated charging periods. We simply could not stay under water for any length of time." Lange turned his bow north to begin the return voyage to France.[8]

* * *

It was Lange's May 15 situation report that had caught the attention of Knowles and his staff at the F-21 tracking room. The course and location they plotted for *U-505* during the days that followed proved to be more accurate than BdU's own estimation of Lange's whereabouts. By May 21, Knowles's estimate was off by only 267 miles; BdU's calculations, however, were 452 miles wide of the mark.[9]

Using Knowles's decrypts, Task Group 22.3 steamed in the direction of *U-505* as Lange cruised slowly northward on his homebound trek. Progress was painfully slow and frequently interrupted by enemy aircraft alerts, forcing *U-505* deep underwater. The increased danger from the skies convinced Lange to spend extended periods submerged. His boat, however, was not equipped with a *schnorchel*, and so he was unable to recharge the boat's steadily draining batteries without running for long periods on the surface. Heat from the balmy equatorial waters clouded the boat's interior with a dense humid fog. With his eye on survival instead of comfort Lange refused to dive deeper in search of cooler waters, choosing instead to remain closer to the surface where his hydrophones were more effective at detecting distant sounds.

By late May *U-505* was northwest of the Cape Verde Islands, well off the coast of Mauritania. Increasing aerial attention was making life aboard the boat almost unbearable. By the afternoon of the penultimate day of May, the U-boat's batteries were virtually depleted and the atmosphere within the pressure hull had grown foul. Lange decided the time had come to risk running on the surface in brief sprints to recharge batteries. It was indeed a risky gamble for it was daylight and the sky held nothing but patches of high cirrus clouds and clear visible horizons. He knew full well the Allies would be on the lookout for U-boats running on the surface to recharge their batteries, but was willing to gamble their vigilance would be relaxed during clear daylight hours. After all, what U-boat would be foolhardy enough to run on the surface under these conditions? Lange's high stake gamble paid off. He routinely interrupted his sprints on the surface with prolonged submergence to allow shelter and effective hydrophone sweeps in search of both hunters and prey. By doing so he recharged his batteries and inched his way across the Atlantic.

Lange continued running in this manner. The steady air cover also continued to haunt his efforts. On June 2 he recorded in his KTB his bewilderment at the endless parade of enemy aircraft: "Continuous A/C night patrol—here under Cape Blanco!"[10]

It was about this time Lange began to suspect he was the focus of a Hunter-Killer group, at the hub of which was an aircraft carrier supplying the irksome airplanes that were tormenting his boat. Events revealed his hunch was indeed correct, but by a quirk of fate he chose a most unfortunate course of action. Lange concluded that if a task force was on his tail, the enemy group was west of his position. Therefore, he decided to turn east toward Africa. His new course carried him in the direction of the still distant American Task Force 22.3.

Lange was now heading east directly into the arms of Captain Gallery and the *Guadalcanal*.

*   *   *

Gallery's Task Force had headed toward its operational area south of the Cape Verde Islands, flying a continuous stream of daytime anti-submarine search patrols while practicing night flying in order to qualify inexperienced pilots for operational patrols during dusk to dawn hours. "[W]e broke the ice on night operations for CVEs," he later wrote, referencing techniques perfected during his previous anti-submarine operation. "So far as I know, we were the first CVE to operate continuously at night as a matter of routine. On this cruise there was one period during which we had planes in the air continuously for 48 hours, and it was during that period that we got both of our kills."[11]

A brief flurry of excitement erupted in the nerve center of *Guadalcanal* when radar contact was made on May 30 with a potential

U-boat, "but it faded quickly. On our next watch another guy had a reading, and we went to GQ. But nothing." Gallery, however, was convinced the signals were the real thing. "We were heading north toward the Bay of Biscay. We kept getting noises on the sonobuoys, and strong transmissions from the sub's radio frequency. We kept getting disappearing radar blips." The U-boat, Gallery noted, "was very cautious."[12]

In Washington, meanwhile, Knowles continued to feed Gallery as much tracking data as he could on *U-505*'s homeward progress. Once again his estimates proved to be much closer than those of Dönitz's staff. On June 1, Knowles reckoned *U-505* to be 175 miles south-southwest of the position logged by Lange in his KTB, while BdU placed him 503 miles to the northwest.[13]

Ultimately the hunt around the Cape Verde Islands proved to be unproductive for Gallery's group. Every boat in the task force was ordered to operate only one-half of its main engineering plant in order to conserve fuel so the group could stay within its operational area for as long as possible. Gallery was convinced time was his ally. He was right. But Gallery was already pushing his luck—and his fuel bunkers—to the brink of exhaustion.

At 2000 on May 31 Gallery ordered Task Force 22.3 to head for Casablanca, taking the opportunity to scour the 20th meridian along the way in a final search for the elusive target. "We planned to conduct continuous night searches so designed that each night we would cover an area 100 miles on each side of the 20th meridian and 250 miles along the meridian," Galley explained. "The searches were to overlap so that if the sub were running surfaced at night anywhere in that area, we would be bound to find him."

Gallery's luck turned on the night of June 2/3 when numerous aircraft made radar contacts with an unknown craft and sonobuoys picked up the sounds of a U-boat's propeller. "We ran north nearly all day June 3 because fuel was getting low and we had to make ground toward Casablanca," explained Gallery. At a conference that afternoon, however, he determined the readings from the previous night "must have been authentic," and that the group could "probably stretch our fuel enough to spend one more night searching that area." Galley turned back and swept the area again on the night of June 3/4. "There were no contacts that night." The pivotal decision to turn back, however, had put the Hunter-Killer group on a collision course with Lange's *U-505.*[14]

Ironically, Gallery's breakthrough arrived shortly after his fuel level reached the critical stage. *Guadalcanal*'s chief engineer, Earl Trosino, warned his commander that fuel was running so low they might not make landfall unless they headed for Casablanca immediately. Frustrated by his inability to find the enemy, Gallery prudently heeded the warning and ordered the task group to sail at economical speed for Africa. A short time later a report from USS *Chatelain* was handed to him. The words rekindled his enthusiasm for the hunt.

*   *   *

U-505 was running submerged on electric motors a little after midday (German summer time) on June 4 when a faint propeller wash was picked up on the hydrophones and passed to Lange. Perhaps an Allied convoy had wandered into the U-boat's vicinity? Maybe the patrol would not be a complete bust after all. Lange ordered to boat to periscope depth and mounted the ladder into the conning tower to take a look around. As *U-505* trimmed into periscope depth an unusual metallic "clinking" noise echoed through the boat. Decker remembered it as "a scraping sound, as if someone were dragging a long cable along the deck above. It stopped, then started again." Most aboard were puzzled; some were terrified the sound was a chain linking a moored mine scraping along their iron flank. The sound ended abruptly only to be replaced by another sound, one that chilled the hearts of all who heard it:

"Destroyer!"

Lange bellowed his warning as he spun the scope around before slamming it back into its well. Valves were turned and diving planes angled to speed *U-505*'s slide into deep water. The strange "clinking" sound was not a chain anchoring a mine but machine gun bullets from two carrier-based airplanes circling overhead firing into the water to mark the U-boat's position for approaching surface ships. In the few seconds available to him Lange had grasped the entire panorama closing in on him: the fighter planes, at least three destroyers, and the distant silhouette of an aircraft carrier.

The odds were heavily stacked against him.

* * *

The message from *Chatelain* passed to Captain Gallery reported a sound contact roughly three miles from the carrier's position. Gallery read the message about the same time Lange was told his own hydrophones had picked up a contact. The course of events that led to the notification was meticulously recorded aboard the destroyer. "The *Chatelain* was patrolling station G-1 of Screen plan 35, and zig-zagging in accordance with the *Guadalcanal*," reported Dudley S. Knox, its commander. "Carrier had hoisted signal 'Queen Queen,' denoting commencing flight operations, when contact was first made at approximately 1109Z; bearing 060°T; range approximately 800 yards; no doppler; bearing width 25°." Dudley immediately changed course to 75° and reduced his speed to ten knots. The target was coming in loud and clear and was off the destroyer's starboard side. Another course alteration to 95° was ordered and at 1110 Gallery was informed *Chatelain* was "investigating possible sound contact." The range to the target was only 600 yards and closing rapidly. Within two minutes the contact was classified as a submarine, though by this time "the range [was] too close to fire." Dudley sounded general quarters but lost the contact "at less than 100 yards"[15]

Within minutes one of two patrolling aircraft that had been airborne for more than four hours arrived at the spot pinpointed by the approaching *Chatelain*. The pilot, Ensign John W. Cadle, Jr., spotted the distinctive outline of a submarine off his port bow running submerged just below periscope depth but clearly visible in the clear Atlantic waters.[15] Excited by what he saw, Cadle radioed precise targeting instructions to the destroyer and then fired bursts from his .50 calibre machine guns into the water at the U-boat. A few minutes later USS *Chatelain* steamed over *U-505*, which was now desperately trying to go deep. Depth charges were dropped in an effort to blow the submarine to the surface or to the bottom.

The U-boat had only reached 50 meters when the first charges exploded "close aboard," remembered machinist Decker. "*U-505* shuddered violently, the lights went out, and amid the din we heard the most dreaded of noises to submariners: water rushing in. Sure enough, someone shouted, 'Ruptured hull in the control room!'" Conditions in the engine room were similarly chaotic, where "flashlights played on streams of oil and water from broken pipe lines. We were in real trouble now," wrote Decker. "More trouble than most of us knew." According to Decker, the boat was out of control and had dropped down to 230 meters. "Take us up, take us up before its too late!" shouted Lange.[16]

Someone blew the ballast tanks and *U-505* began its final ascent into the arms of the waiting Task Group 22.3.

Lange tried to exit as fast as possible, was severely wounded in the attempt, declined to try to defend a doomed boat, and instead issued the command to abandon ship. It was his penultimate decision and perhaps his most controversial, for once the crew abandoned the boat it was much more vulnerable to being captured. Should he instead have ordered the crew to stay on board and fight back?

Jordan Vause

Desperate Decisions

The German Loss of *U-505*

Zhe capture of *U-505* was as surprising to the United States Navy as it was to the crew of the boat. Only Daniel Gallery believed such a thing truly possible. His superiors were skeptical and the *U-Bootwaffe* considered the seizure of a U-boat at sea so difficult as to be impossible and not worthy of serious consideration.[1]

How, exactly, did it take place? How did Gallery's task group and Albert David's boarding party pull off such a high risk maneuver when all the odds for success were against them? Why wasn't the boat blown up or sunk? Was it Gallery's careful planning and audacious execution, as widely advertised in most popular histories, or was there a complete breakdown of discipline and morale inside the boat, as was whispered in the U-boat community?

Most of what has been written about the capture of *U-505* is from an uncritical American point of view. This essay examines the dramatic event from the overlooked German perspective. It concentrates not on the timeline of events (which is hazy at best), or the exact sequence of events (which is even hazier), but on the chain of desperate decisions made within the boat during the last minutes of her existence: the decisions themselves, why they were made, how they could have been made differently, and if the end result in each case would have changed had a different option been followed. The question for historians and leaders is whether any of the decisions made aboard the boat made a real difference, and whether any of them was significant enough to deliver the boat to Task Group 22.3.

Good and bad decision making wasn't all of it. There was indeed bravery and skill on one side and cowardice and incompetence on the other—some of it breathtaking. Substantial credit for the capture of *U-505* must be given to TG 22.3 and especially to Albert David, who was awarded the Congressional Medal of Honor for the bravery he exhibited that day. When David and the members of his boarding party left USS *Pillsbury* and headed toward *U-505*, they had no idea what to expect when they reached the stricken boat. They had every reason to believe German crewmen were still on board, waiting in ambush or preparing for hand-to-hand combat. Even if there was no resistance and they were able to enter the boat, the danger of blasting charges set to destroy it was a very real possibility. David suspected as much and knew that if one or more explosives went off, some in his party would die outright or the boat would carry them all on a fatal plunge to the sea floor. Even without resistance or explosives the situation was perilous. The boat was steadily taking on water, and she would drop like a stone as soon as buoyancy was lost. This could happen quickly and without warning, and if it did there might not be time to get everyone (or anyone) out. These dangers were further complicated because not a single member of the boarding party had ever been inside a U-boat. The sailors were utterly unfamiliar with the narrow passageways, small compartments, and numerous hiding places. David and his men faced a terrible risk.

Some blame for the loss of *U-505* must be placed on the boat's crew. The men had experienced a wide array of successes and failures over the previous two years. The Peter Zschech era ended with his suicide in the boat in October 1943, and the repeated sabotage attempts afterwards had taken a toll on the spirit of the crew (though not as much as some observers believe). Many were young, ill-trained, or inexperienced, and some of the officers suspect. Harald Lange, who captained the boat on her last war patrol, will never be confused with the likes of an Erich Topp or Otto Kretschmer. Simply put, Lange was not very successful as a commanding officer, and his colleagues generally view him with some suspicion for having allowed his boat to be captured. Most of the crew, including Lange, did the best they could under extremely trying circumstances. In the end they were unprepared for the event and their reactions only serve to highlight that fact.

And of course there was the element of luck. Fortune is always a factor in daily life and so it was during the Battle of the Atlantic. Gallery and David enjoyed stunning amounts of good luck—more than they had a right to expect. Harald Lange, on the other hand, had the very bad luck to find himself the target of a hunter-killer group led by a man determined to sink or capture his boat. From the first moment of contact American luck held while Lange's slipped from bad to worse, and his options vanished one, by one, by one.

*   *   *

Virtually everything that occurred on June 4, 1944, centered around one man: Harald Lange. As a commanding officer he was ill-matched for the situation. "*U-505*," mused Jürgen Oesten, captain of three boats during the war (*U-61*, *U-106*, and *U-861*) and a holder of the Knight's Cross. "Not what I would call a lucky boat." He went on to reflect briefly on the various broken careers left behind by *U-505*: Axel-Olaf Löwe, her first captain, who sank six ships, then got appendicitis and never went to sea again; Peter Zschech, who sank one ship and committed suicide in the boat; and finally Lange himself. "A reserve officer," concluded Oesten, as though it explained everything. "No sinkings."[2]

Peter Hansen, a former *Kriegsmarine* officer and sometime member of the *Abwehr*, does not dismiss the reserve officers as easily as Oesten. "There were some very good ones, particularly those that had been merchant marine officers before the war. On the other hand, there were likewise a number of total flops among the active officers who turned into complete failures. One must look first and foremost at the officers involved." Hansen points out that Harald Lange was chosen personally by Karl Dönitz to command *U-505*. It was not something Dönitz often did. A very busy man, he usually allowed U-Boat Personnel Command in Kiel to do their jobs without interference. In this case, he was looking for a man of stability to take over *U-505*, "mainly, one must assume, as he wanted *U-505* to have a dependable commander in view of her history, the suicide of Peter Zschech, and the many technical shipyard problems that had developed," explained Hansen.[3]

Lange was not inexperienced. He received his commission before the war and had served in the *U-Bootwaffe* for almost three years. One year of service was as first watch officer on *U-180* under Werner Musenberg, then a brief stint as the boat's captain, and finally command of *U-505* for ten months before its capture by Gallery. Lange was forty at the time of his capture—which was old for the captain of a frontline U-boat. As Oesten pointed out, Lange had no sinkings to his credit. This was not unusual in 1944, however, when the yardstick for success was measured not by the tonnage sunk but by how long a man could keep his crew alive. In better times he might have done well, if not spectacularly well. But at the bitter end, in the last minutes of his command, Harald Lange made all the right decisions.

The end came late on the morning of Tuesday, June 4, 1944. Located by units of Gallery's Task Group 22.3 and attacked repeatedly by depth charges, *U-505* suffered major damage. There was no reasonable hope of escape. At about 1115 Lange made the decision to surface. It was the first of four decisions he made in approximately ten minutes. Each was made under heavy pressure, and each had far-reaching consequences.

The first question is whether his decision to surface the boat was the correct one. The after torpedo room was taking water. The main rudder was jammed hard over to starboard. The diving planes were stuck in a downward position. Electricity had been knocked out. In other circumstances there might have been a *very* slim chance he could have circled slowly below his pursuers, waiting them out. However, in addition to everything else mentioned his batteries were drained, which meant he could not keep moving and thus could no longer maintain his depth. "When the batteries became empty," wrote ace Siegfried Koitschka about the sinking of his own U-616, "there were only two possibilities: up or down. Up," he added as though explaining it to a child, "is much better."[4] German U-boat crews had a deserved reputation for being loyal, dogged, even heroic in many cases, but they did not have corporate death wishes and very few would have accepted the idea that mass suicide was preferable to capture. The decision to come to the surface was the only reasonable choice Lange could make.

His second decision involved what to do when he surfaced. Lange had two choices: (1) he could make up his mind while coming up to abandon ship immediately upon surfacing; or (2) he could decide to come up, see how bad things looked on the surface, and make a decision at that time whether to leave the boat or to fight. The second choice is essentially a non-decision—a decision to decide later. Either course of action made the other course impossible. Once he committed himself and his crew, Lange would not have an opportunity to change his mind.

Perhaps things might have gone better if Lange had made the decision to abandon ship before he came up. It was often done that way, and there is good evidence it might have prevented the boat's capture. Oesten offers a possible scenario for a Type IX boat:

> By means of compressed air remove remaining water from the diving tanks in order to give the boat as much buoyancy as possible, distribute the crew to the four hatches: torpedo hatches fore and aft, galley hatch and conning tower. Open all the hatches at the same time, crew gets out quickly. Open the air-valves of diving tanks. The period of grace of about two minutes should be sufficient in order to get the crew out of the boat through the four hatches, before the boat has sunk. This, I guess, might work with a good and experienced crew.[5]

If Lange had followed something along the lines of the scenario outlined by Oesten (which of course would have ruled out any defense of the boat), he would have exited from the conning tower hatch while the boat's other officers made their way out of the secondary hatches. Each officer would then have assisted the crew out of the boat. An escape conducted in this manner would have made it impossible for the enemy to concentrate fire against the conning tower alone, and would instead have divided it amongst four separate targets. Lange and Meyer might not have been shot.

This option may not have been available to Lange, however, because there was not enough time for him to prepare for such an intricate maneuver. Oesten's scenario (or any variation thereof) required planning and coordination well in advance of the event. It would have been more practical after a prolonged siege. The time between the first attack by American surface ships and the point at which the boat broke the surface, however, was several minutes at most—and for most of that time everyone was fully occupied trying to keep the heavily damaged boat under control. Even if time had not been a factor, the coordination and split-second timing required to pull off a synchronized four-hatch escape was probably beyond the capabilities of Lange's crew.

Regardless, Lange decided *not* to immediately abandon ship. No matter what the physical condition of the boat (and she was severely injured) he evidently believed there was some hope she could be defended. Nobody will criticize a captain for not wanting to give up his ship without firing a shot. Having made this decision, however, Lange simultaneously ruled out any quick scuttling along the lines described above. And *that* may have given Gallery the extra time he needed to move into position to board *U-505.*

The next decision Lange made was the order in which the men exited the boat. Once *U-505* was on the surface Lange hurried up the conning tower ladder and exited first. Was that the right thing to do? Yes. There was a recognized order involved in leaving a U-boat that differed from a surface warship. The captain was the first to leave for several reasons. "The speed of leaving the boat was very important," explained Koitschka, "It was very possible that shells could hit the tower. There should be no chance that somebody was killed in the tower and blocked the passage through. The crew was trained very well to leave the boat within seconds. The captain took care of the crew jumping very fast out of the bridge."[6] If someone was shooting at the boat the captain would take the bullet. If he were still standing, he would direct traffic as the rest of his men poured out behind him. Finally, the captain sometimes had to move first simply because everyone else was too frightened. He had to lead so they would follow. *U-505* was already under fire from several ships in the task unit and everyone in the boat could hear the enemy shells ricocheting off the control tower or passing through it. Leaving under such circumstances took a lot of courage, and Lange is given scant credit for having done so. "When the boat surfaced," explained Lange after he was captured, "I was first on the bridge and saw now four destroyers around me, shooting at my boat with .50 caliber and anti-aircraft. The nearest one, in now by 110 degrees, was shooting with shrapnel into the conning tower. I got wounded by numerous shots and shrapnel in both knees and legs and fell down. At once I gave the order to leave the boat and to sink her."[7]

Lange tried to exit as fast as possible, was severely wounded in the attempt, declined to try to defend a doomed boat, and instead issued the command to abandon and scuttle. It was his last decision and perhaps his most controversial, for once the crew abandoned the boat it was much more vulnerable to being captured. Should he instead have ordered the crew to stay on board and fight back?

The decision seems not to have been hastily made, nor was it a foregone conclusion. Before he surfaced Lange must have considered putting up a defense of some type because he rejected a quick evacuation and scuttling. After he saw the forces arrayed against him, however, he opted against waging a defense and decided instead to scuttle his boat. Some believe it was a dishonorable decision because the idea of offering no defense at all is contrary to the traditions of most navies. Perhaps it was the duty of the crew to fight for the boat, to defend each hatch and each space, to repel her boarders or to die in the attempt. The image of the German soldier, at least the image held in the West, was consistent with this idea, and it was what would have been expected of any American sailor—including those serving aboard *Pillsbury* and *Guadalcanal*. "Don't give up the ship" is the most famous single phrase in the history of the United States Navy.

This question separates itself neatly into two parts. The first involves those cases when the odds are good that such a defense will be successful. In Lange's case this was clearly impossible and he knew it. There was no way he was going to escape from Task Group 22.3. The second involves mounting a last-ditch defense when the odds are stacked against survival—a defense mounted from within the boat and one that would probably lead to the death of most or all of the crew members. Lange elected not to do this either, and this decision deserves further discussion.

There would have been some benefits to mounting a defense, although Lange probably did not fully appreciate them in the brief moment he had to make his decision. Gallery's well-planned tactic for seizing a boat depended upon landing his boarding party during the narrow window of time after the crew left the boat and before the boat slips beneath the sea. If the crew did *not* leave, however, there would not be an opening to exploit. If David and his boarding party had known for certain armed men were waiting below, they would not have climbed down the hatch as quickly as they did. The speedy snatch of *U-505* would have evolved into a much longer affair, probably one with casualties on both sides. If the defense held firm, Gallery's only other option to take the boat would have been to wait it out. A heavy chain could have been secured to the bridge railing and tossed down the hatch to prevent its complete closure (it is almost impossible to push a chain up out of a hatch), guards would have been posted on the bridge and weather deck, and a shaky armistice would have ensued while Gallery and his men tried to come up with an option for breaking the stalemate.

During all this Gallery's ships would have dealt with the complicated task of maneuvering out of *U-505*'s way. As far as anyone knew her torpedo tubes were still loaded and the boat may have been carrying the newer *Zaunkönig* torpedoes, which homed in on the noise of a warship's screws. And while all this was taking place, *U-505* would have been slowly but steadily sinking. Photographs taken at the point of capture show she was listing heavily, her weather deck awash. Any standoff lasting more than ten or fifteen minutes would have ended with the disappearance of the boat.[8]

On the other hand, defending the boat posed significant tactical problems. The decision to fight would have competed with the primal impulse of survival, an urge not easily overcome by a verbal order on a doomed submarine where drowning is a virtual certainty for those trapped within. In those few minutes before surfacing in a wounded boat, the only consideration in *U-505*'s mad world of darkness and noise was to get up and get out—fast. Planning under such circumstances was virtually impossible; positioning squads of men for defensive purposes unworkable; coordination unachievable. There were technical problems as well. The large weapons on deck were under heavy fire and so could not be manned. In any case, they were unsuited for repelling boarders. The small arms aboard ship were locked up. Beneath the sea the boat was pitching and rolling in darkness (the electricity had been knocked out). Stray bullets discharged in that environment risked hitting fuel or air cells, piercing the boat's hull, and causing collateral damage of every kind.

Finally, there would have been motivational difficulties because any serious defense was nothing more than a kamikaze mission. There was one way into the boat, which was good for anyone planning a defense, but there was also only one way out. Those who fought off boarders would be driven inexorably forward or aft into areas from which there was no escape. And what would a temporary victory achieve? "In our situation," explained Hans Goebeler, a member of Lange's crew, "we were facing a half-dozen enemy warships backed up by air support. Those were impossible odds, even for a U-boat in perfect condition. The *piece de resistance*, of course, was that we were in far from perfect condition. . . . Only a madman or a butcher of a Skipper would have even considered ordering a crew to fight it out under these conditions."[9] As noted above, few German sailors were so driven they would willingly die to keep a boat out of enemy hands. Oesten concurs: the position faced by Lange was hopeless, and "in a hopeless position it would not make sense" to fight back.[10]

The ultimate consideration that makes Lange's decision not to fight entirely proper and supportable is that he knew the boat would not have to be defended at all. She was going to sink. He ordered her scuttled at the same time he issued the abandon ship order. Lange knew there were at least three different ways to scuttle a boat, and he knew there were people still in the boat who would carry the order out. His order to scuttle was the last decision he made that fateful morning. But was it the right thing to do? Absolutely.

Within a few seconds after the order to scuttle *U-505* Harald Lange was wounded and lost consciousness. He was responsible for four major decisions from the time the attack on his boat began. Each was correct (or at least arguably so) under the circumstances as he knew or believed them to be. His conduct in an awful situation was irreproachable. "I could not have done anything better than Lange did," was Jürgen Oesten's honest assessment.[11]

*   *   *

Once Lange fell, command of *U-505* passed to Paul Meyer, the boat's first watch officer.[12]

Meyer was considered by his crew to be an excellent officer. He had started out as the boat's second watch officer and was promoted to his present position in August 1943. "He was immensely well-liked by the crew," remembered Goebeler, "and we were ecstatic that he was now our exec."[13] Part of the reason the crew respected Meyer was that he balanced the wretched excesses of the Peter Zschech era. It was Meyer who brought back both boat and crew safely to port after Zschech shot himself. He must have been disappointed when his superiors did not give him command of *U-505* outright, but he did not complain when Lange arrived. The two of them formed a remarkably well-qualified leadership team at that stage of the war.

Meyer might have been in a position to make several decisions in the minutes after Lange was cut down. As it happened he made only one, but it would turn out to be important. For some reason Meyer decided to follow Lange through the conning tower hatch and out onto the open bridge. He got as far as the anti-aircraft gun in the *Wintergarten* before he, too, was hit. Both the captain and executive officer had been removed from the chain of command in the space of only several seconds. The boat was suddenly leaderless.

Did Meyer do the right thing in following his captain out of the hatch? The best that can be said is that he followed standard *U-Bootwaffe* procedure. When a boat surfaced under normal conditions the bridge watch was always posted immediately, which meant the first watch officer and the entire four-man bridge watch followed the captain onto the bridge. Obviously normal conditions did not exist at this point: the boat was crippled and under intense enemy fire. For some reason it did not occur to Meyer that standard operating procedure may not have applied in this case and it was not a good idea to follow Lange through a hatch into what was obviously a very dangerous situation.

Should Meyer have stayed below? He would have been much better placed in the control room, maintaining order and calm, leading the evacuation, ensuring no bottlenecks formed in the control room or in the tower, and working with the chief engineer to scuttle the boat. More important, he would have been in *command*, able to evaluate information and make decisions. Did his decision to follow Lange affect the course of later events? Almost certainly it did. As will be seen, his absence when a later decision was made by another officer may well have been critical in deciding the fate of *U-505*.

*   *   *

With both Captain Lange and Meyer outside the boat and injured, a critical leadership vacuum developed below. The next officer in the line of command was reservist Kurt Brey. He did little, if anything, to help the situation. Survivors never mention Brey in their recollections of *U-505*'s last frantic minutes of existence. Brey seems to have disappeared during that time. His invisibility is rather unusual because at 37 he was much older than the average *U-Bootwaffe* junior officer. Presumably he was more seasoned as well, and should have been able to shift into a command role without too much difficulty. At the very least Brey might have been expected to bring some order and discipline to the evacuation efforts. In the end he did nothing to change the course of events—or at least he is not recorded as having done anything of substance.

It was at this point that a form of panic set in within the narrow confines of the boat. With no one directing traffic at the foot of the tower, recalled Goebeler, "a great mob of men from the aft end of the boat suddenly stampeded through the control room to scale the ladders to the bridge."[14] Unfortunately, nobody warned them to take cover and they were raked with gunfire when they poured onto the bridge. Those still below could hear their shipmates screaming in pain, which did nothing to calm their own frayed nerves.

And absolutely nothing was being done to carry out Lange's order to scuttle the boat.

*   *   *

The primary responsibility for scuttling *U-505* belonged to her chief engineer, who was still below decks. His name was Josef Hauser.[15]

Hauser is not a sympathetic character. His own engineering skills seem to have been limited—he almost managed to sink *U-505* on several occasions by himself—but he got by because he was surrounded by several very capable engineering petty officers. To be fair, at 23 Hauser was very young and likely too immature for the responsible position he had been given, but by 1944 this had become regrettably commonplace. Known in Goebeler's book only as the "raccoon" for his habit of constantly preening an inadequate beard before a mirror, Hauser was regarded by the crew as an incompetent loser and a second-rate tyrant. Like Paul Meyer, Hauser had the opportunity during the attack to make several key decisions. And like Meyer, he made only one.

There was really only one way to sink a U-boat. Stripped of tedious mechanical detail, the idea was to get a lot of water into the boat as fast as possible. There were different methods of doing this, of course, but the three most often used *in extremis* were the setting of explosive charges, the opening of air valves in the diving cells, and the opening of the seacocks. Any of these methods would have the desired effect of letting water inside the boat, where sooner or later it would cause the boat to sink. All three together would ensure the best result. The frustrating problem was that when you *wanted* your boat to sink, she tended to be very slow about it no matter what you did.

The quickest way was with the largest hole. Most U-boats carried demolition charges along their keels.[16] *U-505* had fourteen charges of five pounds each. These charges were not large enough to actually destroy a boat and were meant instead to weaken the keel and open holes in the pressure hull. They were also small and hard to find—especially in the dark. They were on timers and it took a skilled engineer to set them. It also took time to set them, which is why it was very dangerous for anyone to do so with short fuses after the boat was on the surface under enemy attack. More than once an engineer was lost setting demolition charges. Otto Kretschmer's chief engineer, Gerd Schröder, was killed in this way after he remained to set the charges on the stricken *U-99*.

The demolition charges in a U-boat were not the most reliable things in the world. "Because they usually had been in place a long time," explained Peter Hansen, "not properly checked and serviced, they were unreliable and many officers considered them as not really dependable. Sometimes seawater had reached them and most likely caused them to be neutralized."[17] Once they went off, however, their effectiveness was very high. A breach of the pressure hull was irreparable. The explosions would have damaged many of the onboard systems, cut the electricity, set fires, and filled the boat with smoke. Under these circumstances a boat could not have been saved and no one would have attempted it. In fact, there is little doubt the existence of demolition charges prevented several boats from being captured. The possibility of explosion was a primary concern of the *Pillsbury* boarding party. Albert David showed supreme courage just in entering *U-505*, but he would not have done so if the charges had already detonated, or had begun to detonate.

"Most of us control room mates stayed at our posts, to make sure the scuttling order was carried out," wrote Goebeler. "We kept looking around for the chief engineering officer because we needed to know if he had set the demolition charges."[18] They need not have bothered, for the chief engineer was not even in the boat. His decision was to break and run up the ladder and out of the conning tower soon after Lange and Meyer, "leaving his position in the control room against orders and contrary to naval regulations."[19]

Hauser's departure was a major complication to an already confused situation. It was the custom (if not a requirement) that the chief engineer be the last person out of a boat, not one of the first. His absence precluded the option of setting demolition charges because the three officers authorized to set them were no longer below decks. Hauser was the senior engineer and presumably the most knowledgeable about the location and condition of the charges. His absence made the implementation of other scuttling options that much more difficult. He did not wait to ensure the engineering petty officers in his charge left the boat safely (chief machinist's mate Otto Fricke assumed that responsibility). It is also fair to conclude Hauser did nothing to help the general disarray at the bottom of the conning tower ladder.

Hauser, who survived the *U-505* debacle, maintained thereafter that he believed the boat was sinking when he left, and thus did not see the need to set the timers on the scuttling charges (or do anything else to ensure her sinking). Exactly why he believed this is a mystery. The boat was clearly severely injured and making water, but she was still solidly afloat. As her chief engineer, Hauser should have known this was the case. His youth and inexperience is a mitigating factor only *to a point*; it excuses his belief the boat was sinking, but it cannot excuse his decision to leave his post when he did.

What would have happened if Hauser had not shirked his duty? What if he had stayed below, set the demolition charges, and then assisted in flooding the boat? "It is our impression," explained Oesten (speaking for himself and his own chief), "that the chief engineer is to be blamed for the confusion and there was no serious intention to sink the boat."[20] Perhaps this is so. But Hauser was not the only man who knew how to set those charges, and his past performance suggests he might have failed anyway. At least his decision removed him from the command equation so others could try something without his interference.

It is at this point in the story when Meyer's earlier decision comes into play so dramatically. With both Lange and Meyer on the bridge, there was no effective leadership below decks at a critical time in the sequence of events. If Meyer had remained below, Lange's order to scuttle would have been Meyer's to execute, and not the chief engineer's.

Meyer might not have been able to stop Hauser from leaving the boat, but he could have set the demolition charges himself.

*   *   *

At this point there was very little time left for anyone to do anything that would have changed the ultimate course of events. The quickest and most effective option—the demolition charges—was eliminated primarily because there was no one left in the boat to set them. The captain, the first watch officer, and the chief engineer were all topside. The location and condition of the second watch officer (Kurt Brey) is unknown. If anyone left inside the boat was going to make a decision, it would have to be a member of the crew. As it turns out, members of the crew made the last two important decisions aboard the boat before it was captured.

The crew of *U-505* is often seen as typical of the time: young, inexperienced, "thrown together." More than that, an unlucky streak of bad officers, mechanical difficulties, and outright sabotage, followed by the voodoo-like curse of Zschech's suicide in the boat made them, in some minds, incompetent. Oesten, for example, believes the loss of *U-505* was caused not by the mistakes of the day but by the long term effect of the war. "My guess is that such a blunder would not have happened on a good boat," explained the former ace. "The three commanders were not brought up in the U-boat trade, but they were crash-trained during the war. The crew had to carry a mental burden and might not have had enough stamina to compensate the lack of experience of the commander."[21]

It is a fair observation. Compared with U-boat crews of 1939 or 1940, who were the beneficiaries of years of training and imbued with tremendous morale and the sure knowledge of victory, the U-boat crew of 1944 was a less than perfect bunch. Their training was limited, their prospects grim. They had few illusions and the best they could hope for—and it was a small hope—was a safe return. By 1944 they had lost even that. Compared with the young crews of *Pillsbury*, or *Guadalcanal*, who were well-armed, well-fed, supported at home and apparently limitless in number, the crewmen of *U-505* were weary, cynical, fatalistic, and afraid; their morale was shot and their senses dulled by years of fighting.

At least that is the conventional thinking. According to Hans Goebeler, however, conventional thinking is wrong. "Lange never had a doubt that we were a well-trained and able crew, and was happy that he had us instead of a newly-assembled crew," wrote Goebeler.[22] Paul Meyer had been offered the chance to attend Commanding Officer's School before he became first watch officer on *U-505*. He turned it down because he liked his chances of survival with *U-505*'s crew. While this says something about Meyer, it says more about the men who served under him. Few things would have inspired a *U-Bootwaffe* officer to forego his own command.

It is a credit, then, to *U-505*'s crewmen—and gives some proof to Goebeler's words—that at such a critical stage and without the chief engineer they attempted to sink the boat themselves. After Oesten made his observations about the crew he provided an example of what a better crew might have done under the same circumstances: "I could not have done anything better than Lange did," he wrote. But once Lange and the other officers were gone, "a member of the crew, petty officer or so, might have taken the initiative. I agree this is an odd guess or maybe wishful thinking. Or what I would have expected from my men (more than 55 years ago)."[23] And that is exactly what one of *U-505*'s machinist's mates, a man named Alfred-Karl Holdenried, did.

Unable to set the demolition charges, Holdenried decided to attempt the next most favorable option: flooding the boat's seven large diving cells. In the panic of the moment he stayed put, gathered a few men around him in the control room, and began the operation of opening the valves at the top of each cell, one by one.

The diving cells were essentially huge tanks located outside the pressure hull and open to the sea at the bottom. The air in the cells kept a boat afloat. A surfaced Type IX boat required at least three flooded diving cells to maintain proper trim and a minimum of excess freeboard. This number increased as fuel was burned and the boat became lighter. All remaining empty cells were flooded when the order was given to dive. There was an additional emergency cell of thirty tons used only in crash dive situations. This cell was flooded when the boat had to dive quickly, but it was blown again as soon as she reached a safe depth.

The diving cells were located along the pressure hull and were numbered from aft to forward. The hydraulic levers to open and close them were located in the control room. In order to dive, the levers were pulled and the valves opened, allowing air to escape from the top of the cells and seawater to enter from the bottom. To surface, the valves were closed and compressed air was pumped into the tanks, forcing water out from the open bottoms. It was always possible to dive but it was only possible to come up again if there was enough compressed air in the tanks. (Many boats were lost because they did not have enough compressed air to clear the cells of water.) One of the first things a crew did when a boat surfaced was start the air compressor.[24]

To dive the boat under normal circumstances, the air valves were opened slowly while the boat was underway. A slight downward inclination of the diving planes, along with slow loss of buoyancy in the diving cells, allowed a boat to slip gracefully beneath the water. An emergency (or "crash") dive was nothing more than a normal dive made as fast as possible without killing anyone. A surfaced boat with no way on could be made to sink vertically if the valves were opened (and a submerged boat would come up in a similar fashion), but since there is no water moving over the diving planes, some element of control is lost and the boat will tend to sink or rise out of control. This leads to the familiar effect of a prow shooting out of the water like a whale. It can also lead to wallowing and overturning while sinking.

According to Jürgen Oesten, the best and most efficient way to sink a U-boat was to take her into an emergency dive with all the hatches open. While the crew climbed out through the hatches, the chief engineer would open the valves from the control room that let the air out of the cells. He would then follow the crew out through the tower hatch. Such a dive could normally be done in about thirty seconds, although this depended on the size of the boat, her fuel load, weight, and several other factors. The time it took to get the bridge coaming under water was slightly less than this, and if the hatches were left open the weight of the water pouring into the boat would make her sinking a certainty. An efficient dive, however, depended upon a well-trained crew, good leadership, working equipment, and a moving boat. The faster the boat is moving the faster it will go under water. Performing an emergency dive while simultaneously evacuating the crew would take longer, but Oesten estimates a boat sunk in this manner would go down in as little as one minute.

This maneuver presented special problems in *U-505*'s case. She was moving through the water and her diving planes were jammed in a downward position, which was good. The problem was she was not moving properly for a dive. She was making no headway but was instead steaming in a tight circle because of her jammed rudder. This meant she could not propel herself underwater as she could in a normal dive, but instead would have to drill herself below the surface in a kind of corkscrew motion. In addition to this, she was running on her electric motors rather than her main diesel engines (which were not started up after the boat surfaced). Observers aboard *Pillsbury* estimate she was making only six knots through the water as she turned, which was not enough to execute a proper crash dive. Given these circumstances, *U-505* would have sunk more like a boat stopped in the water (i.e., slower) than like a boat making headway.

Nevertheless taking her into a dive with open hatches was still the best thing to do. There is no mention of the order in which the hydraulic levers were pulled. It probably did not matter anyway. Most of them worked, which would have caused a noticeable settling in the boat, but two of them did not. The levers for the largest two cells, numbers 6 and 7, both forward, were jammed and could not be moved, and the valves at the top of each cell remained closed. Holdenried's men tried to do everything they could to fix the levers, and even tried pulling on the shafts connecting the levers to the valves, but they were stuck solid. It was a critical failure. Both 6 and 7 held huge amounts of air and retained considerable buoyancy. Since they were located forward they had the effect of keeping the bow up, which would have slowed the boat's movement through the water and prevented the planes from driving her below.

Hans Goebeler believes the air in tanks 6 and 7 kept the boat from sinking, but there may have been more to it than that. If the valves for cells 1 through 5 had been opened properly, explained Jürgen Oesten, and the after torpedo room was flooded, the boat would not have retained the buoyancy she needed to stay afloat. Oesten's chief engineer agrees with this assessment. It is entirely possible the valve on another cell failed also, without any indication in the control room, or else there was less water in the boat already than anyone suspected.[25]

Either way luck played a large role in keeping *U-505* afloat. All of the boat's officers were gone and Holdenried's actions were taken under trying circumstances, but he still might have been able to sink the boat. If all of the diving cells had flooded properly, his decision would have been the most important one made that day, and he would have emerged a hero (at least on the German side). Even without success he did more to make Albert David's job a dangerous one than anyone else aboard *U-505*.

Perhaps ten minutes had transpired since Lange made his decision to surface. All of the officers and most of the crew were gone. Despite Lange's hurried order to scuttle, the boat was still afloat. An understandable urgency coursed through the submarine, and the remaining engineers made for the tower hatch.

* * *

At this point the last man out of the boat, Hans Goebeler, made the last decision of the day. He looked for a way to open one of *U-505*'s seacocks—the least effective method of getting water into a boat.[26]

On a theoretical level Goebeler's intent was simple: open a valve somewhere in a line that led directly to the sea. There was more than one valve and more than one line that met this description. The seawater intake valves themselves (often called *seacocks*) are usually the best way to scuttle a boat since they are located at the lowest point in a boat and open directly to the sea, but any good chief engineer could find half a dozen alternates in short order, from any of several fittings along the lines that crisscrossed the interior of the boat to either of the two toilets. It was all too easy, in fact, to sink a boat by accident just by opening the wrong valve at the wrong time, as more than one captain can attest.[27] But there was no time for any of that and no chief engineer, either.

U-boats took water directly from the sea for a variety of reasons: to cool the engines, to run the toilets and showers, to feed the freshwater distiller. This water was taken into the boat through the seacocks. A seacock was connected with a valve to a feeder line, and the line led to a small pump that directed the water to various locations in the boat. In normal operations the valve between the seacock and the feeder line was left open, but it was an uncomplicated mechanism easily closed for maintenance purposes.

Opening seacocks was as good as a demolition charge in sinking a boat, but it was slower and generally effective only when time was not a factor. The German High Seas Fleet in Scapa Flow was scuttled in this manner, but the operation consumed the better part of an afternoon. Many captains scuttled their boats in 1945 by opening seacocks, but time was not a factor and no one was there to stop them. Unlike the first two options, both of which involved positive force, opening seacocks was a strictly passive move, similar in theory to pulling the plug in a bathtub. Water entering the boat would gurgle rather than gush. The seacock itself, and most lines and valves in the seawater system, were small in diameter, which restricted flow and reduced intake. Depending on the number of fittings opened, the number of compartments sealed, the number of hatches open, the buoyancy of the boat, and the amount of water already on board, it could take hours for a boat to go under.

As a *U-Bootwaffe* engineer Goebeler knew most or all of these fine points and fully appreciated the boat would sink only if she took on enough water—but he had barely enough time to make one split-second decision. He had to open something; something close at hand; and he had to do it *fast*. The only thing that occurred to him was the sea strainer.

A sea strainer is just what its name implies: it is a mechanism situated between the seacock and the seawater pump that strains out any large impurities like sand, seaweed, or marine life, all of which might clog the pump or other internal machinery. The strainers are accessible through covers usually bolted or dogged down, and the covers are normally opened only after the intake valves are closed. If the cover is removed without the seacock valve being shut first, or if the seacock is opened after the cover is removed, seawater will begin flowing from the top of the strainer and into the bilges. And so, under enormous pressure, Goebeler removed the cover from the sea strainer under the control room deck plates and opened the seacock valve.

Did Goebeler make the right decision? His instincts were entirely correct, and we can conclude he did the right thing at a theoretical level. He erred only in its execution. A more experienced engineer with more time would probably have selected a different way of doing what Goebeler tried to do, and it is conceivable the boat could have been scuttled this way. For example, if the strainer in the engine room had been opened as well, the flow of water into the boat would have been much higher and would have continued longer. In tearing the cover off the sea strainer, Goebeler performed a completely unrehearsed and *ad hoc* procedure for which he had not been trained.[28]

Goebeler never questioned his decision to open the sea strainer, but he lamented until the day he died the very minor and seemingly inconsequential action he took thereafter. In the haste and terror of the moment, Goebeler tossed the cover of the strainer into the corner of the control room. American sailors swarmed aboard a few minutes later. Zenon Lukosius followed Albert David into the boat, found the cover, and replaced it. This is the same cover now given pride of place in the Chicago restoration. If Goebeler had thrown the cover into the bilges or better yet overboard, Lukosius may not have been able to stem the flow of water and *U-505* might well have gone to the bottom.

Or so goes conventional wisdom. In fact, the seacock valve could easily have been closed just as fast as Goebeler opened it. Unfortunately Lukosius was in just as much of a hurry as Goebeler, and did not think to look for it. If he had not found the cover, there were other ways to stop the water flow. Goebeler's description of the water coming out of the strainer, "a dinner plate-sized stream of water . . . gurgling out of the main pump line into the boat," indicates low pressure and a manageable flow.[29] Any large flat object placed over the strainer, with Lukosius' weight on top of it, might have been enough to reduce the flow until something better could be found by another member of the boarding party to stop it entirely.

Goebeler was the last man out of *U-505*. He left thinking, or perhaps hoping, the strainer would let enough water into the boat to sink her. And it might have been enough to send her to the bottom had the boarding party entered the boat two or three minutes later. It was a very close thing.

*   *   *

In the final analysis, eight significant decisions were made by the officers and men of *U-505* in the last frantic moments before her capture. Each had the potential to affect the outcome. These decisions were:

1. After an intense depth charge attack from surface units of TG 22.3, *U-505*'s captain Harald Lange made the decision to surface. He had little choice and it was the right thing to do. The only alternative was to go down, and as Siegfried Koitschka succinctly put it, "up was much better".

2. Lange made a second almost simultaneous decision not to abandon ship immediately upon surfacing. He evidently believed there was a chance to escape or defend the boat. Lange's decision made any subsequent evacuation longer and more difficult to accomplish.

3. After surfacing, Lange decided to exit the boat first. This was the right decision to make for all the reasons discussed above, although in hindsight it deprived *U-505* of her captain at a critical time.

4. After being seriously wounded, Lange made the decision to abandon and scuttle *U-505* rather than attempt an escape or defend the boat. Again, it was the right decision for several reasons.

5. First watch officer Paul Meyer decided to follow Lange onto the bridge of *U-505*. This was the correct decision under *normal operating procedures*. In this case it was not the best option, though it was a pivotal one. Meyer was hit immediately after Lange went down, which deprived the boat of her second-in-command and the only other competent officer on board.

6. Chief engineer Joseph Hauser made the next significant decision. He was the officer best placed to scuttle *U-505*, and the only man left in the boat who could set the demolition charges. He elected instead to leave, claiming later he did so because he believed the boat was going to sink at any moment. This was a terrible decision for both morale and tactical reasons. The ramifications of Hauser's choice were compounded by Meyer's earlier decision to follow Lange topside.

7. Machinist Alfred-Karl Holdenried made the seventh decision. On his own initiative and with no direction from above, he attempted to open the valves on the diving cells and flood them. This was the correct decision and an admirable move on his part. It might have worked if the valves had not jammed.

8. Hans Goebeler made the eighth and final decision. By opening the sea strainer in the control room he might have scuttled the boat if less air had been in the diving cells or if the men in Albert David's boarding party had waited a little longer to enter *U-505*.

Obviously there was more to the story than these eight decisions. There were fifty-nine men in *U-505*, and each of them made decisions of his own: what to bring and what to leave behind, where to go, what to do after capture. And there were mitigating circumstances for each of the decisions we have discussed: a lack of time, a lack of training, noise, fright, darkness, and confusion.

Time was a critical factor. The decisions considered in this chapter take on a slow motion aspect when picked apart and analyzed, like a movie reel that is stopped and started again, or an instant replay in a sporting event played over and over in slow motion so referees can study it frame by frame. Reality was completely different. Everything discussed herein took place within fifteen or twenty minutes. The boat had been heavily damaged and nearly sunk, the interior was without proper lighting, men were being killed and wounded topside, and large amounts of ammunition were hitting the crippled U-boat. Chaos ensued while the fear of sudden death by enemy fire or drowning pervaded every mind and every action. Choices made and actions executed under tight time restrictions, with the benefit of hindsight, often make the decision maker look foolish or inept.

We have discussed training in general terms, and we can stipulate the crew was not trained as well as they should have been—and as they would have been in, say, 1939 or 1940. But not everyone knows that formal training in at least one specific area was never available. "Nobody received training or even theoretical instruction on [how to scuttle a U-boat]," explained Peter Hansen. "It was considered out of the question and totally unlikely to happen, thus the subject was entirely ignored and never even informally discussed as far as U-boats were concerned."[30] Once again, hindsight makes such an omission incredible. The Germans, however, considered the capture of a U-boat at sea so unlikely training for such an event would be a waste of time. Any skill in the art of scuttling was something picked up along the way, like riding out a depth charge attack. In this sense Lange's crew was as well trained in how to sink its own boat as any crack crew of the early years.

In retrospect it is clear the loss of the boat had nothing to do with the fitness of the officers and men who served aboard her. Many were inexperienced and most made mistakes, but the capture of *U-505* did not come about as a result of their incompetence or a lack of courage or resolve.

The purpose of this chapter is to explain, as best as possible, the capture of *U-505* from the German perspective using as a framework the decisions made inside the boat during its final minutes. If there is a lesson to be learned it is this: every man in a crew can make a difference; every man has the potential, by acting or failing to act, to affect the course of events around him in ways he can not fully appreciate at the time of his actions.

*   *   *

After Albert David's boarding party made it inside the boat and stopped the incoming flow of water, the submarine was taken in tow and hauled across the Atlantic to Bermuda. It was a difficult operation and on more than one occasion the boat was nearly lost. After the war she was restored and put on blocks outside The Chicago Museum of Science and Industry for the edification of the public. *U-505* was the first and only German submarine captured by the United States Navy in either world war.

But as we know now, with a little luck, a little grace, anyone in the boat—from Captain Lange to the lowest fireman—might have written a different ending to one of the most remarkable events in American maritime history.

The German U-boat spent the next 2½ weeks on the beach waiting on its handlers for the final move to the museum. The beached submarine offered a surreal backdrop for beach lovers and the regular crowds of curious people who marveled at the large size of the boat. Now toothless and landlocked, the once-feared shark of the seas was about to assume a new role its builders could never have envisioned. . . .

Keith R. Gill

Project 356

U-505 and the Journey to Chicago

𝔓𝔢𝔬𝔭𝔩𝔢 are often surprised when they discover a German U-boat on display at a science museum in the American Midwest. And they should be, for it is indeed a most unlikely place to find an enemy submarine serving as both a memorial to our nation's sea dead and a premier science exhibit.

U-505's fitful journey from war prize to revered museum exhibit to memorial in Chicago is both logical and fitting. The fascinating story of how it came to rest at 57th Street and Lake Shore Drive is rooted in the logic of the post-World War II and Cold War era. Obtaining title to the U-boat proved to be a frustrating and lengthy process. Transporting the submarine to the Windy City was an adventure requiring large amounts of money, extraordinary seamanship, engineering expertise, the dedicated efforts of dozens of people around the country—and years of patience and hard work. It was so difficult that in 1954, Daniel Gallery exclaimed that the ongoing project was almost as difficult as the boat's capture on June 4, 1944.

This study is an attempt to tell the story, as fully and as completely as space allows, of how *U-505* came to rest outside a Chicago museum and become one of the most visited scientific exhibits and memorials in the world.

The Origins of the Museum of Science and Industry

The Museum of Science and Industry opened its doors to the public on March 1, 1933. It was founded seven years earlier with a $3,000,000 donation by Julius Rosenwald, one of the most influential philanthropists of the 20th Century. The idea for the museum grew out of a Rosenwald family vacation to Europe in the 1920s to visit distant cousins. Once there, they visited the famous Deutsches Museum in Munich and Technical Museum in Vienna. Rosenwald was impressed with his 14-year-old son William's positive reactions and excitement about his experience at the museum, turning cranks and pushing buttons that operated all kinds of machinery. Rosenwald saw the value in this kind of experience and decided Chicago needed a similar museum. The plans were quietly developed and by 1926 he was ready to make them public.

Once the decision to create a science museum in Chicago was made, the obvious question was where to put it. Many options were explored before the only remaining structure left on the site of the 1893 World's Columbian Exposition, the former Fine Arts Palace, was chosen as the new home for what would become the Museum of Science and Industry.

The museum board hired experts in all areas of science to form the core staff and begin developing exhibits. Supporters and museum board members talked about the museum as "education in a new form . . . and never a moment of boredom, nor hint of tedium that often comes with book learning."[1] Some had even talked of a technical training school for prospective workers in modern industrial plants, and that idustry had to find a substitute for the dying practice of apprenticeship. The idea to use real moving machinery as big as locomotives and as small as hand tools was new to America, where most of the exhibits were formally presented and untouchable by the visiting public.

By the end of its first decade it was clear the museum would become a preeminent scholarly institution with important interactive exhibits on the sciences. The staff borrowed heavily from the Munich museum and considered it a sister institution. Detailed photographic surveys of each gallery were produced for later study, and the physical layout of themed wings (or zones) proved very useful in planning the new institution.

The German museum also taught its American counterparts how to involve the visitor with facilitated demonstrations on multiple topics and hands-on, self-guided exhibits whenever the topic made such a thing possible. The Chicago museum took these ideas one step further by increasing interactivity so effectively it is sometimes erroneously credited with pioneering the interactive exhibit concept. It was, however, the pioneer in this field in America, and still presents important new high quality exhibits which other institutions try to emulate. Other institutions around the world were also studied, but the Deutsche Museum remained the principal inspiration.

The first exhibit to open at the Chicago museum was a replica of a working coal mine, inspired by a similar exhibit at the Deutsches Museum. The popular Coal Mine became synonymous with the Museum of Science and Industry until *U-505's* arrival in 1954. The mine defined the museum as an institution specializing in immersive experiences and unforgettable large-scale presentations. Emboldened, many believed no project was too big for the institution. The Munich museum understood that largescale exhibits (such as their cutaway presentation of *U-1*, Germany's first U-boat) were often inspiring in and of themselves and presented an extraordinary opportunity for education as well as a memorable visiting experience. Although the Chicago museum did not copy everything about the Deutsches Museum, work to obtain a submarine to mirror Munich's presentation actually began as early as 1928—long before there was ever a *U-505*. These efforts were carefully documented and the papers stored in Project File 356. No one dreamt that their desire to display a submarine would not be realized until more than two decades later.[2]

The Immediate Post-War life of U-505

Once *U-505* reached Bermuda in June 1944, representatives from several offices of Naval Intelligence arrived to inspect their new prize. Of particular interest were code materials and any new technologies found aboard the boat. The code books, publications, and two enigma machines were rushed off to Washington aboard a Navy plane with Lt. J. W. Dumford from the USS *Jenks* acting as courier. Dumford would provide many eager ears in Washington with their first eyewitness account of what took place during the attack and capture of *U-505*.

The U-boat was tied up at the Navy Yard in Bermuda and the remaining contents of the boat inspected in detail. Fourteen torpedoes, together with their detonating pistols and any other related parts, were inventoried from the boat. Two were T-5 accoustic homing torpedoes (a third had been fired from the #5 tube in the stern) and five were air powered. The torpedoes were sent to Washington on several ships to ensure at least one of the shipments arrived safely. Tests were conducted on the T-5s to discover the frequency upon which they operated. This helped ASW technicians in their quest to make existing foxing gear more effective as a decoy against them.

U-505 was moved into dry-dock for a hull inspection and any repairs necessary to return it to operation. The Navy wanted to get *U-505* on the water with an American crew in order to determine the capabilities of its new prize. The U-boat's forward diving planes had been lost in the tangle with USS *Pillsbury* during the first effort to take *U-505* under tow. New dive planes, an operating shaft, and bearings were constructed and fitted to the boat. The hull had sustained almost no damage whatsoever other than a 20mm shell hole on the water line of Dive bunker #7. It is curious that no problems were reported with the rudders, which supposedly had jammed hard to starboard because of battle damage. Since the rudders were returned to amidships with the emergency steering gear several days after the capture, one must assume they were not actually "jammed to the right" in the literal sense, but merely put at hard right somehow when the Germans abandoned *U-505*.

Once *U-505* was repaired, its batteries charged and air tanks refilled, the boat was returned to water with an American crew for trials. Very little has surfaced regarding these tests, but they must have been quite thorough. Thereafter it is believed *U-505* was utilized to help train destroyers and other surface units preparing to go to sea to hunt U-boats.

Once VE day arrived the secret of *U-505's* capture was finally made public. On May 16, 1945, the US Navy put out a press release detailing the capture. The men who had received medals for their role in the capture could now replace their citations that up until that time read " . . . for reasons which cannot be revealed at this time," with full citations detailing their accomplishments.

U-505 was sent to Portsmouth, New Hampshire, to join other surrendered German U-boats berthed there. Ironically, it shared pier space with *U-858* whose commander, Thilo Bode, had once served as *U-505's* First Watch Officer. *U-505* did not remain in Portsmouth for long. The 7th war bond drive was underway and its organizers were looking for an attraction to encourage citizens to buy more bonds. The story of *U-505* was exactly what they were seeking. Initially the Navy had no interest in the idea but a decision was eventually made to support the effort and an itinerary was put together to have the boat visit ports up and down the Eastern seaboard. The story of how the boat was captured and its pending arrival was announced in advance to drum up interest. The boat stopped in each city for about one week, during which members of the public could tour it if they purchased a war bond. An American crew was on hand to answer questions and assist with the tours. *U-505* was a smash hit. The lines waiting to board were oftens hours long, and people were often turned away at the end of the day. Millions of dollars were raised in New York City alone. When the surrender of the Japanese in August 1945 eliminated the need to sell war bonds, *U-505* was deactivated at Portsmouth and its crew dispersed. Most in the Navy assumed the boat would end up at the bottom of the Atlantic like most of the other surrendered U-boats. No one realized what was in store for the luckiest submarine in the *Kriegsmarine*.

U-505

Legend has it *U-505* eventually ended up in Chicago because of a chance lunch meeting in late 1947 between Father John Ireland Gallery and Lenox Lohr, director of the Museum of Science and Industry. Father Gallery, after explaining to Lohr the story of *U-505's* capture, asked if the museum would like to have the German submarine captured by Captain Daniel V. Gallery in June 1944. In response, Lohr produced the museum's Project 356 file, a one-inch thick folder documenting the institution's various unsuccessful attempts to land an underwater boat for exhibit. Plans had evolved to the point of identifying how to tow a boat to Chicago, how to move it onto land, and where and how to display it. Not only are we interested, Lohr responded, but efforts have been underway to get a boat since the late 1920s! Although the meeting between Father Gallery and Lohr did indeed take place, and plans on bringing *U-505* to Chicago were discussed, the initial effort to bring the U-boat to Chicago preceded that famous luncheon by almost one year.

U-505 first came to the attention of the museum in a letter written January 13, 1947, by Captain Daniel Gallery to Frank Hecht, President of the Chicago Council Navy League of the United States. Would the council, inquired Gallery, be interested in sponsoring an effort to turn *U-505* over to the city of Chicago? Accompanying the letter were three enclosures: an official Navy press release of the capture dated May 16, 1945, a copy of the Presidential Citation, and an issue of the *Saturday Evening Post* with Gallery's compelling account of its capture. Hecht's reply has not yet been found, but discussions were opened as to where to install the submarine should it actually arrive in the city (which coincidently was Gallery's hometown). Several locations in the city were discussed, but the museum was always considered the location of choice.

The man who had originally fought to prevent the Germans from sinking *U-505* was now fighting to keep the boat from being sunk by the American Navy, which had too much surplus war materiel on its hands. Gallery was working several alternatives to install the boat somewhere—anywhere—as a memorial first and later as a museum. Initially he waged this battle outside his official duties, but gradually it became part of his unspoken "official" duties. In September 1944, three months after his spectacular capture, Gallery was transferred from USS *Guadalcanal* to the Pentagon, where he spent 10 months of logistics duty before finally returning to sea in June 1945 as the commanding officer of USS *Hancock* (CV-19), an *Essex*-class carrier. *Hancock* was anchored in Tokyo Bay in August 1945 for the Japanese surrender ceremonies. Gallery participated by piloting one of the 1,500 planes that took part in a massive fly-over to mark the event. After the war he became commander of Carrier Division Sixteen in San Diego, where it remained for a full year undergoing demobilization. Thereafter the captor of *U-505* was called to Washington to serve as Assistant Chief of Naval Operations for Guided Missiles (OP-57). Gallery was responsible for (or his work contributed to) several important navy missile projects. His Pentagon duties kept him busy both politically and socially. Gallery was in demand as a public speaker and enjoyed discussing *U-505's* capture. Thereafter he was transferred to command the Great Lakes Naval Training Center, a new assignment that would prove most helpful in getting the boat to Chicago.[3]

It was about eight months after Gallery mailed Hecht at the Navy League looking for a home for *U-505* that his brother John Gallery phoned the museum on September 25 to arrange a meeting the following day with Director Lohr. Father Gallery and Lohr met on a Friday at 11:00 a.m., sitting down for that legendary meeting. Since Gallery was still working in Washington, D.C., at this time it is reasonable to assume that Father Gallery's role was to act as his brother's representative, and thus assess whether the museum was seriously interested in the boat. He would also be free to lend his own considerable influence among civic leaders and help move the project forward. Together, the brothers worked hard to lay the groundwork to save *U-505* from the scrap heap.[4]

E. R. Henning of the New York-based American Society of Mechanical Engineers had met with Lohr to discuss the project before Lohr's meeting with Father Gallery. Henning visited the Navy on the museum's behalf to discover whatever he could about U-505's physical condition and how to make a formal request for the boat. "From the [Navy] policy angle there appears no objection. Indeed . . . the idea had much to commend it, particularly from the standpoint of naval publicity," reported Henning. The submarine, he continued, had been scheduled for sinking, but the order had been rescinded "for further study of its disposition. Some tentative consideration has been given to placing it at Annapolis."[5] Henning reminded Lohr the Navy was already planning to bring the famous WWII fleet submarine USS *Silversides* to Chicago to serve as a training ship for the local Naval Reserves. While not intended to serve as a museum *per se*, there were plans to open the boat for short periods of time to the interested public as a way to encourage civic interest in the navy and attract potential recruits. That would mean, of course, *U-505* would not be the only game in town. Still, he concluded, there were no technical or policy objections to bringing *U-505* to Chicago, and a formal request to the Secretary of the Navy was in order.[6]

Knowing time was of the essence, Hecht and Lohr dispatched a telegram on October 6 to John Sullivan, Secretary of the Navy:

> We understand Germany submarine *U505* captured June 4, 1944 by Task Force under command of Admiral D. V. Gallery USN is to be destroyed. We feel this craft should be preserved as monument to spirit of the USN and inspiration to youth of our nation. The Navy League joins with the Museum of Science and Industry in requesting the USN to install this submarine at the Museum for public display.

A copy of the telegram was also sent to Chester W. Nimitz, Chief of Naval Operations. "Due to our understanding of the time urgency involved we are sending it [this copy] to you for your information."[7]

U-505 was due to be scrapped soon, and both Hecht and Lohr were doing everything they could to cover every base to avoid that eventuality. To their pleasant surprise Nimitz responded the next day: "Your message to the Chief of Naval Operations quoting your telegram to SECNAV regarding preservation of the captured German submarine *U-505* as an historic relic has been received. Your interest in this matter which is now under study is appreciated and it is hoped that it may be found practicable to carry out your suggestions."[8]

The Navy was now aware of a serious interest in *U-505* but the cost of actually getting a large German submarine to Chicago remained the stumbling block to success. The Navy insisted the city pay all the costs, including all the preparation, the tow itself, and display. Funds would have to be raised, and that could take years. The museum, city, and groups like the Navy League believed their combined influence in Washington would draw enough Congressional support to have the Navy foot most of the bill. Gallery did nothing to disabuse the parties of this fallacy and indeed innocently fostered this false assumption. He tried to sell the project by claiming the Navy would pay for it; an interested party—like the museum, for example—would simply have to supply the display arrangements. "The important thing is to ask the Navy to tow the submarine to Chicago," explained Gallery. "To do this, they will have to put it in shape for the trip, which would cost the Museum a substantial amount of money, but it could be handled by the Navy under their budget without any difficulty."[9] This attitude kept false hopes alive by implying that a payment demand from the Navy was nothing more than a way for it to gauge the seriousness of the request. As Gallery explained it to one interested party, "the first letter from the Navy was more or less of a standard form . . . they always tried to make the other fellow assume the expense." Gallery went on to suggest "that if some pressure could be put on . . . it might be helpful." The Navy, however, never looked at the project in this manner. Although it always professed support for the move, it consistently reminded everyone it would not foot the transportation bill.[10]

And so the dance over expenses began. The early negotiations to land the boat raised the museum's awareness of the potentially high costs involved and, more important for the institution, what it could do to minimize the risk of loss if the project never came to fruition. The museum was justifiably reluctant to launch a major fundraising campaign if there was still a threat of the boat being scrapped. Lohr wanted some assurances the offer of *U-505* would not be withdrawn in the midst of the difficult preliminary investigations required to assemble a budget and begin a broad-based fundraising effort. He shared his thoughts on the matter with Gallery and discussed the idea of having a donor underwrite the project. After all, the cost just to move the boat from the lake shore to the spot along the east side of the Central Pavilion of the museum was estimated at $80,000. An effort was made to find an underwriter and Lohr had Gallery approach Chicago chewing gum magnet William Wrigley. After the effort failed Gallery all but assured Lohr an underwriter was unnecessary. "A move is being started here which I believe will result in the Navy reconditioning and delivering *U-505* to Chicago," Gallery told his eager comrade. "It is too early to say definitely that this *will* be done, but so far it looks promising." Gallery hedged his bets, however, by telling Lohr steps should be taken immediately to begin raising funds to install the boat at the museum. "In the meantime, you can be assured that the Navy will hold the offer of *U-505* open for you."[11]

The Navy also needed some assurances. It required, among other things, that the new owners assume all costs of transfer, future maintenance and upkeep, and that the boat would always be presented so as to shed a positive light on the U.S. Navy.[12] Lenox Lohr had his work cut out for him. He had been recruited by the museum board in 1940 and tasked with reversing the declining finances of that institution, a matter so serious as to threaten the closing of the museum. Determined to keep the doors open, he fired curators to stem the red ink and set about changing the way the museum conducted business. As the director of exhibits for the Chicago Century of Progress World's Fair in 1933-1934, Lohr knew the right venue would attract exhibitors, who in turn would gladly pay a fee for exhibition space. In exchange, the exhibitor received wide exposure and a positive connection to the venue's mission. The Century of Progress had been the showcase for a century of technical and industrial progress in America. The Museum of Science and Industry's mission was much the same—to exhibit the technical ascent of mankind and how the fruits of science and technology impacted the daily lives of society and their potential impact on the future. Lohr knew the institution's mission was a powerful selling tool to industry, and as an outstanding public relations man, rarely found it difficult to sell his ideas. Now he had to sell the institution, the city, and its citizens on *U-505*.

The Navy already had a presence in the museum with permanent and temporary exhibits in the first of what would be to this day a long series of displays highlighting that branch of the service. Lohr looked upon *U-505* as simply an extension of these naval exhibits for which the navy was already paying a maintenance fee. As he saw it, the challenge was to get the Navy to think of it in the same way. About one-third of all naval personnel came from the Midwest and went through the Great Lakes Naval Training Station for their introduction to the service. What better way to cast a positive light on the Navy than to highlight the heroic achievements of the Navy's capture of an enemy submarine? Having 1.6 million annual visitors see and touch the tangible result of that remarkable wartime success would be an enormous publicity coup for the Navy. When looked at in that light, reasoned Gallery and Lohr, why would the Navy not want to help the cause by covering the costs for transporting *U-505* to Chicago? The Museum of Science and Industry was not the only institution forced to cut corners. After World War II, the U.S. Navy was ordered to look for ways to cut its costs. The search for ways to trim the branch's budget was what had set in motion Gallery's pursuit to find "his" submarine a permanent home. And he had an little-known bureaucrat to thank for it.

Maintaining enemy equipment or obsolete weapons was not a priority for the Navy, and once these items outlived their usefulness they were destroyed. Enemy ships were usually used as target practice or sunk outright and stricken from the inventory lists. John F. Floberg, Assistant

Secretary of the Navy for Air and its Controller, was busy signing orders for scrapping obsolete or overstocked items when he came across an unusual nomenclature: "*U-505*." He was used to seeing "DD" for Destroyer, "DE" for Destroyer Escort, "F4F" for Wildcat fighters, and so on, but "*U-505*" was unlike anything he had seen before. Curious, Floberg inquired and discovered *U-505* was "The submarine that Dan Gallery captured." Thinking it would be a shame if the old German U-boat simply disappeared without notifying the man who had brought it into port, Floberg notified Gallery of its pending demise.

Gallery knew how the Navy operated and the last thing he wanted was for the monument to his wartime success to be used as an inglorious target and sent to the bottom. He had no qualms about making his apprehensions known, both inside the Navy and out. As one of the men with whom he corresponded put it, "Dan is afraid that if nothing happens [about making the boat a memorial] the Navy will sink it some afternoon when no one is looking." However, nothing of substance seemed to flow from the initial discussions: months and years slipped past, *U-505* remained unclaimed, and the city and museum remained without funds to finish the task.

On January 20, 1950, Chicago Alderman Clarence P. Wagner introduced a resolution to the council setting in motion the machinery for Chicago's acquisition of title to the war prize. For some reason no action on the resolution was taken but the resolution helped focus the citizens of Chicago on the importance of the project. The *Chicago Daily Tribune* warmed to his plan, eventually running an article on March 8 explaining why U-505 would make a worthy trophy for the city. One reason was obvious: Gallery, its captor, was a Chicagoan. The museum was considered the prime recipient for the boat, and many organizations, including the Navy League, the Irish Fellowship Club, naval reserve units, and others began signing on as official backers of the project. The newspaper reported the museum wanted the submarine as an outdoor exhibit, but other proposals were floating about that included placing it on a concrete platform in Grant Park near Buckingham Fountain, or alongside the naval reserve armory at the foot of Randolph Street. Seabee Unit 9-3 had also worked up plans to place *U-505* near the Lake Shore Drive extension north of Foster Avenue.

Wagner's resolution may have been initially introduced in 1950 to keep *U-505* from being scrapped and to show the Navy Chicago meant

business. At that time the *U-505* committee and museum were not ready
to bring the boat to Chicago. It would take several more years of detailed
investigations and planning before the project was ready to move
forward. When the committee and museum were finally ready to initiate
the actual transfer of the boat, Alderman Wagner reintroduced the same
resolution on March 11, 1953, setting forth for many of the new faces in
Washington the reasons why the city should fight for possession of the
boat. The resolution read as follows:

"WHEREAS, *U-505*, a Nazi submarine prowling the Atlantic
Ocean for Allied shipping, was boarded and captured by the United
States Navy on June 4, 1944, marking the first time that the
American Navy has boarded and captured an enemy ship of war on
the high seas since 1815,"

WHEREAS, Numerous Chicagoans participated in this action,
including the Commander of the task group, the Commanding
Officer of the first vessel to go alongside the submarine, as well as
other officers and men of the task group; and

WHEREAS, A proposal has been made, supported by many
prominent Chicagoans, to bring *U-505* to Chicago for permanent
installation at the Museum of Science and Industry as an exhibit of
outstanding public interest and as a memorial to the many heroic
fighters of the United States Navy who have given their lives for
their country; and

WHEREAS, Submarine warfare constituted a major factor both in
World War I and World War II and still remains a vital part of
modern warfare; and

WHEREAS, The installation of *U-505* at the Museum of Science
and Industry would permit many hundreds of thousands of persons
to see it each year, thus drawing considerable attention to this phase
of the war at sea and emphasizing the importance of maintaining a
strong sea-going force for the protection of our country; therefore
Be It Resolved, That the City Council of the City of Chicago do
hereby make formal request of the Secretary of the Navy to present
U-505 to the City of Chicago for the purpose of installing this vessel
as a permanent exhibit; and be it further

RESOLVED, That the City Council authorize the Mayor of the City of Chicago, if and when such request is granted, to appoint a committee of Chicago citizens to make whatever arrangements are necessary and to prepare plans for appropriate ceremonies attending its installation as one of Chicago's permanent war exhibits."[14]

This time around the Alderman's resolution was seconded by Ald Cullerton of the 38th Ward. Secretary of the Navy Francis Matthews responded a few weeks later with a letter to the City Council confirming receipt and outlining the costs involved in preparing *U-505* for a tow to Chicago from its current berth at the Portsmouth Naval Yard in New Hampshire. Many years had passed since the original interest in *U-505*, but the logjam appeared to be breaking. What nobody associated with the project realized at the time were the problems about to arise because of the use of a few words in the resolution.[15]

Gallery was delighted by the city's renewed enthusiasm for bringing the boat to his hometown but knew if nothing happened soon, the Navy (which was growing impatient by the long delays) was going to scrap the boat because it needed the room occupied by *U-505* at the Portsmouth yard. Gallery suggested $20,000 should be enough to bring the boat through the Great Lakes to Chicago, where "there is plenty of navy space here for its berthing."[16]

The Tribune Company offered the services of one of its newsprint-carrying ships, which could tow *U-505*, and the Quebec and Ontario Transportation Company, which operated the Tribune's fleet between Chicago and its Canadian paper mills, suggested a pair of possible routes: via St. Lawrence and the connecting seaway, or to Lake Erie at the end of the canal and then on to Chicago. These ideas triggered a lengthy discussion about the best route to Chicago vis-à-vis the costs involved, and reopened negotiations with the Navy to determine whether it would perform the task free as a goodwill gesture. Few if any of the major participants fully appreciated the difficulty or expense involved in preparing and moving more than 700 tons of submarine. Their primary focus was getting title to the boat and getting it to Chicago; once that was done they could argue who was going to place it where and for what purpose. The Tribune Company's offer to keep *U-505* at its own riverfront property removed that potential problem from the complex equation.[17]

With local interest increasing Lohr offered up to $25,000 of museum funds to prepare the boat for exhibit at the institution once it arrived. Gallery and Mayor Kennelly agreed between them that the first step should be to get the Navy to transfer custody to the city before the mayor appointed a fundraising committee. Andrew Boemi, president of the Chicago chapter of the Navy League of the Unites States was instructed by the directors of that group to appoint a committee to join in the project to bring the boat to Chicago. The matter seemed to be moving smoothly along.[18]

Unfortunately, the generosity of the Tribune Company would never be realized. J. W. Gulick, Chief of Marine Administration for the Treasury Department's Bureau of Customs, informed the company of a little known clause in the Federal Code that made the tow they offered impossible. Section 36, Title 46 prohibited any vessel of foreign registry, except in case of distress, from towing one of American registry anywhere in the United States. The Tribune's fleet was owned by the Quebec and Ontario Transportation Company, and was thus under Canadian registry. Dismayed by the news, many sought to skirt the law by relying on technicalities. Was not *U-505* a foreign boat? Not as far as the Navy was concerned: "Inasmuch as it appears that *U-505* is in all probability not a vessel of foreign registry . . . it seems the proposed movement is prohibited by this section."[19] *U-505* became a US vessel in June 1944 when Kenneth Knowles had renamed it USS *Nemo* to keep the capture a secret until the war ended.[20]

The disheartening information crushed the spirits of some while sparking others to greater effort. James H. Gately, president of the Chicago Park District Board, was not about to sit idly by and let some obscure law send *U-505* to the bottom of the sea as a wreck. Although Gately recognized the law was the law, he proposed the city seek special dispensation or temporary relief from it in order to allow the tow. "If the maritime laws provisions can't be waived, the whole Illinois delegation in Congress should get behind a special bill to permit the tow," he said. "Chicago should have *U-505*. Certainly it is better to bring it here as an educational exhibit than for the Navy to junk it."[21]

The bad news also increased Mayor Kennelly's determination to land the submarine. Knowing the official transfer request for *U-505* would involve congressional support from both sides of aisle, letters were sent to Illinois Republican Senator Everett Dirksen and Democratic Senator Paul Douglas asking for their joint support. Their backing would help in the upcoming negotiations with the Federal government and the eventual plan by the city to try to have the Navy pay for as much of the project as possible.

On March 30 Mayor Kennelly left for a visit to the White House for a conference with President Dwight Eisenhower and other city officials from around the country dealing with governmental functions and fiscal resources. The timing could not have been better for Chicago to press its case in Washington. Kennelly promised his constituents he would meet with government officials on the matter.[22] It is unknown whether he mentioned the issue directly to the president (or if he even intended to), but the news that followed was promising.

Two days later Kennelly met with John Floberg, the man who had noticed *U-505* on the list of ships to be scrapped. During a discussion of the transfer Kennelly happily learned of Floberg's enthusiastic support for the project—and the high cost of what his city hoped to undertake. The Navy expected the necessary repairs to get *U-505* under tow at an eye-popping $175,000. Floberg sent a telegram several days later reaffirming his support and "co-operation in every practical way. . . . I earnestly hope that under your leadership and that of your committee this war trophy may be preserved in the naval district which furnished the Navy one-third of its personnel during World War II."[23] The amount of money was staggering, but Kennelly was pleased to learn no additional official obstacles had been thrown in the way. Indeed, the US Navy never really objected to the project to the point of refusing to cooperate, (though some individuals felt it was a bad idea or a Dan Gallery self-aggrandizement project) they simply had laws tying their hands about the costs incurred on such project.[24]

On Friday April 3, 1953, a fundraising and organizational drive was kicked off, the former weakly and the latter with vigor. A 42-man committee (which would eventually grow to more than 70 members) of prominent Chicagoans was appointed by Dan Gallery, William M. Goodrich (recently retired from the Goodrich Electric Co.), and Mayor Kennelly. Goodrich sat as chairman. The influential group pledged every effort to bring the U-boat from New Hampshire to Illinois and deposit it safely for display at the Museum of Science and Industry. Other well-known members included honorary chairman Ralph Bard, a prominent Chicago attorney and former Undersecretary of the Navy, Arthur Godfrey, a popular television and radio comedian and a commander in the Naval Reserves, and Dan Gallery's brother, Father John Gallery, priest of Chicago's St. Cecilia's Church.

After Illinois Senator Dirksen held a series of discussions with *U-505* committee leaders he made it known he planned to introduce a bill mandating the Navy to perform the necessary repairs on *U-505*. Gallery had also been intimately involved in these conversations and had encouraged the angle of getting the Navy to pay. Gallery felt that though Federal law stated that the recipient of a stricken vessel assume all costs he felt that the Navy was interpreting the clause too literally. Gallery had in fact disagreed on the high cost estimate of refurbishing the *U-505* for transfer and encouraged Senator Dirksen to try and "persuade the bureaucrats that their estimates . . . were a little on the high side and that it would be good training for the navy to tow it to Chicago for us." For this behind-the-scenes coaching Gallery received a stern warning, but short of what would have been his second reprimand.[25]

In trying to flex the committee's considerable political clout, Goodrich made it clear to the Secretary of the Navy he believed that branch of the service should recondition the boat for towing to Chicago—or at the least assume a large portion of the costs involved: "The Navy should recondition the boat because it was the first enemy vessel captured on the high seas by our navy since the War of 1812." Goodrich also cited precedent in support of the argument. The Navy, he claimed, had delivered the battleship USS *Texas* to its namesake state in 1948 for use as a war memorial. *Texas* was the first surplus ship to become a memorial under a new regulation. However the battleship was transferred under arrangements similar to those that would eventually be worked out for *U-505*: the state provided $250,000 to establish the berthing arrangements and provide all annual costs for maintenance and operation. It has not been determined whether the Navy absorbed the costs for preparing the ship for tow.[26]

Thinking that Goodrich was making a valid point regarding having the Navy pay, the local media enthusiastically agreed. "All Chicagoans should join in this venture," the *Chicago Herald-American* proudly proclaimed in April 1953. "This trophy of war should be brought here because of its historic nature . . . and because it will add immeasurably to the attendance at the museum."[27] An editorial a few days later continued in this vein, adding, "The people of Chicago, now and in the future, would find interest and excitement in seeing and studying this member of the under seas fleet with which the Nazis made such grim and effective war."[28]

Who would pay for what, however, continued to be a major sticking point. Goodrich declared, "I do not think the committee or the city should be obliged to spend this money to put the vessel in towable condition. That should be done by the Navy. We will not engage in any fundraising campaign until we see what the Navy will do. Then we'll know how much money we will have to raise."[29] While this was a fiscally responsible (and perhaps the only appropriate) position to take in the early days of the project, it would prove impossible in practice.

Even without Navy financial backing the optimistic committee members eventually moved forward on virtually all fronts. That April plans were set in motion for a big public welcome of the submarine, which they assumed would arrive just four months later in August. (The month was right but the year was not: the boat would not arrive until August of 1954.) A planning dinner for the 42 committee members was held at the Chicago Athletic Club to discuss the project and assign tasks to the members. The spectacular film of the capture of *U-505* was shown to a delighted group—the first of many public depicting as a way to excite the membership and build enthusiasm for the project. Supposedly, captured German film showing *U-505* in action was also shown, but this claim is doubtful as no such footage is known to exist. The screening of stock footage went hand-in-hand with press reports inflating *U-505's* wartime record. One report claimed *U-505* sank 160,000 tons of shipping, when in fact the total was less than 1/3 that amount at 46,962 tons. The press would continue reporting incorrect figures in the months ahead, but as the date of the boat's arrival in Chicago approached, facts relating to its service edged closer to reality.[30]

After the film was shown the committee broke into an executive committee and subcommittees. One of the latter was tasked with visiting Illinois congressmen and traveling to Washington for negotiations with the Navy. Another was ordered to study the costs of the move and restoration and installation of the boat at the museum. Still a third group, headed by Fred Byington, business manager of the *Chicago Tribune*, was ordered to head for New York City to talk with various companies about the price of towing the submarine to Chicago. Later another committee was formed to produce the welcome and dedication ceremonies.

The cost of towing the boat was not the only major concern facing the committee. A revealing article in the *Chicago American* dated April 22, 1953, pointed out *U-505's* advanced state of decay and that some in the Navy questioned whether it was even feasible to tow *U-505* to Chicago—regardless of the cost:

> Had the city taken action when the boat was first offered to Chicago as a war memorial in 1948, the cost would have been much less. In fairly good condition then and with all its original equipment aboard, the vessel is now a stripped and neglected rusted hulk. Navy officials [hesitate] to move *U-505* too far or to experiment with her diving tanks because of the possibility of it sinking or capsizing. . . . *U-505* could make the trip all right, but it is a mightily dangerous tow. A towline . . . might rip the bow off the sub. Hatches of *U-505* are padlocked and the gangway raised to prevent unauthorized persons from boarding the craft, now considered by Navy men as a bad risk. Below, the musty engine room, crews' quarters, control room and the rest are encrusted with salt and rust. The big diesel engines are still there, but it would cost thousands of dollars to put them in working order again.

The damning article did not stop there:

> Most of the equipment has been cannibalized and sent to France. The German-made periscopes are missing. Several of the ballast tanks contain water but the Navy has no plans for draining them. One of the tanks was tapped a year ago, a naval officer recalled and it immediately began to fill with water. The bottom had rusted. The sub might have sunk right there at the dock if we hadn't immediately plugged the tap. *U-505* was last in dry-dock in 1947, but at that time the bottom was not painted. The Navy Department has thus far refused to allot any money for the upkeep of the vessel. There are no plans at present to dry-dock her and Navy men fear such an operation might result in her destruction. In addition to taking six times the effort to dry-dock *U-505* than for any other submarine, they point out, the keel might give way during the operation. That would mean the U-boat would be cut up on the spot for scrap.[31]

So, could *U-505* be towed to Chicago—or not? Despite these problems, some of which had been sensationalized, the Navy spokesperson conceded the boat would *probably* withstand the difficult journey. But the spokesman did not speak for the inspection team tasked with deciding that question, and whether *U-505* would make it to Chicago as a war memorial or be sunk rested largely with what the team traveling to Portsmouth (which included five committee members) discovered during its evaluation.[32] The blunt frankness exhibited in the *Chicago American* article may have been because the paper had no real stake in whether the boat ended up in Chicago or on the seabed. A rebuttal published in the *Chicago Tribune* two days later refuted some of these claims and offered a less dire portrait of the boat's deteriorating condition.

At the time it was impossible to know which paper was hitting closer to the truth. The *Chicago Tribune*, an enthusiastic supporter of bringing the boat to the city, had and would continue to have a tendency to gloss over some of the more negative aspects of the endeavor throughout the life of the project. This time, though, it was right on the money: the boat was in better shape than reported and had passed the inspection. The estimated price of $200,000 to restore the boat was almost certainly "too high"; the exterior was rusting after eight years of exposure to the corroding sea air, but the inspectors found the interior was still in "very good condition."

According to the *Tribune*, "Reports of the extent to which *U-505* had been dismantled turned out to be exaggerated. The interior is largely intact, most of its equipment is still in place and that it may be possible to round up the missing items." Some missing interior parts had been sent to the Naval Research Laboratory and were reportedly still there. The inspection team found *U-505* lying low and stern down in the water, with a slight list to starboard. Admittedly it was a sorry sight from the outside. Red with rust, the outer hull was deeply pitted with parts completely holed, most noticeably at the stern. A shipyard official claimed the exterior repairs would be hard because the Germans engineered their submarines for only two years of service and used steel ingredients that made welding difficult. Officials estimated repairs would run about $21,000, with another $25,000 to tow the boat to Chicago and another $30,000 to get it into shape for exhibit. The pressure hull was ¾" steel, and because of this the Navy believed it would stand the strain of towing and rough weather.[33] The observation by the shipyard official questioning the suitablility for welding was off the mark. The Germans cut corners in some respects because of the large number of boats required to fight the tonnage war and steadily increasing rate of losses (which is why few boats lasted longer than two years), but their steel was outstanding and the boats were welded as well as any boats afloat.

If Chicago officials hoped this news would end the debate, they were disappointed. The *Chicago Herald American* reported the five-man inspection team had signed off on the move despite caution and pessimism from other naval officials. Captain F. X. Forest reminded the team it would be risky to tow the aging submarine across 1,340 miles of open sea to Quebec and another 1,390 miles to Chicago without first inspecting the boat in dry-dock and preparing her for the journey. Captain R. E. Cronin, commander of the Portsmouth yard, speculated a towing company might not want the job at all—presumably because of the poor condition of the boat. The inspection team, however, dismissed these concerns as too pessimistic.

Other newspaper articles focused on the intricacies found aboard the boat and how well its mechanical features would be received at the Museum of Science and Industry. "There were many wonders to behold. There were the wheels, cogs, lever, gauges, and what not. There were the intricate devices through which this U-boat operated on the high seas . . . Why, youngsters will have a field day with all these things!" exclaimed Cornelius J. Hagan, *U-505* committee member and co-owner of Indian Hill Stone Company. "Even daddies will be craning their necks to get close looks at machinery and torpedo control equipment." For Harry S. Cuttermore, another *U-505* committee member and a civil engineer, "This submarine has appeal for patriotism because it vividly displays that it took courage by our men in uniform to bring it back in one piece."[34]

As enthusiasm coursed through Chicago the issues of where the boat would end up and how it would be displayed began to be more fully explored. On April 27, a headline in the *Chicago American* announced, "Inspiration: Museum Plans U-505 Shrine." Until now it was not exactly clear where or how the boat would be displayed. The museum had offered to spend $25,000 to provide a proper setting and demonstrate to the Navy that everyone was serious about the idea, but the issue had not yet been officially settled. Few, however, doubted that if the boat came to Chicago the museum would indeed be its future home. Its plans included a 200-seat theater to show film of the dramatic capture, after which visitors would walk through covered walkways into and out of the boat. Exhibit galleries before and after the boat tour would display various war trophies. It had already been decided that should the boat end up at the science museum, holes would be cut into the side so visitors would not have to negotiate the difficult hatches. It would also be heated, and artificial lighting would be provided. Those issues were still open to debate, but the reason for exhibiting the boat was clear: "Such an exhibit would be an excellent inspiration because *U-505* represents a triumph of American forces in a war." Now in the midst of an arms race with the USSR and with a successful global war behind the country, the earlier intent to refuse to "glorify war" by exhibiting a military machine seems to have fallen by the wayside.[35]

The committee wasted no time moving its plans along. By April 29 the Chicago Park District Board unanimously agreed to issue any permits necessary to bring the boat ashore and haul it across park land to the museum. This was another important step the committee used to cement commitment from the Navy. Vice Admiral R. F. Good, logistics officer for the Chief of Naval Operations, reiterated again the Navy fully intended to transfer title to *U-505* to Chicago as long as all preparations had been duly performed. Another hurdle had been cleared.[36]

The *Detroit Free Press*, meanwhile, watching the event unfold from afar, published an article wondering aloud why the people of Chicago would invest civic pride and dollars in an old rusty German wreck. "For reasons best known to itself," began the editorial, "Chicago wants the now obsolete old wreck for its Museum of Science and Industry. . . . Every city is entitled to its own enthusiasms. New York, for instance, is in a twitter over the unveiling of a new marble statute of Aphrodite which rivals in beauty the Venus of Milo at the Louvre. . . . Her beauty remains timeless, and unlike a rusty old war relic she will never become obsolete." The observation smacked of sour grapes, at least to the *Chicago Daily News*, which shot back, "It is interesting to note that the *Free Press* is unable to point to any activity in Detroit, either patriotic or aesthetic to match the proceedings in Chicago and New York." The barbs sank to lower levels when the Chicago paper began discussing Detroit's sub-par professional sports teams, namely the "toothless Tigers" who had finished in lowly 8th place the previous year. Even at this early date Chicagoans had an emotional investment in the "obsolete old wreck," which they would soon see as a measure of civic accomplishment and patriotism.

The details were moving forward when suddenly the *U-505* committee experienced a change in leadership. Painted in some accounts as a shake-up, many had reported simply that Goodrich had decided to withdraw his leadership due to health reasons. It did appear that a new approach was desired. "Torpedo," announced one newspaper article. "A fuse has been lit which threatens to sink efforts to bring the captured Nazi submarine, *U-505*, to Chicago. The explosion may result in the resignation . . . of William Goodrich . . . and may singe the epaulets of Rear Admiral Daniel V. Gallery." It was becoming clear the Navy, restricted by law in what it could do financially, was not going to pay for any of the services required to get *U-505* into shape. The course the committee had been following, however, was all about getting someone else to foot the bill instead of digging in to aggressively raise the necessary funds. It was time for a change in direction and leadership. Goodrich, the retired industrialist who had been heading up Mayor Kennelly's *U-505* committee, was replaced by two men—in recognition of just how difficult it would be to raise the needed cash. The co-chairmen were Carl Stockholm, owner of Stockholm Cleaners, and Robert Crown, Vice President of Material Services Corporation.[37]

Two more significant hurdles to acquiring title to the boat were cleared that June. Navy Secretary Robert B. Anderson notified the speaker of the House of Representatives and the President of the Senate of his intention to award *U-505* to Chicago for display at the Museum of Science and Industry. Illinois Senator Everett Dirksen, in turn, notified Chicago Mayor Kennelly of the good news. There was only one stipulation: if another community filed a claim within 60 days of the notification to Congress, the legislators would have to decide which city would get the boat. The second stumbling block knocked aside was an agreement between the Museum of Science and Industry and the Navy. The museum had to agree formally to accept custody of the submarine and be responsible for its upkeep—without any expense to the Federal government. Museum Director Lohr, as previously noted, quickly committed $25,000 to install the boat as an indication of the museum's commitment. With the momentum now fully on its side the committee dispatched another team to Portsmouth over the 1953 Fourth of July weekend to prepare a final engineering report to confirm projected budget estimates in advance of a formal fundraising announcement.[39]

It was Thursday, July 9, 1953, when the fund drive was officially announced. This time Lenox Lohr informed everyone that having *U-505* in Chicago would serve a two-fold purpose: the city would get a permanent war memorial *and* realize the wishes of museum founder Julius Rosenwald. The goal for the fund drive was set high at $225,000—$40,000 of which was needed immediately to ready *U-505* for the 2,730-mile tow to Chicago. And it was a good thing, because some of the boat's problems were more serious than originally believed, and would require more than the early estimate of $100,000. The committee, already emotionally invested in the idea of owning *U-505*, recommended moving ahead with its plans.[40] The additional $125,000 was earmarked for the tow to Chicago, further repairs and restoration, and placing the boat alongside the museum. The grassroots nature of the fundraising was illustrated by the plea to extend the drive to local school children. "The exhibition will be educational, and the kids will love to have a part in bringing this historic relic to Chicago," explained P. F. Brautigan, the Illinois commander of the American Legion.[41] Pledge cards were sent out to hundreds of Chicagoans. Area residents were invited to participate by sending their donations directly to the museum "in care of the *U-505* fund." Some committee members primed the pump by contributing $10,000 on the first official day of the fundraising effort.

The first fundraising meeting was with the Rotary Club of Chicago. Some 350 members were on hand at the Morrison Hotel to hear Admiral Gallery tell his story of the capture of *U-505*. He also discussed the benefits gained from the capture of *U-505*, such as a better understanding of German acoustic torpedoes and the acquisition of code books and "code machines." Gallery, of course, was unable to speak directly about the Enigma machine or matters of intelligence in anything but a very general manner. "With them," he explained, "we sat in on the German frequencies and read their messages for the rest of the war." That generalized explanation was easy to grasp. The deeper truth—of how the British had broken into the Enigma code much earlier and how we had been reading German messages for much of the war—was still top secret and would not be revealed to the world for another twenty years. Ironically, even Gallery probably never realized the full extent of the naval intelligence efforts against the U-boats. Occasionally his overstated claims caused him some embarrassment. British hackles were raised, for example, by his description of the extent of the American contribution to reading German code. Gallery and Lohr, however, were merely barkers at a circus intent on raising funds to preserve a submarine, and were not trying to carve in stone some historical truth to slight our British allies. If the case had to be overstated a tad, so be it. At this stage, the preservation of the boat was more important.

The mayor's committee played the local media well and knew how to use it to advantage. Having the *Tribune* as an official backer on the project certainly helped the cause as well. Press releases and stories appeared regularly throughout the campaign to let the locals know the status of the growing fund. Readers knew when the project was succeeding or faltering, and read with interest the many changes in direction as the project unfolded. The important concept to be grasped was that a grass roots effort was required for the project to succeed, so it was important local citizens felt they had a stake in its success. Interest flourished when articles began discussing the sailors who had pulled off the capture. The search was on for Chicago veterans who had participated in the event and the museum was trying to track down the boarding party from USS *Pillsbury*. Stories of the dramatic capture mesmerized the citizenry and served to energize everyone. As might be expected, one of the most popular fundraising tools was the spectacular film of *U-505's* capture. Utilizing actual combat footage of the event, the Navy created two different films about *U-505* and a third was produced by the museum using both Navy films. The first, clumsily titled "And Now It Can Be Told," was screened to war production plants and assorted patriotic groups to instill patriotism. The second film, "Away Boarders," was a variation of that film. The third movie, "The Story of *U-505*," would eventually find a place in the museum's *U-505* theater to inform visitors about the event before they boarded the submarine. The first two films used much of the same combat footage but were edited differently. Footage recreating certain events was added to all three movies to fill in gaps that were not caught on camera in June 1944. These scenes included staged reenactments of Gallery watching events unfold, the boarding party whaleboat being lowered and ordered away, and similar actions. At least two versions of each film exist in the Museum of Science and Industry archives. They offer an interesting study in the subtle art of film production, editing, and war propaganda. Primary differences include variations of music, narration, and edits depending on the intended audience. On the fundraising trail Gallery often appeared as a star attraction to introduce the film and take questions afterward from potential donors. Later he would pique the interest of audiences by announcing some of the footage had never been seen by anyone outside of naval personnel.[42]

Donors were also impressed by the willingness of the committee members to forego any reimbursements for costs they incurred while traveling or working on the project. Every dime donated for *U-505* would go directly to getting the boat to the museum.[43] As a further incentive, donor recognition levels were established; $500, for example, would get your name on a plaque that would eventually be hung inside the exhibit. When Milwaukee began making noise about landing *U-505*, Chicagoans took it personally and worked harder to raise money. Donations soared.[44]

Gallery, meanwhile, continued beating the drum for Chicago and the museum. He was closely wrapped up in the entire affair and so took it personally when anyone questioned why so much money should be spent to preserve a German submarine. In August the admiral penned a lengthy and thoughtful editorial for the *Chicago Daily News*. "Why collect funds to bring an old German submarine here and install it at the Museum of Science and Industry?" began the Gallery piece. "Admittedly, the U-boat will not improve the comfort and convenience of life in Chicago, nor will it affect taxes one way or the other. In a material sense, it will be of no practical value. But it will have an emotional and historic impact that will be of great and continuing benefit to the community." With a patriotic flare, Gallery explained how these benefits would come to pass:

> *U-505* will serve a dual purpose, commemorating those who have given their lives to maintain our control of the seas, and reminding future generations that this country owes its present greatness to sea power, and even in the atomic age must control the seas to stay alive.
>
> It will do this with a unique symbol of victory at sea—the only German submarine ever boarded and captured, and the first enemy warship so captured by our Navy since 1815.
>
> The Middle West has hundred of memorials commemorating land battles of the Civil, Spanish, and World wars. But there is none recalling the two great battles of the Atlantic in which German U-boats almost drove our ships off the sea. *U-505* will be a fitting

memorial to the 75,000 Americans who lost their lives at sea in those battles. . . .

The principal gainers from this project will be the youngsters. Over 4,000 schools from 39 states send classes to the museum each year, and 200,000 school children visited there last year. . . . This will not be the usual inert, dust-covered, museum exhibit. It will be a dynamic, living one, recapturing for those who see it the heroic mood of the afternoon when our boys made naval history by boarding *U-505.*

In this day and age, too many of us judge every question on the basis of, "What is there in it for me?" There is nothing much in this project for any one individual—no professional fund raisers are being employed in it. But there's a great deal for the community and the future. When a country becomes so absorbed in the present it forgets its heroic past, then its future is in danger.[45]

Gallery's powerful editorial satisfied many but did not fully silence critics. A February 2, 1954, rebuttal to the patriotic theme espoused by Gallery and others appeared in the *Chicago Sun Times*. "I don't agree . . . that acquiring the submarine *U-505* for a permanent exhibit in Chicago will serve to 'instill in the hearts and minds of our young people a knowledge of the sacrifices necessary to make a country great,'" retorted Louis Schoichet. "Let's face it. The submarine would be nothing more than a mechanical curiosity. If we want to do homage to navy heroes, let's record their deeds in literature for posterity, and use the funds necessary to bring the sub here for a worthy charity or a foundation in memory of these heroes."[46] An editorial over the signature "Ex-Sailor" echoed much the same sentiment two days later: "Yes, 2.5 million, mostly children, will see the 'intricate machinery' [of *U-505*] which is now completely outmoded by our own new atomic submarine. The money . . . used for this useless project would be of much more benefit if donated to veterans' hospitals"[47]

As one might imagine, the word "Nazi" could whip up a firestorm in any conversation; using it in conjunction with the boat sparked anger at the idea of preserving one of Hitler's "wolf" boats. The "Nazi" submarine, some said, was "evil" and no amount of money should be used to memorialize such a thing. "If you have a poll on the Nazi submarine matter, put me in the 'no' column," barked one resident. "Some day it, too, will probably end up a neglected piece of rust."[48]

Others, echoing the pre-World War II beliefs of the museum, decried using the U-boat as a memorial. Who, they collectively inquired, wanted a lasting reminder of the terrible nature of war?

Objections about the boat and its potential meaning were relatively small in number and the donation drive continued without interruption. The steady stream of smaller donations was occasionally punctuated with heftier sums: an anonymous $5,000 donation and a $1,000 check from the Chicago-based Hilton hotel chain. Approximately $25,000 was raised during just the first month. Heady predictions were offered that within another four weeks the $40,000 needed to lift *U-505* into dry-dock would be in hand. The early results were impressive but time was running short. The committee's goal was to move *U-505* into dry-dock in Portsmouth, complete the needed repairs (estimated at four weeks), and get the boat underway to Chicago before the fall storms hit the Atlantic Ocean. The initial fundraising success was indeed promising, but the window to accomplish so much so soon was closing rapidly.

With more than $30,000 on hand the committee decided to arrange for the dry-docking of *U-505* on August 5, but the date was bumped back one week because the Navy needed the space for emergency repairs to an active vessel. The dry-docking milestone finally arrived on August 12 when the U-boat left the sea for the first time since it was put into dry-dock in Bermuda in 1944. Five days later 20 committee members flew to Portsmouth to inspect the progress of the work and figure out how to haul the mammoth craft across dry land to the museum—assuming they could get it to the beach along Lake Shore Drive in the first place.

The initial work on the boat began with the removal from the hull of a thick layer of barnacles and seaweed, the sealing of every exterior opening—including hatches, drains, torpedo tubes, and tank openings—and the reinforcement of the boat's towing cleats. The forward and aft diving planes that had ripped a hole in USS *Pillsbury* in June 1944 were removed to allow tug boats room to safely maneuver and stuff the boat into the very tight dimensions of the locks along the St. Lawrence waterway. The sheer magnitude of the project, which was now rapidly becoming reality, hit the team when it got their first view of the boat out of the water. So, too, did the U-boat's deterioration, which was now plainly visible for all to see. Eight years of neglect "had left deep scars on the hull. In addition, sea water has been sitting inside the vessel, creating a coat of rust," recalled one observer. (The water was actually in the external tanks, which were not supposed to have water in them.) "You'd be surprised at the creatures we pumped out of that boat," added a Navy spokesman.[51]

The reality of the boat's condition was not immediately made public, and indeed was played down to keep in check additional and potentially embarrassing questions about the viability of the project. Admiral Gallery and others prevaricated a bit, telling members of the media how impressed they were with the condition of the boat. "It's in much better condition than I had been led to believe," fibbed one member of the committee. "There is more of the original gear than I expected to find," stretched another. "All the essential things are here, and the rest can be replaced easily. With a good cleanup and a coat of paint, it will be ready for visitors." Not quite. In addition to the deep exterior rusting problems and rotted decking, the interior had also been roughly handled. The radio and sound rooms had been stripped, as had the quarters for the officers and men, while the fire control equipment had been removed.[52] The Navy promised all removed equipment would be returned—a promise it would not be able to keep. The crew bunks were present, though in piles on the floors, and the galley was a shambles. The cramped interior made quite an impression on one committee member, who told the media it was little more than a maze of engines, gauges, and dials.[53]

During this inspection trip Gallery added another catch phrase to the growing list liberally used by the media. "It was a rough mission," he said of the effort to capture *U-505*. "But it's been almost as tough a fight to bring the sub to Chicago."[54] The going was about to get a lot tougher.

While laborers unpacked their tools and Gallery wooed reporters with war stories, Seth M. Gooder, a civil engineer from Gooder-Hendrichsen Company in Chicago was already seriously at work. Gooder had come out of retirement by special request to join the project and lend his unique expertise to the adventure. His company had almost 50 years of experience underpinning and moving hazardous buildings. Among its many successful projects was the shoring of the floating foundations of a 70,000-ton building and the successful transfer of a 150-foot tower balanced vertically on barges to a location one-half mile distant. When asked to comment on the current scope of the task before him, Gooder noted dryly, "[it] looks like a large order."[55] Gooder, like Earl Trosino 10 years earlier, would be credited as one of the most critical people in helping save *U-505* and getting it to Chicago and on to dry land next to the museum.

Repairs to the dry-docked boat were completed by the first week of September 1953. Once released back into the water *U-505's* ballast tanks were checked, the boat passed several stability tests, and to the delight of everyone was pronounced fit for an open ocean tow and passage through the St. Lawrence and Great Lakes. Remaining work consisted of fitting the craft with running lights and the installation of towing pads, chocks, and eyes, all of which were to be directed by the towing company doing the actual work. The fitting of an auxiliary anchor and other handling details were also accomplished at this time. Previous assumptions about the condition of the outer hull turned out to be overly pessimistic. The earlier estimate of $40,000 to prepare the hull had dwindled to only $15,000—a savings of $25,000.[56]

By now the *U-505* fund had some $55,000 tucked away and a submarine ready to make the long journey. That is, until an obscure law was raised dashing any hope *U-505* would be in Chicago by year's end. Federal law stipulated Congress had to be in session for 60 days after the Navy Department informed Congress of its intention to transfer title of a Federally-owned vessel. Congress, however, had only been in session 58 days—two days shy of the required total. A last-ditch effort by the museum to avoid further delay with a proposal to lease the boat from the Navy failed when the creative solution was ruled illegal.[57] Crestfallen, officials announced their plan to have the boat in the city by June 4, 1954, in time for the 10th anniversary of the boat's capture. *U-505* would have to spend one final winter in Portsmouth.

Efforts to raise money, however, continued unabated. Gallery visited Milwaukee to speak with that city's council of the U.S. Navy League. His visit came on the heels of the recent acrimonious letters published in the Chicago papers calling into question, among other things, the merits of the Windy City to host the submarine. The president of the council was none other than B.T. Franck, who had attempted to rally Milwaukeeans to support an application requesting the Navy send *U-505* to their city rather than Chicago. Franck had also made a trip to Portsmouth to inspect *U-505* and report on the feasibility of bringing the boat to Milwaukee. Shortly thereafter Chicago's *U-505* committee began reaching out to Milwaukeeans to convince them of the advantages it would bring to the entire Midwest should the prestigious Museum of Science and Industry land the U-boat.

Gallery's speech was well received in the once-antagonistic city. He described the project and its appeal to the greater good of the Midwest Navy veterans, outlined the steps for how the boat would be towed to Chicago, and described how it would be carefully displayed outside the museum. He continued by making a direct plea for cooperation between the cities and promised that when *U-505* was towed through Lake Michigan, Milwaukee could display it for a one week period before *U-505* made it to Chicago. In typical Gallery flair, he described the dedication ceremonies and concluded, "we think [it] will be the biggest whoop-de-doo on the lake front since the Fort Dearborn massacre."[58]

Although disappointed by the delay imposed by federal law, Chicagoans were delighted by an announcement in November that Moran Towing and Transportation Company, Inc., offered to tow *U-505* one-third of the distance—free. The company was based in New York City and headed by Edwin J. Moran, a rear admiral in the Navy Reserve who had responsibility during World War II for planning temporary harbors for the Normandy invasion and who later helped plan invasion operations in the Pacific. Moran's offer was to tow *U-505* during the open ocean portion of the trip from Portsmouth, New Hampshire, to the mouth of the St. Lawrence River—a distance of approximately 700 miles.[59] The offer was seen as a challenge to other companies. Only a few weeks later a "Great Lakes shipping firm that prefers to remain anonymous" offered to tow the boat 1,000 miles from Port Colborne, Ontario, at the eastern end of Lake Erie, through Lakes Erie, Huron, and Michigan, to Chicago.[60]

By the end of 1953 everyone was confident the fundraising would be complete by the following spring and the boat would be safely in Chicago before the summer heat wave enveloped the city.[61] The collection coffers were already bulging with $150,000 which, when coupled with the donations of two legs of the tow and the "unexpected savings on the original estimated hull and tow preparation costs," made a spring arrival feasible.[62] The final and thus far unclaimed portion of the tow through the St. Lawrence and across Lake Ontario was estimated at less than $10,000.[63]

July 4, 1954, was finally set as the date for the dedication ceremonies for *U-505*. The 10th anniversary of the capture (June 4) was more desirable, but because of the normally rough seas in the early spring, the middle of April was the earliest anyone believed a safe tow could be undertaken. After 30 days on the water (during which several exhibition stops were planned along the way), it would take weeks of preparation once in Chicago—in addition to the hauling overland of the boat from the lake's shore to the museum. A dedication on June 4 simply did not leave enough of a margin for error. The Fourth of July, however, added enough extra time and was in keeping with the patriotic theme surrounding the whole project.[64] Indeed, patriotism was being injected into the project almost as fast as money was pouring into the collection fund. After pleading with readers to dig deeply, the *Chicago Tribune* concluded an article with a direct play on emotions: "Anyone who contributes to this cause will be long and gratefully remembered in the community for service to a patriotic cause."[65]

One donation is especially worthy of mention. On January 21, 1954, USS *Nautilus* was launched. The world's first atomic submarine made headlines all over the world while simultaneously making every other submarine obsolete. General Dynamics Corporation, the builder of *Nautilus,* presented the *U-505* committee with a $500 check to help bring *U-505* to Chicago.[66] Although it was likely intended for publicity purposes, someone, somewhere, surely realized the era of the submarine represented by the Type IX *U-505* was now conclusively at an end, and boats of the past would survive only as exhibits in museums like Chicago's Science and Industry. Also left unspoken was another message: our submarine forces had to remain strong and technologically superior to our potential enemies. Ironically, USS *Nautilus* would also become outdated, and when retired was utilized as a museum ship in 1986—a link between the submarine forces of yesterday and tomorrow at the site of her construction in Groton, Connecticut, where the revolutionary boat remains today.[67]

With a date targeted for *U-505*'s arrival, tentative plans coalesced for the dedication ceremonies to mark the opening of the boat as an exhibit. The first thought was to invite President Dwight D. Eisenhower. His presence as both the country's commander-in-chief and former commander of Allied forces in World War II would offer an authoritative and meaningful statement about the significance of preserving *U-505* for posterity. The committee, with all of its connections in Washington, D.C., was confident the President might see fit to accept the invitation and were encouraged by news he had plans to be in the Midwest around the July Fourth holiday.[68] Plans were also made by the Chicago Council of Boy Scouts, which planned to provide thousands of members to act as color and honor guards at the dedication ceremonies.

"This was the first time I ever gave away a ship." Secretary of the Navy Robert B. Anderson's quip accompanied the long-awaited transfer of title from the U.S. Navy to the museum in front of a delegation of interested parties—a dream finally realized when he signed the requisite documents on Tuesday, March 9, 1954.[69] With 40 newsmen, photographers, and navy personnel in attendance Anderson recounted the boat's history, which he labeled as "one of the great outstanding achievements in U.S. naval history."[70] Also present was Means Johnston and Dudley Knox, the former commanders of USS *Chatelain* and USS *Flaherty*, respectively. Both men had been present with their ships during the seizure of *U-505* and both had played important roles in the capture. Illinois Republican Senator Everett Dirksen, who had made it politically possible to transfer the title to the museum, was also on hand, as were prominent members of the committee and many others who had labored so hard to see this day arrive.

In March of 1954 Dan Gallery wrote Earl Trosino to inquire if he would be interested in commanding the *U-505* "convoy" on its last journey to Chicago. "Are you kidding about the convoy?" an excited Trosino responded. "You made me responsible for 'Junior' way back when, and I certainly would like to accompany her to her final resting place." Enclosed with his response was a $500 check for the *U-505* fund. Gallery's reply was not long in arriving: "I'm not kidding a bit on that convoy deal and nothing would be finer, in my opinion, than to have you bring *U-505* to Chicago. It would add a hell of a fine dramatic twist, with a lot of human interest angles to have the first Commanding Officer of the sub after she joined the U.S. Navy deliver her to the Museum! So it's a deal."[71]

Gallery's selection was as obvious as it was perfect. Earl Trosino had served as the chief engineer on the carrier USS *Guadalcanal* during the capture of *U-505*. When the U-boat was forced to the surface by depth charges and boarded by sailors from USS *Pillsbury*, Trosino was put in charge of the salvage effort and instructed to take his crew aboard the disabled submarine and save it. "I want that boat!" declared Gallery. Once *U-505* was secured by the *Pillsbury* boarding party, Trosino led two salvage parties aboard about 70 minutes later and played a critical role keeping it afloat and towing the boat across the ocean to Bermuda. Who better to "bring" the boat to Chicago's premier museum than the man chiefly responsible for keeping it above water across a hostile Atlantic Ocean while under tow? In 1954 Trosino was the chief engineer on the oil tanker S.S. *Maryland Sun*. His employer graciously granted him leave for however long it would take to complete the transportation of *U-505* to Chicago, allowing Trosino to become, in effect, the submarine's "last commander." The museum also conducted a search for other members from Gallery's Task Group 22.3 so they could be present for the ceremonies, and in particular those men who had participated in boarding *U-505*.[72]

With the major arrangements complete, anxious Chicagoans had little more to do than wait for a break in the weather to begin the arduous and dangerous towing process. The committee hoped to begin the move by May 1, but the threat of ice in the Gulf of St. Lawrence pushed the date back. The new target date was set for May 15.[73] The delay was important because it meant the U-boat could not reach Chicago any earlier than June 15. Another six weeks would be necessary to haul the boat to the museum and prepare it for visitors. Holding the memorial dedication ceremony on the Fourth of July weekend now appeared very unlikely.[74] The dedication date was pushed back once again, this time to mid-August, while a dedication sub-committee was formed to work out the final arrangements for the ceremonies.[75]

Journey to Chicago

With all the pomp and fanfare one might expect, on May 12 the diesel-powered luxury yacht *Airbanas*, owned by Ulises A. Sanabria, left the Chicago Yacht Club and headed for Montreal, where it expected to meet *U-505* on May 26. Sanabria had volunteered *Airbanas* as a general utility boat for the towing operation. It would also act as a moving office for reporters and photographers and serve as the sleeping quarters for four sea scouts selected to assist in the operation. The scouts, who had been organized into two groups of four to bring *U-505* to Chicago as a training exercise, had departed earlier by train to meet the boat. The trip was a highpoint for the scouts, some of whom had never been on the water.[76] For many, *Airbanas's* departure was the first tangible evidence *U-505* was really coming to Chicago.

Airbanas was crossing Lake Michigan on its way to Montreal on May 14 when two Navy tugs in Portsmouth, New Hampshire, edged into position to take *U-505* under tow from her dockside station. White draft marks had been painted on the boat's bow and stern to help handlers keep an eye on its trim as final preparations were made to take to the seas again for the first time in a decade. The plan was to move the boat down the Piscatauqua River from the Portsmouth yard to the Atlantic, where Captain Rodney M. Jones and the tug *Pauline L. Moran* would take over. The tug arrived on the morning of the 14th to begin the tow but encountered rough water and strong easterly winds which made moving the U-boat dangerous. Instead of proceeding downriver the Navy tugs guided *U-505* approximately one mile to the harbor at Kittery, Maine, where they tied off the submarine to a buoy for the night and hoped the weather would subside enough to allow towing operations to resume the following day.[77]

Fortune smiled on May 15 when the winds died down and the seas smoothed out. A reporter for the *Chicago Tribune* recorded the details of the transfer:

> At 8:35 a.m. the tug tied up to the buoy where the submarine had been tied up overnight and the tug crew began the tricky job of fastening the nylon tow line to the submarine's heavy tow chain. At Captain Rodney Jones' order, a seaman leaped 10 feet down to the buoy, shackled the towline to the sub's tow chain, and cut the sub loose from its moorings. Pushed by a strong tide the U-boat drifted free and astern the tug, dragging the tow-line along. When some 200 feet had paid out it was made fast, and Captain Jones started for the open sea.

"Jones," the reporter explained, let out the full 1,200 feet of line once the boat reached the mouth of the harbor because, as he explained it, "she'll ride smoother that way." Once the line was fully extended Jones "headed thru the open sea for Nova Scotia."[78]

Assuming the weather cooperated, *U-505's* first stop would be on May 19 in Baie Comeau, Quebec, the hometown of the McCormick Paper Mill, an important publicity stop because the mill supplied its product to the *Chicago Tribune*, one of the most important backers of the project. Thereafter *U-505* would stop in Montreal on May 20 or 21 to prepare to enter Lake Ontario around May 23, again at Port Colburn on about the 25th, and then on to Chicago with stops in Buffalo, New York, Cleveland, Ohio, Detroit, Michigan, and Milwaukee, Wisconsin.[79] With *U-505* finally on the move the national media picked up the story and ran with it in virtually every major news market across the United States.

The journey from New Hampshire to Illinois vaulted Earl Trosino into the public eye. As the "commander" of *U-505* the media naturally focused their attention on him at each stop. Gallery had already ensured Trosino's everlasting connection to *U-505* by attributing to him the boat's survival at sea in 1944. This attention, of course, was not intended to diminish the role played by the other men who participated in the capture: a Medal of Honor, two navy crosses, and six silver stars forever enshrined their brave efforts. But from the moment the towing of *U-505* to Chicago began, the media attention on Trosino and his salvage efforts mistakenly morphed into stories of how he had led the initial boarding party—which he had not. The articles were repeated, twisted, and passed along as fact, much to Trosino's everlasting dismay.

Hounded at every stop for a story, the forty-seven-year-old former navy officer warmed up to his role, meeting with mayors, governors, and other VIPs. He did everything he could, however, to explain he was only one of many who had participated in the capture: "*we* came upon *U-505* and drove it to the surface with a series of depth charges. The German crew tried to scuttle the sub but *we* kept them too busy by firing all around them. *We* boarded the sub in time to close the sea-cocks and stop the water from pouring in." But it was the next sentence (or a minor variation thereof) printed in newspapers that triggered a misconception of his original role: "It was Trosino who led the boarding party. . ."[80] This statement and others like it raised bile in several throats and triggered a rift among members of the *Guadalcanal* Task Group (and modern historians) about who was responsible for the factual misstatements. Ultimately Trosino would take most of the heat, much of it unfairly.

The division between the carrier and DE (Destroyer Escort) personnel over issues relating to the capture of *U-505* did not begin with the move to Chicago. They can be traced all the way back to 1945 when *U-505* was on a war bond tour with an American crew along the East Coast. Trosino was a star attraction when the boat stopped in Philadelphia because he hailed from Pennsylvania. Trosino was also the subject of many news articles at the time and was the victim of inaccurate news accounts. He never claimed he was the first man to set foot aboard the submarine. He did, however, lead the salvage parties from USS *Guadalcanal* that played a distinctly different role than the nine-man boarding party from USS *Pillsbury*. To the ears of the uninitiated, however, there was little or no difference between "the boarding (or salvage) party from *Guadalcanal*," and the "*Pillsbury* boarding party." When the press learned *Guadalcanal* was the main ship around which the Task Group was assembled, the phrase "*Guadalcanal* boarding party" was assumed to mean that the carrier had launched the crew that captured the submarine. In reality, the carrier had turned away from the action and headed for the horizon at top speed (as it should have done to avoid being sunk in a desperate last act by the trapped enemy submarine). Earl Trosino's salvage men did not set foot on *U-505* until some 70 minutes *after* the boat had been secured by *Pillsbury's* crew. But the media was not interested in the finer details of how Hunter-Killer task groups operated, and the hectic dockside interviews conducted by Trosino were not the place for scholarly instruction. Sadly, the lack of understanding only served to exacerbate a situation in which everyone involved had room to bask in the glory of their remarkable achievement.[81]

*   *   *

Daily reports kept Chicagoans abreast of the progress during *U-505's* journey from New Hampshire. On May 16 Captain Jones radioed his position and speed as 30 miles west of Cape Sable, Nova Scotia, at eight knots. The wind, he reported, was blowing at 28 mph.[82] It increased over the next two days, building dangerous ocean swells which, coupled with fog, forced Jones to slow down to a crawl southwest of Halifax, Nova Scotia, on the way to the Gulf of St. Lawrence.[83] Jones intended to cut through the Strait or Gut of Canso between Cape Breton Island and Nova Scotia. Though more difficult to navigate (especially in the fog), it was shorter than going around Cape Breton Island and into the more navigable waters of the Cabot Straight. Without warning, contact was abruptly lost with *U-505* and *Pauline L. Moran*.

The worsening weather, coupled with the sudden loss of contact on May 18 quickened the heartbeat of everyone following the boat's progress. Officials decided if the tug was not heard from within 24 hours, aircraft and ships would be dispatched to locate Jones and his important charge. For the mayor's committee it was nail-biting time. Had they been too eager to get the boat to Chicago by insisting on an early spring passage? Would the final product of their impatience be the loss of *U-505?*[84]

Matters were indeed serious, but thankfully not as critical as many presumed. For 36 hours Jones's tug and *U-505* weathered a heavy storm. Powerful gales and high waves caused the submarine to roll so heavily radio transmitters had flooded and were temporarily out of service. To the relief of everyone contact was reestablished on Wednesday, May 19, when Admiral Gallery finally got through on a radio telephone. Trosino answered his first question by reporting the boat was in good shape after the pounding and had not taken on any significant amount of water. They were at the Cabot Straight heading into the Gulf of St. Lawrence, which meant the heavy fog had convinced Jones to bypass the Straight of Canso and use the longer route around Cape Breton Island. The good news, explained Trosino, was the tug and U-boat were in calm waters and heading for the mouth of the St. Lawrence River. Everyone exhaled a long sigh of relief.[85]

On Friday, May 21, *U-505* approached Cape des Rosiers on the Gaspe peninsula on the way to the first official stop at Baie Comeau, Quebec.[86] *U-505* was not the first U-boat to visit the St. Lawrence area. Many other submarincs, including *U-69, U-106, U-132, U-165, U-517, U-536, U-553, U-802, U-1223, U-1228* had traveled these waters during World War II. Several scored heavily here; many of them litter the ocean floor off the Canadian coast. This was the first time any of that country's citizenry, however, had an opportunity to see what had been lurking in the depths of the lower St. Lawrence only 10 years earlier.[87]

Canadian media, naturally enough, were very interested in the progress of *U-505*, and the people of Baie Comeau put out a grand welcome for the former enemy boat. The 15-piece Baie Comeau brass band assembled in full uniform on the wharf to salute its arrival. Mayor J. A. Duchesneau proudly presented a wooden key to the city mounted on a piece of spruce log to Earl Trosino during a brief ceremony on deck. Some 2,000 curious visitors toured *U-505's* interior that day. The next stop was Father's Point, Quebec, where Jones picked up two river pilots to guide *U-505* and his tug on the 342-mile trip to Montreal.[88] The boats arrived in Quebec on Monday, May 24, and reached Montreal the following afternoon. There, *U-505* encountered the first five of the 28 locks its would have to transit during her voyage up the St. Lawrence River.[89]

The mighty St. Lawrence flows easterly from the Great Lakes to the Atlantic Ocean, a long and natural border between Canada and the United States touching eight states and two provinces. The waterway experiences a 578.5-foot drop in elevation from Chicago to the Atlantic—325 feet of which is accounted for by the Niagara Falls system in the Welland Canal. The drop between Lake Ontario and Montreal alone is 226 feet. The waterway also boasted several unnavigable rapids.[90] In 1954—five years before the completion of the St. Lawrence Seaway Project—ships passing through the waterway traversed a system of locks and canals known as the St. Lawrence/Great Lakes canal system. Each of the 28 locks through which *U-505* had to pass had a depth of 12.5 feet—barely deep enough to move the boat up the river and into the Great Lakes.

Professional seamen from the International Seafarers Union were hired by Trosino to help handle the lines and move *U-505* through the Lachine canal system. The transit took place without incident and on May 26 the German submarine cleared the remaining three locks in the Lachine system before heading for the Soulange Canal locks, which were cleared that afternoon. The journey continued a few more hours to Cornwall, Ontario, where the tug and submarine stopped for the night.[92]

Nine Cleveland naval reservists met *U-505* in Cornwall to provide a volunteer reinforcement for the deck crew until it reached Cleveland. Two days later Admiral Gallery made a surprise visit and was briefed by Trosino on the progress and the boat's condition. The next day Gallery rode *U-505* through the locks at Morrisburg, Ontario, marking the official half-way point of the long journey from Portsmouth to Chicago. By noon that day tug and boat were moving at seven knots and approaching Ogdensburg, New York. City officials rode out on a U.S. Coast Guard ship to greet *U-505*. A delighted Gallery and four excited Sea Scouts were being interviewed by a local radio station when the river pilots were switched for the next leg of the journey to Buffalo.[94]

The passage through the small Canadian locks nearly proved impossible. *U-505* was 23 feet wide and Jones's tug *Pauline L. Moran* was 29 feet wide, a total of 52 feet of width. The locks along the river route, however, were only 45 feet wide. The Canadians insisted the only way through was to use a smaller Canadian tug at the added expense of $5,000. Captain Jones scoffed at the idea and told his employers to save their money: he could do it himself. Both the tug and *U-505* bulge out a bit underwater, but the tug's sides ride higher than those of *U-505*. With winches and old sailor know-how, Jones tied his tug up so tightly next to *U-505* that the tug boat was pulled slightly up onto the hull of the submarine. This pushed the U-boat down a few feet but still allowed the tug's propellers to move both boats forward through the locks and canals. Lashed together, the two vessels had only six inches to spare on each side! The locks varied in length, with some as short as 252 feet—the same length as *U-505*. This problem was solved by inserting the submarine diagonally, or corner-to-corner, instead of simply guiding the boat in head first. It was indeed a tight squeeze, both width- and length-wise.

Back home in Chicago on May 29, the *U-505* Committee announced the good news received thus far and added more of its own: the Coast Guard had agreed to tow *U-505* with its cutter *Kaw* at no charge on the final leg of the trip from Buffalo to Chicago. The only stipulation was that official business came first: if *Kaw's* services were required, the tow would have to be interrupted.[95] That same day *U-505* reached the end of its journey up the St. Lawrence and entered Lake Ontario, the first of the four Great Lakes it would transit (Lake Superior was the only lake the U-boat did not enter on its way to Chicago). The first major American city to host the boat's arrival in the Great Lakes system was Buffalo.[96]

The last group of locks left to traverse was designed to bypass Niagara Falls and connect Lake Ontario to Lake Erie. The Welland Canal, as the various locks are known, was a much wider system than the smallish Canadian locks and thus easier to negotiate. Jones pulled into Port Colbourne, Ontario, on the night of May 31 and entered Lake Erie. All 28 locks were now behind him. The tug pulled out at daybreak on June 1 for Buffalo, where it turned over *U-505* to the U.S. Coast Guard cutter *Kaw*.[97]

The difficult transit of lock and canal system had attracted thousands of Canadians and Americans, all of whom eagerly lined the waterway to watch the boats pass. Almost 30,000 people were said to have looked on as the boat moved through Montreal, and many thousands more witnessed the historic journey at other points along the way. None of them would ever forget it.[98]

Captain Jones and his *Pauline L. Moran* had performed flawlessly. Under his guidance *U-505* had passed through an Atlantic gale with 48 mph winds without damage and transited 28 locks on the St. Lawrence River in one-half the time the Canadians predicted it would take—all without significant incident. It was indeed a remarkable bit of seamanship.[99]

Towed by the cutter *Kaw* and escorted by the tug *Aubrey* (which arrived to lend assistance after the submarine had developed difficulty steering), *U-505* pulled into the Cleveland harbor and tied up to the 9th Street pier on the morning of June 3.[100] Thousands of onlookers cheered the arrival, and 15,000-20,000 more would view the boat over the next three days. Mayor Anthony J. Celebrezze's welcome ceremonies were attended by Gallery, who had flown in from Chicago to join the celebration.[101]

The first man to board the German boat in Cleveland was no stranger to *U-505*. Chester Mocarski had been a Gunner's Mate aboard USS *Pillsbury*'s boarding party when *U-505* was captured in 1944. The attempt to board the submarine during the war did not go well for Mocarski, who slipped and severely injured his back when trapped between the grinding whaleboat and submarine hull. He was lucky to escape with his life. Fellow boarder Wayne Pickels and Zenon Lukosius pulled Mocarski onto *U-505* and put him back into the whaleboat. He was eventually delivered to *Guadalcanal* for further medical treatment. Mocarski was awarded a Silver Star for gallantry but refused a purple heart because his legs and arms were intact where others were not so fortunate.[102]

The next day, June 4, 1954, marked the 10th anniversary of the boat's capture. A ceremony was held aboard the boat and crowds of onlookers elbowed closer to listen while Gallery, Mocarski, and Trosino enthralled everyone with their recollections of the event.[103] "We are gratified by the great public interest in *U-505* all over the country," commented Committee Co-Chair Robert Crown from his home in Chicago. "After years of war time secrecy and an almost forgotten feat of bravery, the submarine's capture has become the most talked about engagement in United States naval history."[104]

U-505 spent several days in Cleveland, during which disappointed visitors learned that because of safety reasons, they would not be allowed on deck or inside the boat. A close-up examination of the boat would have to satisfy the curiosity seekers. Rust holes in the outer hull, especially at the stern, and the dreadful condition of its paint, convinced the committee to give the old war boat a quick paint job so it would look presentable for its triumphant arrival in Chicago. House painters Michael Homyak and Russell Stevenson were flown by commercial airliner from Chicago by Local 396 of the AFL Painter's Union to perform the most unusual request for their services they would ever receive. Their union paid the airfare, Glidden Manufacturing supplied 50 gallons of paint, and Binks Manufacturing Company supplied the compressor and paint spraying equipment. Unfortunately, no effort was undertaken to document how *U-505* was originally painted, so it ended up standard U.S. Navy black—the paint scheme used on many American boats at that time.[105]

A much cleaner looking *U-505* departed Cleveland on Monday, June 7, her restoration fund $3,000 richer thanks to donations from citizens of Cleveland and local businesses. In fact, donations were solicited and received at every stop along the way from Portsmouth to Chicago. The fund was now bulging with $175,000—the goal of $225,000 well within striking distance.[106] After spending two days in Toledo, Ohio, *U-505* left for Detroit and arrived there late in the day on June 10. Sanabria's luxury yacht *Airbanas*, which had left Chicago on May 26 and would accompany the boat back to that city, was on hand to greet it. The submarine spent the weekend tied up at the Brodhead Naval Armory, where visitors again were forced to view the boat from afar rather than from atop or within. This time the slick black finish impressed most of those who saw it. Ironically, the U-boat tied up behind the landlocked USS *Tambor*, a veteran of the Pacific submarine war relegated for use as a training ship for naval reservists. Gallery flew to Detroit a few days later for the final journey to Chicago.[107] However, the media-savvy officer found himself overshadowed by a former opponent. German submariner Hans Wollschlager had sailed on *U-504*, a sister ship to *U-505*. Wollschlager, an employee of Ford Motor Company, brought his wife and two daughters to see the boat "because he couldn't stay away." He told the press if given a choice to serve on *Tambor* or *U-505* he would select the more superior German boat, "because the American sub is too large for quick submerging."[108]

With the Coast Guard cutter *Arundel* now in command of the tow, *U-505* departed Detroit early on Monday, June 14, with *Airbanas* carrying members of the media, Admiral Gallery, and the Sea Scouts. *Arundel's* route took the boats north along the "thumb" of Michigan on the western shore of Lake Huron. The plan was to stop overnight in Alpena, a small community about 250 miles north of Detroit. The announcement sent hundreds to the harbor to catch a glimpse of the German submarine. It was not to be, however, because the schedule was getting too tight to allow the convoy to slip into the small town, even for a few hours. Gallery wisely pulled into Alpena to explain personally the change in plans and play a hand at damage control.[109]

U-505 spent a calm night at Mackinac Island on the 16th of June between the lower and upper peninsulas of Michigan before departing the next day for Milwaukee.[110] With Gallery's two-star flag flying proudly above the conning tower, *U-505* cleared the Lake Michigan breakwater, entered the Milwaukee River under a host of spouting fireboats, and tied up at the city dock. Mayor Frank Zeidler and a contingent of officials welcomed the boat and Trosino with a large crowd and appropriate speeches. In recognition of the efforts of Milwaukee to raise money in an attempt to bring the U-boat there instead of Chicago, the *U-505* committee had graciously agreed to display the submarine for one week before beginning the final leg of the trip to its new home.[111]

The week in Milwaukee witnessed an extraordinary media event. Sol Polk, a local business leader, arranged to sponsor a one-hour live TV broadcast on WBKB from *inside* the U-boat. The affair was hosted by local "ace" newscasters Spencer Allen and Austin Kiplinger. What made it unique was how the broadcast came about. As explained by a Chicago paper, "[The] Crew will actually dismantle a TV camera, haul it piece by piece through the tiny hatch of the captured U-Boat, and put it together to show you via video what it's like inside." Given the size of TV cameras in 1954, it was indeed a remarkable effort on the part of the TV crew.[112] The smashingly successful Milwaukee visit ended in the very early hours of June 26, 1954, when the U-boat was taken under tow by *Arundel* and headed for Chicago.

The Final Water Leg

Elaborate plans had been made to welcome *U-505* into the Windy City on June 26, 1954. Destroyer escort *Daniel A. Joy* (DE 585) and two sub chasers, USS *PC 845* and USS *PCE 894*, met the U-boat about three miles north of Wilson Avenue beach to escort it on the last 20 miles of the tow. The ships were part of the 9th Naval District, the so-called "Corn Belt Fleet," a small group of six Navy ships operating out of Chicago used to train Navy reservists. The veteran submarine USS *Silversides* was also part of this fleet, but was permanently docked at Navy Pier and unable to diesel out to greet *U-505*. More than 100 yachts made the journey to meet *U-505*, more than making up for *Silversides'* absence. They sailed out to welcome the U-boat and Navy ships north of the city off Grosse Point Lighthouse near Evanston and escort them to the mouth of the Chicago River.

And then tragedy struck. A freak storm hit Chicago on the morning of *U-505's* arrival. A sudden squall hit the shore at 9:32 a.m. Heavy rain lashed the ships and a sudden lightning storm crackled across the dark skies. The water level of the lake rose suddenly from three to ten feet in some areas and a rogue series of waves rolled against the shore. The water surged inland as far as 150 feet in some places. One boat sank at its mooring and debris was scattered everywhere. Tragically, the water swept away more than a dozen people fishing on a pier just south of Montrose harbor. Eight lives were lost that morning. The high water receded almost as quickly as it had splashed ashore. *U-505* and its escorts had no idea the freakish conditions caused so much damage and death, and did not learn of the disastrous events until after their arrival.[114]

U-505 arrived ninety minutes late at Navy Pier. It was 1:00 p.m. From there it was towed to a mooring location to participate in ceremonies. Forty members of the *Guadalcanal* Task Group 22.3, including three sailors from the original *Pillsbury* boarding party, staged a re-enactment of the capture. By this time thousands of people had gathered along the pier, shoreline, and anywhere a few feet of space could be found to witness the historic event. After a proud Admiral Gallery shouted "Boarders Away!" through a bullhorn, three whaleboats full of TG 22.3 veterans were lowered over the side of *Daniel A. Joy*. Once in the water, they made their way to *U-505* as it approached the locks of the Chicago River. When the lead whaleboat lurched against its hull Gallery again shouted, "Boarders Away!" Zenon Lukosius grabbed the ladder and was the first aboard. Lukosius, a member of the original boarding party, had returned the cover to the sea strainer the Germans had opened in their attempt to scuttle the boat. He was followed closely by

Wayne Pickels and Chester Mocarski (who had slipped and been hurt ten years earlier). Admiral Gallery brought up the rear. A drum and bugle corps played as the German battle flag sporting the hated swastika was jerked down and the U.S. Ensign raised high. The Nazi ensign was re-installed below it. The reenactment received a roar of approval from the huge crowd, which included more than 260 hospitalized veterans from area VA hospitals, who had front row wheelchair seats for the show.[115]

After this breathtaking display *U-505* was towed to a spot east of the Michigan Avenue Bridge on the north side of the river. Chicago fireboats *Joseph Medill* and *Fred M. Busse* erupted with their carefully rehearsed salute and a mountain of spray carried by the wind offered spectators and participants an impromptu shower. Thousands along the river banks and lake shore cheered as the U-boat approached a decorated barge (the boarding point for all VIPs) to tie up at the foot of the bridge. Committee member Karl Stockholm and Mayor Kennelly officially hailed the sub as it approached. It was 2:00 p.m.

"What ship is that?" Stockholm playfully shouted through his bullhorn.

Admiral Gallery, standing proudly on the bridge, replied. "Nazi submarine *U-505!*"

"Where from and where bound?" asked Crown.

"From Cape Blanco, French West Africa, bound for Jackson Park. We wish to stop here to get our bearings. This ship was 10 years and 22 days en route, and I'm sorry it had to be an extra hour and a half late!" shouted Gallery. The crowd roared itself hoarse.[116]

Speeches and presentations at 2:30 p.m. marked the official ceremony turning over the boat to Chicago. City Council members and some 250 donors to the *U-505* fund served as official guests. Entertainment was provided by the 35-piece Great Lakes Naval Training Center Recruits Band. Spectators were not allowed to board the U-boat during its brief stay in the river, but the view from the South side of the waterway and bridge on Michigan Avenue was spectacular. With all the clamor and excitement it is likely few recalled this same bridge played host to President Franklin D. Roosevelt on October 5, 1937, when he delivered his famous "quarantine the aggressors" speech. The president had urged the isolation of Japan, Italy, and Germany for their actions in China, Ethiopia, Spain, and Austria. Roosevelt's words foretold the threat posed by boats like *U-505*: "In times of so-called peace ships are being attacked and sunk by submarines without cause or notice." And now *U-505* wallowed gently in the Chicago River within a stone's throw of where Roosevelt had uttered his famous words. Once the initial festivities ended a cocktail party and reception was held at the Chicago Yacht Club for the participants of the capture and the Mayor's *U-505* committee.[117]

To Shore!

U-505 remained tied up at the Michigan Avenue Bridge over the weekend. On Monday it was taken in tow to the dockyards south of the city to be outfitted for the move to the museum. These final preparations were challenging. Press reports claimed the stripped-down boat weighed 840 tons and would be the largest object ever moved from a floating base to shore. Plans for exactly how to accomplish such a feat had been underway for months.

While the U-boat was still in Portsmouth, members of the *U-505* committee discussed how to move the submarine over land from Lake Michigan to the museum, a distance of about 300 yards. Seth Gooder, the civil engineer who had come out of retirement to craft this aspect of the project, pondered two proposals. The first involved using the existing Jackson Park lagoon system south of the museum, which was connected to Lake Michigan. This option was the first one shared openly with the public and was deemed the most desireable for quite some time. The difficulties of this alternative were discovered when Gooder explored the option more deeply. Channels would have to be dredged and the sandstone-supported bridge at the lagoon's entrance (a valued remnant of the 1893 World's Fair and one that still carried automobile traffic) would have to be preserved. Squeezing the large boat beneath the structure provided thorny engineering challenges. More complex issues—such as how to turn the boat 90 degrees so it could begin its overland journey to the museum—would face the engineering team once inside the small lagoon. None of the solutions proposed—including cutting off the conning tower to reduce the height, or rolling the boat on its side to avoid cutting off the tower—were deemed acceptable.

The second option, which initially appeared to be less desirable and more dangerous than the lagoon approach, involved moving *U-505* overland across Lake Shore Drive, which at that time was the only north-south highway through the city and a major regional thoroughfare. Hauling the heavy boat along this route risked destroying the pavement and causing serious traffic headaches. The committee heard many proposals and presentations before finally making up its mind on February 13. *U-505* would be moved across Lake Shore Drive on a barge floated to the 57th Street beach close to the museum. The deciding factor seems to have been the fact that the Lake Shore Drive route was all overland once the boat left the lake. Although it was a longer distance than the lagoon route, it posed essentially only one problem: how to move the boat across land to the museum.

The plan called for *U-505* to be floated in and out of dry-docks in order to prepare the moving gear on its underside, and then float it onto a floating dry-dock for its high and dry journey to the beach. Once there, the U-boat would be winched onto dry land on large rollers, pulled across Lake Shore Drive, and then, finally, eased into position alongside the museum and swung into its final position. Gooder decided the best way to haul *U-505* onto land was to carry it aboard a floating dry-dock to the 57th Street beach adjacent to the museum. There, the boat would be hauled off the dock onto a special pier built for that purpose. The lake end of the pier was constructed on steel sheet pilings extending 50 feet out into the lake from the shoreline and six feet above the surface. Pier construction began in the first week of July and required 25 tons of steel pilings, steel rails, and hundreds of feet of wooden beams. Fitzsimmons Dredge and Dry-Dock Company dredged a channel nine feet deep and 80 feet wide so the floating dry-dock could edge as close as possible to the beach. Obviously the devil was in the details, but by the time everyone was ready the details had been impressively and meticulously planned. The final technical hurdle of installing *U-505* as an exhibit had apparently been resolved—at least on paper.[118]

Once the decision was made Seth Gooder compiled a list of the materials and equipment he would need to accomplish the herculean task. House moving equipment, tractors, steel, wood, jacks, rigging, and other large pieces of equipment were required. The American Shipbuilding Company offered the free use of its Calumet harbor dry-dock for preparing the boat for its final move aboard the floating dry-dock, which was being donated by the Great Lakes Dredge and Dock Company.[119]

U-505 was towed to the American Shipbuilding dry-dock on Monday, June 28. The first job was to remove the more than 30,000 gallons of fuel and lube oil still sloshing about in the boat's forward tanks. The fuel had been left there to raise the stern of the boat to bring the propellers up as much as possible for its journey through the shallow canal systems. After the fuel was pumped out the tanks were steam cleaned to eliminate lingering explosive fumes to allow the welding and structural work to safely proceed.

U-505 was moved again under tow on July 2 to the American Shipbuilding Company docks at 101st and the Calumet River for the structural work. There it was guided through an open gate at one end of the dry-dock, which was then closed and the water pumped out. As the boat settled to the bottom, large wooden graving blocks were positioned along the center keel as pedestals to accept its weight. Wooden beams braced between the boat's hull and walls of the dock prevented the U-boat from tipping over. In an effort to further reduce its weight workmen removed 96 tons of iron ballast from the boat's box keel. This would allow *U-505* to float as high in the water as possible and make it easier to place it onto a floating dry-dock and move it onto the beach.

U-505 was refloated in the main dry-dock and towed out into the river. The floating dry-dock was pushed into the main dry-dock and *U-505* was floated back inside. After a complicated series of maneuvers the water was finally pumped from the main dock, allowing *U-505* to come gently to rest on top of the floating dry-dock.

While *U-505* sat in this dry-dock within a dry-dock, the moving cradle and roller-track system was put into place for its movement onto the beach. Two large H-beams, each 135 feet long, were placed on both sides parallel with the length of the boat and 11 feet apart on center. The beams (known as "shoe beams") would carry slightly less than four tons per linear foot.[120] Holes were cut into the keel center and 14-foot transverse beams were passed through and bolted and welded to the shoe beams. The transverse beams were then cribbed from the top of the beam to the underside of the ballast tanks or outer hull of the boat for maximum support and to distribute the load of the move more evenly. Three large steel cradles were also designed and attached to the rear, center, and forward parts of the box keel. These would serve as the main structural component of the concrete support cradles once the boat was in final position alongside the museum.

Once the beams were secure *U-505* was jacked up and several sets of railroad track placed beneath the long shoe beams. House moving rollers (large round steel bars similar to rolling pins) were inserted between the two sets of rails so the boat could be rolled off the barge and onto the beach. *U-505* would be hauled the same way large houses and other buildings were moved across land. Once these complicated moving structures were in place the floating dry-dock was emptied of much of its water ballast, which lowered it to the bottom of the main dry-dock. The main dry-dock/graving dock gate valves were now opened. As the main dry-dock filled with water the floating dry-dock rose, carrying with it *U-505*.

The U-boat now rode high above the water centered in the floating dry-dock with both ends overhanging the dock (the stern, which would be the first part to reach land, by 65 feet). A gravel barge was secured to each end of the dock to provide, among other things, longitudinal stability during the tow on the open lake. Once near the beach the nearest gravel barge would be removed so *U-505* could be transferred off the dock and directly onto the pier. The fluctuating water level in the lake was of great concern to the engineers—especially after the recent freakish waves that had battered the shore without warning. Any sudden misalignment of the moving rails between the pier and floating dry-dock could spell disaster.

By August 2, *U-505* was judged ready for the transfer to land and its new home outside the museum. The display cradles and steel framework were in place and it was now resting on the steel rollers for the move off the dry-dock. To the dismay of everyone, bad weather blew in and delayed the operation for days. The rough waters shifted the lake's sediment, which in turn forced the Army Corps of Engineers to dredge the channel a second time. Ironically, the forecasts promised cooperative weather conditions for August 13—Friday the 13th!

Friday morning arrived with winds hovering around 10 mph and very little wave action. A relieved Seth Gooder gave the go-ahead to proceed. Although the conditions were still less than ideal, they were deemed acceptable. Many of the companies participating in the project were donating their services and postponing paying business; it would be unfair to delay any longer. By 11:00 a.m., with one tug pushing and the other tug pulling, the long-delayed move to the beach got underway. Spectators by the thousands gathered at bridges along the Calumet River and along the shore of Lake Michigan. *U-505* reached the open lake about 12:15 p.m. and was 100 yards off shore near 57th Street shortly after 2:00 pm. A third tugboat met the submarine to assist in the delicate maneuver to the pier, which began around 3:15 p.m. Ashore, meanwhile, 50 engineers and workmen busied themselves with all manner of tasks to ensure the difficult transition onto land went as smoothly as possible.

The tugs made several attempts to push the dock into place, but choppy waves made the effort difficult. After several attempts a decision was made to tie off one corner of the dock and allow the other end to swing into the desired position. As this was being accomplished the genius of Seth Gooder and those who had worked so hard for so long to master the unique and difficult task became evident in a most tangible way. *U-505* could be off-loaded *only* if the rails on the dry-dock and the pier matched. What many spectators failed to realize was that the depth of the lake, height of the pier, wind, dry-dock trim—and a myriad of other factors—had to be taken into consideration. Because of the possible variation in the water level on the day of the actual move, Gooder factored in a margin of error for the transfer. He had estimated that once the dock was aligned with the pier, the bottom of the track on the dock would hover above the top of the pier platform by 4 7/8 inches. How precise was his advance planning? When the dock was finally maneuvered into position, the distance was exactly five inches—a difference of only 1/8 of an inch! Water ballast was increased to lower the rails on the dock into perfect alignment with the rails on the pier. Landing operations were now ready to begin.

The off-loading of the U-boat from the floating dry-dock to the pier offered a mathematical nightmare that had required weeks of calculations and revisions to solve. The issue was how much ballast water would have to be added to the dry-dock to compensate for the loss of weight as the submarine moved onto the pier and shore. It was finally calculated that 27 tons of water would have to be taken into the dry-dock ballast tanks as every four feet of submarine slid off the dock. Because of the tremendous weight involved, a miscalculation would upend the structure and tip *U-505* into Lake Michigan. Several hours of white-knuckle tension followed.

It was nearly 7:00 p.m. when the U-boat was ready to be pulled onto the beach. Six returns of steel cable were run through six compound pulleys attached to the end of the moving cradle and a winch at the end of an International Harvester Company heavy tractor located on the beach. When the winching process began, *U-505* creaked and moaned as if once again diving deep beneath the sea. As it slid forward, the steel rollers under the shoe beams came free in the rear and were brought ahead of the shoe beams patch enabling the lumbering journey to continue without interruption. By 9:00 p.m. the critical halfway point was reached. A few minutes more and the boat's center of gravity forever passed from water to land.[121] Within another hour *U-505* was welcomed ashore by the hearty crowd, which had remained to watch the magnificent engineering feat unfold.

The German U-boat spent the next two and one-half weeks on the edge of Lake Michigan waiting on its handlers for the final move to the museum. The beached submarine offered a surreal backdrop for beach lovers and the regular crowds of curious people who marveled at the large size of the boat. Now toothless and landlocked, the once-feared shark of the seas was about to assume a new role its builders could never have envisioned. The forward half of the boat remained on the pier over the water while the rear half occupied that portion of the pier constructed over the beach. The stern was but a single foot away from the sidewalk running along Lake Shore Drive. Extra police officers were assigned to the area to protect the pedestrians and motorists who paid more attention to the submarine than their own surroundings.

The last major obstacle was crossing Lake Shore Drive. The busy route was the main highway through Chicago in 1954 (the interstate system located farther west did not arrive until two years later). Closing it for any length of time—especially during rush hour—would cause serious headaches for the city and those who relied on it for moving goods and services in the area. Planners estimated it would take three hours for the boat to cross the busy thoroughfare and another three hours to remove the rail system and clear the road for traffic. The city wisely gave the museum a twelve-hour window (from 7:00 p.m. until 7:00 a.m.) to accomplish the task.

The boat was now on the beach but below the surface of Lake Shore Drive. Forty-two 50-ton Buda hydraulic jacks were brought in to lift *U-505* chest-high to prepare for the crossing. The delicate hoisting process took several days to accomplish. Meanwhile, other workmen moved heavy wooden beams and rails to the west side of Lake Shore Drive to construct the platform on which the boat would be transferred after crossing the busy street. Everything was finally ready at 7:00 p.m. on Thursday, September 2. Traffic was rerouted around the west side of the museum and workmen began the backbreaking task of laying wooden timbers and steel track in front of the boat for crossing. The track pieces had to be bolted and welded together to form the strongest connection possible. By 10:28 p.m. everything was ready and the boat began sliding across the road. The 312-foot move took place on 638 steel rollers at the rate of 57 feet per hour. The endeavor offered a grand sight for those fortunate enough to be on hand to witness it: a mammoth U-boat crossing a busy Chicago street in the heartland of its former foe, illuminated by two Chicago Fire Department trucks while some 15,000 people looked on in breathless awe. The sloth-like progress and late hour eventually took its toll and the crowd eventually dwindled to several hundred by the time *U-505* finished the Lake Shore crossing.

Gallery, Lohr, Gooder, Robert Crown, Carl Stockholm and other dignitaries were on hand for the action, posing for photographs throughout the night, especially once the center of U-505 reached the center of Lake Shore Drive. The media-savvy Gallery had a gag ready for the occasion. Signs reading "Drive Carefully, Submarine Crossing," had been installed for the event and *Time Magazine* was on hand to cover the story as the signs were being erected along Lake Shore Drive. The "warnings" offered yet another photo opportunity as the boat inched its way across. The passage was completed at 4:15 a.m., leaving the workmen more than enough time to remove the track and allow the road to resume carrying the traffic it was intended to serve.

With thousands of miles and nearly insurmountable logistical, engineering, and political problems behind it, *U-505* had a mere 375 feet left to traverse in order to reach the museum. The boat would now be guided from the beach to the museum in a southwesterly direction, stern first. Workers placed more timbers and rail to prepare for the move. On September 9 the boat continued the fitful journey until its stern was almost exactly where museum officials envisioned its final position. Using the center of the boat as a pivot point, the bow was swung in a 67-degree arc to bring the boat into a north-south orientation alongside the building and eased over its final position. The only thing left to do was to lower *U-505* by reverse jacking onto the concrete foundation, special display cradles, and pedestals designed to hold it. Nothing having to do with *U-505*, however, was ever simple. A concrete foundation 36" wide and 18" deep had been poured to match *U-505's* flat-bottomed box keel. Only the center cradle for *U-505*, which had been designed to carry 1/3 of the boat's weight, was intended as a fixed mounting point. The bow and stern ends of the keel would be installed on a pair of large rollers to allow for the expansion and contraction of the steel hull during Chicago's hot and cold seasons. If the expansion and contraction had not been accounted for, explained the engineers, the movement of the boat would crack the concrete cradles. The solution was the installation of 20 steel rollers, each eight inches in diameter, on each end of the keel. These, in turn, were placed on top of a steel track resting on top of the concrete foundation. The bottom of the keel in these locations was cut away so the rollers could be recessed into the keel-box and hidden from view. Smaller stabilizing brackets were also affixed in four higher locations to the outer keel to keep the boat from tipping to either side. The rollers at each end and the very center of *U-505's* box keel were the only areas of the boat actually taking its full weight. One can only wonder how this engineering issue would have been solved if an earlier plan to cut away the entire box keel (as a means of lowering the boat to make it easier for visitors to enter and exit via covered walkways) had gone forward.

U-505's remarkable journey—beginning with its birth at Hamburg's *Deutsche Werft* shipyard along the Elbe River in 1940 and continuing through its patrols to and from the hunting grounds of the Atlantic and Carribean, its discovery, attack, capture, American war-bond tour, long sojourn at the Portsmouth Naval Yard in New Hampshire, and difficult final trip inland—had reached an end.

Dedication

Time was now running short. The boat's committee had announced that formal dedication ceremonies would be held September 25. The elaborate plans for the event had been underway for most of the year. It was not until Sunday, September 19, that workers began sandblasting *U-505's* exterior to prepare the proud old boat for a new coat of paint. The old boat could be made to look good on the outside for its unveiling, but its interior—which was to have been open for guests at the ceremony—was not going to be ready. Indeed, there was barely time to erect the raised platform for the dedication ceremonies and install the seating for the VIP guests invited to witness the event.

A pair of tunnels had been built prior to the boat's arrival to connect *U-505* to the east side ground floor of the museum to provide visitor access. Now that the boat was in place, doorways had to be cut into the outer and pressure hulls. Engineers and museum staff decided the best place for the entrance would be through the # 2 port dive bunker, and the exit through the #7 port dive bunker.[122]

A special preview dinner banquet with 500 VIPs was scheduled for Thursday night, September 24, to celebrate *U-505's* successful arrival at the museum. Entertainer Arthur Godfrey served as Master of Ceremonies for the dinner and the memorial service that followed. The keynote speaker, Secretary of the Navy Charles Thomas, had a special connection to the event: his son Hayward was aboard *Guadalcanal* when *U-505* was captured. Admiral Gallery was also on hand to give a speech. The entire boarding party from USS *Pillsbury* (except for Lt. Albert L. David, who had passed away in 1945) had been located and invited to attend as guests of honor. Earl Trosino was given the honor of unveiling a large bronze plaque at the dedication ceremony the following day.[123]

The veterans of the capture of *U-505* were arriving in Chicago for the dedication when local media discovered many of their wives had little or no idea of the historical role they had played during the war. Anne Mocarski learned about her husband's participation only after Gallery visited Cleveland for a fundraiser in 1954 and asked her husband to attend. Until then, she had never heard of *U-505*. Norma Hohne did not learn about her husband's exploits until November 1953, when Gallery sent a letter asking Gordon Hohne to complete a questionnaire and send a photograph. "I thought he was being called back into the Navy," she laughed. Gloria Trusheim learned of the capture when she overheard her husband Phillip telling a friend about it. Margaret Wdowiak stumbled across her husband's role by reading magazine accounts of the capture.[124]

The Thursday night banquet was advertised for 500 guests, but media reported 600-800 in attendance.[125] Everyone enjoyed the event. Secretary Thomas extolled the virtues of a strong military (especially the navy) and credited the captors of *U-505* for their forward thinking and planning. "If the Navy today can match the bravery and ingenuity of the

U-505 captors," he concluded, "I am confident our sea-power will remain superior and our country will remain safe."[126] In a move that surprised everyone save Gallery, who had arranged the special event, Secretary Thomas awarded the Distinguished Public Service Award—the Navy's highest civilian honor—to six members of the citizen's committee responsible for bringing U-505 to Chicago. The prestigious and rarely awarded medal, "is awarded to citizens not employed by the U.S. Navy for heroic acts and significant contributions which help accomplish the Navy's mission." Gallery had arranged for Thomas to do it that night because, "it would be much more satisfactory to all concerned, including the Secretary, and much more effective, if the Secretary could present the people concerned with concrete evidence of the Navy's gratitude, rather than just make a speech about it."[127]

The weather also cooperated when September's last Saturday dawned clear and beautiful. The museum and Chicago Park District expected 20,000 people to be on hand for the ceremonies, but to their surprise 40,000 showed up—packed into every square foot of space they could elbow their way into. The Blue Jackets choir from Pensacola Naval Station entertained the crowd, as did the Great Lakes Naval Training Band. An honor guard of 30 Marines enjoyed the music in stoic silence.

A thunderous flyover by Navy jets kicked off the ceremony at 1:49 p.m. William Kahler, the president of Illinois Bell Telephone, arranged for the telephone company to sponsor live television coverage of one hour of the ceremonies beginning at 2:30 p.m. on local WBBM-TV. The show was carried by the entire CBS television network across the country. Master of Ceremonies Arthur Godfrey guided the event to perfection, reading aloud a letter of greeting from President Eisenhower:

> I am delighted to learn that the Nazi submarine captured on the high seas . . . is to have a home in the Museum of Science and Industry in Chicago," wrote the president. "There it will be a permanent memorial to the tactical skill and gallantry of the men of the Navy. The story of this trophy's capture, as told to me, is a stirring one indeed. It is a saga of initiative, skill and daring. . . . I am certain that this memorial will afford pleasure to all who view it; it will serve as an expression to our sailors of their nation's gratitude.

Godfrey introduced the day's keynote speaker, Admiral William "Bull" Halsey, who was piped aboard the platform. Everyone stood at attention while the *Daniel A. Joy*, anchored off the 57th Street beach, fired a 17-gun salute in his honor. Godfrey recounted the story of the capture, the secrets of the code books and acoustic torpedoes, and how 3,000 men had kept all of this secret. Admiral Gallery also spoke briefly, introducing each member of the boarding party and Earl Trosino, who perhaps was more responsible than anyone for saving the boat. "This is a great day for all of us who took part in the capture of *U-505*," began Gallery. "That day ten years ago when we were struggling to keep this craft afloat . . . is a day none of us will forget. But not even in our wildest dreams could we then foresee the great climax to this ceremony today. We who captured this ship are indeed proud of what you here in Chicago have done with it. . . . It was made possible by the generosity and efforts of many citizens whose only motives were patriotism and the feeling that this memorial is important to future generations."

And then Halsey stood and spoke. "*U-505*," declared the man who had gallantly led American naval forces at Guadalcanal and elsewhere in the Pacific, represented a "tombstone of all Navy men, merchant sailors, and civilians who have gone down to unmarked graves in the sea. . . . It is particularly fitting that this, one of the few Naval memorials in the country, be placed here in Chicago. Almost one-third of naval personnel in World War II came from the great Midwest and the 9th Naval District with headquarters at Great Lakes." The memorial, he continued, will serve to show the Communists that "their challenge for control of the high seas is doomed to failure." He finished to thunderous applause.

The afternoon neared its end when Bishop Weldon, *Guadalcanal*'s former Chaplain, rose to offer a prayer to the Navy's war dead. The last event was left to Earl Trosino, who was given the honor of offering up for posterity the bronze memorial plaque and its image of the capture. National pride could not have been elevated any higher by the time Trosino stepped forward and unveiled the impressive sculpture, which was temporarily mounted to the hand rail on the starboard side deck in the middle of *U-505*. The choir sang the Navy Hymn. The Marine honor guard fired a volley. The striking contrast between the sharp crack of the rifles and what followed—"Taps," played by a solitary Navy bugler standing at attention on the boat's conning tower—tightened throats and brought tears to the eyes of nearly everyone present. The bugler's final note hung for a moment on the autumn air and then faded away.[128] The ceremony heralding the arrival of *U-505* in Chicago was over.

U-505 *as an Exhibit*

Despite not being fully prepared for an eager visiting public, *U-505* opened on Sunday, September 26, 1954. By the end of the first week 7,125 people had paid a quarter each to see the submarine. Thirteen-year-old Sharon Henriksen of Park Ridge, Illinois, became the 1,000,000th visitor in November 1956. As of this writing *U-505* has welcomed more than 23,000,000 visitors. It is by far the museum's most popular exhibit. The boat serves both as a fitting war memorial and a technological wonder—the complexity of construction and mass of valves, wheels, levers, equipment, and crew quarters, all stuffed inside a narrow pressure hull, invariably leaves a lasting impression. Many visitors find it difficult to fully comprehend what their eyes tell them is so. "Is this a real submarine?" many inquire, believing instead the museum had built some kind of elaborate stage set for their benefit. Questions run the gamut one would expect, from how many men served aboard the boat to what they ate, whether they showered, and how they learned to safely operate what appeared to be a very complex piece of machinery.

When visitors see so much gear crammed inside the boat they have a hard time imagining how much of it was actually missing when the submarine arrived in Chicago. Unfortunately, *U-505* was stripped of some of its gear and spare parts as early as 1946, when these items were sorely needed by the French Navy to operate its own confiscated German U-boats. The extent of what was parceled out is still not clear. Thankfully, Lenox Lohr worked hard to return as much of the original equipment (or at least genuine parts) as possible. The most impressive success centers around the boat's two diesel engines. Thanks to the help of volunteers from General Motors' Electro-Motive division, they were placed in running condition by 1956. Lohr had them fired up again in 1968, and the author returned the starboard diesel to operation in 1994; it was last run in 1998. A sound recording of the thumping engines accompanies visitors as they walk through the boat.

The ongoing restoration of *U-505* has been difficult, rewarding, and expensive. In 1953, museum teams discovered the radio and underwater listening equipment were missing. Indeed, the radio and sound rooms had been stripped bare. Even the countertop in these small rooms had been removed, as had the three document safes from the radio room, captain's bunk, and officers' room, which once housed the boat's secret code books. Every bunk frame in the berthing spaces had been removed from their hangers and piled hither and yon. Whether the correct bunks for each room were on board when the boat arrived is unknown. Not even the battery spaces, located beneath the deck plates, had been spared. The tons of heavy batteries had been removed to reduce the weight (and thus draft) of the boat for the towing operation, but the space attracted bits and pieces of equipment pulled from elsewhere in the boat. The main ventilator motors from the Diesel Engine compartment, for example, were found two compartments away in the battery well beneath the Officers Quarters.

The museum immediately pressed the Navy to return any of *U-505's* original parts and equipment—or similar items from other boats if the originals could not be located. A most fortunate stroke of luck occurred shortly after the U-boat was opened when Carl T. Milner toured the craft and sought out museum officials. An electronics junkie, Milner worked with the Naval Underwater Sound Lab at the Portsmouth Naval base. When *U-505's* radio and sound equipment was stripped and sent to the dumpster after the war, Milner intervened. Unable to bear the thought of trashing the equipment, he shuttled most of it into his basement! He offered to return to the museum whatever he still had and even paid the cost of crating and shipping. The returned gear was immediately reinstalled. Unfortunately, Milner did not possess everything that had been removed, so the museum identified what it had and distributed it between the two rooms. In the mid 1990s, a detailed inventory of both rooms was discovered when many classified documents relating to the U-boat war were released to the public. Hopefully, these will allow the museum to obtain the original items and one day return the rooms to their original configuration.

Just how good was German optical equipment? Intelligence officials wanted to find out, so both of the boat's periscopes were removed shortly after the end of the war. Most of this sort of equipment was sent to private industry, whose labs were better suited to carry out investigations and often received authorization to test to destruction. The museum was under the impression this had been done with *U-505's* periscopes, so a British navigation scope was obtained and installed on the boat after it arrived in Chicago. A stainless steel tube was erected to simulate the attack periscope. Both were depicted in fully extended positions so visitors could see the equipment most people closely associate with submarines.[129] However, lightning struck twice when the U-boat was reunited with its original aerial periscope in 2002. The precious piece of optical equipment was returned from a once-secret naval laboratory in San Diego, where it was about to be demolished. Records as to the whereabouts of the pilfered periscopes disappeared and for decades no one knew what had happened to them. As was recently discovered, one ended up in San Diego, installed at the bottom of a giant cold water tank for experiments with submarine technology and materials suitable for submarine warfare beneath the polar ice caps. The author had long sought the originals but would have settled for an authentic (and difficult to come by) German periscope. When officials in San Diego realized what they had they contacted the museum to determine whether the institution was interested in its acquisition. The periscope will not be re-installed in the boat, however, because the low roof in its new home will make it impossible for visitors to see the scope. The periscope will instead be exhibited horizontally alongside the boat as a separate technical exhibit. The museum is still looking for the attack periscope. Hopefully one day it, too, will be found and returned to *U-505*.

   U-505's guns, which had been removed for evaluation in Bermuda, were reunited with the boat at an unknown date. Except for one barrel, the twin 2cm anti-aircraft guns and mounts are original to the boat. The replacement barrel came from *U-858*, a type IXC/40 and the first German U-boat to surrender to the US Navy on May 8, 1945. Ironically, its skipper was Thilo Bode, *U-505's* former *I.W.O.* Bode surrendered to a hunter-killer group off the American East Coast that included four of the five destroyer escorts present during the capture of *U-505*. The destroyer that accepted Bode's capitulation was USS *Pillsbury*, whose boarding party had so valiantly captured *U-505* only 11 months earlier.[130]

U-505's Future

   Structurally speaking, the boat arrived in good condition, if a bit shabby looking. Extensive corrosion damage (as noted earlier in the article) was present, but for the most part major structural components were intact. Many of the compartments were coated with surface rust and many painted areas were chipped and peeling. The Navy had repainted

(Top) The Officers Quarters on *U-505* on the afternoon of June 4, 1944. The small photo on the wall is the destroyer *T-25*. (Bottom) *U-505's* rear torpedo room looks crammed even after 80 days at sea. A spare torpedo is under the starboard bunks and spare parts containers clog the central aisle. The emergency steering control in the center rear of the room was activated by Captain Gallery, and Earl Trosino used it to straighten the boat's rudders.

Museum of Science and Industry, Chicago

This photograph was taken during one of the annual *U-505* members-only events. From left to right: Wayne Pickels (*Pillsbury* boarding party), Keith R. Gill (*U-505* curator), Pete Petersen (*U-518*), Zenon Lukosius (*Pillsbury* boarding party), and historian Timothy Mulligan.

Museum of Science and Industry, Chicago

Former members of the USS *Guadalcanal* Task Group and *U-505* came together for a reunion in 1982. German crewmen are seated in front. Hans Goebeler (with cane) on the far left. Earl Trosino, *Guadalcanal's* engineer who led the salvage team, is visible over Goebeler's right shoulder. This was the German crew's first formal visit to *U-505* since its capture in June 1944.

the vessel black on the outside and white on the inside, without making any attempt to match the boat's original color scheme (which was a two-tone gray exterior and ivory interior). Thankfully, the original *Kriegsmarine* interior colors survived intact beneath several coats of American white paint, which helped the museum significantly in recent restoration efforts. The original paint scheme has been restored to the interior of the submarine, and extensive research helped return the exterior to its original color scheme. Expertise in restoring the boat has been received from many of *U-505's* former crewmen, some of whom emigrated to the United States after the war.

Since its arrival at the museum *U-505* has undergone four restorations: 1954, 1968, 1978, and 1988-1989. Each time the boat was sandblasted to metal, damaged or rusted shell plating was cut out and patched in or doubled over, and a new coat of fresh paint applied. Unfortunately, each restoration required that bits and pieces of the original boat be cut or sandblasted away. Corrosion has been taking its toll on the outer hull plating and complex mechanical equipment located under the main deck. The periodic sandblasting provides a clean and easy-to-paint surface, but removes and thins the metal. The pace of deterioration has been as unrelenting as Chicago's weather.

When tests in the 1990s conclusively demonstrated that *U-505's* outer hull had thinned dramatically during its many decades of outdoor display, it became obvious that something had to be done to preserve the boat for future generations. The successful construction of a massive underground structure to display and protect the 1934 Pioneer Zephyr, the train that had been outdoors alongside *U-505* for 30 years, persuaded museum officials do consider doing the same thing for *U-505*.

Plans were formulated to move the boat to a new location underground on the North side of the East Pavilion, with a roof installed overhead and special exhibits around the boat to tell the story of its heroic capture in June 1944. The controlled atmosphere of the new exhibit will be maintained at 45% Rh and 70 degrees Fahrenheit and greatly reduce environmental damage to the boat while allowing caretakers to maintain *U-505* in its current state in perpetuity. Visitors will be able to observe *U-505's* deck from a balcony, walk around the outside and touch the boat, and participate in many interesting smaller interactive exhibits. Over the past 15 years a determined effort has been made to collect artifacts related to *U-505*. Many of these items—including medals awarded to the Navy personnel and more than 50 artifacts removed as souvenirs—will appear on exhibit for the first time when the new display opens in 2005. At $23,500,000, this new exhibit is the largest and most expensive ever undertaken by the museum.

Other efforts have been made to preserve the boat's history. In 1999, the author and Laura Graedel, a museum archivist, organized an intensive oral history project. More than 100 hours of filmed interviews have now been preserved with surviving American and German veterans who played important roles during the June 1944 capture of the boat. Many members of the crew arrived for a reunion at the boat and took part in the oral history project. Some met for the first time the Americans they had faced in 1944. One of the surviving crewmen from the *Thomas McKean*, which had been sunk by *U-505* more than four decades earlier, attended the 1999 reunion. He, too, met his former enemies for the first time.

To many people *U-505* was an "unlucky" boat. It is hard to agree with that assessment. The U-boat did have the misfortune of several aborted war patrols due to mechanical failures and witnessed the dramatic suicide of one of its captains at sea. But *U-505* survived the bombing attack of November 1942 that would have been fatal to many other boats, sank more than its share of Allied shipping, and every man but one aboard the boat survived June 4, 1944. Considering how many U-boats and crews were lost during the war, leaving on patrol in 1944 and living to tell the tale can hardly be considered an unlucky fate.

The meaning of *U-505* as a memorial has evolved over time. World War II grows more distant by the day. As we lose participants from that era, so too will we lose all direct continuity with that watershed historical event. *U-505* served first as a memorial for the World War II generation established *by* the World War II generation. Yet, even as the memorial was being dedicated a new interpretive framework, the Cold War Communist threat, was employed to alter the symbolism and meaning the veterans attributed to the submarine. The Cold War generation utilized the threat once posed by *U-505* as a clarion call for preparedness against the Soviet Union, whose "challenge for control of the high seas," Admiral Halsey so eloquently noted, was "doomed to failure."

Subsequent generations will look upon, study, and apply their own meaning to *U-505*. As such, the boat will transcend the purpose for which it was built and for which it was saved.

Appendix A

Type IXC U-Boats: Technical Data

(compiled by Eric C. Rust)

Total number built: 54

Designations: *U-66* through *68*; *U-125* through *131*; *U-153* through *166*; *U-171* through *176*; and *U-501* through *524*.

First boat commissioned: *U-66* (January 2, 1941)

Last boat commissioned: *U-524* (July 8, 1942)

Constructed at:

Deschimag Weser, Bremen (*U-66* through *68*; *U-125* through *131*; *U-153* through *160*; and *U-171* through *176*);
Seebeckwerft, Geestemünde (*U-161* through *166*);
Deutsche Werft, Hamburg (*U-501* through *524*)

Displacement:

Surfaced: 1,120 tons
Submerged: 1,232 tons

Hull Dimensions (overall):

Length: 76.76 m (251.83 ft.)
Beam: 6.76 m (22.18 ft.)
Draft: 4.67 m (15.32 ft.)

Pressure Hull:

Length: 57.75 m (189.47 ft.)
Diameter: 4.40 m (14.44 ft.)
Thickness (plates): 18.5 mm (.73 inches)

Diving Characteristics:

Diving depth, safe: 100 meters (328 feet)
Diving depth, tested: 165 meters (541 feet)
Maximum depth, theoretical: 250 meters (820 feet)
Fastest dive: 35 seconds

Engines:

2 MAN 9 cylinder four-stroke diesels, producing up to 2,500 HP
2 SSW electric motors fed by 164 (2 x 62) battery cells, generating
    740 W at 11,300 Ah (based on discharge over 20 hours);
    producing up to 562 HP
Battery weight: 74.90 metric tons

Maximum Speed:

Surface: 19.25 knots
Submerged: 7.46 knots

Maximum Range:

Surface: 13,450 nautical miles at 10 knots
5,000 nautical miles at 18.3 knots
Submerged: 63 nautical miles at 4 knots
128 nautical miles at 2 knots

Fuel Storage Capacity:

Inside pressure hull: 64.35 metric tons
Including diving tanks: 152.42 metric tons
Including diving and trimming tanks: 207.51 metric tons

Weight:

Hull without ballast: 404.78 metric tons
Engines: 291.31 metric tons
Water, lubricating oil, etc.: 10.15 metric tons
Weaponry: 168.30 metric tons
Miscellaneous: 2.00 metric tons
Weight without ballast: 876.54 metric tons
Effective ballast: 78.33 metric tons
Weight (normal load): 958.33 metric tons
Weight (maximum load): 1081.45 metric tons

Weaponry:

Torpedo tubes: 6 (4 in bow compartment, 2 aft), 21-inch diameter
Torpedoes carried: 22
Deck gun: One 10.5cm (4.1 inch) L/45 (removed after 1943)
Anti-aircraft artillery: One 3.7cm, one (after 1943 up to four) 2cm

Complement:

Standard: 48; Officers: 4; Petty officers: 15; Ratings: 29

After 1943, up to 12 additional crew were utilized to man anti-aircraft artillery.

U-505 Combat Chronology

(compiled by Timothy Mulligan)

Abbreviations:

GRT = gross registered tons, the weight of a merchant ship without regard for cargo
I.W.O. = *Erster Wach-Offizier*, First Watch Officer
II.W.O. = *Zweiter Wach-Offizier*, Second Watch Officer

September 25, 1939: German Navy contracts with Deutsche Werft AG Hamburg-Finkenwerder for the construction of five Type IXC U-boats; Construction No. 295 will become *U-505*.

June 12, 1940: Keel laid.

May 24, 1941: Submarine launched.

August 26, 1941: Commissioned into service as *U-505* under *Kaptlt.* Axel-Olaf Loewe.

August 27, 1941-19 January 1942: Training and shakedown cruises in the Baltic.

August 31-October 3, 1941: Acceptance and silent running trials in Kiel, off Bornholm, and in Danzig Bay.

October 4-15, 1941: Operational training off Danzig and Hela.

October 16-November 10, 1941: Torpedo-firing, artillery, and depth-charge exercises with the 25th U-boat Flotilla, Danzig.

November 11-22, 1941: Tactical training in the Baltic with the 27th U-boat Flotilla.

November 27, 1941-8 January 1942: Tied up in Hamburg.

January 12-15, 1942: Outfitting for operations in Stettin.

January 17-19, 1942: Final preparations for departure in Kiel.

January 19-February 3, 1942: Transfer passage from Kiel to Lorient.

First operational cruise; No encounters with enemy forces; total distance traveled = 2,562 nautical miles, of which 2,371 surfaced [92.5%], 191 submerged [7.5%].

February 6: Admiral Karl Dönitz personally inspects *U-505*.

February 11-May 7, 1942: Combat patrol off Freetown and West Africa (second operational cruise).

March 1-April 21: in operations area.

March 5: Sinks British steamer *Benmohr* (5,920 GRT) at 06.05 N/14.15 W with four torpedoes (two hits); crew recovered by British aircraft.

March 6: Sinks Norwegian tanker *Sydhav* (7,587 GRT) at 04.47 N/14.57 W with two torpedoes (both hits); survivors brought to Freetown.

March 16: Unsuccessful attack on unidentified vessel, two torpedoes miss.

March 29: Boat experiences first depth-charge attack.

March 31: Boat crosses the Equator.

April 2-3: Pursues and torpedoes American cargo vessel *West Irmo* (5,775 GRT), bound from New York to Lagos with 4,000 tons of general cargo; the ship sinks 4 April at 02.10 N/ 05.52. W; five torpedoes fired (two hits); all 44 crewmen and Navy gunners survive, but 10 of 65 African longshoremen on board are killed.

April 4: Sinks Dutch merchantman *Alphacca* (5,759 GRT) at 01.50 N/07.40 W with one torpedo hit; no apparent casualties among crew.

April 6: Error during emergency dive leaves bridge and stern exposed above water for five minutes, but *U-505* eludes detection.

May 7, 1942: *U-505* returns to Lorient, completing 86-day patrol.

Total distance traveled = 13,253 nautical miles (12,937 surfaced [97.6%], 316 submerged [2.4%].

May 7-June 6, 1942: Docked at Lorient for repairs and refitting; crew leave.

June 7-August 25, 1942: Third operational cruise, combat patrol in the Caribbean.

June 30-August 1: In operations area (a defective compass affected navigation throughout the patrol).

June 28: *U-505* encounters and sinks US freighter *Sea Thrush* (5,447 GRT), bound from Philadelphia to Capetown via Trinidad with a cargo of Army supplies at 22.40 N/ 61.10 W, three torpedoes fired, two hits; all 41 crewmen, 14 US Army passengers and 11 Naval Armed Guard personnel survived.

June 29: *U-505* encounters and sinks American Liberty ship *Thomas McKean* (7,191 GRT) en route from New York to the Persian Gulf with a cargo of planes, tanks and war supplies for Russia at 22.00 N/ 60.00 W; two torpedoes fired, one hit plus 72 rounds of 10.5cm artillery; 38 crewmen and 13 Naval Armed Guard personnel survived, three of the latter and one crewman were killed or died of wounds.

July 22: Encounters Columbian schooner *Roamar,* recently renamed *Urios* (110 GRT), which tries to flee despite several warning shots and is sunk by 22 rounds of 10.5cm gunfire at 12.24 N/ 81.28 W, 12 miles from Callo Bolivar; all 23 Colombian crew and passengers (including four women) lost; thereafter many *U-505* crewmen attribute the submarine's subsequent bad luck to this incident, although it is not the cause of Colombia's eventual declaration of "belligerency" against Germany in November 1943.

July 31: Loewe's worsening illness (appendicitis) leads him to request permission to break off the patrol and return home.

August 8: Rendezvous with *milchkuh U-463* to receive fuel.

August 20: Chance encounter with outbound *U-214*, to whom *U-505* transfers surplus supply of tea.

August 25: Return to Lorient, completing a 79-day patrol.

Total distance traveled = 13,340 nautical miles (12,842 surfaced [96.3%], 498 submerged [3.7%].

August 25-October 3, 1942: docked at Lorient for repairs and refitting.

September 15: Loewe transfers command to *Oblt.z.S.* Peter Zschech.

October 4-December 12, 1942: Fourth operational patrol, again to the Caribbean.

October 22: Rendezvous with homeward-bound *U-514* to transfer *Kaptlt. (I)* Förster, who returns to Lorient after briefly supervising the new chief engineer, *Oblt. (I)* Josef Hauser.

November 1: Arrives in operational area off Trinidad.

November 6-7: Attacks and sinks British freighter *Ocean Justice* (7,173 GRT) bound from Durban to Trinidad with 600 tons of manganese ore at 10.06 N / 60.00 W; four torpedoes fired, two hits at long range (2000 meters); all 54 crewmen, including nine British naval and military gunners, survive.*

November 7: Unsuccessful attack on unidentified freighter (two torpedo misses).

November 9-10: Problems noted with radar-detection gear.

November 10: *U-505* surprised on the surface SE of Trinidad by British Hudson aircraft (RAF 53 Squadron) piloted by Australian F/Sgt. R. R. Sillcock, who since August has already damaged *U-155* and *U-173* with his attacks; Sillcock releases four depth-charges, one of which scores a direct hit near the aft 3.7cm deck gun; damage includes a puncture in the pressure hull, the loss of the port diesel engine, and leaks in the outer fuel tanks on the port side, as well as the severe wounding of *II.W.O.* Stolzenberg and another crewman; the force of the explosion also destroys the attacking Hudson, killing Sillcock and his four crewmen.

* Because of the differences in maintaining time, *U-505* recorded her attack on *Ocean Justice* in the early hours of November 7 (Berlin time); the crew of her victim placed the time of the sinking during the evening of November 6 (local time).

November 11: Effected repairs allow *U-505* a limited diving capability; return voyage begins.

November 22: Rendezvous with *milchkuh U-462* (*U-68* and *U-332* also present), during which *U-505* receives oil, fresh provisions, and spare parts; *Lt.z.S.* Stolzenburg is transferred to *U-462* for medical treatment and return to Germany, *Lt.z.S.d.R.* Knoke comes aboard as a replacement for the remainder of the patrol; some welding repairs to the hull and bridge of *U-505* are also completed.

November 24: Abortive pursuit and attack on an unidentified Allied merchantman; six torpedoes fired without effect.

November 30: Rendezvous with *milchkuh U-461* for radar detector equipment replacements and medical supplies.

December 12: Return to Lorient, completing a shortened 69-day patrol.

Total distance traveled = 10,876 nautical miles (10,250 surfaced [94.2%], 626 submerged [5.8%]

December 13, 1942-June 30, 1943: *U-505* laid up in Lorient for major repairs and reconstruction of bridge platform to accommodate new anti-aircraft battery.

January 14, 1943: Heavy Allied air raids devastate Lorient, U-boat crews transfer residence to "Lager Lemp" outside the city.

February 10-26, 1943: Entire crew on leave to *U-505* sponsor city Schliersee (Bavaria) and to U-boat recreation facility in Wiessee.

July 1, 1943: Departs Lorient but develops leak on first test dive, returns for repairs July 2.

July 3-13: Departs on patrol, but problems encountered with radar detection gear and hydrophones, later with radio; while transiting Bay of Biscay *U-505* surprised and depth-bombed by aircraft on July 8, followed by depth-charging by Allied warships; though not seriously damaged; a significant oil leak convinces Zschech to return to Lorient.

July 14-31: In port for repairs; investigation reveals complete corrosion of the rubber gaskets on the ballast tanks' ventilation and emergency vent valves, and corrosion of the two new batteries installed.

August 1-2: *U-505* departs again, but unidentifiable cracking noises in the hull during practice dives prompts a return to port.

August 3-13: In port for examination, problem not identified.

August 14-15: Departs again, on first deep practice dive cracking noises return and a tear develops in the air-intake mast, forcing return to base.

August 16-20: In port for repairs.

August 21-22: Departs again, but oil leak causes return to port.

August 23-September 17: In port for repairs, problem again identified as corroded rubber seals to vents on the ballast tanks; new radar detector gear ("Wanze G2," also called "Hagenuk") received. (Note: several sources attribute most of these problems to sabotage by French dockyard workers, several of whom were reportedly tried and shot; the *U-505* war diary contains no information on this subject).

September 18-30: Aborted patrol; on September 19 the starboard exhaust valve proved not watertight, personally inspected and repaired by a visit of the 10th Flotilla Chief Engineer; on September 23 *U-505* crash-dived to elude an aircraft, after which the starboard electrical motor and the main ballast pump fell out of action; the motor was repaired but the pump could not be, compelling another return to Lorient.

During the aborted missions of July 1-September 30, U-505 traveled a total of 3,293 nautical miles, of which 2,649 (= 80.4%) were on the surface and 644 (= 19.6%) submerged.

October 1-8, 1943: In port for repairs to the main ballast pump and other minor problems; new radar detector "Naxos" equipment installed.

October 9-November 7: Curtailed patrol due to suicide of commanding officer.

October 24: After a relatively quiet passage through the Bay of Biscay, *U-505* is apparently attacked in the evening by Allied warships and depth-charged. During this action Zschech shoots himself in the head and is pronounced dead about 90 minutes later. *I.W.O. Oblt*.z.S Paul Meyer assumed command, and after burying Zschech at sea on October 25, returned to Lorient November 7.

Total distance traveled = 2,211 nautical miles (1,254 surfaced [= 56.7%], 957 submerged [= 43.3%].

November 8-December 20, 1943: Refitting and repairs in Lorient.

November 18: *Oblt.z.S.d.R.* Harald Lange assumes command of *U-505*.

December 20-21: Aborted patrol when *U-505* develops a leak on her first practice dive and returns to base.

December 21-24: Repairs in Lorient.

December 25, 1943-January 2, 1944: *U-505* departs on patrol but diverted to rescue operation for survivors of German vessels lost in Bay of Biscay battle of December 28, 1943.

December 28: Audible sounds of artillery gunfire and explosions during the afternoon followed by an evening message from BdU to alter course and join with other U-boats to search for survivors.

December 29: Over the course of the day *U-505* recovers 34 survivors from nine life-rafts of torpedo-boat *T25*, including commanding officer *Korv.Kapt.* Wirich von Gartzen; at day's end *U-505* puts about to return and is directed to the port of Brest.

January 2, 1944: While approaching port a short-circuit results in a fire in the starboard electrical motor, quickly extinguished; while docking the starboard diving plane fin and shaft is accidentally damaged.

Total distance traveled = 865 nautical miles (651 surfaced [= 75.3%], 214 submerged [= 24.7%].

January 2-March 16, 1944: Docked at Brest for repairs and refitting; during this time *U-505* receives new crewmen and three new T-5 acoustic torpedoes.

March 16-June 4, 1944: *U-505*'s final patrol off the west coast of Africa, operational area Freetown, Sierra Leone-Monrovia, Liberia

March 16: Departure from Brest.

March 19-20: While transiting the Bay of Biscay *U-505* crash-dives five times to avoid aircraft indicated by "Naxos" radar detector.

April 7: Rendezvous with homeward-bound *U-123* to provide current radio cipher keys.

April 24-May 23: In operational area; few targets seen, none attacked; during this period *U-505* is hampered by a substandard radar set and a jammed bow-cap on torpedo tube II.

May 23: Begins return passage.

May 30-June 2: While moving east and northeast of the Cape Verde Islands *U-505* crash dives eight times to avoid aircraft indicated by "Naxos" and "Wanze" radar detectors.

June 4: *U-505* attacked and captured by Task Group 22.3 at 21.30' N/ 19.20'W, ca. 150 miles west of Cape Blanco, West Africa.

Total distance traveled prior to capture = 7,977 nautical miles, 6,044 surfaced [= 75.8%], 1,933 submerged [= 24.2%].

Sources

Primary

War diary (*Kriegstagebuch*) of *U-505*; accounts of Allied merchant ship losses among records of the U.S. Tenth Fleet, Record Group 38, National Archives-College Park, Md.; copies of *U-505* administrative records available at the Museum of Science and Industry, Chicago; and *U-505* subject folders at the U-Boot-Archiv, Cuxhaven.

Secondary

Hans Joachim Decker, "404 Days! The War Patrol Life of the German *U-505*," *United States Naval Institute Proceedings*, 86, 3 (March 1960), 33-45.

Hans Jacob Goebeler with John P. Vanzo, *Steel Boats, Iron Hearts: The Wartime Saga of Hans Goebeler and the U-505* (Holder, FL: Wagnerian Publications, 1999).

A shorter chronology is provided in Kenneth Wynn, *U-Boat Operations of the Second World War, Vol 1: Career Histories, U 1-U 510* (Annapolis, Md: Naval Institute Press, 1997), 323-24.

Statement of Commanding Officer
Oblt.z.S.d.R. *Harald Lange, U-505*

given while at sea aboard
USS Guadalcanal on June 15, 1944

On June 4th about 1200 I was moving under water on my general course when noise bearings were reported. I tried to move to the surface to get a look with the periscope. The sea was slightly rough and the boat was hard to keep on periscope depth. I saw one destroyer through West, another through Southwest and a third at 160 degrees. In about 140 degrees I saw, far off, a mass that might belong to a carrier. Destroyer #1 (West) was nearest to me, at about 1/2 mile. Further off I saw an airplane, but I had no chance to look after this again because I did not want my periscope seen. I dove again and quickly, with noise, because I couldn't keep the boat on periscope depth safely. I suppose that I must have been seen by the airplane because if these heavy boats are rolling under the surface they make a large wake.

I had not reached the safety depth when I received two bombs at a distance and then close after them two heavy dashes, from depth charges perhaps. Water broke in; light and all electrical machinery went off and the rudders jammed. Not knowing exactly the whole damage or why they continued bombing me, I gave the order to bring the boat to the surface by pressed air.

When the boat surfaced, I was the first on the bridge and saw now four destroyers around me, shooting at my boat with caliber and anti-aircraft. The nearest one, in now through 110 degrees, was shooting with shrapnel into the conning tower. I got wounded by numerous shots and shrapnels in both knees and legs and fell down. At once I gave the order to leave the boat and to sink her. My chief officer, who came after me onto the bridge, lay on the starboard side with blood streaming over his face. Then I gave a course order to starboard in order to make the aft part of the conning tower fire lee at the destroyer to get my crew out of the boat safely. I lost consciousness for I don't know how long, but when I awoke again a lot of my men were on the deck and I made an effort to raise myself and haul myself aft. By the explosion of a shell I was blown from the first antiaircraft deck down onto the main deck; the explosion hit near the starboard machine gun.

I saw a lot of my men running on the main deck, getting pipe boats (individual life rafts) clear. In a conscious moment, I gave notice to the chief that I was still on the main deck. How I got over the side I don't know exactly, but I suppose by another explosion. Despite my injuries I somehow managed to keep afloat until two members of my group brought a pipe boat and hoisted me into it; my lifejacket had been punctured with shrapnel and was no good. During all this time I could not see much because in the first seconds of the fight I had been hit in the face and eye with splinters of wood blasted from the deck; my right eyelid was pierced with a splinter.

When I sat in the pipe boat I could see my boat for the last time. Some of my men were still aboard her, throwing more pipe boats into the water. I ordered the men around me to give three cheers for our sinking boat.

After this I was picked up by a destroyer where I received first aid treatment. Later, on this day, I was transferred to the carrier hospital and there I have been told by the Captain that they captured my boat and prevented it from sinking.

Notes

No Target Too Far: The Genesis, Concept, and Operations
of Type IX U-Boats in World War II
by Eric C. Rust

1. An online version of the treaty text exists at: http://www.lib.byu.edu/~rdh/wwi/versailles.html.

2. Arguably the best, constantly updated and most convenient resource for information on German submarines in both World Wars is the U-boat Net website at: http://uboat.net.

3. Article IV of the Washington Treaty regulated the size of the naval establishments of Britain, the United States, Japan, France and Italy in a ratio of 5:5:3:1.75:1.75. In other provisions, the treaty placed limits on the tonnage and armament of certain classes of warships. The full text of the treaty is available in print, and online: http://www.ibiblio.org/pha/pre-war/1922/nav_lim.html.

4. This was evidenced in Germany's endless improvisations, compromises, and experiments all the way into the later stages of the Second World War.

5. A summary and discussion of the Z-Plan can be found in Jak P. Mallmann Showell, *The German Navy in World War II: A Reference Guide to the Kriegsmarine, 1935-1945* (Annapolis, MD: Naval Institute Press, 1979), 23-24.

6. For a detailed list of Germany's actual and anticipated naval building program, consult Erich Gröner, *Die Schiffe der deutschen Kriegsmarine und Luftwaffe 1939-45 und ihr Verbleib*, 7th rev. ed. (Munich: Lehmanns, 1972).

7. To avoid possible national embarrassment in case it was sunk by the enemy, the *Deutschland* was later renamed *Lützow*. Scheer and Spee were prominent naval leaders in World War I.

8. August K. Muggenthaler's work, *German Raiders of World War II* (Englewood Cliffs: Prentice-Hall, 1977), remains one of the finest on the subject.

9. Four additional experimental designs were labeled V80, V300, WA201 and Wk202. They relied on the revolutionary "Walter turbine" concept and never saw frontline deployment.

10. Numerous publications and internet websites offer statistics on the characteristics and wartime fate of German submarines. One of the best-researched is Axel Niestlé, *German U-Boat Losses during World War II: Details of Destruction* (Annapolis, MD: Naval Institute Press, 1998). For a reasonably accurate listing of Axis submarine successes against Allied shipping consult Jürgen Rohwer, *Axis Submarine Successes, 1939-1945*, rev. ed. (Annapolis, MD: Naval Institute Press, 1999).

11. National Archives Microfilm Publication T 1022, roll 1724, item PG 32173, Supplement to KTB 1/Skl, Teil C, Heft IV, "Ubootkrieg" (1941), 5.

12. Operation Deadlight involved the deliberate scuttling of surviving German U-boats after the war by the British in the eastern Atlantic, often after or as part of weapons experiments.

13. U-Boot-Archiv Cuxhaven-Altenbruch, "Wasserbombenschäden an U-Booten Typ IX," in Folder "Untersuchungen über Wabo- u. Fliebo-Schäden," 37.

14. Corraborating evidence in Bundesarchiv-Militärarchiv (BA-MA), RM 98/358, KTB *U-154*, entry for July 3, 1943, and post-war testimony.

15. See "The Monsun Boats," at: http://uboat.net/ops/monsun2.htm.

16. Michael Gannon, *Operation Drumbeat: The Dramatic True Story of Germany's First U-Boat Attacks along the American Coast in World War II* (New York: Harper & Row, 1990).

17. Two areas receiving increased attention are the Gulf of Mexico and Caribbean. A fine account of operations here is Gaylord T. M. Kelshall, *U-Boat War in the Caribbean* (Annapolis, MD: Naval Institute Press, 1994).

18. A slightly dated but generally reliable account of these operations and Allied countermeasures is L. C. F. Turner, *War in the Southern Oceans, 1939-1945* (Capetown: Oxford University Press, 1961).

19. The best and most comprehensive book on the May 1943 tragedy is Michael Gannon, *Black May: The Epic Story of the Allies' Defeat of the German U-Boats in May 1943* (New York: HarperCollins, 1998).

A Community Bound by Fate: The Crew of U-505
by Timothy Mulligan

1. Karl Dönitz, *Die U-Bootswaffe* (Berlin: E.S. Mittler & Sohn, 1940), 27.

2. Clay Blair, *Hitler's U-Boat War, Vol. II: The Hunted, 1942-1945* (New York: Random House, 1998), 550.

3. Eric C. Rust, *Naval Officers Under Hitler: The Story of Crew 34* (Westport, CT: Praeger, 1991), 64, 68, 89.

4. Most information is taken from Axel-Olaf Loewe's letters to Daniel Gallery, September 29 and October 18, 1955, among Gallery Papers in the Nimitz Library, U.S. Naval Academy, Annapolis, MD (hereafter Gallery Papers); additional data from *Konteradmiral a.D.* Albert Stoelzel, ed., *Ehrenrangliste der Kaiserlich Deutschen Marine, 1914-1918* (Berlin: Marine-Offizier-Verein e.V., 1930), 211, 214.

5. Data taken from Loewe's letter to Gallery of September 29, 1955; the official publication *Rangliste der Deutschen Reichsmarine Nach dem Stande vom 4. November 1932*, 9, 56; and Walter Lohmann and Hans H. Hildebrand, *Die Deutsche Kriegsmarine, 1939-1945: Gliederung, Einsatz, Stellenbesetzung* (3 vols.; Bad Nauheim: Podzun, 1956-64), III, 291/211.

6. Hans Jacob Goebeler with John P. Vanzo, *Steel Boats, Iron Hearts: The Wartime Saga of Hans Gobeler and the U-505* (Holder, FL: Wagnerian Publications, 1999), 24, 68.

7. Loewe's letter to Gallery, October 18, 1955; Goebeler, *Steel Boats*, 38-39, 56, 65; and Daniel V. Gallery, *U-505*, rev. pb. edition of *Twenty Million Tons Under the Sea* (New York: Paperback Library, 1967), 91-92.

8. Kriegstagebuch (hereafter KTB) *U-505*, August 26, 1941-August 25, 1942, reproduced through November 7, 1943 on National Archives Microfilm Publication T1022, rolls 3065-66, record item PG 30542/1-7 (hereafter cited as T0122/3065-66/PG 30542/1-7); a copy of the KTB for November 8, 1943 - June

4, 1944, is available at the U-Boot-Archiv, Cuxhaven, Germany. See also Loewe's letters to Gallery, September 29, and October 18, 1955.

9. Data on Förster taken from the *Crewbuch 33*, p. 35, maintained by the Wehrgeschichtliches Ausbildungszentrum at the Marineschule Mürwik (with thanks to Mr. Eberhard Schmidt); the Navy *Ranglisten* for 1935-38; and Loewe's letter to Gallery, September 29, 1955.

10. Rainer Busch and Hans-Joachim Röll, *Der U-Boot-Krieg 1939-1945, I: Die Deutschen U-Boot-Kommandanten* (Hamburg/Berlin/Bonn: E.S. Mittler & Sohn, 1996), 171; Frank Binder and Hans H. Schlünz, *Schwerer Kreuzer Blücher* (Herford: Koehlers, 1990), 137, 183; the pursuit of the tortoises is noted in Loewe's letter to Gallery, October 18, 1955; Nollau's relations with Loewe are described in the Museum of Science and Industry's interview with Aloysius Hasselberg in Chicago, March 2, 1999, as part of the *U-505* Oral History Project (hereafter cited as MSI interviews). I am indebted to Mr. Keith Gill, the Museum's Curator for *U-505* and Transportation, for access to these materials.

11. Loewe letter to Gallery, September 29, 1955; Busch and Röll, *U-Boot-Kommandanten*, 236; Nazi Party membership data originally held at the Berlin Document Center, now reproduced in National Archives Accessioned Microfilm (hereafter NAAM) A3340, series MFOK, roll W053, frame 0357, and series PK, roll M043, frames 0500-02.

12. Examples are (in order): Eric J. Grove, *The Price of Disobedience: The Battle of the River Plate Reconsidered* (Annapolis, MD: Naval Institute Press, 2000), 17; Edwin P. Hoyt, *U-Boats: A Pictorial History* (New York: McGraw-Hill, 1987), 51-54; and Jordan Vause, *U-Boat Ace: The Story of Wolfgang Lüth* (Annapolis, MD: Naval Institute Press, 1990), 123-25.

13. On the role of the SA and Party in the merchant marine, see Rust, *Naval Officers*, 54. On Prien, see his autobiography *Mein Weg Nach Scapa Flow* (Berlin: Deutscher Verlag, 1940), 96, and his Party membership application in NAAM A3340, series NSDAP-A, roll 82. The significance of Party membership for reserve officers is explored in the sources noted in footnote 41, below.

14. Kommando der Marineschule Mürwik an Kommando U 505, "Personalpapiere für Offizieranwärter," September 26, 1941, among *U-505* administrative records, copies in the custody of the Museum of Science and Industry (MSI), Chicago; Doedens letter to Keith Gill, MSI, November 21, 2001; MSI interview with Heinrich Klappich in Cuxhaven, Germany, April 1999; and data on Jacobi's fate from Horst Schwenk, U-Boot-Archiv, Cuxhaven, April 25, 2002.

15. Loewe letter to Gallery, September 29, 1955.

16. Data from V. E. Tarrant, *The U-Boat Offensive 1914-1945* (Annapolis, MD: Naval Institute Press, 1989), 103, 116.

17. Zschech data taken from Lohmann and Hildebrand, *Deutsche Kriegsmarine*, III, 292/220; Stoelzel, *Ehrenrangliste*, 1334; and the official Navy *Ranglisten* for 1937 (p. 145) and 1938 (p. 36); Crew 36 data in Rust, *Naval Officers*, 16-17.

18. MSI interview with Mathias Brünig in Chicago, March 3, 1999.

19. The chronology and successes of *U-124* are furnished in Kenneth Wynn, *U-Boat Operations of the Second World War, Vol. 1: Career Histories, U1-U510* (Annapolis, MD: Naval Institute Press, 1997), 100-01; for a general history of the boat see E. B. Gasaway, *Grey Wolf, Grey Sea* (New York: Ballantine Books, 1970), which however errs in assignment dates for *U-124's* officers. On *U-124's* status as the third most successful U-boat, see Bodo Herzog, "Der Torpedoverbrauch von *U-48*, dem Erfolgreichsten Unterseeboot des Zweiten Weltkrieges, in der Zeit von September 1939 bis Juni 1941," *Deutsches Schiffahrtsarchiv*, 1981/4, 124.

20. Goebeler, *Steel Boats*, 68-69. The Knight's Cross (*Ritterkreuz*) of the Iron Cross was worn at the base of the throat, hence the association.

21. KTB *U-505*, August 25-December 12, 1942, T1022/3065-66/PG 30542/4. The observation as to "the most severely damaged U-boat to return" is attributed to the flotilla engineer of the 2nd U-boat Flotilla at Lorient Hans Joachim Decker, "404 Days! The War Patrol Life of the German *U-505*," *United States Naval Institute Proceedings*, (March 1960), 42). Details of the damage can be found in the 1944 summary report prepared for the U-Boat Command, "Wasserbombenschäden an U-Booten Type IX," *passim* (copy in the U-Boot-Archiv, Cuxhaven, subject folder "Untersuchungen über Wabo- und Fliebo-Schäden").

22. KTB *U-505*, December 13, 1942–September 30, 1943, T1022/3066/PG 30525/5; Goebeler, *Steel Boats*, 68ff.

23. The verse is quoted by Heinrich Klappich in his interview with MSI representatives at the U-Boot-Archiv in Cuxhaven, Germany, April 1999; remaining information from the raw interrogation report of *U-172* crewmen (statements by *Mechanikerobergefreiter* Günther Meissner, January 14, 1944), in interrogation materials for survivors of *U-172*, records of the Office of Naval Intelligence's Special Activities Branch (Op-16-Z), Record Group 38, National Archives at College Park, Md (hereafter cited in the format RG 38, NA-CP).

24. List of 2nd U-Flottille U-boats for March 5, 1943 reproduced on T1022/2152/PG 36678; data on losses in Tarrant, *U-Boat Offensive*, 118-19, 123-24; comparison of Crew origin and fates of U-boats lost in Busch and Röll, *U-Boot-Kommandanten, passim*, and the same authors' *Deutsche*

U-Boot-Verluste von September 1939 bis Mai 1945 (Hamburg/Berlin/Bonn: E.S. Mittler & Sohn, 1999), 86-146.

25. Goebeler, *Steel Boats*, 70-80, 104-05, 170; MSI interviews with Wolfgang Schiller and Karl Springer in Chicago, March 1-2, 1999.

26. See MSI interviews with Thilo Bode in Munich, Germany, April 18, 1999; Goebeler, *Steel Boats*, 73ff., 155; Bode's comments copied from *U-505's* guest book and located in folder "*U-505*," Box 38, Gallery Papers; and Hans Herlin, *Verdammter Atlantik. Schicksale deutscher U-Boot-Fahrer* (Düsseldorf / Vienna: Econ Verlag, 1982), 102.

27. KTB *U-505*, October 24-25, 1943, T1022/3066/PG 30542/6; Herlin, *Verdammter Atlantik*, 107-112. The captain of *U-604*, *Kaptlt.* Horst Höltring, reportedly shot himself following the loss of his boat and the U-boat that temporarily rescued him (Paul Kemp, *U-Boats Destroyed. German Submarine Losses in the World Wars* [Annapolis, MD: Naval Institute Press, 1997], 142-43).

28. KTB *U-505*, October 24-25, 1943; letters of Paul Meyer and Willy Englebarth to Daniel Gallery, August 31, 1955 and December 19, 1954, respectively, Gallery Papers; Decker, "404 Days!", 43; and Goebeler, *Steel Boats*, 175-78.

29. Review of listings of actions in "Chronological 1 Sep 43 - 31 Oct 53" and "Attacks on U-Boats - British Assessment No. 4" (October 1943), both in Tenth Fleet ASW Analysis and Statistical Section, Series VIII: Assessments of Probable Damage Inflicted in Specific ASW Incidents 1941-45, Tenth Fleet records in RG 38, NA-CP.

30. Loewe letter to Gallery, September 29, 1955, Gallery Papers.

31. Herlin, *Verdammter Atlantik*, 96-98 (quoting an interview with Meyer); Busch and Röll, *U-Boot-Kommandanten*, 161; Goebeler, *Steel Boats*, 139, 155-56, 167, 176ff.; and Paul Meyer's letter to Gallery, August 31, 1955, Gallery Papers.

32. Data compiled from the KTB of *U-505*, crew list information at the U-Boot-Archiv, Cuxhaven, and crew information contained in folder "*U-505*," Box 38, Gallery Papers; data on naval surgeons from Hartmut Nöldeke and Volker Hartmann, *Der Sanitätsdienst in der deutschen U-Boot-Waffe* (Hamburg/Berlin/Bonn: E.S. Mittler & Sohn, 1996), 150-51, 156-57, 241.

33. KTB *U-505*, October 22, 1942, T1022/3065/PG 30542/4; Goebeler, *Steel Boats*, 69-70, 77; crew information in folder "*U-505*," Box 38, Gallery Papers; and MSI interview with Bode, April 18, 1999 (pp. 46-49), Munich, Germany.

34. KTB *U-505* November 21, 1942, T1022/3066/PG 30562/4; crew list of *U-377* in U-Boot-Archiv, Cuxhaven.

35. See Gallery's praise for Meyer in *U-505*, 193.

36. Background data from "German U-Boat Captain Here, Tells of Sub's Capture," *The Indianapolis Star*, June 7, 1964 (copy in U-Boot-Archiv, Cuxhaven); interview with Hans and Hannelore Schultz, October 19, 2001, Hamburg, Germany.

37. The data in Busch and Röll, *U-Boot-Kommandanten*, 139, is only partly correct as Lange only commanded (successively) V-909 and V-906 in the Ninth Patrol Boat Flotilla (see the KTB of 9. Vorpostenboot-Flottille, 1 Mai 1940 -September 30, 1941, T1022/3724-25/PG 82692); Schultz interview (Hans Schultz was II. W.O. aboard *U-180*); Wynn, *U-Boat Operations*, 135.

38. MSI interviews with Wolfgang Schiller, Chicago, March 1, 1999, and Karl Springer, Chicago, March 2, 1999; Goebeler, *Steel Boats*, 192-93.

39. Dönitz acknowledged this openly in his radio message of November 13, 1943, the significance of which is discussed in the author's *Neither Sharks Nor Wolves: The Men of Nazi Germany's U-Boat Arm, 1939-1945* (Annapolis, MD: Naval Institute Press, 1999), 83-85, 188.

40. NSDAP membership data in NAAM A3340, series MFOK, roll M078, fr. 0384 (Lange), roll C029, fr. 1364 (Brey), and roll H023, fr. 2065 (Hauser).

41. See the preliminary discussions of this in Manfred Messerschmidt, *Die Wehrmacht im NS-Staat: Zeit der Indoktrination* (Hamburg: R.v. Decker's, 1969), 86-87, 226-27, and Bernhard R. Kroener, "Auf dem Weg zu einer "nationalsozialistischen Volksarmee' - Die soziale Öffnung des Heeresoffizier-korps im Zweiten Weltkrieg," in Martin Broszat, Klaus-Dietmar Henke, and Hans Woller, eds., *Von Stalingrad zur Währungsreform: Zur Sozialgeschichte des Umbruchs in Deutschland* (Munich: Oldenbourg, 1990), 651ff.

42. This subject is addressed generally in Charles S. Thomas, *The German Navy in the Nazi Era* (Annapolis, MD: Naval Institute Press, 1990), and more specifically in Rust, *Naval Officers*, 57-59, 70-72, 117-18; Messerschmidt, *Wehrmacht*, esp. 94, 429-30, 437-38, and 475-77; and Mulligan, *Neither Sharks*, 215ff. Lange's NSDAP membership surprised Hans Schultz (interview with latter at Bad Brückenau, May 28, 2002).

43. Interrogation of Thilo Bode, June 14, 1945, among the German POW 201 files, G-2 (Intelligence) Division MIS-Y Branch interrogations and reports, Records of War Department General and Special Staffs, RG 165, NA-CP.

44. Volkmar Kühn, *Torpedoboote und Zerstörer im Einsatz 1939-1945* (Stuttgart: Motorbuch Verlag, 1997), 238-39, 273. The German Navy's debacle in the Bay of Biscay on December 27-28, 1943 is detailed in *Der Marineoffizier im Gefecht*, compiled by the Deutsches Marine Institut (Herford: E.S. Mittler, 1984), 51-103.

45. The KTB for *U-505* from December 25, 1943 to June 4, 1944 was not filmed on Microfilm Publication T1022, but is available on microfilm from the Manuscript Division, Library of Congress (hereafter LC); the original is now located with the complete *U-505* KTB in the Bundesarchiv-Abt. Militärarchiv, Freiburg/Br., with a photocopy at the U-Boot-Archiv, Cuxhaven.

46. The official record of *U-505 's* capture, including a statement by Lange, is found in the Action Report of Task Group 22.3, June 19, 1944, among World War II Action Reports, RG 38, NA-CP; Gallery's memoir account is found in *U-505*, 247-79; the treatment of Lange's wounds is detailed in a medical report among the raw interrogation reports for *U-505* among the records of the Special Activities Branch, RG 38, NA-CP; and Karla Lange's letters are noted in the MSI interview of Werner Reh in Chicago, March 2, 1999.

47. On casualty data for the U-boat force, see Mulligan, *Neither Sharks*, 251-56; information on individuals from folder "*U-515*," Box 38, Gallery Papers, Busch and Röll, *U-Boot-Kommandanten*, 31, 171, 236, and author's telephone interview with Thilo Bode, February 15, 2002. On *U-534*, see Kenneth Wynn, *U-Boat Operations of the Second World War, Vol. 2: Career Histories, U511-UIT25* (Annapolis, MD: Naval Institute Press, 1998), 19, and the website for the boat, http://web.ukonline.co.uk/gaz/u-534.html.

48. *Indianapolis Star* news story, June 7, 1964; Hans Schultz interview, May 28, 2002; Lange letter to Gallery, September 29, 1955, Gallery Papers.

49. This particular figure comes from Goebeler, *Steel Boats*, 169. All other data derive from the sources noted in footnote 50, below.

50. Figures are based on the author's review of the following crew data: crew list for December 1941 (ranks and last names only) attached to Loewe's letter to Gallery, October 18, 1955; crew lists for March 1943 and August 1943 (ranks, full names, birthdates and/or next of kin) and *U-505* veterans' list, ca. 1982, in the custody of the U-Boot-Archiv, Cuxhaven; and crew list of *U-505* prisoners of war (names, ranks, ages) from the logbook of USS *Guadalcanal*, Record Group 24, Records of the Bureau of Navigation and Personnel, NA-CP (hereafter collectively cited as "crew data"). The *U-505* administrative records at MSI (folder "AI" Heft 1, Offene Bootsakte) include the earliest statistical breakdown of the crew's composition (but without names) as of October 1941 (4. U-Flottille an "U505," "Sollvermehrung lt. Abänderungsvorschlag," October 9, 1941). Excluded are nine crewmen identified among the last-named records who only served aboard *U-505* during her training period.

51. See Dönitz's memorandum and accompanying enclosure to the Kommando der Marinestation der Ostsee, "Personalbedarf der U-Boote auf

Grund des Schiffbauneubauplanes," November 13, 1939, T1022/2066/PG 33541.

52. Loewe letter to Gallery, September 29, 1955; Kommando Schlachtschiff "Scharnhorst" an 4. U.-Flottille, February 2, 1942; Loewe's memorandum on "Abkommandierung Maschinenmaat S.," September 28, 1941, and the accompanying responses by 4. U.-Flottille, September 28, 1941 and Admiral der Ostseestation, November 5, 1941, all in folder "AI" Heft 1, Offene Bootsakte, *U-505* administrative records at MSI. The notes on *U-505's* cautious passage patrol comes from her KTB of January 25-26, 1942, T1022/3065/PG 30542/1.

53. Goebeler, *Steel Boats*, 71, 213-14, and the postwar "Besatzungsliste 'U 505'" prepared by the U-boat's veterans (copy in the U-boot-Archiv); MSI interview with Aloysius Hasselburg, March 2, 1999, Chicago; and interrogation of Willi Jung among the rough interrogations of *U-858* crewmen, records of the Special Activities Branch (Op-16-Z), RG 38, NA-CP.

54. See Mulligan, *Neither Sharks*, 82-83, 166-68.

55. Loewe letter to Gallery, September 29, 1955, Gallery Papers.

56. E.g., Lothar-Günther Buchheim, *Zu Tode Gesiegt: Der Untergang der U-Boote* (Stuttgart: C. Bertelsmann, 1988), 56; Michael Salewski, *Von der Wirklichkeit des Krieges: Analysen und Kontroversen zu Buchheims "Boot"* (Munich: Deutscher Taschenbuch Verlag, 1976), 29; and Erich Topp, "Manning and Training the U-boat Fleet," in Stephen Howarth and Derek Law, eds., *The Battle of the Atlantic, 1939-1945: The Fiftieth Anniversary International Naval Conference* (London and Annapolis: Greenhill and Naval Institute Press, 1994), 216.

57. Mulligan, *Neither Sharks*, 169-70.

58. Report B-578, "The Age-Structures of the U-boat Arm and the G.A.F. (British source, January 10, 1944)," February 3, 1944, among intelligence reports, interrogations and materials of the G-2 Division (MIS-Y Branch), Records of War Department General and Special Staffs, RG 165, NA-CP.

59 See the author's "German U-boat Crews in World War II: Sociology of an Elite," *Journal of Military History*, 56, 2 (April 1993): 261-81, and *Neither Sharks*, 114-19.

60. Raw interrogations of *U-505* crewmen among records of the Special Activities Branch (Op-16-Z), RG 38, NA-CP; for information on the socioeconomic classification of occupations in Germany at this time, see Detlef Mühlberger, *Hitler's Followers: Studies in the Sociology of the Nazi Movement* (London and New York: Routledge, 1991), 14-25.

61. The sample of U-boat veterans is described in Mulligan, *Neither Sharks*, 247-50 (two of the 947 crewmen who prepared questionnaires were in fact *U-505* veterans). Where the questionnaires directly solicited places of birth, the *U-505* crew list provides only the residences of next-of-kin, but these overwhelmingly represent their parents. The postwar *U-505* veterans' association name list provides addresses for a larger number of men who served on the U-boat, but as these reflect residences in the 1980s they were not used.

62. Loewe letter to Gallery, December 30, 1955, Gallery Papers.

63. Goebeler, *Steel Boats*, 16-17; MSI interviews with Aloysius Hasselberg and Werner Reh, Chicago, March 2, 1999.

64. Letter of Willy Englebarth to Dan Gallery, December 19, 1954, Gallery Papers.

65. MSI interviews with Karl Springer, Chicago, March 2, 1999, and Heinrich Klappich, Cuxhaven, Germany, April 1999.

66. MSI interview with Wolfgang Schiller, Chicago, March 1, 1999.

67. Interrogation notes for Willi Kneisel, Anton Kern, Hans Rasch, Erich Kalbitz, and Wolfgang Schubert among the raw interrogation reports for *U-505*, Special Activities Branch (Op-16-Z), RG 38, NA-CP; information for Ewald Felix in C. Herbert Gilliland and Robert Shenk, *Admiral Dan Gallery: The Life and Wit of a Navy Original* (Annapolis, MD: Naval Institute Press, 1999), 127.

68. Ewald Felix's (in American accounts his name is often reversed) cooperation with the Americans is attested to by Gallery among his personal papers (Folder D, "Miscellaneous Correspondence," Box 37), the content of which is summarized in Gilliland and Shenk, *Admiral Dan Gallery*, 127-31. Felix's own POW record confirms that he was a German national, born well within the 1923 German boundaries of Upper Silesia. Hans Goebeler claims (*Steel Boats*, 246-47) that Felix contributed little to the American salvage effort, and certainly Felix remained in Germany and an active member of the *U-505* veterans' association. On the Polish-German confusion, see the author's comments in *Neither Sharks*, 137 and 289n.

69. "Auszug aus dem Wachmeldebuch des Wachoffiziers der 2. U.-Flottille vom 3.6.42," in folder "A I" Heft 1, Offene Bootsakte, *U-505* administrative records at MSI.

70. Raw interrogation reports for *U-505*, Special Activities Branch (Op-16-Z), RG 38, NA-CP.

71. See Ludwig C. Hannemann, *Die Justiz der Kriegsmarine, 1939-1945, im Spiegel ihrer Rechtsprechung* (Regensburg: S. Roderer, 1993), 318-22.

72. 2. U.-Flottille, "Laufender Flottillenbefehl Nr. 26," 1 Dezember 1943, among a collection of 2nd U-boat Flotilla standing orders for 1943-44 located in file 24309-U, formerly secret reports of naval attaches, 1941-44, RG 38, NA-CP.

73. See Heinrich Walle, *Die Tragödie des Oberleutnants zur See Oskar Kusch* (Stuttgart: Franz Steiner, 1995), esp. 89ff.

74. See the detailed study by Manfred Messerschmidt and Fritz Wüllner, *Die Wehrmachtjustiz im Dienste des Nationalsozialismus. Zerstörung einer Legende* (Baden-Baden: Nomos, 1987), 63-89.

75. Search of NSDAP membership cards on NAAM A3340, series MFOK; Party data for Albert Weingärtner located on roll Y048, frame 1403.

76. MSI interview with Wolfgang Schiller, Chicago, March 1, 1999.

77. Copies of *U-505's Bücherverzeichnis* and *Schallplattenverzeichnis*, together with one issue of the boat's newsletter, are reproduced on reel 81 of the German Submarine Materials in the custody of the Manuscript Division, Library of Congress, Washington, DC. The list of phonograph recordings was annotated by hand to indicate replacements of titles.

78. Goebeler, *Steel Boats*, 222-23.

79. Based on reviews of U-boat casualty lists in the custody of the U-Boot-Archiv, Cuxhaven; I am indebted to that institution's Horst Schwenk for assistance in consulting the records. Omitted from the final figure of 115 officers and men are those crewmen who transferred off *U-505* during her training period, and *Lt.z.S.d.R.* Knoke, who briefly replaced Stolzenburg for the last three weeks of the patrol in November-December 1942.

80. In addition to Zschech and Fischer, those killed in the war, with their approximate period of service on board *U-505* indicated in parentheses, include: *Lt.z.S.* Werner Jacobi (September 1941-May 1942), lost with *U-973* on March 6, 1944; *Lt. (I)* Erich Altesellmeier (October-December 1942), lost with *U-377* on January 15, 1944; *Btsmt.* Wallfred Gerlach (August 1942-June 1943), lost with *U-154* on July 3, 1944; *Btsmt.* Hannes Bockelmann (September-December 1942), lost with *U-124* on April 2, 1943; *Fk.OMt.* Gottfried Fischer (August 1941-June 1944), KIA on *U-505* on June 4, 1944; *Masch.Mt.* —— Krautscheid (December 1941-December 1942), lost with *U-755* on May 28, 1943; *Masch.Mt.* Lothar Lipka (August 1941-December 1942), lost with *U-504* on July 30, 1943; *Masch.Mt.* Erhard Mosch (December 1941-December 1942), lost with *U-676* on February 12, 1945; *Matr.OGfr.* Werner Marenberg (August 1941-December 1942), lost with *U-336* on October 5, 1943; *Matr. Gfr.* Rudi Nepaschings (August 1941-January 1942), lost with *U-381* in May 1943; *Matrose* Rudolf Heinemann (January-December 1942), lost with *U-1199* on January 21, 1945. For a discussion of the final casualty rates among U-boat crews, see Mulligan, *Neither Sharks*, 251-56.

81. Veteran crew lists, reunion data, and Loewe's comments from the September 1990 reunion all in the *U-505* subject folders, U-Boot-Archiv,

Cuxhaven; data on Hans-Joachim Decker's work at the Museum in Gallery Papers, folder "*U-505*," Box 38.

From the Lion's Roar to Blunted Axe:
The Combat Patrols of U-505
by Lawrence Paterson

1. Loewe's words were recorded in private notes by Hans Goebeler, who wrote his memoirs of his service aboard *U-505* in Hans Jacob Goebeler with John P. Vanzo, *Steel Boats, Iron Hearts: The Wartime Saga of Hans Goebeler and the U-505* (Holder, FL: Wagnerian Publications, 1999).

2. In German naval parlance the word "Crew" refers to the officer class Loewe attended, 1928 being his first year as an officer candidate.

3. Hans Joachim Decker, "404 Days! The War Patrol Life of the German *U-505*," *U.S. Naval Institute Proceedings*, Vol. 86, No. 3 (March 1960), 34. The allocation of U-boats to various flotillas was purely logistical and did not reflect any localised command of the U-boats concerned. BdU (*Befehlshaber der Unterseeboote*—U-boat command) continued to exercise central control over U-boats in action.

4. KTB *U505*, January 25, 1942, U-Boot-Archiv, Altenbruch, Germany.

5. For further details of operations against Freetown by long-range U-boats see specific references in Lawrence Paterson, *Second U-Boat Flotilla* (Naval Institute Press, 2003).

6. See Admiral Dönitz's comments noted in BdU KTB, January and February 1942, 30302–30304b; National Archives Microfilm Publication T1022, roll 3979.

7. Decker, "The War Patrol Life of the German *U-505*," 36. RAF Coastal Command began to step up operations within the Bay of Biscay at the "choke points" that U-boats were forced to traverse to enter and exit the French Atlantic ports. These operations were soon augmented with extended ASW sweeps along the Bay of Biscay, such as Operations Seaslug and Musketry. Aircraft, with improved radar, became the primary threat to U-boats by 1943.

8. Crewmember Hans Goebeler mentions the fractious state of the crew aboard *U-505*, in *Steel Boats and Iron Hearts*, 31-38.

9. Decker, "The War Patrol Life of the German *U-505*," 36. Anderson, his fifty-one crewmen and four gunners were eventually rescued by a Sunderland flying boat of 95 Squadron and landed at Freetown.

10. Goebeler, *Steel Boats and Iron Hearts*, 35, and KTB *U-505*, copy held in U-Boot-Archiv, Altenbruch. See also an eyewitness description left by Thorstein Schau in his article in the Norwegian magazine *Krigsseileren* (2000).

11. Prime Minister Churchill and President Roosevelt conferred often during 1942 regarding the fragile Allied position in the Middle East and Africa, and the very real fear of German occupation of Morocco. See, for example, Winston Churchill, *The Second World War, Volume IV: The Hinge of Fate* (Cassell & Co, 1951), 364.

12. The outbreak of war between Germany and the United States prompted Brazil's severing of diplomatic relations. Despite being treated the same as all other neutral vessels, U-boats accidentally sank seven Brazilian ships between February and April 1942 as the war moved closer to the Americas. Brazil and Germany edged closer to outright hostilities until August 19, 1942, when Brazil declared war. Dönitz discusses this issue in his memoir, *Ten Years and Twenty Days* (Naval Institute Press, 1990), 239-240.

13. A stoker from among the survivors also died of wounds the next day, raising the death toll to fifteen. However, all four lifeboats landed east of Las Palmas and one week later the survivors were taken to Freetown by two Free French corvettes. Survivors' account held in the Royal Navy Submarine Museum, Gosport, papers collected by Gus Britton. Unfortunately, this collection is not yet fully catalogued, and no box or volume number is provided.

14. Goebeler, *Steel Boats, Iron Hearts*, 42.

15. War Diary (*Kriegstagebuch*) of *U-505*, August 26, 1941– November 7, 1943, PG 30542/1-7; ONI roll T-5-F, T-6-F, National Archives Microfilm Publication T1022, rolls 3065-3066.

16. The five boats that launched "Operation Westindien" sank 222,651 tons of Allied shipping, or 70,000 more tons than the celebrated "Operation Paukenschlag." For more on this theater of operations, see Gaylord T. M. Kelshall, *The U-Boat War in the Caribbean* (Annapolis, 1994).

17. *U-157* was only officially listed as missing on August 13, two months after it was sunk. BdU was initially swayed by reports from *U-67*, operating in the same region, suggesting *U-157* was probably still active and that its radio was out of commission. NARA Microfilm T1022, Roll 3980.

18. This, as well as other attacks, prompted Dönitz to issue orders on June 24 that U-boats were to proceed submerged by day and night when crossing Biscay, surfacing only long enough to recharge batteries. BdU Log, NARA Microfilm T1022, Roll 3980.

19. Survivor's account held in Royal Navy Submarine Museum, Gosport, England. Unfortunately, this collection is not yet fully catalogued, and no box or volume number is provided.

20. The development of both centimetric radar sets for aircraft and long range bombers combined during 1942 and 1943 to rob U-boats of their ability to surface in safety and recharge both crew and batteries while in the mid-Atlantic. Air power was a decisive factor in the defeat of the German U-boats.

21. Loewe later became a member of the *Reichsministerium für Rüstung und Kriegsproduktion* from August 1944 to April 1945, and then commanded the *1. Marine Panzerjagdregiment*.

22. Johann Mohr commanded *U-124* between September 1941 and March 1943. On April 2 he was killed with his entire crew after *U-124* was depth-charged by HMS *Black Swan* and *Stonecrop* west of Oporto.

23. Decker, "The War Patrol Life of the German *U-505*," 39. Zschech was not Turkish, despite his birthplace. His father had been part of the German military mission based in Turkey's capital.

24. The "Metox" radar detector was named after the French electronics company Metox-Grandin that produced the apparatus in Paris. Officially designated FuMB-1 (Funkmess Beobachtungs-Gerät 1) the unit consisted of a flimsy wooden cross with wires wrapped around it to provide a horizontal and vertical aerial. Introduced in August 1942, it initially proved successful against early Allied radar sets, but ultimately useless against the centimetric radar introduced later in the war. Despite Germany's ignorance of centimetric radar, Metox's use was discontinued in August 1943 when fears were raised that the radar detector radiated its own signature that was detectable by Allied aircraft. For more on this issue, see Eberhard Rössler, *The U-Boat: The Evolution and Technical History of German Submarines* (Arms & Armour Press, 1981), 196.

25. Nollau took charge of *U-534* in December 1942. His boat was sunk in May 1945, subsequently discovered, and raised in 1993. It is now on display in Birkenhead, England. This makes Nollau the only man to serve on two of the remaining four Second World War U-boats.

26. This aspect of the relationship between Peter Zschech and Thilo Bode remains extremely conjectural with no evidence to support it other than Hans Goebeler's recorded opinion.

27. Hans Goebeler mentions information regarding the extreme disharmony developing aboard *U-505* during this period. Goebeler, *Steel Boats and Iron Hearts*, 6-80.

28. The survivors were later rescued by HMS *Pimpernel* and landed at Santiago de Cuba.

29. Yellow aluminum from the downed Hudson was found all over *U-505's* decking. It was collected and later fashioned into small axes, the emblem of the boat, and used to decorate the crewmen's caps. Goebeler, *Steel Boats and Iron Hearts*, 93.

30. *Ibid.*, 91; Decker, "The War Patrol Life of the German *U-505*," 40-41.

31. Translations of ULTRA intercepted radio traffic for *U-505*, U.S. National Archives, RG38. 10, Box 130, Naval Security Group.

32. The provision of *Milchkuh* tankers to the U-boat service allowed not only the replenishment of U-boats at sea with ammunition and provisions, but also the services of an onboard surgeon who was equipped with the necessary tools and space in which to carry out emergency operations. The limited space available in a combat boat made this almost impossible. For a recent and thorough study of these large boats, see John F. White, *U-Boat Tankers, 1941-1945* (Naval Institute Press, 1998).

33. Decker, "The War Patrol Life of the German *U-505*," 42. In hindsight the looming defeat seems clear. At the time Dönitz treated his strategic withdrawal as a temporary measure that would enable his boats to rest and refit. However, they were never to return in force to the Atlantic battle, although anti-convoy operations were later resumed.

34. The Allied air and naval campaign against France's Atlantic ports escalated into 1944 and culminated in "Operation Kinetic" during August. By that stage U-boats and their small escort craft were regular victims of increasingly aggressive Allied attacks. The narrow "choke points" through which U-boats exited and entered the French bases allowed concentrated attacks by their enemies. This, coupled with air supremacy over the Bay of Biscay by late 1943, spelled the end for Germany's Atlantic flotillas. For more information on the defeat of the German effort against convoys, see Michael Gannon, *Black May: The Epic Story of the Allies' Defeat of the German U-Boats in May 1943* (New York, NY: HarperCollins, 1998).

35. Several reports held in Allied records tell of the execution of several French dockyard workers in relation to these acts of sabotage. These records are held at the Bundesarchiv-Zentralnachweisstelle (BA-ZNS), Aachen-Kornelimünster. See "Anti Submarine Warfare Report," Volume 4 (1943), British Admiralty, RNSM, Gosport.

36. ULTRA intercepts for *U-505*, RG38, 10, Box 130, Naval Security Group, Office of the Chief of Naval Operations, USN.

37. War Diary of *U-505*, PG 30542/1-7; T1022, 3065-3066; Decker, "The War Patrol Life of the German *U-505*," 43. The nickname *Bold* was short for *Kobold*, meaning "deceiving spirit" or "goblin." This clever system used a 15cm diameter capsule filled with calcium and zinc that was expelled from the stern

compartment of a U-boat through a specially built ejector system or *Pillenwerfer* (pill-thrower). The calcium-zinc compound was packed inside a wire bag and stuffed inside an aluminium canister. A hydrostatic valve regulated the entry of seawater into the "pill." Hydrogen gas was produced when the water mixed with the calcium-zinc, and the result was a large rather "solid" mass of bubbles that to Allied sonar vaguely resembled a submarine signature. When they worked properly, Bold capsules could emit bubbles for up to 25 minutes.

38. ULTRA intercepts for *U-505*, RG38, 10, Box 130, Naval Security Group, Office of the Chief of Naval Operations, USN.

39. Goebeler, *Steel Boats, Iron Hearts*, 206-207.

40. Decker, "The War Patrol Life of the German *U-505*," 44. Decker may have confused *U-505's* April 7 meeting with *U-123*.

Deciphering the U-boat War:
The Role of Intelligence in the Capture of U-505
by Mark E. Wise and Jak P. Mallmann Showell

1.   The Allies generally learned U-boat numbers through prisoner interrogation or decrypted radio messages. In particular, information derived from Enigma intelligence would have been classified Top Secret Ultra, a level of classification beyond the photo interpreters' security clearances.

2. National Archives and Records Administration, College Park, MD (NARA), Records of the Chief of Naval Operations, Record Group 38 (RG 38), Messages, message 101047, CTG 22.3 to CINCLANT, June 10, 1944; NARA, RG 38, Records of the Naval Security Group Central Depository, Crane, Indiana; CNSG Library; folder "U-505 (Code Name Nemo) Navy Dept. Documents (memoranda, messages, etc.) re capture and dispositions vessel, crew, and captured materials" (cited hereafter as NARA, RG 38, U-505 Documents); memorandum from Commander J. N. Wenger, USN to OP-20, countersigned by RADM Joseph R. Redman, July 13, 1944, 1. Cited hereafter as NARA, RG 38, U-505 Documents, Wenger Exploitation Memorandum.

3. Captain Wyman H. Packard, USN (Ret.), *A Century of Naval Intelligence* (Washington, DC: Office of Naval Intelligence and Naval Historical Center, 1996), 204; Ladislas Farago, *The Tenth Fleet* (New York: Ivan Obolensky, 1962), 213.

4. Packard, *A Century of Naval Intelligence*, 204; Farago, *The Tenth Fleet*, 214.

5. *Ibid.*, 204.

6. *Ibid.*, 205.

7. *Ibid.*, 204.

8. *Ibid.*, 205.

9. *Ibid.*, 206.

10. Kenneth A. Knowles, Jr., Professor of Weapons Systems Engineering, U.S. Naval Academy, telephone interview with the author, March 13, 2002. For the sake of clarity, "F-21" will be used to denote the Atlantic Section of COMINCH Intelligence throughout this chapter, although that designation did not apply until July 1, 1943, as noted above.

11. Knowles telephone interview.

12. Farago, *The Tenth Fleet*, 215-216.

13. Packard, *A Century of Naval Intelligence*, 206.

14. David Kahn, *Seizing the Enigma: The Race to Break the German U-boat Codes, 1939-1943* (Boston: Houghton Mifflin Company, 1991), 243-244.

15. David Syrett, *The Defeat of the German U-Boats: The Battle of the Atlantic* (Columbia, SC: University of South Carolina Press, 1994), 18-20.

16. Packard, *A Century of Naval Intelligence*, 206.

17. *Ibid.*, 207.

18. NARA, Records of the National Security Agency/Central Security Service, Record Group 457 (RG 457), Lieutenant John E. Parsons, USNR, F-211; Memorandum for F-21, Subject: Functions of "Secret Room" of Cominch Combat Intelligence, Atlantic Section, n.d., 1; Document SRMN-038; United States Navy Records Relating to Cryptography, 1918-1950. Cited hereafter as NARA, RG 457, Parsons Memorandum.

19. NARA, RG 457, Parsons Memorandum, 1.

20. NARA, RG 457, Parsons Memorandum, 1. It is unclear from the memorandum whether "Chief of Staff" refers to Low, who was Chief of Staff, Tenth Fleet, or to Edwards. Since Low exercised routine command over the Tenth Fleet, issuing orders in King's name, he was probably the Chief of Staff in question.

21. NARA, RG 457, Parsons Memorandum, 10.

22. *Ibid.*, 3.

23. *Ibid.*, 3.

24. *Ibid.*, 4.

25. *Ibid.*, 5.

26. *Ibid.*, 5.

27. Packard, *A Century of Naval Intelligence*, 124, 127. "Foreign material exploitation," usually shortened to FME, is the examination of captured, purchased, or stolen equipment for any information of intelligence value.

28. NARA, RG 38, OP-16-Z (Special Activities Branch), U-Boat List, November 1, 1943; U-Boat Officers, October 12, 1943; U-Boat Bases, July 15, 1943.

29. Jennifer E. Wilcox, *Sharing the Burden: Women in Cryptology During World War II* (Fort Meade, MD: Center for Cryptologic History, National Security Agency, March 1998), 7.

30. Kahn, *Seizing the Enigma*, 241.

31. *Ibid.*, 241-242.

32. NARA, RG 457, Office of Naval Intelligence, OP-20-G, *History of Communications Intelligence in the Battle of the Atlantic: Allied Communication Intelligence in the Battle of the Atlantic*, n.d., 3; Document SRH 008; Studies on Cryptology, 1917-1977, hereafter NARA, RG 457, COMINT History.

33. NARA, RG 457, COMINT History, 5-6.

34. *Ibid.*, 6-7.

35. *Ibid.*, 6.

36. Farago, *The Tenth Fleet*, 164-165.

37. *Ibid.*, 174.

38. Packard, *A Century of Naval Intelligence*, 206.

39. Farago, *The Tenth Fleet*, 166-167. In naval parlance, a numbered fleet may be referred to with or without an article prefacing the number; that is to say, one sees "Tenth Fleet" and "the Tenth Fleet" used interchangeably. The term "Tenth Fleet" may also be used to refer specifically to the fleet commander.

40. *Ibid.*, 7-8.

41. *Ibid.*, 174.

42. *Ibid.*, 164-165.

43. *Ibid.*, 169-170.

44. *Ibid.*, 200.

45. *Ibid.*, 213.

46. *Ibid.*, 214.

47. Packard, *A Century of Naval Intelligence*, 206.

48. Kahn, *Seizing the Enigma*, 243-244.

49. Farago, *The Tenth Fleet*, 170-171.

50. Daniel V. Gallery, *Reminiscences of Rear Admiral Daniel V. Gallery, U.S. Navy (Retired)* (Annapolis, MD: U.S. Naval Institute, June, 1976), March 5, 1971 interview, 74-76. Cited hereafter as Gallery, Reminiscences.

51. NARA, RG 457, Commander J.N. Wenger, USN, and others, Memorandum for Director of Naval Communications, Subj: History of the Bombe Project, April 24, 1944, 2; "Bombe History" folder; Historic Cryptographic Collection, pre-World War I through World War II. Cited hereafter as Wenger Bombe Memorandum.

52. Knowles telephone interview.

53. NARA, RG 457, Office of Naval Intelligence, OP-20-G, *History of Communications Intelligence in the Battle of the Atlantic: Technical Intelligence from Allied C.I.,* n.d., 79; Document SRH 025; Studies on Cryptology, 1917-1977; Records of the National Security Agency/Central Security Service.

54. NARA, RG 457, Captain Laurance F. Safford, USN (Ret.), *A Brief History of Communications Intelligence in the United States,* 1952, 3; Document SRH 149; Studies on Cryptology, 1917-1977.

55. Kathleen Broome Williams, *Secret Weapon: U.S. High-Frequency Direction Finding in the Battle of the Atlantic* (Annapolis, MD: Naval Institute Press, 1996), 11.

56. David Syrett, ed., *The Battle of the Atlantic and Signals Intelligence: U-Boat Situations and Trends, 1941-1945* (Brookfield, VT: Ashgate Publishing Company, 1998), xiii-xiv.

57. NARA, RG 457, Office of Naval Intelligence, OP-20-G, *U.S. Navy Communication Intelligence Organization, Liaison and Collaboration 1941-1945,* October 8, 1945, 19-20; Document SRH 197; Studies on Cryptology, 1917-1977. Cited hereafter as NARA, RG 457, COMINT Organization.

58. Williams, *U.S. High-Frequency Direction Finding in the Battle of the Atlantic,* 43.

59. Walter J. Boyne, *Clash of Titans: World War II at Sea* (New York: Simon and Schuster, 1995), 93.

60. Peter Padfield, *Dönitz: The Last Führer* (London: Cassell, 2001), 64-88. Padfield concluded it was Dönitz's fault the boat was lost; Williams, *U.S. High-Frequency Direction Finding in the Battle of the Atlantic,* 9-10.

61. Intercept ZTPGU 26480, June 15, 1944: in DEFE3, Public Records Office, Kew. Quoted in Ralph Erskine, "U-Boats, Homing Signals, and HFDF," *Intelligence and National Security* 2, no. 2 (April 1987), 327, ellipsis Erskine's.

62. Williams, *U.S. High-Frequency Direction Finding in the Battle of the Atlantic,* 288.

63. Kahn, *Seizing the Enigma,* 4.

64. *Ibid.,* 145.

65. Williams, *U.S. High-Frequency Direction Finding in the Battle of the Atlantic,* 120.

66. *Ibid.*, 89.

67. *Ibid.*, 13.

68. Williams, *U.S. High-Frequency Direction Finding in the Battle of the Atlantic*, 13; Safford, 3.

69. Williams, *U.S. High-Frequency Direction Finding in the Battle of the Atlantic*, 11.

70. *Ibid.*, 94.

71. *Ibid.*, 90; U.S. Coast Guard, Mendota (late—HMS Culver, Y-87), http://www.uscg.mil/hq/g-cp/history/mendota_1929.html>, accessed January 8, 2004.

72. Williams, *U.S. High-Frequency Direction Finding in the Battle of the Atlantic*, 94-95; Boyne, *Clash of Titans*, 107.

73. Williams, *U.S. High-Frequency Direction Finding in the Battle of the Atlantic*, 147.

74. Clay Blair, *The Hunted, 1942-1945*, vol. 2 of *Hitler's U-Boat War* (New York: Random House, 1998), 791-792.

75. Farago, *The Tenth Fleet*, 193.

76. Blair, *The Hunted, 1942-1945*, 792.

77. Williams, *U.S. High-Frequency Direction Finding in the Battle of the Atlantic*, 228.

78. William T. Y'Blood, *Hunter-Killer: U.S. Escort Carriers in the Battle of the Atlantic* (Annapolis, MD: Naval Institute Press, 1983), 282-283.

79. NARA, RG 457, COMINT History, 29.

80. Williams, *U.S. High-Frequency Direction Finding in the Battle of the Atlantic*, 208.

81. Boyne, *Clash of Titans*, 96.

82. Jennifer E. Wilcox, *Solving the Enigma: History of the Cryptanalytic Bombe* (Fort Meade, MD: Center for Cryptologic History, National Security Agency, January 2001), 1.

83. Kahn, *Seizing the Enigma*, 68.

84. Wladyslaw Kozaczuk, *Enigma: How the German Machine Cipher Was Broken, and How It Was Read by the Allies in World War Two*, ed. and trans. Christopher Kasparek (Frederick, MD: University Publications of America, 1984), 196-197.

85. Kahn, *Seizing the Enigma*, 222, 224-227.

86. NARA, RG 457, COMINT History, 22. The fourth enigma wheel was introduced at the worst possible time for Germany. Many aspects of the war at sea were changing, and neither Dönitz nor his staff noticed the sudden Allied blackout.

87. NARA, RG 457, COMINT History, 23.

88. Kahn, *Seizing the Enigma*, 53-55, 62-67.

89. Kozaczuk, 53.

90. Kahn, *Seizing the Enigma*, 73.

91. *Ibid.*, 230-231.

92. *Ibid.*, 106-112.

93. *Ibid.*, 132-137.

94. *Ibid.*, 116-118.

95. *Ibid.*, 149.

96. *Ibid.*, 179-182.

97. *Ibid.*, 149, 179-182.

98. Wilcox, *Solving the Enigma*, 14.

99. Kahn, *Seizing the Enigma*, 161, 168-169.

100. Syrett, *The Defeat of the German U-Boats*, 20-21.

101. Blair, *The Hunted, 1942-1945*, 86-87; Kahn, *Seizing the Enigma*, 222, 224-227.

102. Blair, *The Hunted, 1942-1945*, 86-87.

103. NARA, RG 457, Wenger Bombe Memorandum, 5.

104. Kahn, *Seizing the Enigma*, 222, 224-227.

105. NARA, RG 457, Wenger Bombe Memorandum, 4.

106. *Ibid.*, 5.

107. *Ibid.*, 6.

108. NARA, RG 457, COMINT Organization, 38.

109. NARA, RG 457, Wenger Bombe Memorandum, 5.

110. *Ibid.*, 6.

111. *Ibid.*, 8-9.

112. Wilcox, *Sharing the Burden*, 9; NARA, RG 457, Wenger Bombe Memorandum, 8.

113. Wilcox, *Sharing the Burden*, 9, 27.

114. *Ibid.*, 33.

115. *Ibid.*, 29.

116. NARA, RG 457, Commander H.T. Engstrom, USNR, Memorandum for OP-20-G-1, Subj: Bombes - History of., March 24, 1944, 2; "Bombe History" folder; Historic Cryptographic Collection, pre-World War I through World War II.

117. NARA, RG 457, Wenger Bombe Memorandum, 8.

118. *Ibid.*, 9.

119. Wilcox, *Solving the Enigma*, 32-33; Kahn, *Seizing the Enigma*, 239-240.

120. Wilcox, *Solving the Enigma*, 33-34.

121. Kahn, *Seizing the Enigma*, 239-240.

122. Wilcox, *Solving the Enigma*, 35-36.

123. *Ibid.*, 34-35.

124. Kahn, *Seizing the Enigma*, 241.

125. NARA, RG 457, COMINT History, 33; Y'Blood, *Hunter-Killer*, 282-283.

126. Packard, *A Century of Naval Intelligence*, 47, 124.

127. Zenon Lukosius, member of USS *Pillsbury* boarding party, interview with the author, December 9, 2001.

128. Packard, *A Century of Naval Intelligence*, 46. When *U-85* was fatally damaged the order to abandon ship was given. Many crewmen made it out of the boat, which then slipped beneath the surface. Determined to make sure the boat was fatally damaged, *Roper* dropped eleven more depth charges over the spot, killing those men who had been fortunate enough to exit the boat. In addition to the petty officer's notebook, many personal diaries were also recovered from the bodies. For more information, see Michael Gannon, *Operation Drumbeat: The Dramatic True Story of Germany's First U-boat Attacks along the American Coast in World War II* (New York, NY: Harper and Row, 1990), 380-381.

129. Packard, *A Century of Naval Intelligence*, 125.

130. *Ibid.*

131. NARA, RG 38, Translations of Intercepted Enemy Radio Traffic and Misc. WWII Documentation; Translations of German intercepts U-boats (Messages) by Hull; U-475-U-508 box, message 0436/25/42 from U-505, March 25, 1944. Cited hereafter as NARA, RG 38, Intercepts.

132. NARA, RG 38, Records of the Naval Security Group Central Depository, Crane, Indiana; CNSG Library; folder "3270/409–CNSG–HFDF Operations–HFDF Logs for Atlantic Area, 1 Jan-31 Mar 1944;" log page for March 25, 1944. It was standing practice for U-boats to send a signal from 10 degrees West (later from 15 degrees West) to confirm the safe passage of the Bay of Biscay. From these messages British direction finders were able to determine the approximate latitude of each boat, and thus the boat's probable destination.

133. NARA, RG 38, Intercepts, message 0436/25/42; NARA, RG 38, Records of the Naval Security Group Central Depository, Crane, Indiana, folder U-505 (Code Name "NEMO")–Captured Documents: Navigational Charts and Materials, documents "Key to German Naval Grid" and "Mittel-und Südatlantik." Cited hereafter as NARA, RG 38, Navigational Charts.

134. NARA, RG 38, Intercepts, message 1719/28/169/22 to Lange (*U-505*) and Wintermeyer (*U-190*), March 28, 1944; message 1251/29/306/179, March 29, 1944.

135. NARA, RG 38. Second message, see Office of Naval Intelligence, OP-20-GI-A, War Diary, Command "*U-505*," Commanding Officer: *Oblt.z S.*

Harald Lange, 7th War Cruise from 25 December 1943 to (4) June 1944; *U-505* (Code Name "NEMO"); War Diary (Translated Version) folder, 15. Cited hereafter as NARA, RG 38, KTB.

136. NARA, RG 38, KTB, 15.

137. NARA, RG 38, KTB, 16; NARA, RG 38, Records of the Naval Security Group Central Depository, Crane, Indiana; CNSG Library; folder "3270/409–CNSG–HFDF Operations–HFDF Logs for Atlantic Area, 1Apr-31 Aug 1944;" log page for April 1, 1944. Cited hereafter as NARA, RG 38, HFDF Logs.

138. NARA, RG 38, Intercepts, message 0027/4/301 to Lange (*U-505*) and Schroeter (*U-123*), April 4, 1944.

139. NARA, RG 38, Intercepts, message 0121/5/317 to Lange (*U-505*) and Schroeter (*U-123*), April 5, 1944.

140. NARA, RG 38, Intercepts, message 1206/5/326 to Lange (*U-505*) and Schroeter (*U-123*), April 5, 1944; NARA, RG 38, KTB, 20.

141. NARA, RG 38, Intercepts, message 0449/10/394 from *U-505*, April 10, 1944.

142. NARA, RG 38, KTB, 21; NARA, RG 38, Intercepts, message 0914/10/396 to Lange IV (*U-505*), April 10, 1944.

143. NARA, RG 38, Intercepts, message 1253/13/340 to Rudolf (*U-155?*), Wintermeyer (*U-190*), and Lange (*U-505*), April 13, 1944.

144. NARA, RG 38, Records of the Naval Security Group Central Depository, Crane, Indiana; CNSG Library; Inactive Stations; Folder "B.(1): Daily Locations of U-Boats and Groups–30/10/43–1/6/44," March 26, 1944, April 1, 1944, April 6, 1944, April 7, 1944, April 8, 1944, April 10, 1944, April 14, 1944. Cited hereafter as NARA, RG 38, Daily Locations. U-boats were identified by bigram rather than by hull number on the location lists. The bigram "BY" correlates to *U-505* through the commanding officer's name, the serial numbers of message traffic attached to BY, and the HF/DF fixes.

145. NARA, RG 38, KTB, 10; Naval Historical Center, Washington, DC; U.S. Navy; Translation of B.d.U. War Logs for period beginning January 1, 1944, ending June 30, 1944, entries for March 17 through April 14, 1944. Cited hereafter as Naval Historical Center, BdU War Logs.

146. NARA, RG 38, Intercepts, message 2302/14/3— from Lange IV (U-505), May 14, 1944.

147. NARA, RG 38, HFDF Logs, log entry for May 14, 1944; NARA, RG 38, KTB, 45; NARA, RG 38, Intercepts, message 0349/15/372 from BdU, May 15, 1944.

148. Naval Historical Center, BdU War Logs, May 14, 1944.

149. NARA, RG 38, Records of the Naval Security Group Central Depository, Crane, Indiana; CNSG Library; Intelligence Records of Inactive Naval Stations 1941-1945; folder "17 March 1944-19 May 1945;" COMINCH U-Boat Intelligence Summaries #50-80; U-Boat Intelligence Summary 52, April 28, 1944. Cited hereafter as NARA, RG 38, U-Boat Intelligence Summaries.

150. NARA, RG 38, U-Boat Intelligence Summaries, U-Boat Intelligence Summary 53, May 13, 1944.

151. NARA, RG 38, Daily Locations, May 15, 1944. As became his Commander's rank, Knowles probably did not type up the daily location list himself. However, with rare exceptions the list bore a stylized "K" that Kenneth A. Knowles, Jr. has identified as his father's mark (Knowles telephone interview).

152. NARA, RG 38, Records of the Naval Security Group Central Depository, Crane, Indiana; CNSG Library; Intelligence Records of Inactive Naval Stations 1941-1945; folder "COMINCH U-Boat Summaries, 1 Apr-30 Jun 1944;" message 151555, F-21 (Knowles) to CTF 60, CTF 62, CTF 63, CTF 66, CTG 22.11, CTG 22.16, CTG 22.2, CTG 22.3, CTG 41.6, May 15, 1944. Cited hereafter as NARA, RG 38, COMINCH Daily Estimates.

153. NARA, RG 38, Daily Locations, May 16, 1944.

154. NARA, RG 38, Daily Locations, May 17-20, 1944.

155. NARA, RG 38, Daily Locations, May 21, 1944; Naval Historical Center, BdU War Logs, May 21, 1944.

156. Gallery, *Reminiscences*, March 5, 1971 interview, 75-76.

157. Captain Henri H. Smith-Hutton, USN (Ret.), *Reminiscences of Captain Henri Smith-Hutton, U.S. Navy (Retired)*, vol. 2 (Annapolis, MD: U.S. Naval Institute, August, 1976), August 22, 1974 interview, 402.

158. NARA, RG 38, Records Relating to Naval Activity During World War II; WWII Action and Operational Reports; TF 22.2 to TF 22.3; TF 22.3; folder "Task Group 22.3, Serial: 0021, June 19, 1944;" USS *Guadalcanal*; Report to Commander in Chief, Atlantic Fleet, subject: Report of A/S Cruise of Task Group 22.3, June 19, 1944, entry for May 13, 1944. Cited hereafter as NARA, RG 38, TG 22.3 Report.

159. NARA, RG 38, TG 22.3 Report, entries for May 14-15, 1944.

160. NARA, RG 38, TG 22.3 Report, entries for May 18-20, 1944.

161. NARA RG 38, TG 22.3 Report, entries for May 20-28, 1944.

162. NARA, RG 38, TG 22.3 Report, entry for May 28, 1944. *U-505* was approximately 400 miles northeast of the task group at this time; the identity of this contact is unknown.

163. NARA, RG 38, COMINCH Daily Estimates, messages 181450, May 18, 1944; 191550, May 19, 1944; 201537, May 20, 1944, 211451, May 21, 1944.

164. NARA, RG 38, COMINCH Daily Estimates, message 231517, May 23, 1944; NARA, RG 38, Daily Locations, May 23, 1944.

165. NARA, RG 38, KTB, 53.

166. NARA, RG 38, U-Boat Intelligence Summaries, U-Boat Intelligence Summary 54, May 24, 1944.

167. NARA, RG 38, COMINCH Daily Estimates, message 281601, May 28, 1944.

168. NARA, RG 38, Daily Locations, May 28, 1944; NARA, RG 38, KTB, 56.

169. NARA, RG 38, Daily Locations, May 29, 1944, May 30, 1944, May 31, 1944, June 1, 1944; NARA, RG 38, COMINCH Daily Estimates, messages 291515, May 29, 1944; 301605, May 30, 1944; 311552, May 31, 1944; 011500, June 1, 1944.

170. NARA, RG 38, Daily Locations, May 22 -June 1, 1944; Naval Historical Center, BdU War Logs, May 22-June 1, 1944.

171. NARA, RG 38, Commander Task Group 22.3, Report to Commander in Chief, U.S. Atlantic Fleet, subject: Capture of German Submarine U-505, 19 June 1944; folder "Task Group 22.3, Serial: 0021, June 19, 1944;" TF 22.3; WWII Action and Operational Reports; TF 22.2 to TF 22.3; Records Relating to Naval Activity During World War II, 2. Cited hereafter as NARA, RG 38, CTG 22.3 to CINCLANT.

172. NARA, RG 38, TG 22.3 Report, entry for June 1, 1944; NARA, RG 38, KTB, 59.

173. NARA, RG 38, TG 22.3 Report, entry for June 2, 1944; NARA, RG 38, KTB, 59.

174. NARA, RG 38, TG 22.3 Report, entry for June 4, 1944. While the 0520 fix was on the opposite side of the task group from *U-505*, the 0629 bearing could have come from *U-505*. However, Lange mentioned no incoming or outgoing messages in the KTB for this date. NARA, RG 38, KTB, 60.

175. Gallery, *Twenty Million Tons*, 289-290.

176. Gallery, *Twenty Million Tons*, 292. For specific information about the Allied success against *U-505*, see Lawrence Paterson, "Collision Course: Task Group 22.3 and the Hunt for *U-505*," and Jordan Vause, "Desperate Decisions that Doomed U-505," both of which are reproduced elsewhere in this collection.

177. NARA, RG 313, Messages, message 062359, CTG 22.3 to CINCLANT, June 6, 1944.

178. NARA, RG 38, U-505 Documents, Wenger Exploitation Memorandum, 1

179. *Ibid.*

180. NARA, RG 38, Records of the Naval Security Group Central Depository, Crane, Indiana; CNSG Library; folder "CNSG–Enigma Machine–Information Regarding Captured Machines and Code Lists, 22 Jun 1944-19 Jun 1945;" memorandum from OP-20-G to F-21, June 22, 1944.

181. NARA, RG 38, U-505 Documents, Wenger Exploitation Memorandum, 2.

182. *Ibid.*, 2-3.

183. *Ibid.*, 3.

184. NARA, RG 38, U-505 Documents, memorandum from OP-20-GI-A for FX-01, October 21, 1944.

185. NARA, RG 457, COMINT History, 225-226.

186. NARA, RG 38, Messages, Memorandum for Distribution List Attached, serial 001786, June 18, 1944.

187. NARA, RG 38, Messages, message 141817, NOB BERMUDA to COMINCH, August 14, 1944.

188. NARA, RG 38, Messages, message 301957, August 31, 1944.

189. NARA, RG 38, U-505 Documents, memorandum "U.S.S. NEMO," December 11, 1944. Cited hereafter as NARA, RG 38, *Nemo* Documents, *Nemo* Memorandum.

190. NARA, RG 38, Nemo Documents, *Nemo* Memorandum, 3.

191. Y'Blood, *Hunter-Killer*, 197.

192. NARA, RG 38, Messages, message 242045, COMINCH to COMDT NOB BERMUDA, June 24, 1944.

193. *Ibid.*

194. NARA, RG 38, Messages, message 271437, COMINCH to COMDT NOB BERMUDA, June 27, 1944; NARA, RG 38, Messages, message 042143, COMINCH to Admiralty, July 4, 1944.

195. NARA, RG 38, OP-16-Z (Special Activities Branch); 1941-1945; Interrogations: U-505 to U-512; folder "U-505;" U-505 Rough Interrogations; interrogation of *Mechanikerobergefreiter* Karl Heinz Werner Hönemann. Cited hereafter as NARA, RG 38, Interrogations.

196. NARA, RG 38, Messages, message 012111, COMINCH to CINCLANT, July 1, 1944. Emphasis added.

197. NARA, RG 38, Messages, message 282217, NOB BERMUDA to COMINCH, June 28, 1944.

198. NARA, RG 38, Messages, message 081330, NOB BERMUDA to COMINCH, July 8, 1944; message 031834, NOB BERMUDA to COMINCH, July 3, 1944; message 171457, NOB BERMUDA to COMINCH, July 17, 1944.

199. NARA, RG 38, Messages, message 061617, BAD to Admiralty, September 6, 1944.

200. NARA, RG 457, COMINT History, 229-230.

201. NARA, RG 38, Interrogations.

202. NARA, RG 38, Interrogations, interrogation of Hönemann.

203. NARA RG 38, Interrogations, interrogations of Hönemann and *Maschinenobergefreiter* Willi Karl Kneisel.

204. NARA, RG 38, Interrogations, interrogations of *Funkobergefreiter* Erich Wilhelm Kalbitz and *Funkgefreiter* Erich Hans Laun.

205. NARA, RG 38, Interrogations. The crew was apparently interrogated further after their arrival in the United States, but the author could not locate any notes for smooth interrogations in RG 38.

206. NARA, RG 38, Messages, Memorandum for the Chief of Staff, U.S. Army, from Deputy Commander in Chief, U.S. Fleet, January 25, 1945; C. Herbert Gilliland and Robert Shenk, *Admiral Dan Gallery: The Life and Wit of a Navy Original* (Annapolis, MD: Naval Institute Press, 1999), 129.

207. NARA, RG 38, U-505 documents, message 051407, GCCS to OP-20-G, June 5, 1944. Emphasis added.

208. NARA, RG 38, memorandum from Wenger to Smith-Hutton, June 5, 1944, attached to message 051407, June 5, 1944.

209. *Ibid.*

210. NARA, RG 38, COMINT History, 227.

Collision Course: Task Group 22.3 and the Hunt for U-505
by Lawrence Paterson

1. NARA, RG 38, U-Boat Intelligence Summary 52, April 28, 1944. For a good history of these offensive carrier groups and their operations, see William T. Y'Blood, *Hunter-Killer: U.S. Escort Carriers in the Battle of the Atlantic* (Annapolis, MD: Naval Institute Press, 1983).

2. Daniel Gallery, *Twenty Million Tons Under the Sea* (Chicago, IL: Regnery, 1956), 273. An outstanding biography of Werner Henke and the history of *U-515*, including its final days and aftermath that led to the death of

this U-boat ace, can be found in Timothy P. Mulligan, *Lone Wolf: The Life and Death of U-Boat Ace Werner Henke* (Westport, CT: Praeger, 1993).

3. TG22.3, "Report on Capture of German Submarine *U-505,*" Action Report of Task Group 22.3, June 19, 1944, RG 38, NA-CP (TG22.3 Report); Gallery, *Twenty Million Tons Under the Sea*, 247-79.

4. "Oral History—Battle of the Atlantic, 1941-1945"; Daniel V. Gallery Interview, recorded May 26, 1945, Box 11/World War II Interviews, Operational Archives Branch, Naval Historical Center, Washington (hereafter Gallery Interview, May 26, 1945).

5. Captain Henri H. Smith-Hutton, USN (Ret.), *Reminiscences of Captain Henri Smith-Hutton, U.S. Navy (Retired)*, 2 vols. (Annapolis, Md.: Naval Institute Press, 1976), vol. 2, August 22, 1974. Interview, 402, provided courtesy of Mark E. Wise, USNR.

6. War Diary of *U-505*, PG 30542/1-7; T1022, 3065-3066.

7. *Ibid.*, 4186.

8. Hans Joachim Decker, "404 Days! The War Patrol Life of the German *U-505,*" *U.S. Naval Institute Proceedings*, Vol. 86, No. 3 (March 1960), 44-45.

9. NARA, RG 38, Daily Locations, May 21, 1944; Naval Historical Center, BdU War Logs, May 21, 1944, provided courtesy of Mark E. Wise, USNR.

10. NARA, RG 38, KTB, 59.

11. Daniel V. Gallery Interview, May 26, 1945.

12. Diary Excerpt from V. J. Verdolini, RM2/c, USS *Guadal-canal* (CVE-60).

13. NARA, RG 38, Daily Locations, May 22-June 1, 1944; Naval Historical Center, BdU War Logs, May 22-June 1, 1944, provided courtesy of Mark E. Wise, USNR.

14. TG22.3 Report.

15. NARA, RG 38, TG22.3 Report, entry for 4 June 1944, Commander USS *Chatelain* to Commander Task Group 22.3; VC-8, ASW6 After Action Report.

16. Decker, "404 Days! The War Patrol Life of the German *U-505,*" 45.

Desperate Decisions: The German Loss of U-505
by Jordan Vause

1. A pair of other U-boats had been captured by the time of Gallery's exploit. The details of their seizure, however, were kept secret and BdU (German submarine command headquarters) never knew anything about them. *Kptlt.* Fritz

Julius Lemp's *U-110* was temporarily captured by British forces after several depth-charge attacks (even her crew did not realize the boat was boarded by enemy forces) but sank while under tow. Unfortunately for the Germans, records found aboard included a top secret Enigma machine and secret documents relating to it. On August 27, 1941, *U-570* was damaged by a British Hudson aircraft and her commander, Kptlt. Hans Rahmlow, surrendered to the plane without any surface ships in the vicinity. The British towed her to Thorlakshafn, Iceland, and converted her into the HMS *Graph* on September 19, 1941.

2. Jürgen Oesten, E-mail, 27 July 1998. Oesten, a recipient of the Knight's Cross, was the commander of *U-61*, a Type II boat, and *U-106* and *U-861*, both Type IX boats. *U-106* was very similar to *U-505*. Oesten is an outspoken man who will not hesitate to share his views on anything, including the *U-505* affair. His input is always helpful.

3. Peter Hansen, Letter, September 12, 1998. Hansen was a *Kriegsmarine* officer who worked for the *Abwehr* during the war. For that reason he seems to know a lot more about the men and the affairs of the *U-Bootwaffe* than most people would suspect. When *U-505* was hit with sabotage in Lorient, Hansen was part of the investigative team and had the opportunity to speak with several of her crew.

4. Siegfried Koitschka, Letter, September 6, 1991. Koitschka, another Knight's Cross holder, was the captain of two boats, *U-7* (a Type II U-Bootschulflottille, or school boat) and *U-616* (a Type VIIC). He was captured two weeks before the *U-505* incident when his *U-616* was hunted to exhaustion for three days east of Spain in May of 1944. He surfaced, saved everyone in his crew, and his U-boat sank. Koitschka died in 2002.

5. Oesten, E-mail, October 13, 1999.

6. Koitschka Letter.

7. Statement of Commanding Officer, *U-505*. This can be found online at http://uboat.net/allies/ships/uss_guadalcanal-5.htm, or in Appendix C herein.

8. Taking *U-505* in tow with some or all of her crewmen still aboard would have been foolhardy. If the boat went down while attached to a towing hawser, major complications would have ensued for the towing ship. If the boat fired a torpedo up the hawser at the towing ship, it could not miss.

9. Hans Jacob Goebeler and John Vanzo, *Steel Boats, Iron Hearts: The Wartime Saga of Hans Goebeler and the U-505* (Wagnerian Publications, 1999). Goebeler was a *Maschinengefreiter* (fireman) who had served in the crew since the days of the boat's first skipper, Axel-Olaf Loewe. On the morning *U-505* was bombed to the surface he was in the control room, one of the team who tried so hard to pull the boat out of its uncontrolled dive just before she surfaced. Some controversy surrounded Goebeler in his later years (he died shortly after his book

was published). To put it bluntly, he was not entirely trusted by certain elements of the *U-Bootwaffe* community who thought he exaggerated his role during the final minutes of *U-505*. Goebeler's firsthand version is the most complete German account we have of the events of June 4, 1944. Many of the concerns about Goebeler can be traced to the political squabbles within the *U-Bootwaffe* community (and to some of those outside this exclusive community who think fancifully they are part of it). Like several other U-Boat veterans, Goebeler has become a symbol of a greater struggle.

10. Oesten, E-mail, July 27, 1998. As a follow-up to this comment, Oesten was asked whether it was more important to save the crew or to prevent the boat's capture. His response was interesting and reflects the cynicism he began to experience as the war progressed. "My answer is bound to be pure speculation—to be or not to be a hero . . . and the answer might differ whether it concerns my first, second, or third boat. As I knew that the war was definitely lost since the beginning of 1942, I guess I would not have taken an unnecessary risk on the third boat and would have tried to save my crew."

11. Oesten, E-mail.

12. Information on members of *U-505*'s crew was taken from Naval Archives Record Group 38, Records of the Office of the Chief of Naval Operations, Office of Naval Intelligence (OP 16-Z), 1942-45.

13. Goebeler, *Steel Boats, Iron Hearts*, 96.

14. *Ibid.*, 152.

15. Engineering officers in the Kriegsmarine were trained differently than line officers, and normally did not rise to command. It is worth noting, however, that any officer, Hauser included, would have been expected to take command in the absence of an eligible line officer. The most striking example of this occurred in 1943, when U-441 was brought home under the command of its doctor after her other officers had been incapacitated in a firefight.

16. Not all boats were outfitted with explosive charges. Jürgen Oesten states flatly that none of the three boats he commanded had demolition charges on board. Oesten, E-mail, November 24, 1999.

17. Hansen, Letter, September 12, 1998.

18. Goebeler, *Steel Boats, Iron Hearts*, 152.

19. Hansen, Letter, December 18, 1999.

20. Oesten, E-mail, November 24, 1999.

21. *Ibid.*

22. Goebeler, 126.

23. Oesten, E-mail, November 24, 1999.

24. This point was emphasized well in Lothar-Günther Buchheim's novel (and movie) *Das Boot.*

25. Oesten, E-mail, November 24, 1999.

26. This is the point where some people start to get edgy about Hans Goebeler's credibility—after all, he was the only one present. But when the onion is peeled back and the circumstances examined closely, there does not seem to be any real debate about the facts he presented.

27. Jordan Vause, *U-Boat Ace: The Story of Wolfgang Lüth* (Annapolis, MD: Naval Institute Press, 1990), 81-85. In February 1941, *U-43* sank at her berth in Lorient, a victim not of torpedoes or bombs, but of the wrong sequence of valves being left open by an unknown crewman. She took at least twelve hours to go down.

28. For what it is worth, Oesten cannot think of a better fitting to have selected if there was time to open only one.

29. Goebeler, *Steel Boats, Iron Hearts*, 152.

30. Hansen, Letter, September 12, 1998.

Project 356: U-505 and the Journey to Chicago
by Keith R. Gill

1. Jay Pridmore, *Inventive Genius: The History of the Museum of Science and Industry* (Chicago, IL: Museum Books, 1996), 16.

2. *U-1* is presented in full cutaway view so visitors can see into the boat for its entire length. This helps them understand the more important compartments and how sailors lived and worked in a foreign environment. *U-1* was commissioned on December 6, 1906, and eventually used as a training boat for WWI crews. The museum attempted unsuccessfully to acquire several different submarines. These included Simon Lake's historic *Argonaut* and a variety of different classes of American boats (H, L, O and S), including *O-12*, which was renamed *Nautilus*.

3. The summary of Daniel V. Gallery's postwar assignments was taken from C. Herbert Gilliland and Robert Shenk, *Admiral Dan Gallery: The Life and Wit of a Navy Original* (Annapolis, MD: Naval Institute Press, 1999), 132-139.

4. Lenox Lohr Appointment Calendar for September 25 and 26, 1947, File 1069, Museum of Science and Industry Executive Calendar, Jan.-Dec., 1947, University of Illinois Chicago Special Collections Department.

5. Letter from E. R. Henning to Lenox R. Lohr, October 6, 1947, Box 5/12, Series IV, file 5-4, Correspondence 1954, Bringing *U-505* to Chicago, Museum

of Science and Industry Archives, hereafter referred to as MSI Archives. It is likely Gallery was working behind the scenes in Washington to do everything he could to save *U-505*. At this time Gallery did not have any meaningful connection with MSI, and the correspondence between Gallery and museum staff was of a formal nature. Once Gallery and Lohr began a regular discussion about *U-505*, however, they grew to admire each other, quickly moved to a first name basis, and even shared many inside jokes.

6. Dan Gallery's fingerprints coat Henning's report. He had long been pushing the publicity angle, was the officer behind the temporary sinking stay, and had originally pushed for the most obvious place to exhibit the boat—Annapolis. *U-505* did appear at Annapolis on the Navy's 150th anniversary in 1945.

7. Both telegrams are located in Box 5/12, Series IV, file 5-4, Correspondence 1954, "Bringing U-505 to Chicago," MSI Archives.

8. *Ibid.*

9. Letter from Harry C. Watts to Charles C. Dawes, October 20, 1947, Box 5/12, Series IV, file 5-4, Correspondence 1954, "Bringing U-505 to Chicago," MSI Archives. Watts was quoting Gallery's letter. Gallery's letter to Watts was not available to the author.

10. *Ibid.* It would take almost seven years of letter writing, lobbying, telegrams, and discussions before the museum finally altered its tack and followed the recommended procedure for gaining title to the elusive boat. The indefatigable Gallery, meanwhile, even with the actual move to Chicago underway, was still laboring to have the Navy pay for part of the tow. He finally met with some success when the U.S. Coast Guard agreed to tow the boat at its expense on the final third of its trip.

11. Letter from Daniel Gallery to Major Lohr, November 24, 1947, Box 5/12, Series IV, MSI Archives.

12. Letter from Lenox Lohr to Admiral Daniel V. Gallery, November 21, 1947, Box 5/12, Series IV, Bringing U-505 to Chicago, MSI Archives.

13. Letter from Harry C. Watts to Charles Dawes, February 18, 1948, Box 5/12, Series IV, File 5-4, Correspondence 1954, Bringing U-505 to Chicago, MSI Archives.

14. Journal, City Council, Chicago, "Secretary of Navy Requested to Present Nazi Submarine *U-505* to City of Chicago and proposed resolution," January 20, 1950, 5,782.

15. Journal, City Council, Chicago, Communications, "Transfer of Nazi Submarine *U-505* to City of Chicago, April 13, 1950, 6028.

16. "City Told: Act or Lose U-boat as War Trophy," *Chicago Daily Tribune*, March 8, 1953.

17. "Tribune Offers Use of Ship to Tow *U-505* Here," *Chicago Daily Tribune*, March 18, 1953. Lenox Lohr told the press a previous proposal from the Naval Reserve to bring the submarine to Chicago failed principally because of lack of interim storage facilities, a problem the Tribune Company's offer seemed to solve.

18. "Praise Tribune Offer to Tow Nazi Sub Here, Spur Drive to Get *U-505* as War memorial," *Chicago Daily Tribune*, March 19, 1953.

19. "Kennelly Vows New Efforts To Bring Sub Here," *Chicago Sunday Tribune*, March 29, 1953.

20. This name change appears first in a memo from Francis Low, head of 10th fleet to the Commander of the 10th fleet. Two new names were being offered for consideration. "Under the assumption that *U-505* is successfully towed to Bermuda, it is suggested that she be given an appropriate cover name of which the following are submitted: a) *Ark* and b) *Nemo*." The name *Ark* was likely a biblical reference to the literal boat load of information contained in the submarine. The final decision on USS *Nemo* is credited to a fascination with Jules Verne and was transmitted in a secret radio message to CTG 22.3 that *U-505* should be referred to as USS *Nemo*. On several occasions reminders went out when *U-505* was used in some messages instead of *Nemo*. Both items in NA RG38 CNSG Library.

21. *Ibid.*

22. "Kennelly to Fly to White House for Conference," *Chicago Herald Tribune*, March 30, 1953.

23. "Navy to Help City get *U-505*," *Chicago Herald-American*, April 9, 1953.

24. See Gilliland and Shenk, *Gallery*, 187.

25. Gallery, Daniel V., *U-505* (Paperback Library, 1956), 282-283. (originally titled *Twenty Million Tons Under the Sea*). See also, Gilliland and Shenk, *Gallery*, 188, which cites a letter to Gallery from R. A. Ofstie dated April 1, 1953, at the Nimitz Library in the Gallery Papers: "It was the view of the Chief [CNO] that your action in going outside the Department with the intent of applying pressure toward the accomplishment of this business was quite inappropriate. I think, Dan, that you can readily understand this conclusion, which seems obvious to me as well. 'Nuff said!'" In an unrelated incident Gallery won an official reprimand that almost resulted in a court martial hearing in January 1950. It is this 1950 reprimand during the "Revolt of the Admirals" crisis that the author believes has been confused by some historians who state that Gallery was almost court-martialed by E. J. King for threatening to blow the scheduled Normandy invasion when he captured *U-505* without authorization— a preposterous claim.

26. The transfer of *Constellation* to Baltimore provides an interesting example of how the Navy worked. The media made it appear as though the Navy was picking up the tab for much of the preparation and towing of that frigate, when in fact, the city of Baltimore was paying the Navy for the work it did on the ship. The author thanks Gloria Carvahlo of the U.S. Navy, Naval Sea Systems Command, Navy Ship Donation Program, for providing the transfer agreements for the USS *Texas* BB and the USF *Constellation* which provided the source of these statements.

27. Hy Delman, "Drive Opens for Nazi Sub," *Chicago Herald-American*, Friday April 3, 1953, 5.

28. *Ibid.*, Tuesday, April 7, 1953.

29. Hy Delman, "Historical Relic Sought: U-Boat Aid Asked Navy, City Group Wants Sub Put in Tow Able Condition," *Chicago American*, Tuesday April 7, 1953, 3.

30. Hy Delman, "42 to Dine, Plan *U-505* Strategy," *Chicago American*, Thursday April 16, 1953, 7.

31. "Chicago's U-Boat, If City Acts Fast," *Chicago American*, April 22, 1953.

32. *Ibid.*

33. Harold Smith, "*U-505* Passes Inspection by Chicago Group: Finds it in Better Shape Than Reported," *Chicago Daily Tribune*, April 24, 1953, Hy Delman, "Problem of Whale on Land, *U-505* Move Giant Task," *Chicago American*, April 26, 1953, 15.

34. Hy Delman, "Full Speed on *U-505!*" *Chicago Herald American*, April 24, 1953.

35. "Inspiration, Museum plans *U-505* Shrine," *Chicago American*, April 27, 1953. One of the reasons the museum had not added a submarine to its collection was the attitude of many post-WWI Americans, who opposed involvement in another international war and were against celebrating machines built to kill people. Museum officials, therefore, decided to focus on the scientific aspect of submarines. Their initial efforts were spent searching for submarines that had been utilized for scientific research. Candidates suitable for exhibit, naturally enough, were very scarce. Eventually the museum found ways to justify exhibiting submarines with military connections, but by this time the best opportunities were no longer available and other priorities occupied their time and resources.

36. "Approve Plans for Moving Nazi Sub to Museum, Park Board Authorize Necessary Permits," *Chicago Daily Tribune*, April 29, 1953.

37. "Torpedo," *Chicago American*, June 14, 1953, 19.

38. Late in the game Milwaukee, Wisconsin, flirted with making a bid, and even began raising money to preserve *U-505* there, but in the end no other city made a counter proposal. "Clear 2 Legal Steps to Bring Nazi Sub Here," *Chicago Daily News*, June 26, 1953.

39. "Mayor's Group to Hear U-boat Trophy Report," *Chicago Daily Tribune*, July 8, 1953, pt. 1, 2.

40. "Continue Drive for *U-505* Though Cost Doubles: Seek $40,000 to Fix Sub for Trip," *Chicago Daily Tribune*, July 9, 1953, pt. 1, 5. According to Jack Manley, the president of the International Ship Master's Association of Chicago who inspected *U-505* at its berth in Portsmouth, the boat's topside exterior was in extremely bad condition, and considerable work on the interior would also be required.

41. "$221,000 Goal, *U-505* Fund Drive Opens," *Chicago American*, July 9, 1953, 3.

42. Kathry Loring, "U-boat Epic Will be Told at Benefit," *Chicago Daily Tribune*, November 23, 1953, Section F, pt. 5, 2, "Film of *U-505* Capture Shown in Fund Drive," *Chicago Daily Tribune*, July 15, 1953, pt. 1, 17.

43. "$225,000 Drive for *U-505* to Begin Today," *Chicago Daily Tribune*, July 16, 1953, pt. 1, 4.

44. "Wagner Name to Go on *U-505* Donor Plaque," *Chicago Daily Tribune*, July 17, 1953, pt. 3, 2.

45. Gallery, Daniel, "Adm. Gallery Answers Question: Why Bring *U-505* to Chicago?" Letters to the Editor, *Chicago Daily News*, August 13, 1953, 10.

46. "*U-505*," *Chicago Sun Times*, February 2, 1954.

47. *Ibid.*

48. Grace, H. H., "Reader Votes No on Submarine Project," *Chicago Daily News*, August 5, 1953.

49. "Hilton Hotels Act: New $1,000 Gift to U-Boat Fund," *Chicago Daily News*, July 28, 1953.

50. "Repair Delay Holds Up U-Boat's Trip To Chicago," *Chicago Daily Tribune*, August 7, 1953.

51. "May Bring U-boat Here in September," *Chicago Daily News*, August 18, 1953, 6. This was in keeping with *U-505's* "tradition" when two pairs of pants, loose bolts, and debris were removed from the boat's tanks by Kriegsmarine dockyard personnel in early 1944!

52. Robert Howard, "Chicago Group Pleased with Sub's Condition," *Chicago Daily Tribune*, August 19, 1953, pt. 1, 20F. Accompanying the team were three members of the Seabee battalion, who had presented the two options for moving the boat onto land. With them was C. Thomas Kelly, the Chicago Park District assistant engineer, with blueprints of the bridges affected by the

lagoon move option. The task was to confirm the dimensions of the boat to determine if the lagoon option was feasible. The following men made the trip: Seth Gooder, Robert Crown, Carl Stockholm, Dan Gallery, C. Thomas Kelly, Fred Joyce, Jr., Albert E. Hill Jr., Harold E. Peterson, Luther C. Mueller, Maurice L. Horner Jr., B. T. Franck, Dan McMaster, and Thomas F White, Jr. The list appears in *Chicago American* article "*U-505* Safe, Seaworthy," August 19, 1953, 4, and additional names in "Chicago Naval Experts Study *U-505* in East: Admiral and Engineers Fly to Portsmouth," *Chicago Daily Tribune*, August 18, 1953.

53. John Justin Smith, "Find U-Boat's Voyage Here Will Be Tight Sque-e-eze: Conning Tower Must Come off," *Chicago Daily News*, August 19, 1953, 38.

54. *Ibid.*

55. John Justin Smith, "Delve Into U-Boat Problems: Chicagoans at Navy Dry-dock Study How to Bring Ship Here," *Chicago Daily News*, August 18, 1953, 6.

56. News Release for Wednesday, December 30, 1953, Fred A. Joyce and Son Public Relations, Chicago, MSI Archives, *U-505* PR Box.

57. "Legal Snag Delays Bringing German Submarine Here," *Chicago Sun-Times*, September 20, 1953.

58. "U-Boat, Captured in War II, to be Exhibited Here," *Milwaukee Sentinel*, October 28, 1953. Support for *U-505* would eventually come from Milwaukee, Wisconsin, as well as Minneapolis, Minnesota, Akron, Ohio, New York City, New York, Detroit, Michigan, New Orleans, Louisiana, and Los Angeles, California, to name just a few of the more prominent cities around the United States. Much of this support was the result of national efforts by the various chapters of the Navy League. "Other Cities Boost Fund for *U-505*," *Chicago American*, December 28, 1954.

59. "700 Mile Tow Offered Free to *U-505* Fund: New Yorker Cuts Cost of Voyage 33%," *Chicago Daily Tribune*, November 16, 1953.

60. "Aid Drive to Bring *U-505* Here: Free Tow Offer, $500 Received," *Chicago Sunday Tribune*, November 29, 1953.

61. "Early Spring U-505 Goal," *Chicago American*, December 30, 1953, 4. See also, News Release for Wednesday, December 30, 1953, Fred A. Joyce and Son Public Relations, Chicago, MSI Archives, *U-505* PR Box.

62. "U-Boat Fund hits $150,000," *Chicago Daily News*, December 30, 1953; "Launch Final Drive for Case to Move *U-505*: $100,000 is pledged, $50,000 is needed," *Chicago Daily Tribune*, December 30, 1954, pt. 1, p. 10.

63. News Release for Wednesday December 30, 1953, Fred A. Joyce and Son Public Relations, Chicago, MSI Archives, *U-505* PR Box.

64. "Tentative Date for Dedication of *U-505* is Set," *Chicago Sunday Tribune*, January 17, 1954, pt. 1, 36H.

65. "Souvenir of Souvenirs," *Chicago Daily Tribune*, February 6, 1954, pt. 1, 10H. To encourage continued donations, donors at the $100 or more level received a Plank Owner's card. The small card featured a drawing of the *U-505* boarding party with an inscription bestowing lifelong membership to the "prize crew," and entitled the bearer to "board and seize any enemy submarines that attempt to molest him on the high seas," and free admission to *U-505*. The initial admission fee was .25 cents. "You Can Be *U-505* "Plank Owner," *Chicago Sun Times*, February 20, 1954. A plank owner card is also available in the MSI archives.

66. *Chicago Daily News*, January 21, 1954.

67. http://www.ussnautilus.org/history.htm.

68. "Crown to Ask Ike to *U-505* Fete on July 4," *Chicago Daily Tribune*, January 23, 1954, pt. 1. 2.

69. "Museum Given title to *U-505* by Navy Chief," *Chicago Daily Tribune*, March 10, 1954, pt. 1, 5.

70. Paul Leach, "Title to *U-505* Issued to Museum," *Chicago Daily News*, March 9, 1954.

71. Letter, Earl Trosino to Dan Gallery, March 31, 1954, and Dan Gallery reply to Earl Trosino, April 2, 1954, UIC Archives, Lenox Lohr papers.

72. Gene Byer, "Nazi U-Boat Captured by Springfield Man," *Chester* [PA] *Times*, May 11, 1954, 1.

73. "Nazi U-boat to Head for City May 1," *Chicago Daily News*, April 13, 1954, 20; "*U-505* to Start Long Trip Here About May 15," *Chicago Daily Tribune*, May 3, 1954, pt. 1, 7F.

74. "*U-505* Captors to Share in Dedication," *Chicago Daily Tribune*, May 6, 1954.

75. *Ibid*.

76. "Big Yacht Starts Cruise to Bring Nazi Sub Here," *Chicago Sun-Times*, May 13, 1954; "Yacht to Meet *U-505*," *Chicago American*, May 12, 1954, 25.

77. "Bad Weather Holds Up Tow Trip Of *U-505*," *Chicago Daily Tribune*, May 15, 1954, and "Winds halt *U-505* Trip," *Chicago American*, May 14, 1954; "Leaves Yard: Halt Trip Of *U-505* To Chicago," *Chicago Daily News*, May 14, 1954.

78. "German U-Boat Begins its Long Trip To Chicago: Tug Pulls Submarine Toward Nova Scotia," *Chicago Sunday Tribune*, May 16, 1954, pt. 2, 12F.

79. "U-Boat Heads for Chicago Museum," *Jamestown* [N.Y.] *Post Journal*, May 14, 1954.

80. "He'll Tow Nazi U-Boat He Helped To Capture," *Philadelphia Daily News*, May 11, 1954, is just one example of many that followed.

81. Few realize just how difficult it was to keep *U-505* from foundering during the critical hours after its capture. The boarding and salvage parties struggled for hours to keep the boat above water. During the two-week tow to Bermuda, salvage crews paid daily visits to *U-505* to keep the boat from sinking. Their tasks included, but were not limited to: pumping bilges, blowing ballast, and re-charging batteries all of which was magnificently directed by Earl Trosino.

82. "U-Boat Moving Along, Captain of Tug Radios," *Chicago Daily Tribune*, May 17, 1954.

83. "*U-505* Slowed By Fog Bank Near Halifax," *Chicago Daily Tribune*, May 18, 1954, pt. 1, 15.

84. "Fog Shrouds *U-505*, Tug, Radio Silent," (no publishing information is available, but a copy of the article exists in MSI archives, *U-505* newsclip collection).

85. "*U-505* Goes Back 'On Air,'" *Chicago American*, May 20, 1954; "*U-505*, Escort Resume Contact After Storm," May 20, 1954 (no publishing information is available, but a copy of the article exists in MSI archives, *U-505* newsclip collection). "*U-505* is Safe After Storm of 36 Hours," *Chicago Daily Tribune*, May 20, 1954.

86. "Report *U-505* off Gaspe Peninsula," *Chicago Daily News*, May 20, 1954.

87. See http://www.uboat.net, an extraordinarily thorough and well organized web site about U-boats from both WWI and WWII; http://www.vac-acc.gc.ca/general/sub.cfm?source=history/secondwar/battlegul f/intro.

88. "2,000 in Baie Comeau Visit Captured *U-505*," *Chicago Sunday Tribune*, May 23, 1954, pt. 1, 3.

89. "*U-505* To Reach Montreal Today," May 25, 1954, 9 (no publishing information available).

90. http://www.great-lakes.net/lakes/stlaw.html.

91. "Guide *U-505* Through Canada Canal," May 27, 1954 (no publishing information available).

92. "Chicago-Bound Submarine Lures Canadians to Canal," (paper unknown), May 28, 1954 F, pt. 1, 5.

93. "Captured U-Boat Delayed in Locks en Route to City," *Cleveland Plain Dealer*, May 29, 1954.

94. "Adm. Gallery Rides *U-505* Thru Locks on Trip Here," *Chicago Sunday Tribune*, May 30, 1954.

95. "*U-505* Aid Promised," *Chicago American*, May 30, 1954.

96. "En Route Here, Sub Gets Tight Squeeze," *Chicago Sun Times*, May 31, 1954; "Captured U-Boat Delayed in Locks en Route to City," *Cleveland Plain Dealer*, May 29, 1954.

97. "Former U-Boat Due in Buffalo," *New York Times*, June 2, 1954.

98. "Chicago-Bound Submarine Lures Canadians to Canal," (paper unknown), May 28, 1954 F pt. 1, p. 5.

99. "Tug Pauline L Moran Tows Ex-Nazi Sub Portsmouth, NH to Port Colborne, Ont.," Tow Line, Moran Towing and Transportation Co, Vol. VII, No. 3.

100. "Nazi Sub Docks, Scars Tell Tale: Hundreds on Hand as Prize of War Arrives," *Cleveland Plain Dealer*, June 3, 1944.

101. "Nazi Submarine at E. 9th Pier," *Cleveland News*, June 3, 1954.

102. Author's interview of Mrs. Chester Mocarski, December 2002. Various accounts that describe Mocarski's injuries as a crushed leg, two broken legs, or a broken back are incorrect. Interview with Chester Mocarski family with the author, May 2001, Chicago. Wayne Pickles Questionnaire, 1954, MSI archives. It was during this effort to help Mocarski that Pickels dropped the tool box loaded with machinist tools and gear. It plunged into the depths of the sea and was lost. The heavy tool box was attached to a long chain. Pickels was going to attach one end of the chain to the boat and lower the tool box down the hatch to keep any waiting Germans from closing it behind them.

103. "U-505 Ceremony to Mark Capture by U.S. Navy," *Chicago Daily News*, June 4, 1954.

104. "U-505 Seized 10 Years Ago, Ceremony Set," *Chicago Daily Tribune*, June 4, 1954, pt. 1, p. 11.

105. "Two Chicago Painters in Cleveland Spray Exterior of *U-505*," *Chicago Sunday Tribune*, June 6, 1954, pt. 5, 36F; *U-505* would not be painted in its original colors until 2003.

106. "U-505 Leaves Cleveland on Way to Toledo," *Chicago Daily Tribune*, June 8, 1954, pt. 2, 2F.

107. "Boards Sub: Admiral Gallery Greets U-505 at Detroit," *Chicago Daily News*, June 11, 1954.

108. "German U-Boat's Visit Stirs Veteran's Memory," *Detroit Michigan Times*, June 14, 1954.

109. "Town Talk," *Alpena Michigan News*, June 16, 1954; "Nazi Sub Fails To Stop in City," *Alpena Michigan News*, June 15, 1954.

110. "*U-505* Heading for Milwaukee From Mackinac," *Chicago Daily Tribune*, June 18, 1954.

111. "*U-505* Docks at Milwaukee on Way Here," *Chicago Sunday Tribune*, June 20, 1954, pt. 1, 34F.

112. *Chicago Daily News*, Thursday June 24, 1954.

113. http://www.kacm.com/Tidalwave.htm

114. The scientific name for what took place is "seiche," a phenomenon that strikes enclosed bodies of water when oscillations at the right frequency occur. The result is something akin to water in a bathtub sloshing back and forth. This phenomenon is relatively rare and only a few natural locations in the world, including the Great Lakes, Lake Geneva, Loch Earn in Scotland, and Lake Vattern in Sweden, are subject to them.

115. "Four Local Men Helped Take Nazi Sub," *The South End Reporter*, June 30, 1954, 1.

116. Clay Gowran, "Chicago Roars Its Welcome to Captured Sub," *Chicago Sunday Tribune*, June 27, 1954, 1, 6, 7

117. This internet address was active when checked for this article: http://tucnak.fsv.cuni.cz/~calda/Documents/1930s/FDR_Quarantine_1937.htm l.

118. "Engineers Plan on Rolling Sub Across Street," *Chicago Sunday Tribune*, February 14, 1954; "How *U-505* will be 'landed' at Museum," *Chicago American*, February 21, 1954; "A Cheaper Way Found to Bring *U-505* Here," *Chicago Daily News*, February 20, 1954.

119. "Big Machines Needed To Help Transfer *U-505*," *Chicago Sunday Tribune*, March 21, 1954.

120. Letter from D. M. McMaster, May 3, 1954, for general PR use. Correspondence file 1953-54, 5-3, 99, MSI archives.

121. "Submarine Moved Onto S. Side Beach," *Chicago Daily Sun Times*, August 14, 1954.

122. The portions of the submarine's outer hull and pressure hulls removed were cut into small square pieces and sold as souvenirs in the gift shop for many years.

123. The bronze memorial plaque has an interesting history. The museum was approached by Leonard Grosse of Chicago's Bronze Incorporated Company to create the plaque, which was intended to remind future visitors of the importance of the boat. The upper 1/3 is a bas-relief based on the proud tradition of the U.S. Navy. The ghostly sailing ship in the background represented USS *Peacock's* 1815 capture of HMS *Nautilus* in the Straits of Sunda. The plaque's middle portion depicts USS *Guadalcanal* and *U-505*, the latter with its bow poking out of the water and a salvage party hard at work. Sculptor Fred M Torrey and at least eight others worked on the plaque. Grosse generously donated the finished piece of art, which cost about $5,000 in 1954

dollars. The title block in the middle of the plaque originally read "Nazi Submarine *U-505*," but after the dedication the museum decided to change the wording on the plaque to read "German Submarine *U-505*." This was in deference to the feelings of many German companies who, in the 1950s, were working hard to rebuild Germany with the assistance of the U.S. Government. In addition, some of these companies were being asked by the museum to contribute knowledge or materials for *U-505's* restoration. Some had expressed an interest in helping but objected to the connection to the "Nazi" past exhibited in the wording of the original plaque.

124. These stories are compiled from various news articles at the time and follow up interviews with Mrs. Hohne, Mrs. Wdowiak, and Mrs. Trusheim.

125. "Discloses U.S. Preparations for U-Boat War," *Chicago Daily Tribune*, September 24, 1954, pt. 2, 3; "*U-505* Speaker Warns Russians Build Big Sub Fleet," *Chicago American*, September 24, 1954.

126. *Ibid.*

127. Gallery letter to R. A. Beecher, September 11, 1954, UIC Archives; "*U-505* Passes Preview, Dedication is Tomorrow, Navy Secretary Praises Men Who Captured it in War," *Chicago Daily News*, September 24, 1954. The awardees were: Robert Crown and Carl Stockholm as co-chairs of the *U-505* committee; both were Naval reserve officers and active in the Navy League (Crown was the Vice President of Material Services Corporation and Vice President of the Navy League, and Stockholm the Regional President of the 9th Region); Seth Gooder (civil engineer who skillfully transferred *U-505* onto land); Lenox Lohr (President of Museum, conceived of the idea in 1947 and kept it alive); William V. Kahler (President of Illinois Bell and Chairman of the dedication committee); and Ralph Bard, Sr. (a former Undersecretary of the Navy and prominent Chicago attorney who served as Honorary Chair of the *U-505* committee and raised the the most money for the project). Secretary Thomas told the crowd, "The awarding of these medals was kept almost as secret as the capture of *U-505* by the men in the task force."

128. "*U-505* Dedicated as War Tribute; 40,000 Watch," *Chicago Sun Times*, September 26, 1954; "U-505 Dedication Viewed by 45,000: Admiral Halsey Calls Sub Warning to Reds," *Chicago American*, September 26, 1954.

129. The attack periscope was for spotting and attacking enemy ships with torpedoes, and the other—the periscope recovered from San Diego—was an aerial-navigational periscope.

130. *U-858* was not the only German submarine that contributed parts to *U-505*. Spare parts were also salvaged from *U-3008*, a Type XXI boat, for use in the mock-up conning tower located in the exit ramp from *U-505*.

Contributors

Erich Topp

A member of Crew 34, Topp served as a U-boat commander and is best remembered as the captain of U-552—the "Red Devil" boat. After the war he studied to become an architect and after a short career in that field entered the West German navy. He retired from active service in 1969 with the rank of Rear Admiral. Topp's memoir was published as *Odyssey of a U-Boat Commander* (Praeger, 1992). Savas Beatie will publish Topp's forthcoming book (co-authored with Eric C. Rust) on Oskar Kusch, the only U-boat commander executed by the Nazi regime. Admiral Topp lives in Remagen, Germany, in a home he designed that overlooks the Rhine River.

Eric C. Rust

Dr. Rust, a native of Lübeck, Germany, holds a doctorate in History from the University of Texas and has been teaching at Baylor University since 1984. His late father Horst Rust, and his mother's first husband, Kptlt. Hans-Jürgen Oldörp (Crew 35), who perished with all his men as the commanding officer of *U-90* in 1942, were active Kriegsmarine officers. The author himself served in the Federal German Navy in 1969-70.

Rust has published numerous books and articles, including *Naval Officers under Hitler: The Story of Crew 34* (Praeger, 1991). He translated Erich Topp's memoirs into English under the title *The Odyssey of a U-Boat Commander* (Praeger, 1992), and contributed to other works, among them *Silent Hunters: German U-boat Commanders of World War II* (Savas, 1997). Dr. Rust is completing a book with Erich Topp on Oskar Kusch, the only U-boat commander executed by the Nazis for opposing the regime. It will be published by Savas Beatie in 2005.

Professor Rust resides with his wife Karen and their two sons in Waco, Texas.

Timothy P. Mulligan

Tim is an archivist specializing in captured German records at the National Archives in College Park, MD. He holds an M.A. and a Ph.D. in diplomatic history from the University of Maryland and is the author of *Lone Wolf: The Life and Death of U-Boat Ace Werner Henke* (1993) and *Neither Sharks Nor Wolves: The Men of Nazi Germany's U-Boat Arm, 1939-1945* (1999), among other publications.

Lawerence Paterson

Lawrence Paterson has enjoyed a lifelong affinity for the sea. The native of Matamata, New Zealand, spent years exploring the world's oceans and has worked as a professional diver. Encouraged by grandfathers who served in both world wars, Paterson developed a keen interest in military history. He gravitated to France, where he and his wife Sarah began researching the wrecks of the Kriegsmarine vessels that litter the Biscay coastline. This interest produced several books, including *First U-Boat Flottila* (Naval Institute Press, 2002), *Second U-Boat Flotilla*, (Naval Institute Press, 2003), and *U-Boat War Patrol: The Hidden Photographic Diary of U-564* (Greenhill, 2004), a remarkable record detailing a 1942 combat patrol aboard Reinhard "Teddy" Suhren's boat.

Paterson resides in Gosport, England, where he indulges in his two other passions: music and motorcycles.

Mark E. Wise

Mark is a graduate of the University of Minnesota and the Joint Military Intelligence College. His Master's thesis, *Intelligence Support in the Capture of U-505*, formed the basis of his contribution to this book.

An enlisted intelligence specialist in the U.S. Naval Reserve, Mark was deployed to the Republic of Djibouti for nine months in support of Operation Enduring Freedom. Before turning to history, Wise published articles about such diverse subjects as aircraft maintenance, classical music, severe weather, and biography. The Bloomington, Minnesota, native lives in nearby Rosemount with his wife and son.

Jak P. Mallmann Showell

A teacher and science adviser for thirty years, Jak specializes in design technology and computing. His father (also named Jak) was *Stabsdieselobermaschnist* on *U-377*. According to the author's research, the boat was sunk in the North Atlantic by one of its own circling acoustic (T5) torpedoes on January 15, 1944—three months before he was born.

Jak is the author of nearly two dozen books on World War II naval-related matters. His first study, *U-boats under the Swastika* (Ian Allan Publishing, 1973), is one of the longest selling naval books in Germany; his second, *The German Navy in World War Two* (Arms and Armour Press, 1979), was named as one of the outstanding books of the year by the United States Naval Institute. Jak works closely with the International Submarine Archive (U-Boot-Archiv) in Germany and has been awarded the Silver U-boat Badge by the German Submariners' Association in Munich for furthering international relations and maintaining naval traditions. He is widely recognized as a respected authority on the Battle of the Atlantic.

Jordan Vause

A 1978 graduate of the United States Naval Academy, Jordan Vause is the author of two books on the Battle of the Atlantic: *U-Boat Ace: The Story of Wolfgang Lüth* (Naval Institute Press, 1990) and *Wolf: U-Boat Commanders in World War II* (Naval Institute Press, 1997).

History is fascinating but it doesn't pay the bills, so in real life Jordan works as an engineer for Lockheed Martin Corporation. He lives in Maryland with his lovely wife Carmel and five charming children, none of whom has the slightest interest in his avocation. He spends his free time reading, working on his genealogy, and trying to get his computer to operate properly.

Keith R. Gill

Keith is the Curator of U-*505* and Transportation for the Museum of Science and Industry in Chicago. He graduated in 1988 with a BS in Archeaology and Public History from Western Michigan University, Kalamazoo, and will be awarded his MA in Public History from Loyola University, Chicago, in 2004. Keith was hired at MSI in 1988 as Assistant Registrar and immediately began working with *U-505* during the final stages of the 1988 restoration project. His documentation of *U-505's* rich history has resulted in the collection of an important archives at MSI. Keith was named Curator of *U-505* in 1997.

In 1994, to mark the 50th anniversary of the capture of the boat, Keith returned the starboard diesel engine to operation and has run it on several occasions since. He is currently working on the $35,000,000 restoration effort to move *U-505* indoors. His tasks include conducting structural repairs, supervising its move, and repainting and returning its interior and exterior it its 1944 configuration and condition. The other part of Keith's title (Curator of Transportation), reflects his passion for antique and classic cars; one of his primary responsibilities includes restoring the institution's 42-car collection.

Keith's private interests include collecting military souvenirs from the U.S. 76th Infantry Division (in honor of his father's participation in WWII as a rifleman with that division), and the restoration of his 1956 Triumph TR-3 sports car, which he occasionally drives in vintage races. One day he hopes to open his own micro-brewery. Keith is married to Chris, his wife of eight years, and they have a two-year old daughter named Valerie—the light of their lives.

About the Editor

A 1986 graduate of the University of Iowa College of Law, Theodore P. Savas operated his own law practice in San Jose, California, for more than a dozen years. He currently teaches evening law-related college classes.

Savas has written many articles for a variety of periodicals, more than 100 book reviews, and has authored, edited and/or co-authored more than a dozen books, including *Nazi Millionaires: The Allied Search for Hidden SS Gold* (Casemate, 2002), *Silent Hunters: German U-Boat Commanders of World War II* (Naval Institute Press, 2003), and *The Red River Campaign: Union and Confederate Leadership and the War in Louisiana* (Parabellum Press, 2003).

Ted lives in El Dorado Hills with his wife Carol and their two children, Alexandra Maria and Demetrious Theodore.

INDEX

Achilles, Albrecht, 78
Admiral Graf Spee, German pocket
 battleship, 8, 29
Admiral Hipper, German heavy
 cruiser, 7
Admiral Scheer, German pocket
 battleship, 8
Affermain, Hans-Jürgen, 74
Airbanas, 193-194, 201
Allen, Spencer, 202
Alpena, Michigan, 202
Alphacca, steamship, 66, 225
Altesellmeier, Erich, 36, 245
American Shipbuilding Co. 206-207
American Society of Mechanical
 Engineers, 167
Anderson, David Boag, 63
Anderson, Robert B., 192
Anglo-German Naval Agreement of
 1935, 6-7
Armed Forces High Command (OKW),
 27
Article 188 and 191 of the Treaty of
 Versailles, 1, 4
Arundel, USCG cutter, 201-202
ASW Organization (ASWORG), 98
Atlantis, German raider, 9, 32
Aubrey, tug, 200

Bachstelze, gyro-kite, 19-20
Baie Comeau, Quebec, 194, 197
Bard, Ralph, 176
Battle of the Atlantic, 23
Bay of Biscay, 23, 34, 62, 67, 74, 83, 84,
 87, 90, 113, 129, 133, 228, 229, 230,
 246, 256
Benmohr, steamship, 63, 225
Bergen, Norway, 12
Berlin Document Center, 29
Binks Manufacturing Company, 201

Birkenhead, England, 40
Bismarck, Otto von, 2
Bismarck, German battleship, 7, 9, 57, 58
Bletchley Park, xxi, 94-95, 97, 99, 105,
 107-109, 111, 122-123
blockade, 3
Blücher, German heavy cruiser, 7, 29
Bockelmann, Hannes, 45, 245
Bode, Thilo, 36, 39, 73-74, 83, 165, 218,
 248; command of *U-858*, 40, 45;
 departure from *U-505*, 35; Josef
 Hauser, 36; Zschech as ally, 34
Boemi, Andrew, 174
Bogue, U.S. escort aircraft carrier, 104,
 111-112, 126
Boland, John V., 95
bombe, 107, 109-111, 253
Borcherdt, Ulrich, 104
Bordeaux, France, 12, 23
Brautigan, P. F., 183
Bremen, Germany, 14
Breslau, German cruiser, 101
Brest, France, 12, 39
Brey, Kurt, 36, 38, 83, 146-147, 150
Buffalo, New York, 195, 199
Bureau of Ordnance Torpedo Design
 section, 120-121
Busignies, Henri, 103
Byington, Fred, 177

Cadle Jr., John W., 135
Camp Ruston, Louisiana, 40, 123
Canaris, Wilhelm, 39
Cape Blanco, 204, 231
Cape Breton Island, 196-197
Cape des Rosiers, 197
Cape Palmas, 116
Cape Verde Islands, 116-117, 131-133
Card, U.S. escort aircraft carrier, 126
Carter, U.S. destroyer-escort, 40

Casablanca, 118, 124, 133
Celebrezze, Anthony J., 200
Chaffee, U.S. destroyer-escort, 121
Chatelain, U.S. destroyer-escort, 115,
 118, 126, 134-135, 192
Chevalier, R.B., 95
Chicago American, 178-179, 180
Chicago Athletic Club, 177,
Chicago Council Navy League of the
 United States, 166
Chicago Daily News, 181, 185
Chicago Daily Tribune, 171
Chicago Herald-American, 176, 180
Chicago Museum of Science and
 Industry, xx, xxii, 159, 162, 165, 168,
 170, 172, 175, 180-182, 184-185,
 190-191, 211-212, 217, 238
Chicago Park District Board, 174, 181
Chicago Sun Times, 186
Chicago Tribune, 177, 179, 184, 191,
 194
Chicago Yacht Club, 193, 205
Chicago, Illinois, *U-505* arrives,
 202-207, 209-210
Christophersen, Erwin, 82
Churchill, Winston, 247
Cleveland, Ohio, 195, 198, 200, 213
Combat Intelligence Division (F-2), 93
Construction Bureau of the German
 Navy, 11
Convoy and Routing Division (F-0),
 98-99
Copinsay, HMS, escort, 66
Cornwall, Ontario, 198
Cronin, R.E., 180
Crown, Robert, 182, 200, 211, 270
Culver, HMS, cutter, 104
Cuttermore, Harry S., 180
Czygan, Werner, 112

Dakar, 117
Daniel A. Joy, USS destroyer, 202, 215
Daniel, Thomas E., 75
Das Boot, movie, 11
David, Albert, 137-139, 143, 148, 154,
 156-157, 159, 213
Decker, Hans-Joachim, 54, 59, 62-64,
 72, 76-77, 79-80, 84-86, 90, 131,
 134-136
demolition charges, 148
Deschimag AG Seebeck, 14
Deschimag AG Weser, 14
Detroit Free Press, 181
Detroit, Michigan, 195, 201
Deutsche Werft AG, 14, 17, 27, 57, 91,
 224
Deutschland, German pocket battleship,
 8, 27, 29
Dietz, Otto, 45, 52
Dirksen, Everett, 175-176, 182, 192
dockyard sabotage, 33, 82
Doedens, Horst, 30
Dönitz, Karl, xx, 6, 13, 65, 92, 133; "a
 community bound by fate", 25;
 "tonnage war," 7; admits defeat, 80;
 centralized system of control, 101;
 decision to employ U-boats in the
 Indian Ocean, 22; early boats tended to
 dive sharply, 102; front line strength,
 31; heavy U-boat losses, 46; inspects
 U-505, 225; introduction of 4-rotor
 Enigma, 106; Loewe as staff officer,
 30; Loewe's staff skills, 27; memoirs,
 247; no help from the Luftwaffe, 18;
 overall strategy, 22; Peter Zschech, 31;
 planned expansion of U-boat fleet, 46,
 push-pull situation, 21, sacrificed
 younger crews, 47, sea war going well
 in 1941, 58; sinking of the *Roamar*, 71;
 sinkings off Brazil, 65; submarine as
 an almost perfect weapon, 13; submarines battling aircraft, 79; suspected
 Enigma code was compromised, 129;
 Tonnagekrieg, 14; *U-505*'s first patrol,
 67; U-boat presence off Freetown, 62;
 wanted *U-505* to have a dependable
 commander, 140; what U-boats could
 accomplish, 21
Douglas, Paul, 175
Duchesneau, J. A., 197

Dumford, J. W., 164
Dunedin, HMS, cruiser, 32

Edwards, Richard S., 95
Eisenhower, Dwight, 175, 191
Emden, German cruiser, 27
Engelmann, Kurt-Eduard, 77
Englebarth, Willy, 51
Enigma cipher, xxi, 80, 91, 96-97, 101,
    115, 117, 119, 124, 126, 128, 250;
    BdU refused to consider it com-
    promised, 106, 129; blackout of 1942,
    94, 101, 108-109; breaking the cipher,
    100, 105; capture of U-505 major
    windfall, 92; ciphering possibilities,
    105; development of a high-speed
    cipher machine, 109; Indian Ocean
    keys captured on U-505, 118;
    introduction of 4-rotor system, 106,
    108; Lange receives orders to meet
    with U-123 to pick up new key, 113;
    machine captured on U-110, 108, 263;
    mathematical method for deter mining
    keys, 106; protection of, 95; resulted
    in sinking 54 U-boats, 104; rotors
    captured from Krebs, 107; rotors
    captured from U-33, 107; sharing
    intelligence, 99; still top secret in
    1953, 183; two machines   captured
    on U-505; 164, U-505's failure to
    destroy, xviii
Erek, T.H., 122

F-0, F-2, etc., see Intelligence
    Organizations.
Felix, Ewald, 51, 244
Fessenden, USS destroyer-escort, 121
Fischer, Gottfried, 48, 245
Fitzsimmons Dredge and Dry-Dock
    Company, 206
Flaherty, U.S. destroyer-escort, 115,
    126, 192
Floberg, John F., 170-171, 175
Flotillas, 1st, 12, 89; 2nd, 23, 33, 39, 46,

52, 60, 62, 79, 82, 131; 3rd, 12; 4th, 59;
    5th, 88-89; 6th, 12, 82; 7th, 12; 9th, 12;
    10th, 23, 74, 82, 229; 11th, 12; 12th,
    12; 13th, 12; 14th, 12; 23rd, 12; 29th,
    12
Forest, F. X., 180
Förster, Fritz, 28-29, 36, 40, 66, 73-74
Franck, B. T., 189, 270
Fred M. Busse, fireboat, 204
Free Press, 181
Freetown, Sierra Leone, 60, 64, 66, 90,
    114, 129-130
Freiwald, Kurt, 18
Fricke, Otto, 46, 76, 149
Friedrich Ihn, destroyer, 31, 72
FXR "Foxer" Mark IV countermeasure
    device, 121

Gallery, Daniel, 112, 166, 168, 171, 174,
    195, 270; captures U-505, 40, 91, 137,
    142, 167, 192; commander of USS
    Hancock, 166; commissions USS
    Guadalcanal, 128; did not know about
    ULTRA, 128; finds U-505, 135;
    intelligence estimates, 123-124; inten-
    tion to capture a U-boat, 115, 126-127,
    144; Lange steams toward him, 132;
    meets with Smith-Hutton, 115; naval
    experience, 127-128; official repri-
    mand, 267; operational decisions, 124,
    opinion of Zschech's suicide, 46,
    orders Task Group 22.3 to Casablanca,
    133-134; post war, 166; received
    intelligence from Knowles, xxi,
    128-129; running low on fuel, 117;
    sank U-68, U-515 and U-126;
    separated Ewald Felix from the rest of
    the crew, 51; significance of items
    recovered from U-505, 118; steams in
    direction of Lange's position, 131;
    stunning amount of good luck, 139;
    tenth anniversary of capture of U-505,
    200; Tenth Fleet situation reports, 115;
    Task Group 22.3 running low on fuel,
    117-118; tracking U-505, 133; U-505

arrives in Chicago, 203-204, 211; *U-505* dedication, 212- 216; *U-505* movement to Chicago, 192-202; *U-505* museum, 161, 169, 173, 182, 184; *U-505* museum fundraising, 175, 185; visits Milwaukee, 189-190

Gallery, Fr. John I., 165, 167, 176

Gately, James H., 174

General Dynamics Corporation, 191

Geneva Convention, 122-123

Gerlach, Wallfred, 245

Gherardi, H. T., 122

Gleaner, HMS, minesweeper, 107

Glidden Manufacturing, 201

Gneisenau, German battle cruiser, 7, 51

Godfrey, Arthur, 176, 213-215

Goebeler, Hans, 34, 37-38, 50, 53-54, 66, 70-71, 73, 85, 89, 145, 147-148, 151, 153-156, 244, 246, 248, 263-265

Good, R. F., 181

Gooder, Seth M., 188, 205-209, 211, 270

Gooder-Hendrichsen Company, 188

Goodrich, William M., 175-177, 182

Government Code and Cipher School (Bletchley Park), 94

Graedel, Laura, 220

Graf Zepplin, German aircraft carrier, 7

Great Lakes Dredge and Dock Company, 207-208

Great Lakes Naval Training Station, 167, 170, 204, 214

Greger, Eberhard, 112

Griffin, HMS, destroyer 107

Guadalcanal, U.S. escort aircraft carrier, 115, 117-118, 126-128, 132, 134-135, 143, 150, 166, 192, 195-196, 200, 203, 213, 215, 274

Guggenberger, Fritz, 17

Gulf of St. Lawrence, 197

Gulick, J. W., 174

Guppy class submarines, 13

gyro-kite (mini-helicopter), 19-20

Hagan, Cornelius J., 180

Halifax, Nova Scotia, 196

Halsey, William, 214-215, 220

Hamburg, Germany, 13-14, 17, 57

Hamburg-America Line, 37

Hancock, U.S. aircraft carrier, 166

Hansen, Peter, 139-140, 158

"Happy Times," xvii, 24

Hart, H. H., 122

Hasselburg, Aloysius, 45, 50

Hauser, Josef, 36, 38, 81, 147, 149, 157, 264

Hecht, Frank, 166-168

Heidtmann, Hans, 108

Helgesen, Nils O., 64

Henke, Werner, 82, 126, 261

Henne, Wolf, 67

Henning, E. R., 167

Henriksen, Sharon, 216

Hermann Schoemann, German destroyer, 31, 72

Huff/Duff, 94, 100-102, 113-115, 116, 118, 124-125; benefited from technological advancements, 102; facilitated by BdU's centralized control, 106; resulted in sinking 22 U-boats, 104; shipborne, 104; technology, 103

High Seas Fleet, 2, 5

Hill Jr., Albert E., 270

Hinsley, Harry, 107

Hitler Youth, 53

Hitler, Adolf, seizure of power, 5, 7; "Fortress Europe," 9; appoints Dönitz, 6; Operation Barbarossa, 59; renunciation of the Versailles Treaty, 5, 7; replaces Raeder, 6

Hohne, Gordon, 213

Hohne, Norma, 213

Holdenried, Alfred-Karl, 151, 153, 157

Homyank, Michael, 201

Hood, HMS, battlecruiser, 58

Horner Jr., Maurice L., 270

human intelligence (HUMINT), 112

Höltring, Horst, 240

Ibbeken, Hans, 18

Idaho, U.S. battleship, 115, 128

Indian Hill Stone Company, 180
Ingersoll, Royal E., 98
Intelligence Organizations: *F-0*, 99; *F-2* (Combat Intelligence Division of ONI), 93; *F-11*, (fleet intelligence staff), 93; *F-20*, 93, 115, 128; *F-21*, 93, 94-97, 99, 113, 115-117, 119, 124, 128, 131, 251; *F-22*, 93; *F-23*, 93; *F-35* (Operational Information Section of ONI), 93, 98; *F-211* (The Secret Room), 94-97, 111, 114, 116;
International Red Cross, 54
International Ship Master's Association of Chicago, 267
Irish Fellowship Club, 171

Jacobi, Werner, 30, 245
Janssen, Gustav-Adolf, 82
Jenks, U.S. destroyer-escort, 115, 118, 126, 164
Johnson, Means, 192
Jones, Rodney M., 194, 196-198, 200
Joseph Medill, fireboat, 204
Joyce Jr., Fred, 270
Jung, Willi, 45
Jutland, Battle of, 2, 27

Kahler, William, 214
Kaiser Wilhelm Canal, 59-60
Kalbitz, Erich Wilhelm, 85
Kals, Ernst, 83, 87
Kaw, USCG cutter, 199-200
Kelly, C. Thomas, 270
Kennelly, ?, 174-175, 182, 204
Kentrat, Eitel-Friedrich, 59
King, Ernest J. 95, 128, 251, 267; commander of Tenth Fleet, 98; orders ships equipped with HF/DF, 104; U.S. naval intelligence operations, 92-93; unified control over antisubmarine operations, 98
Kiplinger, Austin, 202
Klappich, Heinrich, 45, 51
Kloevekorn, Friedrich, 90
Klüver, Pasche, ixx

Knocke, R., 78, 228, 245
Knowles, Kenneth A., xxi, 93, 96-97, 99, 113-117, 120, 123-124, 128-129, 131, 133, 174, 251
Knox, Dudley S., 135, 192
Koitschka, Siegfried, 140, 142, 156, 263
Komet, German raider, 9
Kormoran, German raider, 9
Kraus, Hans-Werner, 17
Krebs, whaler, 107
Kretschmer, Otto, 12, 139, 148
Kriegsmarine, 5, 9, 25, 44, 58, 107, 124; grid-square system, 97; refused to consider Enigma compromised, 106; what to do with the crew of *U-505*; 36
Kusch, Oskar, 17, 52, 277-278
Königsberg, German cruiser, 27

La Pallice/La Rochelle, France, 12
La Spezia/Toulon, France, 12
Lachine canal system, 198
Lake Ontario, 199
Lange, Harald, 88, 90, 134, 159; assumes command of *U-505*, 37, 45, 86, 146, 230; can't recharge batteries, 117, 131; chosen by Dönitz, 139; collision course with Task Group 22.3, 134; compared to Loewe, 38; could be a dependable commander, 140; decision to exit conning tower first, 141, 157; decision to surface only reasonable choice, 140, 156; decisions made after he surfaced, 141; defense was hopeless, 145; despaired over contin- uous night patrols, 117, 132; did best under circumstances, 139; eye on survival instead of comfort, 131; first position report, 113; found by Task Group 22.3, 134; fourth decision after he surfaced, 141; high stake gamble pays off, 132; ill-matched for the situation, 139; last chance to sink a ship passes, 130; loss of options when attacked, xx-xxi; May 14 situation report, 115; May 15 situation report, 131; member of the

Nazi party, 38-39; no doubt about ability of his crew, 151; no way to escape Task Group 2.3, 143; not given credit for courage, 142; not very successful commanding officer, 138; nothing being done to scuttle *U-505*, 147; ordered to Freetown, 129; orders abandon ship, 141-142, 145, 157; orders scuttling, 145, 151, 154, 157; orders *U-505* to surface after attack, 136; portegé Otto Dietz, 52; position on June 1, 117; quirk of fate, 132; radio transmissions providing intelligence, 125; receives final orders, 114; receives orders to meet *U-123*, 113; rejects quick evacuation, 143; replaces Zschech, 37; rescued survivors from *T25*, 39; reservist advanced through the ranks, 38; salvages morale, 38; second decision after he surfaced, 141; statement aboard USS *Guadalcanal*, 232; steams directly for Task Group 22.3, 132; third decision after he surfaced, 141; tries to defend against overwhelming odds, xvii; very bad luck to be found by a Hunter-Killer group, 139; would he have better luck? 87; wounded, 40, 145-146, 149, 157, 242

Lange, Karla, 40, 54
Lauenburg, trawler, 107
Leigh Light, 24
Leipzig, German cruiser, 29
Lemp, Fritz-Julius, 27, 108, 263
Leningrad, Battle of, 80
Liebe, Johannes, 78
Linz, Austria, 13
Lipka, Lothar, 245
Livecchi, Samuel P., 95
Loewe, Axel-Olaf, 28, 31, 46, 139, 224, 238, 246, 263; first commander of *U-505*, 27; "U-boat duty was by command," 50; a select professional, 38, appendicitis, 30, 71, 226; as staff officer, 30, 58; commissions *U-505*,

27, 29; concern for the good of the boat, 37; final opportunity to meld boat and crew, 60; first U-boat command, 59; liaison officer to Albert Speer, 40; logo shield bearing a raging Lion, 33, 59, 86; months of training for *U-505*, 59; opinion about Zschech suicide, 35, 46; ordered to follow Merten, 65; original crew, 45; post-war, 41; proven a capable captain, 72; relieved of command, 72; respected "good luck" traditions, 34, 62; sinks sailing vessel *Roamar*, 71; sinks SS *Alphacca*, 66; sinks SS *Benmohr*, 63; sinks SS *Sea Thrush*, 68; sinks SS *Sydhav*, 64; sinks SS *Thomas McKean*, 68, 70; sinks SS *West Irmo*, 65; spots fast convoy, 63; transfers command to Zschech, 227; U-505 museum, 54

Lohr, Lenox, 165-170, 174, 182-184, 211, 216, 266-267
Lorient, France, 23, 28, 36, 46, 60, 67, 78-79, 81-83, 86-87, 131, 228-229
Low, Francis S. "Frog," 93, 95, 98, 119-122, 251, 267
Lukosius, Zenon, 156, 200, 203
Lusitania, RMS, 2
Lüdecke, Werner, 54
Lüth, Wolfgang, 22

Mainz, Johann, 52
Malaya, HMS, battleship, 62
Marenberg, Werner, 245
Maryland Sun, steamship, 193
Matthews, Francis, 173
McCormick Paper Mill, 194
McDiarmid, John B., 94
McMaster, Dan, 270
Mendota, USCG, 104
Merten, Karl-Friedrich, 62, 64-65, 78
Messmer, Johannes, 37
METOX passive receiver, 19, 73, 75, 81, 248
Meyer, Paul, 35-36, 40, 47, 83-86, 113, 141, 145-147, 149-151, 157, 229

Milner, Carl T., 217
Milwaukee, Wisconsin, 195, 202, 269
Mine Disposal Group, 120
Mk 24 "Fido" homing torpedo, 18
Mocarski, Chester, 200, 204, 213, 273
Mocarski, Anne, 213
Mohr, Johann, 32, 72
Monfalcone, Italy, 13
Montreal, Canada, 195, 197
Moran Towing and Transportation
    Company, 190
Moran, Edwin J., 190
Morrisburg, Ontario, 198
Mosch, Erhard, 245
Mueller, Luther C., 270
Muir, U.S. destroyer-escort, 40
Musenberg, Werner, 140
Möller, Heinz, 46
München, German weather ship, 107

Narvik, Norway, 12
National Socialist German Workers
    Party (NSDAP, NAZI), 29
Nautilus, U.S. submarine, 13, 191
Naval Mine Warfare Test Station, 121
Naval Research Laboratory, 102, 179
Navy League of the U.S., 171, 174
NAXOS, 117, 230-231
Nazi party, 53
"Nemo," code name for *U-505*, 120, 174
Nepaschings, Rudi, 245
Nikolaev, Ukraine, 13
Nimitz, Chester W., 168
Nollau, Herbert, 29, 31, 40, 45, 62, 71,
    73, 238, 248
Norway, invasion of, 8
Nova Scotia, 194

Ocean Justice, steam ship, 74-75, 227
Oesten, Jürgen, 62, 139, 141, 145, 149-
    153, 263-264
Office of Naval Intelligence, 92-93, 95-
    96, 99, 112, 119-120, 122, 169
Ogdensburg, New York, 198
Oldörp, Hans-Jürgen, 277

Operation Deadlight, 15, 236
Operation Barbarrosa, 59
Operation Drumbeat, 21, 128
Operation Intelligence Centre (Admir-
    alty), 95
Operation Kinetic, 249
Operation Monsoon, 21
Operation Weserübung, 20
Operational Information Section (F-35),
    93
Operational Intelligence Centre, 97
Operational Intelligence Sections,
    OP-16-F-9, 96; OP-16-Z, 95-96, 112,
    119-120, 122; OP-20-3-GI-A: The
    Atlantic Section, 97; OP-20-G, 97,
    109, 111, 113, 118-123; OP-20-GI-2,
    Enigma section, 95-96; OP-20-GI-A,
    119; OP-38W, 93
Orion, German raider, 9

Panama Canal, 70
Panzerschiffe, name for pocket
    battleship, 8-9
pars pro toto, ixx, xxii
Parsons, John E., 95
Paukenschlag Wolf Pack, xvii
Paul Jones, U.S. destroyer-escort, 93
Pauline L. Moran, tug, 194, 196, 198,
    200
PC 845, 894, U.S. patrol craft, 203
Petard, HMS, destroyer, 108
Peterson, Harold E., 270
Pickels, Wayne, 200, 204
Piening, Adolf, 82
Pillsbury, U.S. destroyer-escort, 115,
    120, 126, 138, 143, 148, 150, 153, 164,
    184, 187, 192, 196, 200, 203, 213, 218
Pimpernel, HMS, destroyer, 248
Pinguin, German raider, 9
Polk, Sol, 202
Pope, U.S. destroyer-escort, 115, 116,
    118, 126
Port Colbourne, Ontario, 195, 199
Portsmouth Naval Yard, 173, 187, 190
Prien, Günther, 12, 30

Prince of Wales, HMS, battleship, 58
Prinz Eugen, German heavy cruiser, 7, 58
Project 356, 161, 163, 166
Python, German supply ship, 32

Quebec and Ontario Transportation Company, 174
Quebec City, 197
Quine, Willard Van Orman, 96

Raeder, Erich, 6
Rahmlow, Hans, 263
Reh, Werner, 50
Reichsmarine, 5
Reinig, Alfred, 46
Rejewski, Marian, 106-107
Renig, Alfred, 130
Roamar, sailing ship, 71, 226
Roeder, B. F., 119
Rommel, Erwin, 58, 80
Roosevelt, Franklin D., 247
Roper, U.S. destroyer-escort, 112, 256
Rosenmeyer, Dr. Friedrich-Wilhelm, 36
Rosenwald, Julius, 162, 183
Royal Oak, HMS, battleship, xvii
Rudderow, U.S. destroyer-escort, 121
Rueben James, U.S. destroyer, xvii
Rösing, Hans-Rudolf, 72, 86

Salamis, Greece, 12
Sanabria, Ulises A., 193, 201
Scharnhorst, German battle cruiser, 7, 45
Schepke, Jochen, 12
Schiller, Wolfgang, 51, 53
Schmidt, Hans-Thilo, 106
Schmidt, Willi, 46
Schoichet, Louis, 186
Schröder, Gerd, 148
Schuch, Heinrich, 67-68, 78
Schuirmann, Roscoe E., 93, 95
Schulz, Wilhelm, 32
Sea Thrush, steam ship, 68, 226
Seydlitz, SMS, German battleship, 27
Short Signal Cipher, 108, 119, 113

Short Weather Cipher, 107, 119
Sierra Leone, 60
Sillcock, R.R., 75, 227
Silversides, U.S. submarine, 167, 203
Smith-Hutton, Henri H., 93, 95, 115, 123, 128
snorkel technology, 13, 16
Somali, HMS, destroyer, 107
Soulange Canal locks, 198
Special Activities Branch, 95
Special Intelligence Section, 96, 112
Speer, Albert, 40
Sperry, U.S. destroyer, 121
Springer, Karl, 34, 51
St. Lawrence River, 190, 197, 200
St. Lawrence Seaway Project, 198
St. Nazaire, France, 12
Stalingrad, Battle of, 80
Stevenson, Russell, 201
Stockholm Cleaners, 182
Stockholm, Carl, 182, 204, 211, 270
Stolzenburg, Gottfried, 29-30, 38, 70-71, 75, 245; has respect of the crew, 73; transferred to *U-462*, 78; wounded in depth charge attack, 32, 36, 76-77, 83, 227-228; Zschech, 74
Submarine Design and Sonar Design section, 120
Submarine Tracking Room (Admiralty), 94
submarines, "a community bound by fate," 25; improvements in technology, 5; myths, 10; ungentlemanly weapon, 2; weapon suited for naval underdogs, 4
Sullivan, John, 168
Sydhav, steamship, 64, 225

T-5 acoustic torpedo, 121, 130, 164
T25, torpedo-boat, 39, 88-89, 230
Tambor, U.S. submarine, 201
Task Group 22.3, xxii, 40, 90, 112, 115-117, 123, 126-128, 131-132, 134, 156, 193, 203, 231; captures *U-505*, 136, 138, 140; finds *U-505*, 134-135

Tenth Fleet, 92, 94, 97-99, 115, 124, 128, 251-252, 267
Texas, U.S. battleship, 176
Theodor Riedel, German destoyer, 73
Thetis, U.S. destroyer-escort, 67
Thomas McKean, steamship, 68, 70, 220, 226
Thomas, Charles, 213
Thor, German raider, 9
Toledo, Ohio, 201
Topp, Erich, xxi, 12, 139, 277-278
Torrey, Fred M., 274
Toulon, France, 13
Treaty of Versailles, 1, 4-7
The Tribune Company, 173
Tripitz, German battleship, 7
Trondheim, Norway, 12
Trosino, Earl, 117-118, 134, 188, 192-193, 195, 197, 198, 200, 202, 213, 215
Trusheim, Gloria, 213
Trusheim, Phillip, 213

U-Boats: *Type IA*: 11, 14; *Type II*: 11, 14, 17; *Type IIA*: 11; *Type IIB*: 11; *Type IIC*: 11; *Type IID*: 11; *Type VIB*: 17; *Type VII*: 11-12, 14, 17, 23; *Type VIIC*: 17, 90; *Type IX*: 12-13, 17, 20-23, 79, 151, 191, 263; built in three German shipyards, 14; carnage inflicted upon American shipping, 21; deployment of, xx; description of, 15; designed for long-distance missions, 14; designed interwar, 14; prowled as "one wolves," 14; withdrawal from East Coast, 21; *Type IXA*: 15-16, 23; *Type IXB*: 6, 23; *Type IXC*: 16-18, 23, 28, 41; *Type IXC/40*: 16, 40; *Type IXD*: 15-16, 23; *Type IXD1*: 37, 86; *Type IXD2*: 17; *Type IXD42*: 15; *Type XIV U-tankers*; 12, 15, 7, 22, 71; *Type XXI*: 13, 17, 46, 275; *Type XXIII*; 13, 17, 46; *U-1*: 265; *U-72*: 63; *U-11*: 30; *U-25*: 14, 101; *U-26*: 14; *U-33*: 107; *U-39*: 101; *U-43*: 265; *U-47*: xvii; *U-61*: 139, 263; *U-65*: 62; *U-67*: 247;

U-68: 62, 64-65, 78, 126, 128, 228; *U-69*: 197; *U-74*: 27, 59; *U-81*: 14, 17; *U-83*: 17; *U-85*: 112, 256; *U-90*: 277; *U-99*: 148; *U-103*: 17, 82; *U-105*: 67; *U-106*: 39, 62, 139, 197, 263; *U-110*: 27, 108, 263; *U-118*: 112; *U-123*: 113, 129; *U-124*: 32-33, 45, 72, 245; *U-126*: 19; *U-132*: 197; *U-154*: 17, 52, 78, 90, 245; *U-155*: 82, 114, 125, 227; *U-157*: 67, 247; *U-163*: 77; *U-165*: 197; *U-168*: 81; *U-172*: 46; *U-173*: 227; *U-176*: 17; *U-177*: 20; *U-178*: 18; *U-180*: 37, 45, 86, 140; *U-181*: 16, 18, 22; *U-183*: 81; *U-190*: 114, 125; *U-195*: 16; *U-199*: 18; *U-214*: 71, 226; *U-228*: 82; *U-332*: 78, 228; *U-336*: 245; *U-373*: 90; *U-377*: 36, 245; *U-441*: 264; *U-461*: 228; *U-462*: 77-78, 228; *U-463*: 71, 226; *U-471*: 90; *U-504*: 201, 245

U-505: 14, 219; "a community bound by fate," 25; an unlucky boat, 26; battery trouble, 131; boarding parties equipped with maps, 112; built by Deutsche Werft AG, 14; capture of, xviii, 137, 140, 143, 146, 150-151, 158; cheerless mission, 6; Chicago: arrival, 202-207, 209-211, movement to, 193-202; code material captured, xviii, 118, 164; code-named "Nemo," 120; commissioning, 58; crew: 1942 crew, 41; American, 164; blame for loss goes to crew, 138; civilian occupations, 48; final crew, 41; grew older with time, 48; held incommunicado, 123; interrogation, 122; not as well trained as they should have been, 158; original crew, 45; residences, 49; sent to POW camp at Ruston, Louisiana, 123; crosses equator on last mission, 129; deactivated, 165; decision to surface only reasonable choice, 140; defending posed tactical problems, 144; depth charged, 65, 67, 75-76, 81, 84-85, 135-136; F-21 started estimating position on May 21, 115; final action, 40; final ascent, 136; found by Hunter-Killer group, xvii, 124, 134-135; four-hatch escape plan, 142; Goebeler last man out, 156; HF/DF plays part in capture, 104, 116; human intelligence related to capture, 112; in film, 184; last chance to sink a ship passes, 130; launch on May 24, 1941, 57; life and fate mirrors transformation, 24; list of documents captured, 119; Loewe as first commander, 27, 59; luck played a roll in keeping her afloat, 153; Meyer as acting commander, 35; months of training, 59; motivation and morale, 52, 64, 150; Museum development: dedication ceremony, 212-216; early plans to take to Chicago, 166; exhibit, 181; committee, 175, 180, 199; condition of boat, 188; cost to move to Chicago, 178; fundraising, 182-185, 189; future, 218, 220; guns returned, 218; hole in Number 7 ballast tank, 120; Mil- waukee, 202; museum, 15, 171-174; objections to the museum, 187; dedication ceremony in Chicago, 190; planned move to Chicago, 173, planned museum, 170; planned tow to Chicago, 179; preparation to move to Chicago, 176; raising money for museum, 173; return of missing items, 217; no mail allowed by survivors, 40; not a lucky boat, says Oesten, 139; off Freetown, 66, 130; officers, 26, 40, 73; only managed 32 days at sea in the summer of 1943, 33, 46, 83; operations, 152-153; ordered scuttled, 145, 151; patrols: October 4, 1942, 74; June 7, 1943, 67; July 1, 1943, 80; July 3, 1943, 81; August 1, 1943, 82; September 18, 1943, 82; October 9, 1943, 34, 84; October 9, 1943, 84; December 20, 1943, 87; December 25, 1943, 39; March 16, 1944, 39, 90, 129;

planned disposal, 168; position on June 1, 117; progress being tracked, 133; rammed by USS *Pillsbury*, 120; reaches Bermuda, 164; rendezvous with *U-461*, 228; rendezvous with *U-462*, 78, 228; rendezvous with *U-463*, 226; returns to builder's yard, 60; sank three ships in Caribbean, 28; scuttle, 147-148, 151; seashell tower insignia, 39; sent to pick up survivors from *Z27*, 87-88; serious defense would be a kamikaze mission, 144; sinks A*lphacca*, 66, 225; sinks *Benmohr*, 63, 225; sinks *Ocean Justice*, 74, 227; sinks *Roamar*, 71, 226; sinks *Sea Thrush*, 68, 226; sinks *Sydhav*, 64, 225; sinks *Thomas McKean*, 68, 70, 236; sinks *West Irmo*, 65, 225; subject of Allied intelligence reports, 91; T-5 torpedoes, 121; table with crew classification, 43; tenth anniversary of capture, 200; tracking its position, 113; trails an oil slick, 77; transits Kaiser Wilhelm Canal, 59; travels across the Atlantic, 68; typical submarine, xx; U-Boat Intelligence Summary for April 28, 114, 125; U.S. Navy announces capture of, 165; under tow, 164; used to help train American ships, 165; very lucky boat, 54; wartime record, 177; Zschech takes command, 32

U-513: 18; *U-514*: 36, 74, 81; *U-515*: 82, 126, 128, 251; *U-517*: 197; *U-524*: 40; *U-533*: 81; *U-534*: 29-30, 45, 248; *U-536*: 197; *U-544*: 128; *U-552*: 277; *U-553*: 197; *U-554*: 30; *U-559*: 108; *U-565*: 51; *U-570*: 263; *U-587*: 104; *U-604*: 240; *U-616*: 140, 263; *U-676*: 245; *U-755*: 245; *U-802*: 197; *U-845*: 30; *U-852*: 122; *U-858*: 40, 73, 83, 165, 218, 275; *U-861*: 20, 139, 263; *U-862*: 16; *U-973*: 30, 245; *U-1199*: 245; *U-1223*: 197; *U-1228*: 197;